**Straight
from the heart**

Reverend
JESSE L. JACKSON

Straight
from the heart

Edited by Roger D. Hatch and Frank E. Watkins

FORTRESS PRESS PHILADELPHIA

Designed by Phyllis Carson

Library of Congress Cataloging-in-Publication Data

Jackson, Jesse L. 1941–
    Straight from the heart.

    1. Afro-Americans—Politics and government.
2. Afro-Americans—Civil rights.   3. United States—
Politics and government—1981–   .   4. United
States—Foreign relations—1981–   .   5. Racism—
United States.   6. Jackson, Jesse, 1941–   .
I. Hatch, Roger D.   II. Watkins, Frank E.   III. Title.
E185.97.J2457   1987   973.92'092'4   86–19422
ISBN 0–8006–0862–3

2658G86   Printed in the United States of America   1–862

To my grandmother, Matilda, who in her lifetime will never read this book because she can neither read nor write—but who gave *me* encouragement to do so. To my mother, Helen Jackson, who, along with my grandmother, took me to church. To Charles Jackson who adopted me and gave me his name, his love, his encouragement, discipline, and a high sense of self-respect—who has since gone to be with God, but whose presence in my life assures me that heaven smiles upon our sincere efforts. Their love, concern, affection, sacrifice, and discipline helped, in my formative years, to shape my values.

Contents

Preface

In my preaching, teaching, and activism over the past quarter of a century—and hopefully in this book—I have tried to illustrate that the issues of life flow primarily from the heart, not from the head, and that at the center of every political, economic, legal, and social issue is the spiritual, moral, and ethical dimension.

Thus, those who would build this national house, these United States, and make a difference in the world, must build on the solid foundations of truth, justice, mercy, peace, equality, and freedom. They must fight for humane priorities at home and human rights abroad measured everywhere by one yardstick.

I identify with the school of thought that says "right is might," not with the school that argues "might makes right." I live "on the boundary" and with the inevitable tension that comes with trying to synthesize and put in their proper relationship, in a pluralistic society, the "religious and the secular," the "spiritual and the material."

My religion obligates me to be political, that is, to seek to do God's will and allow the spiritual Word to become concrete justice and dwell among us. My politics do not make me religious. Religion should *use* you politically to do public service. Politics should not *misuse* religion. When the Word (the spiritual) becomes flesh (the actual) and dwells in our hearts, that's called good religion.

It is this human struggle to have good religion and good politics that I hope you will sense throughout this collection of speeches. We see through a glass darkly. As we struggle with the public issues confronting the men and women of our day, none of us has achieved perfection and none is beyond redemption. We must constantly rebuild relationships, revive broken spirits, redeem, forgive, and move on to the next challenge.

I am very proud of this book. There have been other books *about* me and what I think, but this is *my* statement. It is a comprehensive, representative collection of my thoughts and ideas.

All of these speeches, of course, were written for a particular occasion and audience and within a concrete moral, political, and historical context—and, I might add, mostly on the run. They have all been preserved in their original form and flavor, subject only to grammatical corrections and small editorial considerations for purposes of this book.

I want to especially thank my longtime press secretary and colleague in the struggle, the Reverend Frank E. Watkins, and Dr. Roger D. Hatch, a person I have learned to love and respect, and with whom I have worked for over a decade, for their hard work in assembling this book and for their relentlessly seeing this project through.

I want also to thank my publisher, Harold W. Rast, my editor, Davis Perkins, and Stephanie Egnotovich, all of Fortress Press, for conceiving this project and approaching me with the proposal. Despite the difficulty of tying me down—because of the hectic pace of my schedule—they remained diligent, committed, and enthusiastic about the book throughout. For their faithfulness, wisdom, guidance, and professionalism I shall always be grateful.

I hope that the urgency of *now* and the fervency of spirit with which I gave these speeches is conveyed and experienced by you as you read each page. In the midst of our present protracted moral and civilizational crisis, perhaps some inspiration, some insight, some idea contained in these pages will inspire or convince you to keep on struggling for the bright new day of peace and justice.

REVEREND JESSE L. JACKSON
December 6, 1986

Editors' Introduction

Reverend Jesse Louis Jackson was born on October 8, 1941, in Green-ville, South Carolina. After graduating from Greenville's Sterling High School in 1959, he attended the University of Illinois on a football scholarship. He left after his freshman year due to racial discrimination, transferring to North Carolina A & T, where he received a B.S. degree in sociology.

While a leader in the student sit-in movement of the sixties to desegregate public facilities, Jackson was also a student-government leader, a star athlete, and an honor student. After graduation, he attended the Chicago Theological Seminary for two years. In recognition of his leadership and achievements, more than thirty-five colleges and universities have conferred honorary doctoral degrees on Jackson, including Pepperdine, Oberlin, Oral Roberts, Rhode Island, Georgetown, Howard, Han yang University, Seoul, Korea, and his alma maters, North Carolina A & T and Chicago Theological Seminary.

An integral part of the man is his religious calling. Jackson delivers the spiritual keynote address for most Saturday-morning meetings at the Operation PUSH national headquarters and regularly preaches in churches across America on Sundays. Ordained a Baptist minister in 1968, Reverend Jackson is presently on leave as a co-pastor of the Fellowship Missionary Baptist Church in Chicago, where the Reverend Clay Evans is pastor and senior minister. He and his wife, Jacqueline, are the parents of five children.

Operation PUSH

Jesse Jackson has devoted all of his adult life to the human rights movement. National recognition for this activity began in August 1967 when he was appointed national director of Operation Breadbasket (the economic arm of the Southern Christian Leadership Conference) by Dr.

Martin Luther King, Jr. He worked in this capacity until December 1971, when he and seventy prominent national black leaders founded Operation PUSH (People United to Serve Humanity) in Chicago on Christmas Day, 1971.

Operation PUSH has employed as many as 120 staff members, but it is through the thousands of volunteers that PUSH has made its impact. PUSH has over seventy affiliates in large and small cities across the country, and its Saturday-morning national forum, which Jackson conducts on a regular basis, is broadcast by several radio stations. PUSH completed payment on the mortgage on its headquarters in 1981 and now owns the $2.5-million facility.

PUSH is not a church; rather it is an ecumenical action arm of the church devoted to furthering the cause of human rights internationally. It believes that injustice anywhere is a threat to justice everywhere. PUSH's approach to social change is holistic, though. It believes that a spiritual and moral crisis is at the core of every material evil. Grounded in the love ethic of the Judeo-Christian tradition and the militant non-violent activist tradition of Thoreau, Gandhi, and Dr. Martin Luther King, Jr., PUSH seeks to be a positive moral authority in the struggle for freedom and liberation. Whereas *civil rights* was the cutting-edge issue for social change in the fifties and sixties, PUSH has made *economic rights* the fundamental issue of the seventies and eighties.

One dimension of this struggle for "silver" rights in addition to civil rights may be glimpsed in Jackson's PUSH for Excellence education program. Using mass student motivation and parent-community mobilization, Jackson has developed one of the most innovative education programs in the country.

PUSH has perhaps made its largest impact economically. Through PUSH's Economic Justice Campaign, Jackson has negotiated multimillion dollar covenants with companies such as Coca-Cola, Anheuser-Busch, Burger King, Avon, Quaker Oats, General Foods, and, a first of its kind, a PUSH-LULAC (League of United Latin American Citizens) Black-Hispanic agreement with the Southland Corporation in order to ensure that blacks, other minorities, and women receive their fair share of new jobs and economic opportunities in return for their considerable consumer dollars spent.

While PUSH is a not-for-profit corporation, it is *not tax exempt;* so it can and does involve itself in politics. Massive voter-registration campaigns, grass-roots political organizing, and participation in party and independent politics locally and nationally are among PUSH's political activities. Jackson broke new ground by giving a major address (contained in this volume) before the Republican National Committee in 1978 (he has consistently maintained that blacks have no permanent friends and no permanent enemies, only permanent interests) /and received national attention for leading the delegation that ousted the Mayor Daley-led Cook County delegation from the 1972 Democratic convention in Miami. The next morning the new PUSH headquarters was fire-bombed.

Presidential Campaign

After conducting a Southern crusade for voting-rights enforcement focused in Mississippi with an assistant attorney general from the U.S. Justice Department and expanding his voter-registration drive to G.I.s on U.S. bases in Europe, Jackson launched his campaign for the Democratic nomination for the presidency of the United States on November 3, 1983. His candidacy marked the first full-scale effort by an African American to capture the nation's highest office. His campaign was given a significant boost in January 1984 when he successfully negotiated with Syrian President Assad for the release of downed air force pilot Lt. Robert Goodman. This feat was expanded and duplicated in the summer when Jackson's discussion with Cuban President Fidel Castro led to the release of forty-eight American and Cuban prisoners.

The keystone of the Jackson presidential campaign was the Rainbow Coalition. Through the Rainbow Coalition, Jackson intends to give a united voice to those blacks, browns, Native Americans, Asian Americans, Arab Americans, Jewish Americans, and Caribbean Americans, and the poor who lack *power*. Jackson's fundamental assumption here is that these groups do not lack work habits, discipline, education, training, health care, housing, etc. They lack *power* in one form or another. Poor people are poor because they are powerless (and as Jackson points out, there are quantitatively more poor white people than poor black people, so the Rainbow Coalition aims to embrace people of all colors).

Hence the Rainbow Coalition sought to give those who have traditionally lacked power a larger voice in government. Assuming that these people are unable to purchase power economically, Jackson endeavored to let them purchase it politically through the ballot box.

The success of the presidential campaign can be seen, in part, through the numbers. Jackson won sixty-one congressional districts, five states (he placed second in five more), and he garnered 3.5 million votes (21 percent of the total cast). The Rainbow Coalition lived up to its name inasmuch as 21 percent of the Jackson vote was nonblack (neither Hart nor Mondale had greater nonwhite support), and Jackson confounded the political analysts by capturing 465.5 delegates rather than the projected 175–200 delegates. Jackson accomplished all this while spending less than $3 million, making his campaign the most cost-efficient in American history. His speech at the Democratic National Convention in

San Francisco on July 17, 1984 (contained in this volume) electrified the convention and the country.

Since the presidential campaign, Jackson has continued to champion the causes of the Rainbow Coalition. He continues to advocate a consistent human-rights policy internationally that would preclude U.S. support of the minority-run government of South Africa and he has been increasingly involved with the burgeoning farm crisis in this country. His commitment to improving the quality of life for the underprivileged everywhere is undeniable and, in the view of many, unparalleled in America today. The reader of this volume will have no trouble in discerning that this commitment is rooted in Jackson's religious-ethical vision.

A Religious-Ethical Vision

At the heart of Jackson's approach lies a consistent religious-ethical vision of a just society and a peaceful world. He expressed it succinctly in his speech announcing his candidacy for the Democratic party's 1984 presidential nomination:

> We are here to heed the call of this nation's highest and noblest principles that we might fulfill our mission to defend the poor, make welcome the outcast, deliver the needy and be the source of hope for people yearning to be free everywhere.
>
> Today, we are here that we might fulfill the promise of democracy and assure equal protection under the law and equal regard within the law for all; that we might serve the ends of justice and lift those boats that are stuck on the bottom full of unpolished pearls; that we might elevate the lot of common humanity and build a functional new rainbow coalition spanning lines of color, sex, age, religion, race, region, and national origin. . . .
>
> Thus I seek the presidency to serve the nation at a level where I can help restore a moral tone, a redemptive spirit, and a sensitivity to the poor and dispossessed of this nation. . . . We must appreciate that the world has become a global village where military resources alone will not supply peace. Accordingly, my foreign policy proposals will seek to emphasize respect, talk, and negotiations over confrontation, gunboat diplomacy, big-stick diplomacy, military adventurism, and racial insensitivity; and we will seek to measure human rights for all human beings by one yardstick.[1]

Racism as a Central Problem in American Life

Some may be surprised at the range of issues and topics Jackson addresses in the speeches included in this volume. It would be possible (but incorrect) to conclude that, as Jackson moved into the realm of electoral politics, he expanded the range of issues and topics he addressed. The actual situation is quite different. For two decades, Jackson has been an outspoken opponent of American racism in all of its dimensions. In his view, racism has become institutionalized into virtually every aspect of American life: politics, education, economics, the military, housing, health care, religion. Accordingly, opposing racism has meant that Jackson has had to oppose it as it appeared in each of these diverse areas of American life. Thus it has been Jackson's opposition to racism in its many forms—not his entry into electoral politics—that has caused him to address so many areas of American life.

Jackson believes that racism is "fundamentally a moral problem, a problem of human values, running from our minds to our local communities and to our international community."[2] It is the belief that some people are superior and others inferior as a consequence of their race. Jackson argues that racism is scientifically untrue, theologically immoral, psychologically unhealthy, and economically and politically unfeasible.[3]

> It gives white people an unjustified sense of superiority and black people a false sense of inferiority. It is economically untenable because racism costs more than justice. Racism costs this country in terms of production and in terms of a climate conducive to good business. In the final analysis, Dr. King's words are as true today as they were . . . when he spoke them: "We will either learn to live together as brothers and sisters or we shall surely die apart as fools."[4]

Jackson sees racism as connecting many, if not most, of America's social problems. Because of this, eliminating or ameliorating racism would not simply help blacks; it would benefit the entire nation and, thus, the world.

> The resolution of the race question in this country would liberate us to liberate others around the world. For until white America is what it ought to be, black America cannot be what it ought to be. And until black Americans are no longer prohibited by race from achieving their potential, all Americans will be poorer as a result.[5]

Jackson makes a similar argument in the area of politics: justice for black people means more humane policies for all Americans. As he said to a joint session of the Alabama legislature, "We must remove the cataracts of race from the eyes of our people and lift them out of poverty, ignorance, disease, and fear. . . . We must elevate people from the [racial] battleground, find a common ground, and then move on to a higher ground."[6] Jackson believes that racism has distracted Americans and has obscured many of America's most fundamental problems. Promoting racial justice allows many white Americans to see what is in their best economic and political interest.

Jackson does not believe, however, that all American social problems can be reduced to the problem of racism. Other social problems—such as sexism, war, corporate irresponsibility, and economic injustice—have their own distinctive aspects. Yet they usually are compounded by their connections with racism, so that creating more racial justice would ameliorate some social problems and would allow citizens to deal more directly with others.

The Nature of Reality

Jackson opposes racism most forcefully when he describes his religious-ethical vision of a just society and a peaceful world. Rather than appealing directly to his own understanding of God as the source of this vision, Jackson claims that it is grounded in the nature of reality itself. In this way, he undercuts the criticism of some who claim that he inappropriately has interjected religion into political issues and merely is seeking to impose his own private religious beliefs on the rest of the country. While his political campaigning did employ religious language and imagery, he asked Americans to examine what they believed about themselves and their country as citizens, not as church members. He claims no particular religious authority for his political program. He believes that there are many ways that Americans can come to hold a similar vision—not just by sharing his particular belief in God. He calls on those who share his vision—however they may have come to their positions—to join with him in his political campaigning.

By appealing to the nature of reality rather than to his belief in God as the source of his vision of a just society and a peaceful world, Jackson appeals to public principles with which Americans can agree or disagree rather than to private beliefs. He believes that we can discover the nature of reality by observing what holds true over the long run. He often repeats Martin Luther King, Jr.'s statement, "though the arc of the universe is long, it bends toward justice,"[7] or claims that "right makes might," not vice versa,[8] or speaks of the lessons of history.[9]

For most people in public life, describing "the nature of reality itself" in speeches would be difficult, perhaps impossible—and it would make for dull, plodding speeches, not the kind demanded in this television era.[10] Jackson, however, is at home with symbolic language and regularly creates phrases that express the nature of reality in memorable ways.

Jackson's understanding of the nature of reality has three principal elements: (1) the importance and worth of each individual, (2) the interrelated nature of reality, and (3) the importance of vision.

"I Am Somebody"

Jackson believes that each individual is important and has worth because all people are God's children. For nearly two decades, he has

opened his speeches to students and his weekly addresses at Operation
PUSH's Saturday morning community forum with a chant:

I am somebody.
I may be poor,
    but I am somebody.
I may be uneducated,
I may be unskilled,
    but I am somebody.
I may be on welfare,
I may be prematurely pregnant,
I may be on drugs,
I may be victimized by racism,
    but I am somebody.
Respect me. Protect me. Never neglect me.
I am God's child.

Jackson believes that self-respect is a "fundamental factor in one's mental and spiritual health"[11] and is the basis from which mutual respect
can be established. "People who feel good about themselves will care
about and help other people."[12]

Just as good interpersonal relationships depend upon a sense of self-
worth, so do good political relationships. A sense of self-worth, coupled
with a clear understanding of one's self-interest, is the beginning of
sound political coalitions.

The Rainbow Nature of Reality

While individual differences are important, finally all people and institutions and dimensions of life are interrelated. As he noted in his
speech at the 1984 Democratic National Convention, "America is not
like a blanket, one piece of unbroken cloth—the same color, the same
texture, the same size. It is more like a quilt—many patches, many
pieces, many colors, many sizes, all woven and held together by a
common thread."[13] The image Jackson most frequently has used to
express this interrelatedness is, of course, the rainbow.

But it is not just individual people who are interrelated—all of reality
has this character. In one campaign speech, for example, he connected
the loss of 25,000 jobs in the rubber industry in Akron, Ohio, with U.S.
tax policy, multinational corporations' search for higher profits by ex-
porting jobs abroad to cheap labor markets, U.S. foreign policy, the
federal government's budget deficits, the abdication of governmental
responsibilities for domestic needs (such as education, cleaning up the
environment, and rebuilding cities and roads), resistance to affirmative
action programs, and the current hostility toward labor unions.[14]

"Without Vision, the People Perish"

In Jackson's view, vision is an essential component of reality. It has three principal purposes: (1) it provides hope and the grounds for perseverance, (2) it allows reality to be seen clearly, and (3) it provides substantive standards of individual and societal fulfillment.

(1) *"Don't Let Them Break Your Spirit."*[15] Sometimes Jackson talks about vision as "the dream that sustains us through the dark times."[16] The conclusion of his speeches typically contains this line: "I believe that suffering breeds character, character breeds faith, and in the end faith will not disappoint."[17] In a related vein, he often says, "[We] must not only have the courage and the conscience to expose the slummy side. We must have the conviction and vision to show America the sunny side, the way out."[18] Thus vision provides hope and the grounds for perseverance.

(2) *"Remove the Cataracts."* Vision also helps people see reality without distortion. Jackson believes that in the United States reality currently is being distorted by racism, nationalism, and false religious appeals:

> We must remove the cataracts of race from the eyes of our people and lift them out of poverty, ignorance, disease, and fear. . . . We must not blind them with prayer clauses, drape them in flags, and give them hot feelings of false racial pride when they remain hungry, ignorant, and diseased in the wealthiest nation in the history of the world.[19]

(3) *"Leave Racial Battleground, Come to Common Economic Ground, and Rise to Higher Moral Ground."* Finally, vision provides the basis for going beyond narrow self-interest and, indeed, beyond racism. Vision provides the standards by which to judge individual and organizational efforts:

> There must be a new litmus test for measuring the nation's greatness. It must not be measured by economics, political and military might alone. Our nation's greatness must be measured by our ideals and principles—and how closely we approximate them.[20]

Jackson speaks of "excellence" as "doing your best against the odds"[21] and of "sin" as "doing less than your best."[22]

Vision introduces substantive, rather than merely procedural or formal, standards for judging values and provides ideas of fulfillment for both individuals and society. To individuals he offers this challenge:

> Live beyond the pain of reality with the dream of a bright tomorrow. Use hope and imagination as weapons of survival and progress. . . . Young people, dream of a new value system. Dream of teachers, but teachers who will teach for life, not just for a living. . . . Dream of a world where we measure character by how much we share and care, not by how much we take and consume.[23]

Jackson articulates his vision of a transformed society most forcefully when he calls for a redefinition of national "greatness."

> It's not the size of our GNP. It's not our military might. It's not our educational and technological achievements—as great and as necessary as each of these may be. More fundamental to greatness, by my definition, is how we treat children in the dawn of life, how we treat poor people in the pit of life, and how we treat old people in the sunset of life. If we treat them with respect and dignity, we'll be a great nation. If we care for our young, insuring their proper nutrition and educate them to work in tomorrow's world, we'll be a great nation. If we provide decent, safe, and sanitary housing and food for the poor, then we'll be a great nation. If we provide health care and food and show respect for our elderly and allow those who are able and willing to continue to contribute something meaningful to our society, then we'll be a great nation. Greatness is in how we value and care for our people.[24]

Note how this last quotation contains all three of the principal elements in Jackson's view of reality: (1) We must respect ourselves and others. (2) Issues such as nutrition, education, housing, health care, and meaningful employment are all interrelated. (3) Greatness lies in acting on the basis of a vision beyond self-interest.

Social Change

While Jesse Jackson may have a consistent religious-ethical vision of a just society and a peaceful world, it is clear that many changes will have to occur in order for these to be achieved. Jackson's vision is not a utopian vision; it serves to judge the present condition of American society and the world, and it provides some guidance about how to achieve a society that is more just and a world that is more peaceful. A just society and a peaceful world are not going to be established through the *outside* intervention of God; nor will they be established through the natural progression of the laws of history or of some particular historical forces. Jackson believes a more just society and a more peaceful world can only be established as God works through the strivings of human beings. This is part of what is implied in his oft-repeated phrase, "Nobody will save us for us but us."[25]

Three ideas are central to Jackson's understanding of how social change occurs: (1) there is a dialectic between "effort" and "opportunity," (2) rejected people have a special role, and (3) coalitions are important.

(1) *The dialectic between "effort" and "opportunity."* Social change involves a dialectic between inner, individual change and outer, institutional change. Jackson agrees with conservatives by believing we must change hearts and minds in order to bring about social change, but he

also agrees with liberals by insisting that changes in institutions and public policies are essential. He believes that both changed minds and changed institutions are necessary. This is part of the reason he avoids· current political labels and calls himself a "progressive."

A clear example of this dialectic occurs when Jackson considers educational issues. The first matter to address, he argues, is the public policy question of equal educational opportunity, of equal access to quality desegregated multicultural education. But, while this is essential, it is not enough. "Effort must exceed opportunity for change to occur. . . . What does it really matter if we have a new book or an old book if we open neither? So motivation is at least as important as opportunity."[26] Thus Jackson simultaneously addresses changing public policies and changing individual hearts and minds.

To those who believe they are powerless, Jackson tells them that "there is nothing in the world more powerful than a made-up mind."[27] Freedom originates in the mind and the will:

> We can never be made truly free from without. . . . If our minds are not free, then they can remove the chains of slavery, but we will still be in bondage. However, if our minds are free and our spirits determined, no external force can enslave us.[28]

Over the years, Jackson has been criticized by those who mistakenly believe Jackson has "blamed the victim" rather than the victimizer for social injustices. To these critics, Jackson responds:

> I'm not arguing that the victimizers abdicate their responsibility, and I challenge victimizers everywhere I go. While I know that the victimizers may be responsible for the victims being down, the victims must be responsible . . . for initiating change, determining strategy, tactics, and timing, and being disciplined enough to pull it off. No one has a greater self-interest than the victims in getting up, while the victimizers do not perceive it to be in their self-interest.[29]

Thus Jackson simultaneously argues that all parts of American society must be opened up to include all those who have been left out and that "effort must exceed opportunity for change to occur."

(2) "The rejected stones will form the cornerstone." Jackson believes that those rejected by society—for their race, their gender, or their economic situation—have a special role in bringing about social change. First, they provide a helpful perspective on the way things are. Black people, for example, "receive the first and the most of whatever is bad and the least and last of whatever is good."[30] Jackson, however, cautions people not to misinterpret this: "Be clear; blacks alone are not the victims of [bad government policies]. We simply are the weather vane, signaling what is ahead for the rest of society."[31]

Second, the needs of the rejected have a claim with moral priority. The true test of national greatness, Jackson argues, is how we treat children, poor people, and old people. Greatness lies beyond self-interest; it lies in meeting the needs of "the least of these."[32] But beyond the moral benefits there also are pragmatic benefits to this approach: meeting the needs of America's rejected will benefit the entire nation. "If the boats stuck on the bottom can rise, all of us will rise."[33]

Third, America's rejected hold the keys to progressive social change. Jackson believes "the rejected stones can become the cornerstones of a new progressive coalition in America who will help to reshape a new domestic and world order."[34] To those who wonder how this could possibly be, Jackson replies with a biblical image: "We must focus on the strength and courage of David, not just on the tyranny of Goliath. . . . David has unused rocks just lying around. Goliath won with a perverse coalition of the rich and the unregistered."[35] Among the most important of these "unused rocks" is the ballot. Jackson argues that the old minorities constitute a new majority. Another "unused rock" is skillful use of consumer power, and much of Jackson's work with Operation Breadbasket and Operation PUSH dealt with developing this potential source of power.[36] Jackson believes that social change comes from the bottom, not from the top.

> To expect change to come . . . from the top down is a false expectation. . . . It is unrealistic to think that the slave master will voluntarily bring an end to slavery. Freedom does not come from the Big House or the White House but from your house and my house. . . . There is a greater correlation between pressure and progress than there is between presidents and progress.[37]

In sum, Jackson's approach to social change involves several steps. First, rejected people must change their minds about themselves and recognize that they are important rather than impotent. Second, through self-discipline, they must develop whatever powers and resources they possess. Third, they must use this power to gain leverage to bring about changes. Jackson makes much of this idea of leverage. While rejected people rarely have a majority of the political or economic power in a particular situation, they frequently have enough to determine where the balance of power will lie. For example, in the economic arena, black consumers often account for sales far in excess of the margin of profit. Thus a small, disciplined group can bring about a great deal of change.

The change Jackson seeks is a "renegotiation" of the current arrangements in society which favor certain people based on their race, sex, or class. The goal is equity and parity in all areas of life, a just society, and a peaceful world.

Building Coalitions

In order for America's rejected to bring about progressive social change, Jackson argues that they must join together in coalitions. As a first step, they must form a Rainbow Coalition of the rejected. Such a coalition would be based on self-interest—and, as Jackson understands it, self-interest is the basis for all political organizing. But the Rainbow Coalition also would be based on self-respect: the rejected have much more potential power than they realize.

Jackson then calls for creating a second kind of coalition. The Rainbow Coalition of the rejected should join with others seeking progressive social change and finally with the middle class. This coalition also would be based on self-interest. To these people who are not among America's rejected, Jackson argues that race, class, and sex have distorted their vision and have kept them from seeing their true self-interests. In seeking to build this second-level coalition, Jackson also appeals to the interrelated nature of reality:

> There are too many unregistered and non-participating potential poor voters, and there are too many poor and middle-class voters voting for the interests of the rich. The rich use the middle class as a buffer against the poor, but the national interest can best be served and protected with a coalition built from the bottom up. The poor and the middle class have more in common than they have in conflict, and—though the short-term greed of the rich often prevents them from seeing it and keeps them resisting with all their might—such a coalition and change of course is in their long-term interest as well, because only productive, prosperous, and employed people can buy their products.[38]

Jackson sounds a cautionary note, however, about entering into coalitions: be clear about your own interests and don't let your sight be obscured or diverted by others. For example, he argues:

> As black people, we have only varying degrees of access to the Republican and Democratic vehicles. But we can't ride to freedom in Pharaoh's chariot. Neither vehicle has as its primary commitment our liberation and development. . . . It is better that we lose a political race and keep our self-respect than to win the race and lose our soul.[39]

Although self-interest is the first principle of political activity, politics finally must be informed by vision, by something more than self-interest. For example, Jackson calls for politicians to mold public opinion rather than just follow public opinion polls.[40] Perhaps the statement that best expresses Jackson's position here is his call to "move from racial battlegrounds to economic and political common ground and to moral higher ground."[41] Because the vision of so many Americans is obscured by race, sex, or class, a great deal of work needs to be done to help people understand just what their common economic and political interests actually are. Only after that is done can Americans hope to rise to higher moral ground.

Acknowledgments

The editors wish to acknowledge the kind and persistent assistance of those individuals, groups, and institutions who have helped make this volume possible. Operation PUSH and the Rainbow Coalition graciously made their files available. JoAnna Brown-el, who transcribed many of these speeches while she was a staff member of Operation PUSH, and Dorothy Payton, who typed the manuscript, painstakingly transformed the oral word into the written. Marcia R. Sawyer, members of the Department of Religion at Central Michigan University, and members of the Social Ethics Seminar encouraged work on this project and offered consistently constructive comments. Central Michigan University, by means of a sabbatical leave and a university research professor grant, provided Roger Hatch with the time to work on this volume. Davis Perkins of Fortress Press offered encouragement and editorial suggestions at several crucial points. Harold W. Rast, Director and Senior Editor of Fortress Press, and his staff demonstrated enthusiasm for this project, accommodated its special problems, and worked diligently and creatively to make publication possible more quickly than we had envisioned.

NOTES

1. "The Quest for a Just Society and a Peaceful World," Washington, D.C., November 3, 1983.

2. "Service and a New World Order."

3. "We Must Act, Not Just React"; "Save Our Children"; "In Search of a New Focus and a New Vision"; and "Overcoming New Forms of Denial."

4. "A Case for Continuing Affirmative Action," Saturday Morning Community Forum, Operation PUSH, Chicago, Illinois, September 15, 1978.

5. Ibid.

6. "From Battleground to Common Ground to Higher Ground."

7. Ibid.; and "Service and a New World Order."

8. "Service and a New World Order"; and "Forty Years Later—Liberation, But Not Yet Joy."

9. "In Search of a New Focus and a New Vision"; "Foreign Policy But Not Foreign Values"; and "Forty Years Later—Liberation, But Not Yet Joy."

10. Ronald Reagan is a notable exception. Jackson understands this well and during his 1984 campaign argued that, in order for the Democrats to defeat Reagan, it was not enough to be anti-Reagan. They had to offer a "superior vision." As Jackson argued in "The Keys to a Democratic Victory in 1984," a

campaign position paper, "Reagan has offered the American people a coherent vision, an ideology based on fighting communism and promoting the growth of American corporations around the world. We must offer an equally coherent vision based on fighting poverty, disease, and oppression and promoting economic development that meets the needs of people around the world."

11. "The Rejected Stones: The Cornerstones of a New Public Policy," National Press Club, Washington, D.C., May 10, 1983.

12. "From Battleground to Common Ground to Higher Ground."

13. "The Candidate's Challenge."

14. "An End to Corporate Blackmail."

15. "From Battleground to Common Ground to Higher Ground."

16. "The Candidate's Challenge."

17. Ibid.; "In Search of a New Focus and a New Vision"; "Service and a New World Order"; "Binding Up the Wounds"; and "Forty Years Later— Liberation, But Not Yet Joy."

18. "The Candidate's Challenge."

19. "From Battleground to Common Ground to Higher Ground."

20. "The Keys to a Democratic Victory in 1984," campaign position paper, n.d. See also "The Candidate's Challenge."

21. "In Pursuit of Peace."

22. "Challenge to the New Generation," *Ebony* (June 1978).

23. "The Candidate's Challenge."

24. "The Keys to a Democratic Victory in 1984." See also "The Candidate's Challenge."

25. "Religious Liberty"; "The Ten Commandments for Excellence in Education"; "It's Up to You"; and "From Battleground to Common Ground to Higher Ground."

26. "Save Our Children."

27. "In Search of a New Focus and a New Vision"; "Service and a New World Order"; "Dreaming New Dreams"; and "The Candidate's Challenge."

28. "A Call to Action," Saturday Morning Community Forum, Operation PUSH, Chicago, Illinois, June 16, 1979.

29. "Challenge to the New Generation," *Ebony* (June 1978).

30. "In Pursuit of Peace."

31. "The State of the Nation: An Alternative View," Northeastern University, Boston, Massachusetts, January 31, 1984.

32. "Binding Up the Wounds"; "The Candidate's Challenge"; "Save the Family Farm and the Farm Family"; and "Protecting the Legacy."

33. "Dreaming New Dreams."

34. "From Battleground to Common Ground to Higher Ground." See also "Service and a New World Order."

35. "Dreaming New Dreams."

36. See, for example, "Black Americans Seek Economic Equity and Parity."

37. "A Call to Action," June 16, 1979.

38. "The Rejected Stones: The Cornerstones of a New Public Policy," May 10, 1983.

39. "The State of Black America and the Challenge to Overcome Against the Odds," Morehouse College, Atlanta, Georgia, February 15, 1983.

40. "The Candidate's Challenge."

41. "From Battleground to Common Ground to Higher Ground"; "The Candidate's Challenge"; and "Forty Years Later—Liberation, But Not Yet Joy."

POLITICAL
PROGRESSIVE

"We must build a coalition that goes beyond
the recognized labels. We must not fight for
Democrats alone, but fight for democracy. We
cannot simply support the Republicans, we must
support the republic. Our goal cannot simply be
to fight for liberals, it must be to fight for total
human liberation, in all of its varied forms. We can
only become a greater generation by serving the
needs of our day. Service is power. Service is
God's will."

The Candidate's Challenge: The Call of Conscience, the Courage of Conviction

Jesse Jackson ran for the Democratic party's presidential nomination in 1984. He finished with 465.5 delegates (about 11 percent of the total) and came in third among the eight original candidates. His surprisingly strong finish garnered him a major speaking assignment at the Democratic National Convention in San Francisco. This speech, given in prime time on national television on July 17, electrified the convention and the nation. It had the largest television audience of any speech at the 1984 Democratic or Republican conventions.

Tonight we come together, bound by our faith in a mighty God, with genuine respect and love for our country, and inheriting the legacy of a great party—the Democratic party—which is the best hope for redirecting our nation on a more humane, just, and peaceful course. This is not a perfect party. We are not a perfect people. Yet we are called to a perfect mission: to feed the hungry, to clothe the naked, to house the homeless, to teach the illiterate, to provide jobs for the jobless, and to choose the human race over the nuclear race. We are gathered here this week to nominate a candidate and write a platform which will expand, unify, direct, and inspire our party and the nation to fulfill this mission.

My constituency is the damned, the disinherited, the disrespected, and the despised. They are restless and seek relief. They've voted in record numbers. They have invested faith, hope, and trust in us. The Democratic party must send them a signal that we care. I pledge my best not to let them down.

The Call of Conscience: Redemption, Expansion, Healing, and Unity

Leadership must heed the call of conscience—redemption, expansion, healing, and unity—for they are the keys to achieving our mission. Time is neutral and does not change things. With courage and initiative, leaders change things. No generation can choose the age or circumstances in which it is born, but through leadership it can choose to make the age in which it is born an age of enlightenment—an age of jobs, peace, and justice. Only leadership—that intangible combination of gifts, discipline, information, circumstance, courage, timing, will, and divine inspiration—can lead us out of the crisis in which we find ourselves. Leadership can mitigate the misery of our nation. Leadership can part the waters and lead our nation in the direction of the Promised Land. Leadership can lift the boats stuck at the bottom.

I have had the rare opportunity to watch seven men, and then two, pour out their souls, offer their service, and heed the call of duty to direct the course of our nation. There is a proper season for everything. There is a time to sow, and a time to reap. There is a time to compete, and a time to cooperate. I ask for your vote on the first ballot as a vote for a new direction for this party and this nation—a vote of conscience and conviction. But I will be proud to support the nominee of this convention for the presidency of the United States. I have watched the leadership of our party grow and develop. My respect for both Mr. Mondale and Mr. Hart is great. I have watched them struggle with the crosswinds and cross fires of being visible public servants, and I believe that they will both continue to try to serve us faithfully. I am elated by the knowledge that, for the first time in our history, a woman, Geraldine Ferraro, will be recommended to share our ticket.

Throughout this campaign, I have tried to offer leadership to the Democratic party and the nation. If, in my high moments, I have done some good, offered some service, shed some light, healed some wounds, rekindled some hope, stirred someone from apathy and indifference, or in any way helped someone along the way, then this campaign has not been in vain. For friends who loved and cared for me, for a God who spared me, and for a family who understood me, I am eternally grateful.

If, in my low moments, in word, deed, or attitude, through some error of temper, taste, or tone, I have caused anyone discomfort, created pain, or revived someone's fears, that was not my truest self. If there were occasions when my grape turned into a raisin and my joy bell lost its resonance, please forgive me. Charge it to my head and not to my heart. My head is so limited in its finitude, but my heart is boundless in its love for the human family. I am not a perfect servant. I am a public servant, doing my best against the odds. As I grow, develop, and serve, be patient. God is not finished with me yet.

This campaign has taught me much: that leaders must be tough enough to fight, tender enough to cry, human enough to make mistakes, humble enough to admit them, strong enough to absorb the pain, and resilient enough to bounce back. For leaders, the pain is often intense. But you must smile through tears and keep moving with the faith that there is a brighter side somewhere.

I went to see Hubert Humphrey three days before he died. He had just called Richard Nixon from his dying bed, and many people wondered why. I asked him. He said, "Jesse, from this vantage point, with the sun setting in my life, all of the speeches, the political conventions, the crowds, and the great fights are behind me now. At a time like this, you are forced to deal with your irreducible essence, forced to grapple with that which is really important to you. What I have concluded is this: when all is said and done, we must forgive each other, redeem each other, and move on."

Our party is emerging from one of its most hard-fought battles for the Democratic party's presidential nomination in our history. But our healthy competition should make us better, not bitter. We must use the insight, wisdom, and experience of the late Hubert Humphrey as a balm to heal the wounds in our party, this nation, and the world. We must forgive each other, redeem each other, regroup, and move on.

Our flag is red, white, and blue, but our nation is a rainbow—red, yellow, brown, black, and white—and all are precious in God's sight. America is not like a blanket, one piece of unbroken cloth—the same color, the same texture, the same size. It is more like a quilt—many patches, many pieces, many colors, many sizes, all woven and held together by a common thread. The white, the Hispanic, the black, the Arab, the Jew, the woman, the Native American, the small farmer, the businessperson, the environmentalist, the peace activist, the young, the old, the lesbian, the gay, and the disabled make up the American quilt. Even in our fractured state, all of us count and fit in somewhere. We have proven that we can survive without each other. But we have not proven that we can *win* or *make progress* without each other. We must come together.

From Fannie Lou Hamer in Atlantic City in 1964 to the Rainbow Coalition in San Francisco today, from the Atlantic to the Pacific, we have experienced pain, but progress, as we obtained open housing; as young people got the right to vote; as we lost Malcolm, Martin, Medgar, Bobby, John, and Viola. The team that got us here must be expanded, not abandoned. Twenty years ago, tears welled up in our eyes as the bodies of Schwerner, Goodman, and Chaney were dredged from the depths of a river in Mississippi.* Twenty years later, our communities, black and Jewish, are in anguish, anger, and pain. Feelings have been hurt on both sides. There is a crisis in communications. Confusion is in the air, but we cannot afford to lose our way. We may agree to agree, or agree to disagree on issues, but we must bring back civility to the tensions. We are copartners in a long and rich religious history—the Judeo-Christian traditions. Many blacks and Jews have a shared passion for social justice at home and peace abroad. We must seek a revival of the spirit, inspired by a new vision and new possibilities. We must return to higher ground. We are bound by Moses and Jesus, but also connected with Islam and Muhammed. We are bound by Dr. Martin Luther King, Jr., and Rabbi Abraham Heschel crying out from their graves for us to reach common ground. We are bound by shared blood and shared sacrifices. We are much too intelligent; much too bound by our Judeo-Christian heritage; much too victimized by racism, sexism, militarism, and anti-Semitism; much too threatened as historical scapegoats to go on divided one from another. We must turn from finger-pointing to clasped hands. We must share our burdens and our joys with each other once again. We must turn to each other and not on each other.

Twenty years later, we cannot be satisfied by just restoring the old coalition. Old wineskins must make room for new wine. We must heal and expand. The Rainbow Coalition is making room for Arab-Americans. They too know the pain and hurt of racial and religious rejection. They must not continue to be made pariahs. The Rainbow Coalition is making room for Hispanic-Americans who this very night are living under the threat of the Simpson-Mazzoli immigration bill and farm workers in Ohio who are fighting the Campbell Soup Company with a boycott to achieve legitimate worker rights.

The Rainbow is making room for the Native Americans, the most exploited people of all and a people with the greatest moral claim among us. We support them as they seek to preserve their ancestral homelands and the beauty of a land that once was all theirs. They can never receive a fair share for all that they have given, but they must finally have a fair chance to develop their great resources and to preserve their people and their culture.

---

*Fannie Lou Hamer led the Mississippi Freedom Democratic party, which challenged the regular Mississippi Democratic party about their exclusion of blacks from the delegation at the Democratic National Convention in Atlantic City, N.J., in 1964. The others named all were civil rights advocates who were assassinated: Malcolm X; Martin Luther King, Jr.; Medgar Evers, chairman of the NAACP in Mississippi; Robert F. Kennedy; John F. Kennedy; and Viola Liuzzo, a white woman from Detroit killed while assisting in the Selma-to-Montgomery march for voting rights in 1965. Michael Schwerner, Andrew Goodman, and James Chaney were young civil rights workers murdered near Philadelphia, Mississippi, in the summer of 1964. Schwerner and Goodman were Jewish.

The Rainbow includes Asian-Americans, now being killed in our streets—scapegoats for the failures of corporate, industrial, and economic policies. The Rainbow is making room for young Americans. Twenty years ago, our young people were dying in a war for which they could not even vote. Twenty years later, young America has the power to stop a war in Central America and the responsibility to vote in great numbers. Young America must be politically active in 1984. The choice is war or peace. We must make room for young America.

The Rainbow includes disabled Americans. The color "chrome" fits in the rainbow. The disabled have their handicap revealed and their genius concealed, while the able-bodied have their genius revealed and their disability concealed. But ultimately we must judge people by their values and their contribution. Don't leave anybody out. I would rather have Roosevelt in a wheelchair than Reagan on a horse.

The Rainbow is making room for small farmers. They have suffered tremendously under the Reagan regime. They will either receive 90 percent parity or 100 percent charity. We must address their concerns and make room for them. The Rainbow includes lesbians and gays. No American citizen ought to be denied equal protection under the law.

We must be unusually committed and caring as we expand our family to include new members. All of us must be tolerant and understanding as the fears and anxieties of the rejected and of the party leadership express themselves in so many different ways. Too often what we call hate—as if it were deeply rooted in some philosophy or strategy—is simply ignorance, anxiety, paranoia, fear, and insecurity. We must be long-suffering as we seek to right the wrongs of our party and our nation. We must expand our party, heal our party, and unify our party. That is the means to our mission in 1984.

The Courage of Conviction: The Misery Index, the Danger Index, and Reaganomics

We are often reminded that we live in a great nation—and we do. But it can be greater still. The Rainbow is mandating a new definition of greatness. We must not measure greatness from the mansion down but from the manger up. Jesus said that we should not be judged by the bark we wear but by the fruit we bear. Jesus said that we must measure greatness by how we treat the least of these.

President Reagan says the nation is in recovery. Those 90,000 corporations that made a profit last year but paid no federal taxes are recovering. The 37,000 military contractors who have benefited from Reagan's more than doubling the military budget in peacetime are surely recovering. The big corporations and rich individuals who received the bulk of the three-year multi-billion-dollar tax cut from Mr. Reagan are recovering. But no such comparable recovery is under way for the least of these. Rising tides don't lift all boats, particularly those stuck on the bottom.

For the boats stuck at the bottom, there is a *rising misery index*. This administration has made life for the poor miserable. Its attitude toward poor people has been contemptuous. Its policies and programs have been cruel and unfair to working people. It must be held accountable in November for an increasing infant-mortality rate among the poor. In Detroit, one of the great cities of the Western world, babies are dying at the same rate as in Honduras, the most underdeveloped nation in our hemisphere. This administration must be held accountable for policies that contribute to the growing poverty in America. Under President Reagan, there are eight million more people in poverty. Currently 15 percent of our nation is in poverty, 34 million people. Of the 34 million poor people, 23 million are white, 11 million are black, Hispanic, Asian, and others. More and more of the poor are children. By the end of this year, there will be 41 million people in poverty—more people than at any time since the inadequate War on Poverty program began in 1965. We cannot stand by idly. We must fight for change, now.

Under President Reagan, the misery index has increased.

Social Security. The 1981 budget cuts included nine permanent Social Security benefit cuts totaling $20 billion over five years. Now he says we may need more.

Small Businesses. Approximately 98 percent of all businesses in America can be considered "small"—employing fewer than 500 workers. Yet under the Reagan tax cuts, only 18 percent of total business tax cuts went to them—82 percent went to big business.

Health Care. Reagan sharply cut funding for screening children for lead poisoning—which can lead to retardation, behavioral difficulties, and learning disabilities—from $9.1 million in 1981 to $5.8 million in 1983. Estimates for 24 states indicate that the number of children screened dropped from 1.1 million to 600,000.

Education. He cut real spending for education by $6 billion, or 25 percent. Four million three hundred thousand handicapped children are receiving delayed or reduced services. One hundred twenty-four thousand fewer college students receive Pell Grant assistance from the federal government.

Women. There are now 9.7 million female-headed families. They represent 16 percent of all families, but half of all poor families. Seventy percent of all poor children live in a household headed by a woman. Working women make less than men in every job category, at every educational level, yet Mr. Reagan sees no need for the Equal Rights Amendment.

Environmental Protection. This administration has cleaned up only 6 of 546 priority toxic-waste dumps in three years.

Farmers. In 1983, real net farm income was only about half its level of 1979 and was lower than at any time since the Great Depression.

Many say that the race in November will be decided in the South. President Reagan is depending on the conservative South to return him to office. But the South, I tell you, is unnaturally conservative. The South is the nation's poorest region and therefore has the least to conserve. In his appeal to the South, Mr. Reagan is trying to substitute flags and prayer clauses for jobs, food, clothing, education, health care, and housing. But apparently President Reagan is not even familiar with the structure of a prayer. We must watch false prophecy. He has cut energy assistance to the poor, he has cut food stamps, children's breakfast and lunch programs, the Women, Infants, and Children (WIC) program for pregnant mothers and infants, and job training for children; and then says, "Let us pray." In a prayer, you are supposed to thank God for the food you are about to receive, not for the food that just left. I take prayer very seriously—I've come this way by the power of prayer. So we need to pray. But we need to pray to remove the man that removed the food. We need a change in November.

Poor people and working people—black, white, and brown—all across America, but especially in the South, must resist the temptation to go for Mr. Reagan's social placebo as a substitute for jobs and economic justice. Cotton candy may taste good, it may even go down smoothly, but it has no substance and it's not good for you.

Under President Reagan, the misery index has increased dramatically for the poor, but the danger index for everyone has escalated. The military budget has been doubled to protect us from the Russians, yet today Soviet submarines are closer to our shores, and their missiles are more accurate. Tonight we live in a world that is more miserable and dangerous.

The Reagan administration has failed to achieve any agreed-upon nuclear arms reductions whatsoever. The Reagan administration's attempts to regain military superiority, to achieve a first-strike capability, its plans and preparations to launch and win a limited nuclear war, and its commitment to "Star Wars" have left the world a much more unstable and dangerous place in which to live. We are at a nuclear standoff in Europe. We are mining the harbors of Nicaragua and attempting to covertly overthrow a legitimate government there—actions which have been condemned by many of our allies and by the World Court. Under this administration we have been at war and lost the lives of American boys in Lebanon, Honduras, and Grenada. Under this administration, one-third of America's children have come to believe that they will die in a nuclear war. The danger index for everybody is increasing—and it is frightening.

But it is not enough simply to react to the effects—a growing misery and danger index. We must dig deeper and comprehend the underlying cause of the growing misery and danger index—Reaganomics. We must distinguish between Mr. Reagan's political appeal and his economic deal. Mr. Reagan's economic program is a combination of cyanide and Kool-Aid, jelly beans and poison. It may taste good, but the results are disastrous. We must distinguish between Reaganism and Reaganomics.

While Reaganism is largely subjective, supply-side economics is more objective. Reaganism was used to impose Reaganomics. Reaganism is the perception. Reaganomics is the reality. We are fatter now, but less secure. Many who were once basking in the sun of Reaganism have now been burned to a crisp with Reaganomics. In 1980 many thought they saw a light at the end of the tunnel in Reaganism. But in 1984 we now know it was not sunshine, but a train coming this way.

In 1980 then-candidate George Bush called Mr. Reagan's economic plan to get America back on track "voodoo economics." Third-party candidate John Anderson said that the combination of massive military spending, tax cuts, and a balanced budget by 1984 could only be accomplished with blue smoke and mirrors. We now know they were both right.

President Reagan declares that we are having a dynamic economic recovery. And we are having a recovery of sorts. After three and a half years, unemployment has inched just below where it was when he took office in 1981. But there are still 8.1 million people officially unemployed, and 11 million working only part-time jobs. Make no mistake about it, inflation has come down, but let's examine how and at whose expense this was achieved—and how long it is likely to last.

President Reagan's 1984 economic recovery has come after the deepest and longest recession since the Great Depression. President Reagan curbed inflation by cutting consumer demand. He cut consumer demand with conscious and callous fiscal and monetary policies. He used the federal budget deliberately to induce unemployment and curb social spending. He then urged and supported the tight monetary policies of the Federal Reserve Board deliberately to drive up interest rates—again to curb consumer demand created through borrowing.

Unemployment reached 10.7 percent; we experienced skyrocketing interest rates; our dollar inflated abroad; there were record bank failures, record farm foreclosures, record business bankruptcies, record budget deficits, record trade deficits, and more. President Reagan brought inflation down by destabilizing our economy, disrupting family life, and wreaking havoc on the poor.

Remember President Reagan's central promise of the 1980 campaign—to balance the budget by 1984? Instead of balancing the budget, in 1984 we are having record budget deficits and looking at record budget deficits for as far as the eye can see. Under President Reagan, the cumulative budget deficits for just his four years in office will be virtually equal to the total budget deficits from George Washington to Jimmy Carter—equal to all past presidents' budget deficits combined. I tell you, we need a change. Reagan's economic recovery is being financed by deficit spending—nearly $200 billion a year. Yet military spending, a major cause of the deficit, is projected over the next five years to be nearly $2 trillion and will cost about $40,000 for every taxpaying family.

When the government borrows $200 billion annually to finance the deficit, this encourages the private sector to make money off of interest rates rather than investing in economic development and growth. Even worse, we don't have enough domestically to finance the debt, so we are borrowing money abroad from foreign banks, governments, and financial institutions—$40 billion in 1983; $70 to $80 billion in 1984 (40 percent of our total); over $100 billion in 1985 (50 percent of the total); and rising. By 1989, it is projected that 50 percent of all individual income taxes will be going just to pay for the interest on the debt. The U.S. used to be the largest exporter of capital, but under President Reagan we soon will become the largest debtor nation. About two weeks ago, on July 4, we celebrated our Declaration of Independence and our freedom. Yet every day supply-side economics is making our nation more economically dependent and less economically free. Five to six percent of our gross national product is now being eaten up with President Reagan's budget deficit.

To depend on foreign military powers to protect our national security would be foolish and make us less secure. Yet Reaganomics is increasingly making us more dependent. By increasing our economic dependency, Reaganomics decreases our ability to control our own economic future and destiny, decreases our security, and decreases our self-respect. A great nation must be measured by its ability to produce, not just its ability to consume. We are negotiating away our independence. Freedom and independence are the result of self-determination, self-reliance, self-discipline, and self-respect. Under President Reagan, America is less economically free and more dependent.

President Reagan's consumer-led, but deficit-financed, recovery is unbalanced, artificial, and will be short-lived. President Reagan's recovery is an economic "quick fix" that is based on foreign borrowing and will end in another recession. The boom of '84 will become a boomerang. If we continue down the road of supply-side—with a "dead-end" sign in front of us, with no brakes, and a cliff behind the sign—we will deserve our inevitable fate.

Reaganomics is economic opium that is destroying us from within. President Reagan's recovery is like Santa Claus's wish list at Christmas time—buy now and pay later. President Reagan's recovery may bring the joy of Christmas morning in 1984, but there will be sadness, sacrifice, and suffering when the generation of your children, and your children's children, have to pay for it. Our adult generation should not be so selfish and self-centered as to burden our children with our indulgent and short-lived behavior. It is short-term pleasure, but it's leading to long-term pain.

Yet an artificial recovery is merely the beginning of our problems. The record Reagan budget deficits drive up interest rates. High interest rates overvalue the dollar abroad. Because of an overvalued dollar, our prices have increased relative to all of our competitors by about 35 percent over the last three years. We cannot give our competitors a 35-percent subsidy, or give ourselves a 35-percent tax, and remain competitive in the world market. An overvalued dollar is good for the American consumer because it subsidizes imports, but it is bad for American exports (farm products and machinery in particular) because it taxes Americans out of jobs and competition. The trade imbalance this year is projected to be close to $120 billion. For every $1 billion of trade imbalance, it costs Americans about 25,000 jobs. Thus President Reagan's record trade imbalance alone will cost Americans nearly 3 million jobs. We need a balance of trade, because another four years of Reaganomics will bring on the greatest tide of protectionism in American history.

Record budget deficits, high interest rates, and an overvalued dollar are contributing to the international debt crisis in the Third World. The greatest threat to our national security in Central America is not the East-West conflict. It is the international debt crisis, created principally by President Reagan's record budget deficits. They are threatening to destabilize the world economy, including the U.S. economy. In light of the international debt crisis, the International Monetary Fund and the big multinational banks are imposing austerity programs on the developing nations. Some developing nations cannot even pay the interest on their debt. These governments are unable to meet the basic needs of their citizens, and the people are rebelling. The buildup of our large interventionary forces is mainly for the purpose of putting down these economic and social rebellions in the name of stopping com-

munism, but it is largely of our own making—and heightened under
Reaganomics.

The Candidate's Challenge: Plan a Way Out
with Justice, Peace, and Jobs

Democracy guarantees opportunity; it does not guarantee success. Democracy guarantees the right to participate; it does not give a license to
either a majority or a minority to dominate. The victory for the Rainbow
Coalition in the platform debates today was not whether we won or lost
the vote but that we raised the right issues. We could afford to lose the
vote. Issues are negotiable. We could not afford to avoid raising the right
questions. Our self-respect and our moral integrity were at stake. Our
heads are perhaps bloody but unbowed. Our backs are straight, and our
vision is clear. We can go home and face our people. And when we
think, in this journey from slave ship to championship, that we have
gone from the planks of the boardwalk in Atlantic City in 1964 to
fighting to help to write the planks in the Democratic party platform in
San Francisco in 1984, there is a deep and abiding sense of joy in our
soul, in spite of the tears in our eyes. Although there are missing planks,
there is a solid foundation upon which we can build.

The real challenge to our individual and collective Democratic leadership is to do three things: (1) provide hope, which will inspire people
to struggle and achieve, (2) provide a plan that shows the people a way
out of our dilemma, and (3) courageously lead the way out.

There is a way out. *Justice.* The requirement for rebuilding America is
justice. The linchpin of progressive politics in America is not new programs in the North but new power in the South. That is why I argue
over and over again, that from Lynchburg, Virginia, around to Texas,
there is only one black congressperson out of 115. Nineteen years after
passage of the Voting Rights Act, we're locked out of the House, the
Senate, and the governor's mansion. The key to unlocking Southern
power is getting the Voting Rights Act enforced and ending the new
forms of political disenfranchisement.

The key to a Democratic victory in 1984 is enfranchisement of the
progressive wing of the Democratic party. They are the ones who have
been devastated by Reaganomics, and, therefore, it is in their self-
interest to vote in record numbers to oust their oppressor. Those already
poor and those who are being impoverished do not simply want a
change in leaders, they want a change in direction. The poor are not
looking to be embellished, they have a need to be empowered. The key
to political enfranchisement is enforcement of the Voting Rights Act.
Gerrymandering, annexations, at-large elections, inaccessible registrars,

roll purges, dual registrations, and second primaries—these are the schemes that continue to disenfranchise the locked-out. Why do I fight these impediments? Because you cannot hold someone in the ditch without lingering there with them. If the Voting Rights Act is enforced, we'll get twelve to twenty black, Hispanic, female, and progressive congresspersons from the South. We can save the cotton, but we've got to fight the boll weevils. We've got to make a judgment.

It's not enough to hope ERA will pass. How can we pass ERA? If blacks vote in great numbers, progressive whites win. It's the only way progressive whites win. If blacks vote in great numbers, Hispanics win. If blacks, Hispanics, and progressive whites vote, women win. When women win, children win. When women and children win, workers win. We must all come up together. We must come up together. I tell you, with all of our joy and excitement, we must not save the world and lose our souls. We should never short-circuit enforcement of the Voting Rights Act at every level. If one of us rises, all of us must rise. Justice is the way out.

There is a way out. *Peace.* The only way we can have jobs at home is to have peace abroad. We should not act as if nuclear weaponry is negotiable and debatable. In 1984, other nations have nuclear weapons too. Now if we drop the bomb, six to eight minutes later, we, too, will be destroyed. The issue now is not about dropping the bomb on somebody; it's about dropping the bomb on everybody. We must choose developed minds over guided missiles and think our way out, not fight it out. We must develop a coherent strategic nuclear strategy. We used nuclear weapons once before on Japan. But we must declare that never again will we be the ones to engage in the "first use" of nuclear weapons. Our real security is in developed minds, not guided missiles.

Our foreign policy must be demilitarized. We must choose mutual respect, talk, negotiations, diplomacy, trade, and aid, and measure human rights by one yardstick as the way of resolving international conflicts. We should support a legitimate Solidarity labor movement and oppose martial law in Poland. But then we cannot become the number-one trading partner with South Africa when they impose martial law and violently crush a black solidarity labor movement—especially while they are developing a nuclear capability. The U.S. must apply a new formula in assisting South African liberation—enfranchisement, investment; disenfranchisement, disinvestment. Our present relationship with South Africa is a moral disgrace.

Beyond the liberation of South Africa, we must fight for trade and aid for development in all of Africa, as well as in Europe and the Middle East. We must be as concerned about the preservation of democracy in Africa as we are in Europe. We've turned our heads and our backs when democracy has been dealt blows in Africa. This indifference must not be allowed to happen in the future.

Our present formula for peace in the Middle East is inadequate and will not work. There are twenty-two nations in the Middle East, and we must be able to talk, act, influence, and reconcile all of them. Currently we have too many interests and too few friends. We must have a mutual recognition policy, built on the Camp David agreement, which was a good first step, and measure human rights by one yardstick.

We should not be mining the harbors of Nicaragua and trying to covertly overthrow that government. Military aid and military advisors (who will give military advice) should be withdrawn from El Salvador. We should use our strength to get FDR-FMLN and President Duarte to agree to a cease-fire and negotiations. We should not be establishing military bases in Honduras and militarizing the nation of Costa Rica. It was wrong for our nation to invade tiny Grenada. And if we can have diplomatic relations with the Soviet Union and China, as we should, we can have diplomatic relations with Cuba. Just this week, we have seen progress as a result of our moral appeal. In addition to the Americans returned, the political prisoners released (and more to be released), negotiations, at this very moment, are being conducted over the Mariel prisoners, a Cuban family-reunification program, and President Castro has agreed to exchange ambassadors without preconditions. Let's give peace a chance.

There is a way out. *Jobs.* If we enforce the Voting Rights Act as a way of achieving justice; and if we achieve peace through cutting the defense budget without cutting our defense, respect other nations of the world, and resolve conflicts through negotiations instead of confrontations; then we will have enough power and money to rebuild America. We can use the money we are currently squandering on the arms race to save the human race. We can use that money to build millions of new houses, to build hospitals, to train and pay our teachers and educate our young people, to provide health care and health-care training, to rebuild our cities and end rural poverty; use that money to rebuild 250,000 bridges, rebuild our railroads, and build mass-transit systems; use that money to put steelworkers back to work; use that money to rebuild the infrastructure of our country: repair our roads, our ports, our riverbeds, our sewer systems, and stop soil erosion; use that money to clean up our environment: our land, our water, and our air; use that money to make "America the Beautiful." We could put America back to work.

The Motivation: Vision, Dreams, and Hope

Ronald Reagan claims the votes of the South. I say to you this night that the soil is too rich and the people are too poor for Ronald Reagan to have the votes of the South. The South is going to rise up and move from racial battlegrounds to economic common ground and moral higher ground. We love our God, and we love our country too, but we want moral values with material substance. Black and white together, men and women, we will take the South.

We have fought hard to build our Rainbow Coalition of the rejected over the last eight months. We have fought hard for party justice and for our minority planks because we believe that expanding our party to include the locked-out is the key to victory in November and to developing the progressive politics of the future.

What this campaign has shown above all else is that the key to our liberation is in our own hands and in our dream and vision of a better world. It is the vision that allows us to reach out to each other and to redeem each other. It is the dream that sustains us through the dark times and the dark realities. It is our hope that gives us a *why* for living when we do not see *how* to live.

In the final analysis, however, we must be driven not by a negative—the fear of Reagan—but by the positive leadership and programs of the Democratic party. It is not enough motivation just to vote against Reagan, we must inspire our constituency to vote for us. We must offer our people the vision of a just society and the dream of a peaceful world. We must inspire the American people with hope. We must put forth the vision of a government that cares for all of its people, the vision of a people at work rebuilding its nation. We must not be forced to choose between the two valid principles of seniority and affirmative action. We must put all of America back to work.

With courage and conscience, conviction and vision, we can win. If we don't raise the issues, if the truth is locked away, the people won't get excited. But when the truth is lifted up, they'll come running. Across lines of race and sex, they'll come running to vote for us. If we lift up before this nation a plan to wipe out cheese and bread lines, to feed our hungry and malnourished people, they'll come running. If we lift up a plan to house the homeless and educate the illiterate, they'll come running. If we reach out to the Vietnam veteran, to the disabled, to the poor, to the widow, to the orphan, and tell them that help is on the way, they'll come running.

When I was a child in Greenville, South Carolina, the Rev. James Hall used to preach a sermon, every so often, about Jesus. He would quote Jesus as saying, "If I be lifted up, I'll draw all men unto me." When I was a child I didn't quite understand what he meant. But I understand it a little better now. If you raise up truth, it's magnetic. It has a way of drawing people. With all this confusion in the convention—bright lights, parties, and big fun—we must raise up a simple proposition: feed the hungry, and the poor will come running; study war no more, and our youth will come running. If we lift up a program to put America back to work as an alternative to welfare and despair, the unemployed will come running. If we cut the military budget without cutting our defense and use that money to rebuild bridges and put steelworkers back to work; use that money to provide jobs for our citizens; use that money to build schools and train teachers and educate our children; use that money to build hospitals and train doctors and nurses—the whole nation will come running to us.

As I lived in the ghettoes, in barrios, on reservations, and in the slums, I had a message for our youth. Young America, I know you face a cutback in jobs, large reductions in housing and food, inferior health care and education, and a general environment that tries to break your spirit. But don't put dope in your veins; put hope in your brains. Don't let them break your spirit. There is a way out. Our party must not only have the courage and the conscience to expose the slummy side. We must have the conviction and vision to show America the sunny side, the way out. When I see urban decay I see a sunny side and a slummy side. A broken window is the slummy side. Train that youth to be a carpenter. That's the sunny side. A missing brick? That's the slummy side. Train that youth to be a brick mason. That's the sunny side. The hieroglyphics of destitution on the walls? That's the slummy side. Train that youth to be a painter or an artist. That's the sunny side. Then unions must open up, embrace, and train our youth so they can help to rebuild America.

Conclusion

I am more convinced than ever that we can win. We'll vault up the rough side of the mountain—we can win. But I just want the youth of America to do me one favor. Exercise the right to dream. You must face reality—that which is. But then dream of the reality that ought to be, that must be. Live beyond the pain of reality with the dream of a bright tomorrow. Use hope and imagination as weapons of survival and progress. Use love to motivate you and obligate you to serve the human family.

Young people, dream of peace. Choose the human race over the nuclear race. We must bury the weapons and not burn the people. We are the first generation that will either freeze the weapons or burn the people and freeze the planet.

Young people, dream of a new value system. Dream of teachers, but teachers who will teach for life, not just for a living. Dream of doctors, but doctors who are more concerned with public health than personal wealth. Dream of lawyers, but lawyers who are more concerned with justice than a judgeship. Dream of artists, but artists who will convey music and message, rhythm, rhyme, and reason. Dream of priests and preachers, but priests and preachers who will prophesy and not profiteer. Dream of writers, but writers who will ascribe, describe, prescribe, not just scribble. Dream of authentic leaders who will mold public opinion against a headwind, not just ride the tailwinds of opinion polls. Dream of a world where we measure character by how much we share and care, not by how much we take and consume. Preach and dream. Our time has come.

We must measure character by how we treat the least of these, by who feeds the most hungry people, by who educates the most uneducated people, by who cares and loves the most, by who fights for the needy and seeks to save the greedy. We must dream and choose the laws of sacrifice, which lead to greatness, and not the laws of convenience, which lead to collapse.

In your dreaming you must know that unearned suffering is redemptive. Water cannot wash away the blood of martyrs. Blood is thicker than water. Water makes grass and flowers grow, but blood makes sons and daughters of liberation grow. No matter how difficult the days and dark the nights, there is a brighter side somewhere. In Angola, Mozambique, Nicaragua, El Salvador, South Africa, Greenville, South Carolina, and Harlem, there is a brighter side.

Jesus was rejected from the inn and born in the slum. But just because you were born in the slum does not mean that the slum was born in you. With a made-up mind, which is the most powerful instrument in the world, you can rise above your circumstances. No mountain is too high, and no valley is too low; no forest is too dense, and no water is too deep—if your mind is made up. With eyesight, you may see misery. But with insight, you can see the brighter side.

Suffering breeds character, character breeds faith, and in the end faith will not disappoint. Faith, hope, and dreams will prevail. Weeping may endure for a night, but joy is coming in the morning. Troubles won't last always. Our time has come. No graves can hold our bodies down. Our time has come. No lie can live forever. Our time has come. We must leave our racial battlegrounds, come to economic common ground, and rise to moral higher ground. America, our time has come. Give me your tired, your poor, your huddled masses yearning to breathe free. And come November, there will be a change, because our time has come.

Dreaming New Dreams

This speech was given August 27, 1983, at the Lincoln Memorial in Washington, D.C., at a march held on the twentieth anniversary of the 1963 March on Washington for Jobs, Peace, and Freedom Now. A little more than a month later, Jackson resigned his position at Operation PUSH to pursue the Democratic party's 1984 presidential nomination.

Twenty years ago, Dr. Martin Luther King, Jr., had a dream of freedom for all Americans. Twenty years later, the power of his dream has drawn this generation together and inspires us to keep on dreaming. We must continue to dream, but the dream of 1963 must be expanded to meet the realities of these times. We must dream new dreams, expand the horizons of our dreams to meet the realities of these times, and remove any ceiling or barrier that would limit our legitimate aspirations. Democracy at its best provides a floor for everyone—but imposes limits upon no one. The sky is the limit. Let us continue to dream. Dreaming is a gift of the spirit that can lift you above misery to miracles and allow you to smile through tears.

Freedom to Equality

Twenty years ago, we came to these hallowed grounds as a rainbow coalition to demand our freedom. Twenty years later, we have our freedom—our civil rights. On our way to Washington today we didn't have to stop at a friend's house or a church to eat or use the bathroom. Apartheid is over. But, twenty years later, we still do not have equality. We have moved in. Now we must move up.

Twenty years ago, we were stripped of our dignity. Twenty years later,

19

we are stripped of our share of power. The absence of segregation is not the presence of social justice or equality.

Twenty years ago, there were no blacks in Congress or in statewide offices in the nine southern states where 53 percent of blacks live.

Twenty years later, we still have none, because the Voting Rights Act has been sabotaged. It has been reduced to an Indian treaty—an unfulfilled law. The Democratic party is violating the law. The Republican party is not enforcing the law. We're still looking for allies who will be fair as our struggle shifts from welfare to our share—from aid to trade, from social generosity to economic reciprocity.

Twenty years ago, there were fewer than 400 black elected officials in the land. Twenty years later, we have 5,200—but that constitutes only 1 percent of the 512,000 officials in this nation. We are still more than 50,000 short of our share. And at the present rate—1 percent every 18 years—it will take us 198 years to achieve equality.

Twenty years later, no longer do the blatant forms of voting rights denial dominate the news—poll taxes, grandfather clauses, literacy tests, and violence. Now the new forms of voter denial go unreported— dual registration, second primaries, gerrymandering, annexation, at-large elections, and registrars who function arbitrarily. The forms of voter denial are different, but the effect is the same.

In Mississippi, blacks are 40 percent of the population. Yet, of five members of Congress, none is black; of nine Supreme Court Justices, none is black; of eight statewide officials, none is black; of eighty-two tax assessors, one is black; of eighty-two registrars, two are black; of eighty-two sheriffs, three are black. The pattern is the same in Virginia, North Carolina, South Carolina, Georgia, Florida, Alabama, Louisiana, and Arkansas. We want our share.

Defend the Poor

We must defend the poor—the boats stuck on the bottom. Mississippi is still the litmus test of democracy, the Democrats, and the Justice Department. We cannot measure our progress by a few more captains on ships on high seas. We must focus on the masses of boats stuck on the bottom. If the boats stuck on the bottom can rise, all of us will rise.

If the boats stuck on the bottom rise, corporate America will be held accountable; the Equal Rights Amendment will rise; health, education, and housing programs will rise; peace, jobs, and a clean and safe environment will rise; those at the sunrise of life, our young, and those in the sunset of life, our elderly, will rise.

If the boats stuck on the bottom can rise, blacks and Hispanics and women can go to Congress, progressive candidates—whites, blacks,

Hispanics, and women—can go to the Senate, and collectively we can determine who will go to the White House.

Twenty years ago, we were together, and we made progress. Twenty years later, apart, there has been regression. On this day, we must revive our coalition. We must remind each other from where we have come, forgive each other, redeem each other, and look to the future. We have proven that we can survive without one another, but we have not proven that we can win without each other. The rainbow coalition must be resurrected.

A New World Order

But the rainbow coalition of the rejected cannot accept the status quo. We must have a new vision. At home, we must fight for one set of rules—equal protection under the law. Abroad, we must measure human rights by one yardstick. We can't define democracy as majority rule in North America and as minority rule in South Africa.

We can't impose economic sanctions in Poland because of martial law and then become South Africa's number-one trading partner. We just want the game played by one set of rules. We must choose the human race over the nuclear race. El Salvador is our neighbor, not our nemesis. They are our next-door neighbor, not our backdoor threat.

The rainbow coalition must seek new values and a new world order. Twenty years ago, blacks, Hispanics, youth, and the military were denied the right to vote. But, twenty years later, American democracy has made a marvelous adjustment—it has made room for all of us. Now we don't have to explode through riots or implode through drugs. We can seek change through orderly elections and not through bloody revolutions.

We Can Win

The rainbow coalition represents promise and power, but we must focus on the strength and courage of David, not just on the tyranny of Goliath. The repressive Reagan regime won because David did not use all of his political rocks and his slingshot. David has unused rocks just lying around. Goliath won with a perverse coalition of the rich and the unregistered.

What do I mean? In the North, Reagan won Massachusetts by 2,500 votes, but there were 64,000 unregistered blacks; he won Illinois by 176,000, with 600,000 unregistered blacks; he won Delaware by 5,400, with 20,000 unregistered blacks; and he won New York by 165,000, with 900,000 unregistered blacks.

In the South, Reagan won Alabama by 17,000, with 272,000 unregistered blacks; he won Arkansas by 5,000, with 85,000 unregistered blacks; Kentucky by 17,000, with 62,000 unregistered blacks; Louisiana by 84,000, with 256,000 unregistered blacks; Mississippi by 11,000, with 131,000 unregistered blacks; North Carolina by 39,000, with 505,000 unregistered blacks; South Carolina by 11,000, with 292,000 unregistered blacks; Tennessee by 4,700, with 158,000 unregistered blacks.

He won these eight southern states—states with 72 electoral votes, 27 percent of what he needed to win—with a cumulative total of 192,000 votes—and there are 3,000,000 unregistered black voters in the South alone! Rocks just lying around.

But we've changed our mind. He won Mississippi by 11,000 votes in 1980, but we've registered 40,000 new Mississippi voters since May. Hands that picked cotton in 1964 will pick a president in 1984.

Don't Let Them Break Your Spirit

If we will but hold on, God has promised us a rainbow after the flood—the Reagan flood of a denial of jobs, peace, and freedom. There is a balm in Gilead. He has given us a formula—turn to each other, not on each other. Separately, we may be poor, but when we come together we aren't poor any more. We have been born and bred in the slums, but the slums are not born and bred in us.

David, don't let Goliath break your spirit! Hold on to your dreams! Don't give up! Hold on to your dreams! Use what you've got. Don't complain about what you don't have. Hold on to your dreams! David, pick up your rocks. Stand up! Stand tall! Stand proud! Use your rocks. Little David, your time has come.

Make up your mind. There is nothing more powerful than a made-up mind. Run toward freedom! Don't stand still! Run! Steal away to freedom! Run! You may lose if you run, but you're guaranteed to lose if you don't. Run! At the worst you'll gain your self-respect, and at the best you'll help to save a nation. Run! Take the chains off of your ankles, but don't shift them to your mind. Run! Run from disgrace to amazing grace. Run! Run from the outhouse to the statehouse to the courthouse to the White House. Run! But hold on to your dreams.

Political Votes,
Economic Oats

Jackson gave this speech before the Republican
National Committee, meeting in Washington, D.C., on
January 20, 1978. Fourteen months earlier, the black
vote had put Jimmy Carter in the White House.

Last month your chairman, Mr. Bill Brock, sent me a
letter. In that letter he indicated that the Republican party was embark-
ing on a new program to open its doors to greater participation by black
Americans. He indicated, on behalf of the party, a willingness to listen
and a desire to respond to our needs.

He also indicated that this platform would give us the opportunity to
meet personally with leading Republicans across this nation and to
discuss with them our organization, Operation PUSH, and its "PUSH for
Excellence" in education program. Many of you may have heard of our
work in this and other areas and desire to get involved. We welcome
your participation.

Further, Mr. Brock said that he felt the American political process was
on the threshold of historic change, and that black people should play
an important role in shaping that future. We agree. So, after serious
consideration and deliberation, I decided to accept your invitation. I
view my presence here today as an indication of a new realization by
this party that blacks do exist and are here to stay. Even more important,
I hear you saying that our presence or absence does make a political
difference.

Mutual need is the basis of an alliance. Black people need the Republican party to compete for us so that we have real alternatives for
meeting our needs. The Republican party needs black people if it is ever

to compete for national office or, in fact, to keep it from becoming an extinct party.

Since 1964, with very few exceptions, the Republican party has turned its back on the black vote and black interests. Yet we have both a right and an obligation to expand our political options. We must now exercise that right and obligation with regard to both the Republican and Democratic parties and create external pressure upon both.

I want to discuss four basic points today:

● Political enfranchisement—the right to vote;
● Political power—our political options;
● Political program—our areas of vested interest;
● Beyond partisan politics—a new America.

I want to state my premise at the very beginning. *The only protection people have politically is to remain necessary.* We must pursue a strategy that prohibits one party from taking us for granted and another party from writing us off. The only protection we have against political genocide is to remain necessary.

Political Enfranchisement:
The Right to Vote

For blacks, political participation historically has involved a struggle to gain equal access to the political arena. Our state of slavery meant we were property, not persons, and therefore could not enjoy the rights and privileges of citizenship—including political rights. During the First Reconstruction, black registered voters actually outnumbered white registered voters in ten southern states, and we won elective office at all levels of government, including the Congress. This progress, while nothing short of amazing, was short-lived and by the turn of this century had been reversed. It was not until the protest movement of the 1960s, led by Dr. Martin Luther King, Jr., culminating in the 1965 Voting Rights Act, that we again began to make political progress.

Thus in thirteen short years we have gone from 400 black political officials to over 4,000, but it is still less than one-half of 1 percent of all public officials.

In 1965 we had fewer than five black congresspersons; now we have sixteen. We had no black U.S. senators; now we have one, Senator Edward Brooke. We had no black justice on the Supreme Court; now we have one, Justice Thurgood Marshall. A black serves as U.S. Treasurer and as chairman of the Civil Service Commission. We had no black lieutenant governors; now we have two.

While much progress has been made to eliminate the external barriers denying our right to vote, there are still some barriers remaining. We can't even play the game adequately until our entire team shows up on the field. We have sixteen million black people eligible to register and vote, but only about nine million are in political uniform—registered. We must press on toward full voter registration—and against the odds, I might add.

The Democrats have no incentive to register us because we already comprise one-fourth of their total vote, and they are afraid we will vote black. The Republicans feel they have no incentive to register blacks because we tend to vote Democratic. Many of the same people who opposed our right to vote also oppose our being fully registered to vote.

The natural energy crisis is not the only energy crisis before us. There is a human energy crisis. In the natural energy field we are rapidly using up our fossil fuels. But in the human energy crisis the problem is the exact opposite—we have unused fossils. The seven million unregistered black voters are the unwanted and wasted political energy potential in our community and country. We cannot be useful unless we are used, yet our problem is that one party has capped the pipeline and allows this potential energy to lie dormant while the other party's pipeline is overflowing, wasting energy. We want our energy to be used by being useful to ourselves and others, not misused through the waste of over-flow or nonuse.

We have the *right* to vote in 1978, but the *ability* to exercise that right through full voter registration is still the unfinished work of political enfranchisement.

Political Power: Our
Political Options

Power is simply the ability to achieve purpose. Our purpose is both simple and complex. Simple because our goal is equity and parity (our share). Complex because we must begin where we are and use what we've got to take us to where we want and need to go.

If the Republican party is to attract black voters, it must involve us in the party and in the process of developing the political strategy to attract the black vote. An all-white Republican national, state, and county leadership apparatus designing a strategy to attract black voters will not work. We must be involved in the party and political strategy development. We must be made a part of policy development and in putting forth programs. Only such a serious and genuine effort on the part of the Republican party will result in effectively attracting black voters.

One of the first questions black voters and potential candidates will ask is, "How has your party dealt with those committed black Republicans who have labored in your ranks through hard and often bitter years?" Have your companies rewarded them with good jobs and contracted for their goods and services, or are they now being ignored by

Democratic politicans and abandoned by Republican businessmen? Bob Brown, Jim Cummings, Sam Jackson, Gloria Toote, Jewel LaFontant, Art Fletcher—these tried and true black Republican warriors are the bridges to the untapped black resources.

Black people have three strategies available to them relative to the use of their political power. First, we can "not vote." We can adopt a cynical point of view which says "neither party is putting forth the perfect candidate for us," therefore we will vote for neither. I do not accept this option as viable for us. While black impatience with, and indifference toward the political process is understandable, it is a fact of life that nonparticipation only makes matters worse. So I reject the "no-vote" posture as a strategy.

Second, we can adopt a strategy where we give all of our votes to one group of people based on blind loyalty, rather than vested interest and reciprocity. I can't endorse this strategy either because it gives us power but no leverage. A football team that runs *all* its plays on the ground and never throws a pass can be defensed and stopped. A team that runs the same play all the time doesn't need to huddle. We've got to diversify our game plan.

A third option and strategy, which I do suggest we pursue, is that we exercise all our political options based on vested interest and reciprocity. We must, without cynicism but with realism, exercise every available political option open to us.

President Carter was elected in 1976 because 6 million black Americans gave President Carter over 90 percent of their votes—not to mention the fact that it was the black vote that secured his nomination. Black voters provided Mr. Carter with the crucial margin of victory in several closely contested states, without which he could not have been elected. Mr. Carter defeated then-President Ford by less than 2 million votes and won the electoral college by the slight margin of 297 to 241. A change of 28 electoral votes would have allowed Mr. Ford to remain president. And if the Republican party had nominated Senator Edward Brooke as its vice-presidential candidate, a man fully qualified, Republicans would probably still be in power. If President Ford had won one state, Pennsylvania, he also would still be president, because Pennsylvania's 29 electoral votes would have tipped the scales. Carter's margin in Pennsylvania was 128,456, but blacks cast 274,141 votes for the Democratic presidential candidate (87.2 percent of the black vote). One state, where a change of just 65,000 votes would have made the entire difference in the election. And some of those 65,000 votes Republicans did not get simply because they did not go after them.

It should be remembered that the nearly 6 million black votes for

Carter represented more than three times his popular-vote margin of 1.7 million.

The Democratic presidential nominee won, not just because blacks tend to vote Democratic, but because there was an enthusiastic black vote. The apathy anticipated did not materialize, and an estimated 64 percent of the registered black voters voted, compared to only 58 percent of registered blacks who actually voted in the 1972 election, 87 percent of which went to the Democratic nominee. Black apathy and political indifference cannot be counted on in the future. So the difference was not just the black Democratic vote but the *enthusiastic* black Democratic vote. In thirteen states—Alabama, Florida, Louisiana, Maryland, Mississippi, Missouri, New York, North Carolina, Ohio, Pennsylvania, South Carolina, Texas, and Wisconsin—the black vote was the margin of victory.

Let me come back to the point of these 7 million unregistered black voters. Only five presidents—Herbert Hoover (1928), Franklin Roosevelt (twice, 1932 and 1936), Eisenhower (1956), Johnson (1964), and Nixon (1972)—have defeated their opponents by more than 7 million votes. Of the fifty states in the union, only eight have populations of 7 million or more. Few countries on earth, and only a handful of world capitals, have populations exceeding 7 million. Hands that picked cotton in 1966 did pick the president in 1976 and could very well be the difference in 1980.

It's a mystery to me why Republicans have had the attitude that blacks will not vote for them. Blacks vote as intelligently and as diversely as any other group. We vote our vested interests, and only when we are ignored or when race is brought into a campaign as an issue does the black vote polarize. Mr. Ford lost Ohio and many other states because there was no real effort to attract the black vote.

I'm not just speaking theoretically when I say that blacks will vote for Republicans who appeal to their vested interests and engage in reciprocity. Blacks contribute significantly to Senators Percy, Mathias, Javits, Brooke, and Baker. Blacks did vote for Governor Milliken in Michigan, Governor Bond in Missouri, and Governor Thompson in Illinois. In the past we have contributed considerably to Governor Winthrop Rockefeller in Arkansas and Governor Nelson Rockefeller in New York. These persons felt and feel that we are necessary, and we felt and feel that they were worth putting in office. There is evidence that we will vote our vested interests.

We must use the political franchise and power that we have to propel us to where we have to go.

Political Program: Our Area of Vested Interest

Where do we have to go? Just as we must demand equity and parity within political parties, we will support political programs that address our vested interests and lead to equity and parity in the society. We are behind, and the gap must be closed. Our political votes must be translated into economic oats.

Business. We do not have economic equity nor do we receive economic reciprocity for what we contribute financially to the American society. What black people own or control is nowhere in proportion to the more than $90 billion of expendable income we spent last year in the American market. In the larger cities of this nation, like Chicago, blacks are 35 to 50 percent of the day-to-day shoppers and 85 percent of the weekend trade. Yet we do not have our share of the nation's banks in the country—and three of that small total were lost last year. We don't control our share of the nation's business wealth, since our businesses claim only 0.8 percent of the total business receipts and less than 1 percent of business assets, and we hire fewer than 3 percent of the black labor force. The Office of Minority Business Enterprise (OMBE) is a bastard budget, an insult to our economic intelligence. We need targeted investments, co-venturers, priority access to the divestitures of holding companies by banks, television stations, and favorable interest rates.

Health. We do not have our share of the nation's trained doctors. We are only 1.6 percent of the nation's physicians, and, while there is 1 white physician for every 649 whites, there is only 1 black physician for every 4,298 blacks. The life expectancy in 1973 for white males and black males was 69 and 62 years, respectively, and for white females and black females 76 and 70 years, respectively. In 1969, the death rate from all causes in the U.S. was 731 per 100,000 people. The rate for whites was 695 per 100,000 and for nonwhites was 1,046—a difference of 351 per 100,000. In 1971, the white infant-mortality rate was 17 per 1,000 births, compared to 30 per 1,000 for nonwhites, a difference of 13. According to the American Medical Association's Annual Report on Medical Education, there are only 1,447 black medical residents out of some 42,000 in the nation. There are fewer than 550 black interns out of a total of 24,000. At the same time, there are over 15,000 foreign medical-school students in graduate training programs. There are 50 percent fewer American black doctors than foreign doctors in this nation.

Professionals. We do not have our share of the nation's architects or engineers. A recent survey by the American Institute of Architects showed only 400 of 45,000 licensed architects to be black, less than 1 percent of the total. Blacks are only 4.2 percent of bank tellers; 3.1 percent of the electricians; 3.1 percent of the social scientists; 1.8 percent of insurance brokers; 1.3 percent of lawyers and judges; 1.3 percent of stock and bond salespersons; and 1.2 percent of engineers. In the skilled labor field, we are only 2 percent of the carpenters and 0.9 percent of sheet-metal workers.

Education. We have been denied our share of the nation's educational resources. While whites complete an average of 12.1 years of school, blacks still only complete an average of 9.4. Our college enrollment has suffered a 25-percent decline in the past four years. The dropout rate for blacks is 43.8 percent, and blacks constitute fewer than 2.9 percent of all college and university instructors. A study of the National Assessment for Educational Progress reveals we are 46 percent of the functionally illiterate youths nationwide.

Land. We do not hold our fair share of the nation's land. The Black Economic Development Center and the U.S. Census Bureau report a land loss among blacks in the past twenty years of over 7 million acres.

Media. We don't approach equity in the mass media. A recent study by the U.S. Commission on Civil Rights discloses that we are still locked out of the top-level decision-making positions in the media, particularly in the television industry. While minority male employment has increased by 42.6 percent and minority female employment by over 30 percent, only 6.5 percent of the officials and managers were minority; only 4.8 percent were minority females. Only 2.7 percent of department heads at stations surveyed by the U.S. Commission on Civil Rights were black males or females.

Youth. There are 400,000 men and women in America's jails. Over 300,000 of these are black and brown, and the overwhelming majority is young. Thousands are there because they are poor and can't afford bail bond. Others are victims of long delays that often surpass the length of the penalty. The liberties extended to the privileged of Watergate heighten the trauma. Our black young people are confronted with reduced life options. They are disproportionately occupying our jails (three out of four); languishing on the corners unemployed (65 percent); or going to early graves—when they ought to be in school or employed and becoming productive citizens. *It costs more to incarcerate our young people than it does to educate them.* If a young person is sent to jail in Illinois for four years, it will cost approximately $52,000, and the chances are that he or she will only become a hardened criminal. If you send that same young person to the University of Illinois for four years, it will cost approximately $20,000, plus you have a taxpaying, law-abiding, productive citizen. The choice? Education and employment or ignorance and incarceration.

What are blacks asking for in return for their votes? One thing we're *not* asking for is an exclusive black program. You will note, I hope, that each of the issues about to be discussed is not limited to black people but will benefit all Americans. If I might make a suggestion, I would advise that you cannot "anti-Carter" your way into power. Your challenge is to chart a new course of action that addresses itself to the needs of the maximum number of people.

1. *Economic Security.* Jobs are the creative alternative to welfare. We will not have reached our goal until every American willing and able to work is provided with a meaningful job doing socially useful work and making a livable wage—and affirmative action must aid our upward mobility. Blacks seek jobs as the most viable alternative to unemployment, welfare, and despair. Jobs in both the public and the private sectors must be provided. The government that uses our youthful energy in war, collects our taxes when we work—that same government, if it is a government of, by, and for the people, must aid us in an unemployment crisis.

2. *A Comprehensive and Coherent Urban Policy.* There has never been a suburb without a city. We need a domestic Marshall Plan to rebuild our cities. We need a plan, a timetable, and a financial commitment. A coherent urban policy, with an adequately financed housing and community development component that is perceived as a rational investment and a duty, is needed. Cities need the latter to improve the quality of life and the former to increase the quantity of life's benefits to all of its citizens. We seek a policy which prioritizes the rebuilding of our cities. Our cities have a trainable work force that is disproportionately idle because industry and jobs have fled to the suburbs—and frequently, overseas. Massive amounts of federal revenue-sharing funds are needed to finance this immediately. This investment would in turn attract people and other monies from the private sector.

3. *Welfare Reform.* Any welfare-reform package must have incentives to earn and learn, with a commitment to protect the dignity of those receiving government assistance. This is a concern of blacks because of the large percentage of black families in poverty. While 8 percent of the nation's families are poor, 32 percent of black families are strapped by this disability. We seek a system that provides incentives to earn and to learn. We want jobs and job training and retraining. We need a balanced approach. It must be remembered that only 10 percent of those presently receiving public aid are able to be employed.

4. *Business Development.* Blacks need business development as well as jobs. We are looking for a commitment to help build our economic institutions (our banks, insurance companies, etc.) and access to capital. Presently, even the monies targeted for our communities remain in downtown banks rather than in black banks. Today black businesses

claim a mere 0.8 percent of the nation's business receipts and employ less than 3 percent of the black and minority labor force. We have two political parties but one economic system. There are people in this room who represent the power of that economic system. You need not wait until 1980 to wield that private-sector power in the interest of blacks. You can do this through support for black financial institutions and businesses, through joint ventures and acquisitions, and through using your tax incentives to provide job and business opportunities in our depressed urban and rural areas. And, whereas government may not be able to do all things, it should be clear that government has to be more than a passive partner.

Blacks need access to the Commerce Department, both in terms of facilitating contractual relationships with other departments and agencies of the federal government and in terms of providing opportunities for such things as foreign trade, purchase of divested property, access to national markets, development of joint ventures, etc. Black banks need major investments from the public and private sectors. There are now eighty black banks, but three were lost in the last three years, and federal deposits in them have been decreasing over the last year. Black banks need at least $4 billion to begin the work of reconstruction in our communities. We want to serve as development banks in target communities. We will teach the so-called unteachable. We will black-line the red-line and make it a green-line. We have survived with little help. We could flourish with support. Help us make flowers bloom in the desert. Black retail and wholesale firms need greater business opportunities and ability to leverage themselves and to have the benefits of increased capital formation.

5. *Education.* Our right to equal opportunity and access to education must be protected, and enough money to provide a quality education for all must be provided. Education is the major passport to economic independence. Yet, while whites average 12.1 years of schooling, blacks average only 9.4 years, and the dropout rate among blacks is 43.8 percent.

In the past four years there has been a 25-percent decline in black college enrollments. Blacks have been entrapped by *Bakke* and Bakkeism—or a groundswell against affirmative action.* This has already

---

*Alan Bakke, who is white, applied to medical school at the University of California–Davis. As part of an affirmative action program, UC-Davis had set aside ten seats in each entering class for economically disadvantaged students. In the past, all of these had gone to minority students. Because a black student who entered in this way had scored lower on the medical-school aptitude tests, Bakke sued, arguing that he was the victim of "reverse discrimination." In July of 1978, a divided U.S. Supreme Court ordered Bakke admitted. They noted that racially conscious methods could be used in college admissions programs; this one, however, they found discriminatory and pointed to a plan used by Harvard that was not. Jackson uses the term "Bakkeism" to refer to the spirit of anti-affirmative action set loose in the country because of the massive publicity surrounding this case.

resulted in a 9.1-percent drop in the number of first-year black medical students, the Institute for Health Resources Development reports. The costs of discrimination rob this nation of $13 billion annually, and at present rates of progress it will take forty-three years to remove job discrimination alone, according to an Equal Employment Opportunity Commission (EEOC) study.

6. *Health*. We are looking for a program that provides a high standard of health care which is affordable by all Americans.

7. *Housing*. There must be a commitment and a program to provide decent, safe, and sanitary housing in a healthful environment. We must protect the housing we have and build the housing we need, including an expanded program of government-assisted housing for low- and moderate-income families. Too few Americans can afford the prices of the present housing supply.

8. *Tax Reform*. A fair and equitable tax reform package that assures that business and individuals pay their fair share.

Business, labor, government, and the consumer *all* must play a part and have a role in addressing these issues and developing these programs. People who are ill-informed or are ill-intentioned speaking on the role of government are often demagogic and divisive, and their hand ought to be called. *Those who argue that there is too much government end up having their businesses subsidized by government, having their house note insured by government, attending schools receiving government monies, living in suburbs built on government incentives, riding to work on highways subsidized by the government, taking government-subsidized public transportation to their jobs, and taking vacations or business trips on subsidized airlines.*

We've got to be consistent. You can't argue that government subsidies and investments should end just as soon as *your* needs are met. It's clear business and labor can't do it by themselves. There's no use trying to turn back the clock. It can't and won't be done. Government's purpose is to protect and distribute justice and life and liberty and the pursuit of happiness to *all* its citizens. Government has been used to protect the interests of business and various other interests in this society. We can't all of a sudden degrade government intervention when it is used to protect the interests of the poor. It must be used to fulfill its essential purpose. So let's get on with the creative role of the proper relationship and balance between business, labor, government, and the consumer that is fair and equitable for all.

In the international economy, we support free trade *and* fair trade. We are concerned about the flight of capital and jobs. Last year, of $164 billion invested by American corporations, $32 billion went abroad, often to cheap labor markets under the control of authoritarian governments. We are not willing to trade jobs paying livable wages for Comprehensive Employment Training Act (CETA) jobs. Every American has the right to a meaningful job doing socially useful work making a livable wage.

Whoever is most willing to address themselves meaningfully to this agenda through a political program deserves our vote. Black people behave politically just like everybody else. We supported Lincoln (by joining the Union Army) because he was the vehicle for deliverance from slavery. We supported Roosevelt because his New Deal addressed our needs. Many supported Eisenhower because he brought the boys back home. We supported Kennedy because he got Dr. King out of jail at a critical juncture and expressed an interest in our interests. And even then, in 1960, the black vote of Fulton County, Georgia (Atlanta), carried the county for Mr. Nixon. The grandfather of Maynard Jackson, mayor of Atlanta, had laid the groundwork. We are growing up now. We are maturing. We know how to split our tickets. Wise political parties and politicians exploit (in the best sense) the openings in the other team's offense and defense.

Beyond Partisan Politics:
A New America

There are two great traditions: the political and the prophetic. The two are sufficiently distinct until both have valid roles of service to people. Prophets need politicians—they keep reminding us of how things are. Politicians need prophets—they keep reminding us of how things ought to be. It is this creative tension that makes us healthy, alive, sensitive, alert, and accountable.

Partisan politics has its place, but ultimately Democrats must be more concerned about democracy than the Democratic party. And Republicans must be more concerned about the republic than the Republican party. We must save our children, our families, our sanity with a foundation of spirituality. For beyond both Democrats and Republicans we need a new America, characterized more by ethical values than ethnic separation. We must have a transcendent agenda. Some values all of us must hold dear. We must choose the high road rather than the low. We must turn a bad situation around.

Enough of assassinations, Vietnams, Watergates, and Koreagates. We must turn around the social decay and reverse the social despair. We must create a society where life is meaningful and people do not have to turn to violence, drugs, intercourse without discourse, alcohol, and other forms of escape just to cope. We must have the will and spiritual stamina necessary to fight the good fight. We must rekindle motivation, put forth the effort, and engage in the discipline necessary to achieve our goals.

More vital than the economic crisis is the spiritual and moral crisis facing us. It doesn't matter if the Democrats or the Republicans are holding the bucket if the bucket has a hole in the bottom. We have lost the confidence of this generation's youth through war and scandal. Who in a government leading a war with no moral justification could tell our young people not to engage in violence and vandalism? What political leader involved in lying, cheating, cutting corners, and other forms of scandal and venality has the moral authority to challenge a lost generation tripping out on angel dust, cocaine, and alcohol?

The challenge of this generation of adults is to regain the lost confidence and trust of this generation's youth. We would be much better off if this generation of young people were in the streets marching and protesting for jobs, housing, health care, the environment, for the rebuilding of our cities, and for reforming the criminal justice system—all of which happen to be socially redemptive programs—rather than mired in their present indifference and turning inward, so often putting dope in their veins rather than hope in their brains. Even when our young people are marching and protesting, too often they're doing it in the name of personalism and a morally decadent agenda. Paralyzed by cynicism, they're fighting to lower the drinking age to eighteen, fighting to extend their personal sexual habits, fighting to legalize dope, fighting to live together without assuming the responsibilities of mature adults in marriage, and other forms of decadence.

It is interesting that, in spite of economic magnets, if the legislative and legal realm has not made life liveable and safe, if social institutions have not provided complementary services, and if religious institutions have not set a moral tone—people will never gravitate to the economic magnet. In other words, nations need money and jobs—but they need more than this. Neither people nor nations can live by bread alone.

Ultimately the concern for the quality of life must prevail. Homes outlast houses, and faith outlasts fact. Once there was a long and arduous biblical journey called the exodus—as people sought to move from slavery to freedom. It is significant that the fertile soil of Canaan was not considered the kingdom (the millennium) without the ten ethical commandments of a sound society, the moral laws by which people live. The issue and teaching of these laws was a forerunner to national development. In other words, the death of ethics is the sabotage of excellence. Without an ethical foundation, economics become unfeasible, education loses purpose, and purpose loses power.

Our country resembles Canaan, but, without the ethical commandments and a decent moral tone and a safe environment, we will fail— even if the schools are new, the administration honest and dutiful, and the budgets balanced.

The loss of ethical values adversely affects economic value. Usually an ethical collapse precedes an economic collapse. Crime in the suites often precedes crime in the streets. We are taking the ethical crisis too lightly. No one includes it in their job description, and thus no one assumes the responsibility for analyzing it or using creative energy to resolve it.

It is this revival of the spirit of the people that will attract industry and jobs.

It is an alert and sober people that will pressure the federal and state governments—and both parties—for sound priorities. A handful of sober and sane people wield more power than densely populated cities of drugged and alienated people.

I say to blacks, put pressure on the political system and on the politicians in both parties. We select them, elect them, and now we must collect from them. I urge blacks to register fully and to join both parties and broaden our political options.

But there is a missing factor that must be derived from the governed, not the government—the will to live, the urge to EXCEL. The power of the human spirit must take this national caterpillar and turn it into a butterfly. We must break out of the marshy meadows of mediocrity into the clear paths of the solid foundation of excellence. We must:

• Tell the people of our nation that the only protection against genocide is to remain necessary.

• Tell them that the laws of convenience lead to collapse, but the laws of sacrifice lead to greatness.

• Tell them if you can conceive it, and believe it, you can achieve it.

• Tell them it is not your aptitude, but your attitude, that will determine your altitude, with a little intestinal fortitude.

• Tell them not to be servile, for it is humiliation, but to be of service—for service is power.

• Tell them to desire to work and then demand to work and then insist that they get paid for the work they do. A servant is worthy of his hire, but more than money is derived from work. For from it comes the joy, the security, the fulfillment, and the self-esteem of doing a job well.

I still believe the country can be saved with bold and courageous leadership. A flower can bloom in the desert if we dig deep enough to find the roots down beneath the soil—beneath the corruption, the corrosion, the hunger, and the hurt. There is a taproot connected to an underground water supply from which all water flows. If we dig deep enough and wide enough, we can turn the desert into fertile soil and make flowers bloom. Dig, dig, dig for new values and new vision.

If we seek new values in the nation, we will add new value to the nation. We need:

Doctors whose concern for public health is greater than their desire for personal wealth.

Lawyers with a greater concern for justice than for judgeships.

Teachers who teach for life and not just for a living.

Politicians who seek not merely an office but seek to be of service.

Preachers who prophesy, not just profiteer.

There must be love of the nation and love in the nation. But, unless God builds the house, we labor in vain.

If a nation is to survive, it must be a nation with solid foundations—whose builder and maker is God.

Thank you very much.

We Must Act, Not Just React: The Present Challenge of Our Democracy

Six months after his speech to the Republican National Committee, Jackson addressed the liberal Americans for Democratic Action on June 11, 1978, showing something of the range of his political appeal.

Politicians, fellow activists, and friends. On behalf of the National Board of Operation PUSH, our staff, and organization, I wish to express to you our deep appreciation for the opportunity to speak before the Americans for Democratic Action. I want to peg my thoughts today on three key concepts:

- The challenge of progressive change in a democracy.
- Threats to progressive change within our democracy.
- The unfinished task of democracy.

I have chosen to speak on the subject of "We Must Act, Not Just React."

The Challenge of Progressive Change in a Democracy

Recently I have been fortunate enough to speak before a variety of groups with quite diverse social, political, and economic views and philosophies, representing a black perspective. As a result, I have come to two conclusions. First, American society is becoming more interdependent and complex, and thus the American political arena is becoming more complex. Second, the black vote is becoming more critical—thus more necessary—in local, state, and national elections.

As an advocate for the interests of black people specifically, and human rights generally, I see the new competition for our vote as healthy for us, for the nation, and for the political system. My fundamental perspective is that *mutual need* is the basis for political alliances.

Increasingly, political parties and politicians of all persuasions will have to compete for our vote or risk extinction.

The only protection that people, politicians, or political parties have is to remain necessary. Black people must pursue a strategy that prohibits one party or one element within a party from taking us for granted or another party or element from writing us off. We have both a right and an obligation to expand our political options. We must now exercise that right and obligation with regard *to* and *within* both parties, and create external pressure upon all involved.

If we follow a strategy of blindly giving our vote to one political faction, we will have power but no leverage. If we write any particular element off, we again sacrifice leverage. So "power" or "no power" will not allow us to pursue our vested interests if we do not have *leverage.*

Black people have three strategies available to them in the use of their political power.

1. We can "not vote." We can adopt a cynical point of view which says "neither party is putting forth the perfect candidate for us," therefore we will vote for neither. I do not accept this option as viable for us. While black impatience with and indifference toward the political process is understandable, it is a fact of life that nonparticipation only makes matters worse. So I reject the "no-vote" posture as a strategy.

2. We can adopt a strategy where we give all of our votes to one group of people based on blind loyalty rather than vested interest and reciprocity. Again, I say I can't endorse this strategy either, because it gives us power but no leverage. A football team that runs *all* its plays on the ground and never throws a pass can be defensed and stopped. A team that runs the same play all the time doesn't need to huddle. We've got to diversify our game plan.

3. We can exercise all our political options based on vested interest and reciprocity. We can, without cynicism but with realism, exercise every available political option open to us. I suggest we pursue this option.

The reason the black agenda and black interests specifically must be raised and taken into account—in addition to our being people like all other people—is that what is good for black Americans is good for *all* Americans. We have never argued for black jobs, but for jobs; never for black housing, but for housing; never for black health care, but for health care. In other words, we have never argued for an exclusive or exclusionary political program. On the other hand, what is good for the ruling elite in this country is not necessarily good for all Americans. It has often been said, and it is correct, that blacks are a weather vane for this society. Because of racism, we are in the front and bear the brunt of social and economic deterioration and in the rear of social and economic development. Whatever is happening to blacks today will be happening to whites tomorrow.

In politics, definition is important. If someone can define you, they can confine you. Increasingly, black people are breaking out of traditional definitions. Labeling is simpler and requires less thought, but it is more productive to analyze, think, and build reconciling bridges across the labels of race, sex, and political party. Thus we are increasingly defining ourselves around our vested interests in our quest for equity and parity within this society.

The issue confronting black people now is beyond freedom. It is equity—our fair share. And we cannot judge the executive branch of government—the president, one man—without putting it in proper context. We cannot afford to be locked into myopic vision where we view all progress or retreat as the responsibility of one branch of government or one person. We must develop peripheral vision and look at the legislative and judicial branches, business, labor, and the mass media simultaneously, which are all very influential, interrelated, and controlling forces over the lives of our people.

The overwhelmingly Democratic Congress is more indebted to us than is the president, yet they are largely unresponsive to our needs. The Nixon Supreme Court—in the Detroit school desegregation suit, the Arlington Heights housing case, and the Teamsters Union job discrimination case—has shifted the burden of proof from the *effects* of discrimination to the *intention* to discriminate; thus discrimination cases are becoming more expensive and more difficult to win. The business community is pursuing its own selfish interests and turning its back on us and affirmative action.

Organized labor resists our inclusion or our upward mobility within the labor movement and even denies us access to job training. The mass media mentally disenfranchises us through deletion and distortion. Of the 1,769 daily newspapers, only 5 have blacks in executive editorial positions; of 40,000 print journalists, only 1,700 are black (about 1,300 of them have been added since the riots); and of 133 television network executives, only 1 is black. Since we are excluded or on the periphery of almost every major institution in America, we cannot afford to limit ourselves to myopic vision. We must run a multiple offense and defense.

There Are Threats to Our Democracy

Many blacks are disappointed and have become disillusioned because we contributed a large number of *votes* to parties and candidates who are not responding in kind with *oats*. Many who were in need asked for and received our votes but have now turned their backs on us on such issues as affirmative action.

Bakke

Bakke and "Bakkeism" is racism and a threat to our attempt to catch up and close the economic and educational gaps. If our goal is educational and economic equity and parity, and it is, then we need the assistance of affirmative action to catch up. We are behind as a result of discrimination and denial of opportunity. There is 1 white attorney for every 680 whites, 1 black attorney for every 4,000 blacks; 1 white physician for every 649 whites, 1 black physician for every 5,000 blacks; 1 white dentist for every 1,900 whites, 1 black dentist for every 8,400 blacks. Less than 1 percent of all engineers are black. Blacks make up less than 1 percent of all practicing chemists. We need affirmative action to help us close these and other gaps. Cruel and dispassionate injustice sets us back. We need creative justice and compassion to close the gap.

Actually, "reverse discrimination" in the American context is illogical and a contradiction in terms. Never in the history of humankind has a majority, with power, engaged in programs and written laws to discriminate against itself. The only thing whites are giving up because of affirmative action is unfair advantage—something that was unnecessary in the first place. The issue is not reverse discrimination but the reversal of the effects of historic and present discrimination.

Blacks are not making progress at the expense of whites, as news accounts tend to project, because there are 49 percent more whites in medical school today and 64 percent more whites in law school than at the beginning of the affirmative action programs some eight years ago.

Bakke does not really challenge preferential treatment, for there is no challenge to the preferential treatment of the children of the rich, of alumni, of the faculty, of athletes, or of the very talented—only minorities.

It has been asked, "Why do you resist being judged on merit?" We do not resist being judged on merit, but white America resists judging us on merit. Being *born* black in the United States is to be born with *de*merits. We are not enslaved and are not discriminated against today because, individually or collectively, we lack merit. We were and are discriminated against because of race. It didn't make any difference if you were a Ph.D. or a "No-D"; if you were black, you sat in the back of the bus, used the colored drinking fountain and washroom. It is more subtle but no different with the discrimination of today. This nation went out of its way to enslave us as a group but now wants to free us through individual effort and merit. We need a solution that is consistent with and comprehensive of the problem.

We argue for special protection under the law because we have, in this society, a special problem—racism. Free citizens ought to be able to live without fear of loss of rights or life—yet we needed federal troops in the South after the Emancipation Proclamation to protect us. And, after they were removed in 1877, America entered its most violent period, and we were the victims. We needed a special amendment to the Constitution, the thirteenth, to guarantee our citizenship.

After education was made mandatory in this country, we needed a special law (the *Brown* decision in 1954) to guarantee our equal educational opportunity. Citizens have the right to use public facilities, but we needed a special law in 1964 to gain access. Citizens have the right to vote, yet we needed, and still need, a special law (the 1965 Voting Rights Act) to ensure our right to vote. Even now it must be renewed in 1982 rather than guaranteed into perpetuity. We needed the special law of the 1968 Open Housing Act, not because we lacked merit, but because of racism. We need special legal protection. We would like to be judged on merit, but the special problem of racism has given us demerits; thus we need the protection of special laws.

Jarvis

All of us have a right to be concerned about the recent vote in California on Howard Jarvis's amendment, Proposition 13, which cut property taxes that had risen because inflation had dramatically increased the price of housing. First, the analysis was correct, but the solution was incorrect. It is an example of cutting off your nose to spite your face. Make no mistake about it, massive tax reform is needed. The diagnosis is sound, but the prognosis reflects a national suicide complex. If you are having severe pains in your *left* arm and the doctor's diagnosis indicates that you need an operation, the doctor puts you to sleep and amputates an arm. If you wake up with your *right* arm missing, you will only have compounded your problem. You will have a hurting left arm and a missing right arm.

In the face of a crisis, California voters panicked and seemed willing to throw out the baby with the bath water. The vote represents short-term pleasure for the few, but it will ultimately lead to long-term pain for the many. A text without a context is a pretext. Proposition 13 must be seen in the context of a move toward the text of general, fair, and equitable tax relief, or we have a pretext. It was irrational to the extent that many people voted against their own interests.

Second, Proposition 13 was deceptive. Of the $7 billion of tax relief given to Californians, $2.5 billion went to homeowners, but $4.5 billion went to corporations. It represents the trickle-down theory of economics, and that philosophy has never worked for black and poor people. Government is more likely to share and serve the real needs of people than is big business because the purpose of government is to serve all of the people. The public's challenge is to pressure government into being democratic enough to live up to its highest and best potential.

The business of business is to make a profit, and business, we have seen, will use its tax savings in one of three ways: (1) it will buy more capital-intensive equipment rather than invest in labor-intensive ventures, even though the latter would have a better overall impact on the society; (2) it will abandon the American worker and go to cheap labor markets abroad—of $164 billion invested by American corporations last year, $32 billion was invested abroad, 1 of every $5; or (3) it will simply hoard its profits.

Third, Proposition 13 represents a frightened rather than a thoughtful response to the pinch of inflation. Inflation somehow is seen as a greater threat than unemployment, yet full employment would do more to curb inflation than almost anything else.

Fourth, we must separate the *language* of Proposition 13 from its *message*. The language of Proposition 13 is dreary, but the message is clear. People want relief, and battle lines are being drawn. The cold war between public workers and taxpayers is heating up. The public wants increased service with decreased cost; workers, too often, want increased wages with decreased production. The cold war is heating up, and if this war continues to heat up, public workers will lose. At this hour, we need strong moral leadership that will reconcile and heal. The politics of expediency can kill the dream. The despairing voices that say, "Let each fetch education, transportation, health care, and housing for himself," is a far cry from the spirit of Kennedy's New Frontier, of Dr. Martin Luther King, Jr.'s "dream," or of Lyndon Johnson's Great Society.

Public workers must demand of themselves accountability against institutional mediocrity and featherbedding. In other words, we must demand excellence and be exemplary models of excellence in administration, attitude, creativity, and production, or we will be subject to the external audit—the people's tribunal—as expressed in Proposition 13, which will always be much more harsh and arbitrary.

Fifth, the Jarvis Amendment is an expression of classism to the extent that nonhomeowners stand nothing to gain and services to lose. It may benefit an elite few but will eliminate and exasperate the many. A CBS survey revealed that 69 percent of California's voters wanted cutbacks in welfare first, which is an anti-black (because welfare and blacks are erroneously perceived as synonymous) and an anti-poor attitude.

Sixth, even though some blacks got caught up in the stampede and voted for Proposition 13, it is racist to the extent that, having abandoned the inner cities and taken their tax money with them, white homeowners are willing to allow blacks and browns to suffer disproportionately because of a situation largely beyond their control. It's a covert way of fighting affirmative action.

The black middle class is not built on land, business development, or monied interests. The black middle class is largely a product of the public sector—government workers, social workers, post office employees, educators, nurses, etc. When they freeze people out of jobs in the public sector, who is it that needs jobs? Blacks. When they stop promotions, who is it that because of discrimination will be stuck in the lower-classified and lower-paying jobs? Blacks. When they cut back on jobs in the public sector, who is it that will be last hired and first fired? Blacks. When funds for education are cut back and class sizes and teacher-student ratios increase, whose classrooms will become the largest and most overcrowded? Blacks. When they cut back on health services, who is it that has the worst health and needs the most health care? Blacks. When they cut back on police and fire services, who suffers the most crime and lives in the most fire-plagued buildings? Blacks. Make no mistake about it, this is an anti-black move with dangerous ramifications for the entire society.

Seventh, Proposition 13 is an anti-program. And we can't "anti" a free, fair, and just society into existence. The end result will simply be to create more of what those who voted for the Jarvis Amendment resented in the first place—alienated young people, despairing poor people, angry blacks and browns, and women who will feel disillusioned after ten years of civil rights activity. It does not solve our problems, it simply escalates them. The less education we get in the short run, the more rehabilitation we will need in the long run. The less *constructive* recreation we have now, the more *destructive* socialization we will have in the future. Proposition 13 is not Democratic, it is demagogic. It is not Republican, it is ridiculous. It is suicidal. If we adopt a negative attitude, it will lead to a negative altitude, and we will crash as a society.

Eighth, if the Proposition 13 people are serious about economic relief and waste, then they ought to go after the military budget and inspect it. Let's be consistent about waste, and let's have our priorities straight about who is most wasteful in this society—both economically and in human terms.

Ninth, the "circuit breaker" approach to tax relief for homeowners is a more creative and just approach to tax reform. Beyond even that, however, it must be said that the whole approach of financing education through property taxes is a bit antiquated and contributes to the inequitable distribution of education funds. The rich pay a smaller percentage of their income for public education yet expend more per capita for the education of their children while the poor pay a higher percentage of their income for education, but expend a much smaller amount per capita. Thus *equity* and *adequacy* are undermined.

Last, the real tragedy of the Jarvis initiative is its orientation toward punishment rather than redemption. It is punitive rather than redemptive. It has a selfish concern about it. It expresses a "my thing" philosophy. "My house"—not housing—is its focus. "My school"—not schools—is its focus. It has a concern for self alone, to the detriment of society as a whole. Our challenge is to be about the business of building a society that is sane, just, and redemptive, and Proposition 13 is neither sane, just, nor redemptive.

The Unfinished Tasks of This Democracy

There is plenty of room for bloom. The mountains seem high and cold, and the valleys seem deep and marshy. We have two choices before us. We can either regress *because of* or progress *in spite of*. The antidote to detachment and apathy is involvement and action. It is precisely because of Proposition 13 that we must be more aggressive, more involved, and more active rather than allow our discouragement to turn to cynicism and escape, where we choose to cop out rather than to use our willpower to cope with.

Those who are concerned about the new direction in which the country is heading must do four things: (1) Recognize the *need* to come together; (2) *come* together; (3) *work* and *plan* together; and (4) *act* together.

Race is still the number-one unfinished task of this democracy. It splits the forces that potentially have the ability to save this democracy. Race has sapped our spirits and absorbs valuable energy. Race has brought tension. Race makes many of us feel uncomfortable. Race makes some feel superior and others inferior. Race has brought negative publicity and images upon us. Race has divided families, communities, and our concept of justice. Race has split religious institutions and distorts the image of God. Race has wrought distress and suspicion.

Race has caused us to build schools where we don't need them and has pitted parents against parents. Race has allowed boards of education to waste taxpayers' money paying lawyers to fight immoral legal battles. Race has allowed politicians to exploit our emotions for their political gain but at our social, economic, and political expense. Race has polarized our children, forcing them to take sides.

Too often, we have only heard about the damage done to black people as a result of racial discrimination and segregation. Blacks *are* damaged spiritually and emotionally as a result. But guess what? Whites suffer emotional, spiritual, and moral damage that is just as devastating. The perversion of personality is just as negative whether one believes he or she is superior or inferior. Both are false psychological identities that damage all of us.

Racism, a philosophy of superiority, is untrue scientifically, immoral theologically, and unhealthy psychologically.

PUSH has set a goal of registering 5 million voters over the next two years. Through our EXCEL program, we contend that citizenship education is as critical as general education. Therefore, upon graduation, we are attempting to get schools and boards of education to adopt a policy that, when our children graduate from high school (and 3.1 million did last year), they receive a diploma in one hand, symbolizing knowledge and wisdom, and a voter registration card in the other, symbolizing power and responsibility. We also contend that, in addition to having 100 percent registration of seniors, they be taught how to operate a voting machine. We are submitting a resolution to you for your consideration. We hope you will pass it and fight all across the country for its implementation.

There is no question about the political program we support. We must defend public education against the attacks of the Packwood-Moynihan legislation providing tuition tax credits for parochial education and the Proposition 13s, for they are creating a three-tiered school system: a suburban school system based on class, a private school system based on race, and a public inner-city school system based on rejection and alienation.

We not only must have a comprehensive and rational urban policy, but it must be adequately funded. We believe in the right of every person to live in safe and sanitary housing in a healthful environment. We know that health care should be provided on the basis of need and that greater efforts should be made in a preventive way, rather than waiting until after the fact and then servicing well only those who can pay. We know we must have more money and greater planning in public transportation and stop wasting our land and our environment on gas guzzlers.

We know that we have moved from neglect to lip service relative to Africa, but now we must aggressively move to relieve the suffering and toward aiding their economic and agricultural development.

We accept and support the economic, social, and political goals of the counterculture. We are intimately a part of it. But we don't accept many of the negative values as a necessary corollary. We cannot allow the noble goals of the counterculture to be synonymous with the use of drugs, alcohol, sexual promiscuity, violence, and vandalism. If we do, we will be defeated, however noble our goals.

We must recognize that the crisis we are facing is dialectical in nature. We have external economic, social, and political problems on the one hand, but internal moral and spiritual problems on the other. We must address ourselves to both. People need hope and help. Hope without help will lead to despair, but help without hope will lead to motion without progress. We cannot live by bread alone.

Every bit of progress we have ever made has come as a result of our initiating the action. We have faced Proposition 13s before. The "separate but equal" legal principle was a Proposition 13, but we took action in the courts and overturned the principle. Denial of public accommodations was a Proposition 13, but we marched and got the 1964 Civil Rights Act. The denial of our right to vote was a Proposition 13, but somewhere on the road between Selma and Montgomery we got a 1965 Voting Rights Act. The denial of open housing was a Proposition 13, but we marched in Chicago and got a 1968 Open Housing law. The Vietnam War was a Proposition 13, but we acted—and Johnson and Nixon reacted—and we brought that tragic war to an end. We must not panic, freeze, or retreat in the face of Proposition 13s. WE MUST ACT.

The challenge of this generation is not simply to be a "New Generation," because that takes no effort. That is simply a consequence of birth. The challenge of this generation is to be a greater generation, and the only way we can be a greater generation is through service.

We must build a coalition that goes beyond the recognized labels. We must not fight for Democrats alone, but fight for democracy. We cannot simply support the Republicans, we must support the republic. Our goal cannot simply be to fight for liberals, it must be to fight for total human liberation, in all of its varied forms. We can only become a greater generation by serving the needs of our day. Service is power. Service is God's will. We must feed the hungry people if we are to be a greater generation. To be a greater generation, we must educate more people. To be the great generation that we are capable of, we must provide decent and safe housing for all of our people. If we are to be a great generation, we must beat our swords into plowshares. Nonviolence must be seen as an alternative to hostility and violence in solving our conflicts if we are to be a truly great generation.

Education is a key in the preservation of democracy; therefore if education is in trouble—democracy is in trouble. We cannot take this civilizational and educational crisis too seriously.

We must know that if we sow short-term pleasure, we will reap long-term pain. But if we sow short-term pain, we will reap long-term pleasure. Hedonism is close to heathenism, and neither is a liberating philosophy. Motivation must be seen as important and critical to turning this crisis in our society around. We must know that if we can conceive it and believe it, we can achieve it. We must know that it is not our aptitude but our attitude that will determine our altitude, with a little intestinal fortitude—or guts. We must know that our mind is a pearl, and we can learn anything in the world.

We must have progressive social change, but we must have a revolution in values as well. We must close the quantitative *and* qualitative economic and educational gaps.

We must believe in ourselves, believe in our ability to bring progressive social change. We must believe in the American people, believe that, if they are educated, organized, and involved, change will occur.

And, finally, all of us must believe that in the final analysis life is not accidental, it is providential. We must know that life has meaning and purpose, if we will but hold on and seek a new and brighter day.

Know that you are somebody, that you are God's child. For unless God builds the house, we who labor, labor in vain.

We *can* save our democracy—it is possible.

We *ought* to save our democracy—it is our moral responsibility.

We *must* save our democracy—it is today's imperative.

Thank you very much.

Liberation and Justice:
A Call for Redefinition,
Refocus, and Rededication

This was Jackson's presidential address at the tenth
annual convention of Operation PUSH, held in
Chicago, Illinois, on July 9, 1981, six months after
Ronald Reagan took office. These annual speeches
typically sum up the year's activities and lay out the
directions for future action.

This is our tenth-year celebration. We give thanks to
God, whose grace and mercy have sustained us through these difficult
and challenging years. During this period the community of civil rights
leadership has made room for PUSH at the table. We have our rightful
place, and we accept our responsibility. As our struggle intensifies, we
must have a redistribution of responsibility for the ongoing of our
human rights movement. There are still vacant seats at the banquet table
for liberation and justice. There is no shortage of crosses or crowns, but
you must pick them up in that order. There is room for more organizations than we have. The harvest is ripe. We need business, labor, journalistic, governmental, and spiritual leadership.

That is why we have done our best to weave into the very fabric of our
convention—but especially in the insightful and exciting session we had
last night at the Leadership Roundtable—the very best of black leadership and black organizations. The work of liberation is great, diversi-
fied, and challenging. We all have something significant to contribute.
Some contribute social service, some social change. Some of us do
research, others work in job placement and job training. But we must
use all of our resources—litigation, cogitation, demonstration—but all
of us must engage and agitate, all of us must participate. We have one

48

goal—liberation and justice—even though we may play different roles. We can be diverse and directed at the same time. When we serve our people, we have a right to expect thirty million black Americans, who comprise seventeen million eligible voters, with $140 billion in disposable income, to support our black organizations. We can't expect our adversaries to finance our army. If they do, they will split our loyalties, dilute our power, and conquer us.

Today I want to speak on the subject "Liberation and Justice: A Call for Redefinition, Refocus, and Rededication." This is a period of intense anxiety, fear, and doubt. The blood at the bottom of the American pool keeps coming to the surface. Centuries of crime and terror upon which this nation was built are beginning to show their effect and result. There is a crisis of confidence and moral bankruptcy. All people and nations must live with the consequences of their choices. God is not mocked. Whatsoever a man soweth, that will he also reap.

America was built on five economic and social pillars. After it cleared the Native Americans away through terroristic genocide, enslaved blacks as the first major American industry, annexed Hispanics against their will, the foundation of the five pillars was laid. These five pillars were: (1) cheap labor, (2) cheap energy, (3) cheap raw materials, (4) an exploited labor market divided on the ideology of race or skin worship, and (5) expensive exports. Each of these pillars is now crumbling, the nation's foundation is shaking, and the people are in a state of panic.

Economic panic caused by new world competition has begun to break the strong hold of economic monopoly. This nation has no monopoly on intelligence, resources, energy, wealth, or the will to be free. White America is suffering from an acute case of cultural shock. The people who hold our lifeline are mostly black, brown, yellow, non-Christian, and don't speak English. World isolation and dependence are replacing world domination and the illusion of independence. America is having to make the basic psychological adjustment from being superior over the world to being equivalent with and, increasingly, dependent on the rest of the world. America has just 4 percent of the world's population; 96 percent of the world lives beyond our borders.

Thus our nation's leadership must stop looking in the mirror more and more, seeing less and less, and begin looking more objectively out of the window at who else occupies the world and how the world really is. Our nation has become divided with narcissism, self-love, and white-skin worship. In this demonic and divided state, blacks are looked upon as scapegoats; in reality we are mountain lions. The American structure must be accurately analyzed and then revitalized. The current American style, peppered with amnesia and false hope, is an inadequate substitute for substance.

About two years ago, there was an American Airlines crash in Chicago in which many people were killed. Reporters and investigators raised questions while everyone was in a state of trauma and shock, trying to understand what happened, what had gone wrong. They asked, Was there a bomb explosion? Did the pilots make an error? Was there a mechanical or human failure in the control tower? Was another plane in the area? Was there an adverse wind? Upon closer examination they found that the bolts that held the engine on the plane were too short and too weak. The plane could not take the pressure. The structure of the plane was inadequate. The in-depth diagnosis led to a prognosis that has prevented further crashes.

In the November elections, in my judgment, too many Americans thought the problem was only pilot-deep, thus they were willing to settle for a cosmetic change—a change of pilots. They said, in many instances, that any change is better than our present predicament. But the U.S. structure, its bolts, its underpinning, is in trouble in the emerging new world order. There is a new wind blowing, and no pilot controls the wind. The problem is more than pilot-deep. The entire American presupposition of wealth, labor, resources, race, and religion must be reexamined. Out of such a blurred vision and confused minds comes a Tarzan policy for Africa. Two sets of rules are applied, both in the name of democracy: *majority rule in America where whites are a majority and minority rule in South Africa where whites are a minority.*

Two definitions for killing. The good killers are called "soldiers" and kill in defense of their nation. The bad killers are called "terrorists" and engage in acts of aggression. Blurred vision and confused minds lead us to accept warmed-over bread and outmoded ideas in the Middle East, where we control neither the heat nor the recipe, even though it's our ingredients and our most essential nutrition—oil—that are at stake and that threaten our national security. Blurred vision and confused minds lead us to conduct surgery on the American poor without anesthesia, to engage in gunboat diplomacy and manifest destiny in place of human rights in the world arena. Blurred vision and confused minds lead us to accept a "no-talk" policy and selective preemptive strikes as acceptable diplomatic art forms. The ideology of might over right dominates our foreign policy. The massive, wasteful, and foolish arms race allows us to engage in the thrill of overkill. This mosaic of conduct—born of economic panic, cultural shock, and amnesia—puts America on a collision course with most of the rest of the world and their legitimate quest for self-respect and self-determination. Last November, people stumbling in the dark, motivated by fear, frustration, and desperation, said there is a simple way out of the darkness. Thus they accepted an "anything is better" philosophy and were willing to go for the first light they saw at the end of the tunnel. They thought it was sunlight, but instead it was a train coming their way.

Reaganism vs. Reaganomics

Perception is one thing, reality is often another. When perception and reality are one, things run smoothly. When perception and reality are different, conflict and increased tension are usually the result.

Accurate vision is in order. Without vision the people perish; but happy is he that keepeth the law. My analysis is not a challenge to the president's integrity or intent but rather to his vision and judgment.

A distinction should be made between Reaganism and Reaganomics. Reaganism is subjective. It is a spirit conveyed through personality. It is the reason nobody can sell Reaganism like the then-candidate and now-president Ronald Reagan. Reaganism is conveyed to the nation and the world through a consummate actor who projects well on television.

There are appealing features in Reaganism—visions of hope, power, prestige, and conquest. Reaganism speaks of no more humiliation—such as that endured by the U.S. victims in the Iranian hostage crisis. It says to the American people, we are no longer going to be pushed around in the world—an appeal to our collective ego. It projects self-confidence and assurance—we're number one, the best, don't be second-class. A significant number of Americans have embraced this "new beginning" in new and subtle ways. With Vietnam, Watergate, and Iran behind us, a new search for patriotism is trying to emerge and erase history. But "new beginnings" must be built on the foundation of truth. Unless God builds the house, they labor in vain.

The basis of this new patriotism often is delicately selected and revised history. It takes pride in the American Revolution but forgets about Crispus Attucks.* Reaganism appeals to a past pride of industrial development but overlooks its foundations—the exploitation of cheap labor, cheap energy, and cheap raw materials. It remembers and looks with pride at the antebellum houses but ignores the dominant character of that age—slavery. You will recall that it was candidate Ronald Reagan who said he only recently discovered that there was a racial problem in this country. Thus insensitivity, not insincerity, may be a part of our communications problem with the president.

The spirit of Reaganism stands for forgetting, even dismissing, the past and concentrating simply and exclusively on recovery, rehabilitation, and national revival. Through projecting optimism and advocating a positive mental attitude among Americans, it tries to convince people that Reaganism can change water into wine. It is an appealing spirit.

---

*Crispus Attucks, a runaway slave killed by the British in the Boston Massacre in 1770, was the first colonial casualty of the Revolutionary War.

While Reaganism is largely subjective, a spirit and attitude conveyed, Reaganomics is more objective. Reaganism is being used to impose Reaganomics. Reaganism—an appeal to national pride—is the perception; Reaganomics is the soon-to-be-faced reality. Many who are now basking in the sun of Reaganism soon will be burned to a crisp with Reaganomics. Reaganism and Reaganomics are on a collision course. Why?

Reaganomics wants to use the powers of the federal government to redistribute income and wealth upward from the poor to the rich. Reaganomics wants to reduce the budget for social programs in order to finance tax cuts for the rich. Reaganomics wants to kill federal grants—Comprehensive Employment Training Act (CETA), Head Start, Title I, welfare, food stamps, and Social Security—in order to give contracts to the big corporations that make military weapons. Reaganomics believes in federal spending as much as anyone. The only difference is that they want to spend the money for a different purpose. We must not allow the powers of the federal government to be used to take from the needy and give to the greedy.

Reaganomics stands for the increased concentration of wealth, with a decreased responsibility to distribute it broadly. In Reaganomics, the economic body will not have health problems because of anemia, weakness in the blood or an inadequate supply, but because of a blood clot—too much blood concentrated in one spot.

Reaganomics will seriously hurt and damage black and poor people, but it will also have a negative impact on most middle-class Americans. It will increase economic disparities between rich and poor, black and white, male and female—thus increasing racial, sexual, and class tensions in the society. Reaganomics doesn't cut the budget, it shifts the budget from needed social programs to unneeded military ones—which will make America less secure at home and abroad.

In the past when the nation was confronted with an economic crisis and used blacks as scapegoats, white America was fed Jim Crow and ate cold turkey. In the current crisis we are being entertained and mesmerized by the Al Jolson syndrome. Once upon another time, there was a white actor who knew the ways of white people. He could manipulate them—make them laugh, make them cry, or make them mad—simply by putting a black face on a white body and acting. The perception was black. The reality was white. Al Jolson eventually had to wash his face, but for a while all could escape and project various emotions on the black face. He did it so well until even some blacks laughed, even though we were victimized by the anti-black meanness mania that often accompanied his entertainment.

Many white leaders are now exploiting the Al Jolson syndrome.

Reaganomics uses economic programs that mainly benefit whites— CETA, welfare, food stamps, public education, minimum wage, legal services—and puts a black face on them. Many whites believed the perception and voted against their own economic self-interest, biting on the race bait. They soon shall wake up to the reality of their own economic nightmare. Born in meanness and bred in madness, what was designed to be an act of genocide quickly will become an act of suicide.

When the gap between perception and reality closes, resistance to the unprecedented economic dislocation, which Reaganomics will bring, will start. The poor are the recipients of welfare, food stamps, legal aid, and more; but it is the middle class who comprise the delivery system— welfare workers, food stamp administrators, medicaid doctors, and legal aid lawyers. When this group is unemployed—an educated and trained group of workers with high expectations and middle-class values, a group not used to coping with real economic adversity—anything may happen. The illusion created by class distinctions will meet. The welfare recipient and the welfare worker, the Title I child and the Title I teacher all eat out of the same public economic trough. When the bottom develops a hole, the delivery bureaucracy and all above it fall through as well. There is a divine law of reciprocity which says that it is impossible to hurt someone without hurting yourself in the process—just as it is impossible to help someone without helping yourself.

At carnivals, white people used to put a black face on a target at which they would throw baseballs. When they hit the target—the black face— it released a lever and dropped the person sitting on a board into a large tub of water. It was great fun for white people to hit the black face and see the person fall into the water. Many whites have had great fun at this year's economic carnival throwing baseballs at the black face. However, some whites are going to be surprised when they get home from this year's carnival and find out that their own sons and daughters are dripping wet.

Renewal of the Voting Rights Act

The executive, judicial, and legislative branches of government are hedging on renewing the Voting Rights Act. They say that the Voting Rights Act should apply to all fifty states. We agree, because it already does. After all, we are the group that fought for blacks, whites, Hispanics, women, and teenagers to have the right to vote.

Poll taxes and literacy tests were not enforced in fifty states. Grandfather clauses were not enforced in all fifty states, and thus their generosity is interesting. They are offering us more, it seems, than we are asking for. But without Section 2, the ban on all forms of racial discrimination, and Section 5, the preclearance provision designed to stop

racially motivated structural changes in government, we would be legislated in but regulated out.

*The predicament of former slaves must be viewed differently from the predic-
ament of former immigrants.* Without these regulations, we would have
equal protection under the law without having equal protection within
the law, and thus the Voting Rights Act would remain a modern-day
Indian treaty—a legal right signed into law but never honored. The lack
of enforcement of Sections 2 and 5 has permitted new forms of denial to
emerge and become as dominant as, but more deceptive than, the old
forms of denial. Jim Crow, Esq., verbally supports the right to vote but
denies the impact of the vote through at-large elections, annexation
schemes, and gerrymandering.

The same people who do not want us to live at-large, worship at-
large, marry at-large, or go to school at-large want us to vote at-large.
That is a change of language but not a change of heart. The result is that
cities like Columbia, South Carolina, and Jackson, Mississippi, have no
black elected officials. Annexation schemes simply mean that every time
a black person comes to bat, they move the walls back. The Justice
Department has not been an aggressive monitor, trouble-shooter, and
enforcer for the disenfranchised as it was mandated to do in the Voting
Rights Act.

The court, by shifting its focus from effect to intent, shifted the burden
of proof from the government to the individual. In *Mobile v. Bolden* (see
"In Search of a New Focus and a New Vision," below) the judge
essentially said that we have a right to vote, but we don't have a right to
have our vote counted. That was a throwback to *Dred Scott* (see "*Brown
Twenty-five Years Later*," below), for then they were saying that a black
person has no rights that a white person is bound to respect.

If the president wants some information on the Voting Rights Act, we
appeal to him to summon those of us who are members of the despised,
rejected, and disenfranchised caste and ask us to share it with him. We
will tell him that the 1965 Voting Rights Act was not a black act, that
whites, Hispanics, and teenagers, as well as blacks, gained from the act
and that the most fundamental tenet in democracy was realized—the
right to speak and be heard. We will tell him that the South has not been
singled out—that twenty-four states, or parts thereof, are being moni-
tored and that Section 5 is applicable everywhere. An earlier race by
Mayor Hatcher in Gary, Indiana, was saved because of the Voting Rights
Act. We will tell him that history and need, not regions, trigger the
regulations and that regional pride is not more sacred than racial justice.

We will tell him that the same people who want states' rights, because
they say that it brings government closer to the people, don't want ward
and district rights because they say it brings government too close to the

people. We will tell him to come with us to Mississippi, where 40 percent of the state is black without any congressional representation. We will take him to Sunflower County, Mississippi, where people must register twice—once at the courthouse and once at the city hall. They must drive sixty miles to Indianola to register with the county and sixty miles back to register with the city.

We will take him to South Carolina where one-third of all eligible voters are black, where there are no blacks in Congress, and where there is not one black in the state senate because the judge approved a reapportionment plan that gerrymandered against blacks, but the state attorney general never filed an objection. We will take him to Edgefield County, the home of Senator Strom Thurmond, which is 60 to 70 percent black, where no blacks have held an elected office in this century and where the last two elections have been held in violation of Section 5, but the Justice Department has never enforced the law there.

I hope the president will send us a copy of the letter that he sent to Attorney General Smith. We can fill in all the blank spaces.

Renewal of the Voting Rights Act in its present or expanded form is in trouble. Some are trying to kill or weaken the law through dilution (applying it to all fifty states), others through deletion (weakening or eliminating Sections 2 and 5). Whatever the scheme, there is an interesting parallel between what happened with the sixty-three Democrats (mostly Southerners) who voted with the Republicans on the Reagan budget and the twenty-nine Democrats (mostly Southerners) who voted for the supplementary budget cuts and what happened in the Hayes-Tilden Compromise of 1877. Tilden won the popular vote by a 250,000 vote margin, and the electoral vote was even more decisive, with Tilden needing only one more vote for victory. Instead, Southern Democrats cut a deal and joined hands with Republicans to deny Tilden the victory. Hayes promised to withdraw federal troops from the South and to appoint at least one Southerner to the cabinet. This was the origin of the Northern Republican–Southern Democratic regressive coalition that has existed in various degrees to this very day.

It looks as if President Reagan has cut a similar three-point deal with Southern Democrats: (1) he promised those Democrats who voted with him on his budget that he would support their pet projects (similar to Southern internal improvements); (2) he promised them that he would not campaign against them in 1982 (similar to appointing a Southerner to his cabinet); and (3) he promised them that he would withdraw federal legal protection from the South by opposing renewal of the 1965 Voting Rights Act in its present or strengthened form—just like Hayes withdrew federal military protection from us one hundred years ago. It's nothing but a Hayes-Tilden Compromise all over again.

The litmus test that in large measure will determine the future of the black-Democractic coalition is the Democratic party's position on the 1965 Voting Rights Act. A strong position advocating extension and strengthening of the bill will build the coalition and the Democratic party generally. A weak or equivocating position will weaken both. Many Democratic legislators are going for the Hayes-Tilden trade-off.

A major problem within the Democratic party, with its current weak-kneed position, is that the black vote is the only factor that stands as a buffer to a Republican takeover of the South. Republicans can win the South with the white vote, but the Democrats cannot win the South without the black vote, and therein lies the Democrats' dilemma. Should it oppose or weakly support the 1965 Voting Rights Act and jeopardize the black-Democratic coalition and probably its chances for national office in the foreseeable future? Or should it advocate that which is morally right and politically beneficial to itself and the nation? How it decides that question will have profound consequences for the black-Democratic coalition and the nation.

We must go back to the streets en masse. Our right to vote and participate in government is nonnegotiable. Taxation without representation is tyranny. We must resist.

Black Leadership vs. White Leadership

Recently I have read several articles asking the question, "Where is black leadership in the 1980s?" Typically these articles name the top five or six civil rights leaders, analyze each of their strengths and weaknesses, and conclude, "Things are not as good with today's black leaders as they were when Dr. Martin Luther King, Jr., was around."

Such analyses always strike me as spurious and romantic. They are spurious because they imply that there was a time when the black community was homogeneous and united behind Dr. King while today it is heterogeneous and divided, with no black leader or leaders to unify it. They are romantic because they deny historical facts and reality. Dr. King was a great leader not because a majority of the black community was solidly unified and marching behind him but because a man in his time rose above disunity and attacks by both blacks and whites to achieve significant social change.

Those who analyze Dr. King from such a romantic perspective actually do him a disservice. Most of those who commemorate his birth date and assassination date and praise his courage and accomplishments today in death were silent and afraid to identify, let alone march, with him in life. The government and white leadership isolated and humiliated him through character assassination—which almost always precedes physical assassination. Blacks loyal to President Lyndon Johnson attacked him, and his own church's denominational body rejected him. He was labeled a Communist, and when he spoke out against the Vietnam War, liberal whites and blacks withdrew their support from his organization. Dr. King, Harry Belafonte, and Aretha Franklin went on an eleven-city tour to raise money in the black community, and in only one city, Chicago, did they make a profit.

Many journalists who could get little space or time to analyze white leadership are all of a sudden getting sizable space and time to criticize black leadership. Many politicians are capitalizing on the current anti-black meanness mania in the country and are using the black masses as scapegoats (affirmative action, etc.) for the country's economic woes. Many in the media with appraisal power are doing the same with black leadership. In part we're victimized by allowing those who compete with us for the mind of the American people to be our judges. The other team has judge, referee, and scorekeeper.

There are several fundamental errors in such approaches. The first error is to focus on 6 civil rights leaders rather than on the 6,000 black elected officials and the breadth and depth of black leadership that has emerged over the last two decades—church, athletic, labor, business, legal, medical, educational, and journalistic.

A second mistake is to equate visibility and responsibility with power. Whites sometimes project a fly in the buttermilk as if it were a whole glass of chocolate milk. There is more visible black leadership, and greater numbers of black leaders are being asked to assume the responsibility for changing things. However, the power of leadership has not shifted in proportion to the burden of leadership.

Where is black leadership, which has limited power—6,000 black public officials out of 512,000 nationally—compared with white leadership's virtual monopoly power on the great issues of our day? While blacks are fighting for a humane policy and majority rule under one set of rules, white leaders define democracy one way in the United States and another way in South Africa. While white leaders, including 63 Democrats, voted for the Reagan budget cuts, the Congressional Black Caucus introduced the fairest and most humane budget but got virtually no coverage and few white supporters.

While black leaders are arguing for job training, white leaders are voting for military training. Black leaders are fighting to increase educational options; white leaders are voting to close schools and build jails. Black leaders have put forth a peace plan in the Middle East accepted by most nations of the world; white leaders are again threatening to engage in gunboat diplomacy and manifest destiny around the world.

Where is black leadership in the 1980s? Fighting for a domestic agenda that would benefit all Americans. Pleading for a foreign policy that is in the long-term security interests of the nation and world peace. Speaking and marching on behalf of stopping a suicidal arms race. Often enduring humiliation from its primary beneficiaries.

Black leadership is in the forefront of humane and progressive change. But it must always be remembered that blacks are only one out of every ten Americans. The fundamental question is not where is black leadership, with its limited power and unlimited burden, but where is white leadership with its virtually unlimited power?

It is white leadership, not black, that is in control of fiscal and monetary policy. It is white leadership, not black, that determines import/ export policy. It is white leadership, not black, that is mapping this nation's foreign and domestic policy. It is white journalists, not black, who are interpreting domestic and world events with their appraisal power. Since the country is in such trouble, it is apparent that white leadership is without vision to lead the country.

A Way Out

It's not enough to analyze our misery and our adversaries; we must seek a way out. Documentation of our predicament alone leads only to a paralysis of analysis. We must act. We must avoid turning inward, avoid turning on each other, and avoid escaping through the various forms of dope and disillusion. We must join hearts and hands, use what we've got, and fight. There's no shady spot in hell. So don't let them send you to hell and then act like you're cool about it. Act like you're mad, act like you don't like it—scream and kick and yell all the way there.

We are running against a stiff headwind. In spite of the odds, we must EXCEL. The odds are such that we must be superior to be equal. Excellence is achieving your best against the odds. It will require strong minds and wills.

What do we have to fight with? Let me suggest eight ways to fight.

1. *Coalitions.* We must rebuild a resistance network in the top 50 markets where 68 percent of black people live and spend between $94 and $100 billion. We must first coalesce among ourselves, turn black tribalism into black federalism, and then coalesce with other groups who are going our way. PUSH supports and will be joining the AFL-CIO, the NAACP, and other civil rights and religious organizations in the march on Washington on September 19. PUSH was glad to see over 5,000 people in the streets to greet the president Tuesday night in Chicago. The first thing we must do is get the president's attention. Coalitions are built on mutual need, self-interest, and reciprocity.

2. *1982 Congressional Election.* Those who oppose or are undecided on the Voting Rights Act must be put on a political dishonor roll. We must conduct aggressive voter education and voter registration drives in their

districts. We must also demand our fair share of congressional seats in reapportionment. In 1982, all 435 members of the House and one-third of the Senate must face their constituencies for reelection. It is going to be difficult explaining that they are bringing home fewer jobs and services, higher interest rates, and continuing inflation. The interesting thing in a democracy is that everything that goes around must come around. We are asking each one of you here today to urge your city council and state legislature to endorse the Voting Rights Act extension. In that regard, we will be asking you to take back to your home city our model resolution for this purpose.

   3. *Consumer Power.* We must use our $140 billion in disposable income as a lever for liberation in the 50 key markets where 68 percent of the black population lives, claiming 75 percent of the black income. We must demand our fair share of "supply-side" economics—wealth, ownership, employers, and producers—not merely settle for being employees of those companies where we spend our consumer dollars. We vote with a ballot every two, four, or six years, but we vote with our dollars every day. In this regard, under the able leadership of Rev. B. W. Smith of Buffalo, New York, the National Selective Patronage Council has submitted a list of ten companies to whom we will send an initial inquiry. At this moment we are in intense negotiations with the Coca-Cola Company, based in Atlanta. Black consumers must renegotiate our relationship with corporate America and the international business community. We must use our consumer demand as a lever for liberation. We will begin immediately to plan for a trade mission to Japan to be led by PUSH, black labor leaders, and black businessmen to negotiate our relationship to the Japanese in light of the tremendous impact that Japanese imports have had on the displacement of black workers.

   4. *The Courts.* We must continue to press our case through the courts. The Supreme Court has shifted the burden of proof from effect to intent, thus making the legal route more difficult and more costly, but we must continue the struggle. There is a direct relationship between votes, political climate, and court decisions.

   5. *Direct Action.* Every major gain we ever made came as the result of the drama, education, and climate setting of marching. We must not get too cute to fight. Reaganomics will force more and more people back to the streets to protect themselves. Direct action is still a legitimate and effective tool in the liberation struggle. The target may change, but the means is still valid.

   6. *Media.* We must demand our fair share of journalists, our fair share of time and space to tell our story, and support the growth of an independent black press, all at the same time. We must not tolerate 2 blacks out of 134 top television network executives, and 7 blacks in

executive editorial positions on 1,769 daily newspapers. We must confront and challenge the white monopoly of the media.

7. *Education.* President Reagan has cut the education budget by 25 percent; he is proposing a voucher or tuition tax credit scheme to use public money for private racial habits; he has cut back on the school lunch program and is refusing to enforce desegregation of the nation's schools. Yet we must confront diminished educational options with an increased will and determination to learn. PUSH takes the position that if the universities cut us out of the Basic Educational Opportunity Grants in the academic area, we must begin to meet with our top athletes and encourage them not to allow their bodies to be used as gladiators to fill up stadiums for white people's entertainment when their black peers cannot receive an education and a diploma at that same university. We will continue to fight for the survival and improvement of black colleges, and we will convene a National Black Students' Congress in August prior to the opening of school to address this concern.

8. *International Affairs.* First, realizing the urgency of the situation in the Middle East and the absolute necessity of Palestine Liberation Organization involvement in any solution, we urge the State Department to continue the dialogue with the PLO in a serious effort to bring about a fair, just, righteous, and lasting peace. A policy of no-talk and preemptive strikes is an impractical, unprincipled, and unproven approach to diplomacy that will only aggravate an already dangerous situation. If we negotiate for peace with one set of rules with a commitment to eliminate terrorism on both sides, and if we as a nation become aggressive mediators rather than helpless instigators, our nation can make a difference. If we talk, we can act; if we act, we can change things and thus protect the interests of Americans and Israelis.

Second, we stand unmoved and immovable in reiterating our unconditional stand on the question of human and political rights in South Africa. The issue is really very simple—one person, one vote, for our brothers and sisters in South Africa and immediate independence for Namibia.

Last, there is no more dangerous and devastating tendency in the world today than that of the escalating arms race. This senseless tendency can only lead to worldwide destruction. Therefore we urge this nation to begin serious dialogue in the international community directed toward stopping and de-escalating the arms race. We must put down our arms and study war no more.

Levers of Liberation

I remind you over and over again about the slave/slavemaster and the victim/victimizer relationship. Slavemasters require submissive slaves.

That's why they use money, jobs, status, and the threat of losing them to whip slaves in line. If that doesn't work, they use jail cells, death, or the threat of death to intimidate—all to break the spirit of the slave. When the spirit is broken and despair replaces hope, then the quantity of the slave's life becomes more important than the quality, and the master is in control.

Willpower—the resistance syndrome on the part of the slave—is the greatest threat to the master. Dependence and fear are the slave's greatest enemies. The master must kill the slaves' will through intimidation, violence, and diversion by making them impotent with alcohol, drugs, obligation through debt, or through deceit destroying their credibility among their neighbors and neutralizing their allies.

When slaves stand up, the master will fall off their backs. The victim's responsibility is to resist. Cooperation with the master is the victim's enemy. It is a sin to cooperate with evil. When we drink the master's liquor, resist education, leave our children to raise themselves—we are the master's unwitting agents. But when we don't sit in the back of the bus or go to the back of the restaurant or be denied the right to vote—in other words, when we don't cooperate with evil—we serve the cause of liberation. The victim is responsible for noncooperation. Accept the fact that slavemasters do not perceive it to be in their self-interest to free you, to pay you your due, your worth. Nobody will save us for us but us. We must not measure progress by the expansion of things but by resistance to them and the lack of dependency upon them.

Just as we have a moral obligation to resist evil, we have a moral obligation to cooperate with good. People who reject this believe in the oppressor's promises, courts, politics, religion. But progress will not come in such a manner. Progress will come in proportion to our struggle and resistance, not the oppressor's goodness. The oppressor will get off our back when it becomes too dangerous or too costly to stay there.

We contribute to this mastery when we kill each other, when we impregnate our women and then walk away, when we refuse to buy from or save with each other, and when we tear each other down.

The masters will contribute to any cause except the development of our willpower. They'll give you jobs and positions, even titles and chauffeurs, just as long as our dependency is extended. The development and perpetuation of the dependency syndrome is the object of the master. Anybody who is dependent upon you is subject to enslavement and exploitation by you.

Martin Luther King, Jr., Gandhi, and Jesus all argued that the kingdom is within. Soul force and *satyagraha* are the true levers of liberation. Suffer, not because the master is oppressing you, but suffer because you are breaking away. Malcolm argued that the master is only disturbed when slaves make other slaves restless.

Slaves are not responsible for their condition, but they must be responsible for changing it. The patients may not be responsible for getting sick, but they will be for getting well. Health is more in the will than in the pill. If master-control is slavery, then self-control is freedom. Freedom is in self-reliance, self-initiative, and self-discipline.

You must not allow the master to control your thoughts through decadent values—salaries, liquor, drugs, debt, insensitivity, cynicism, escapism, fear, hate, finance, superstition, radio, TV, or newspapers. You must be able to resist.

Last, we live in our Father's world. We're not slaves brought here to serve white folks. We're God's children sent here to save the human race. We demand a "talk" policy in the Middle East. We demand "one person, one vote" in Southern Africa.

They may take away the budget for a while, they may take away your land, they may take away your property, but don't let them break your spirit.

They may break your back, but don't let them break your spirit.

They may call us black and ugly, big-lipped, nappy-haired; we may be rejected and despised; but don't let them break your spirit.

You may be an orphan, adopted, a motherless child, but don't let them break your spirit.

It may be kind of rare and kind of odd, but the Lord can turn a rejected stone into a cornerstone. Don't let them break your spirit.

Say "My mind is a pearl, I can learn anything in the world." Say, "I can learn, I ought to learn, I must learn." Don't let them break your spirit.

Humiliation can lead to tears, but remember, weeping may endure for a night, but if you hold on, joy will come in the morning. Don't let them break your spirit.

There was an old biblical hero who said, I know I'm old, but I'm leaning on God's promise. Give me this mountain. I know it's tough, but he didn't bring us this far to leave us now. Don't let them break your spirit.

We don't know where the economy is going, but I've never seen the righteous forsaken nor their seed beg for bread. Don't let them break your spirit.

Like Jesus, you may have been born in the slum, but the slum was not born in you. Don't let them break your spirit.

Don't let anybody stop you from dreaming, hoping, aspiring, and planning. Don't let them break your spirit.

Like a balloon, it is not the color on the outside that matters, it's what's on the inside. If you've got the right stuff on the inside, if there's a little wheel turning, if there's a soul yearning, if your heart is burning, you can rise above your circumstance. Don't let them break your spirit.

They put nails in his hands and thorns on his head, and yet he rose from the grave. He went from disgrace to amazing grace. He wouldn't let them break his spirit.

Jacob wrestled with the angel all night long. They broke his leg, but they didn't break his spirit. Don't let them break your spirit.

Job. They took away everything he had. But he said, Yea, though I have lost it all, yet will I trust him, because deep down on the inside of me, that which makes me me, where my friends can't reach and where my family cannot discourage, way down, I know my redeemer lives because he lives in my soul. Don't let them break your spirit.

If my people, who are called by my name, will humble themselves and pray and turn from their wicked ways, then they'll hear from heaven. God bless you. I am somebody. I am God's child.

The Advantages of a Black
Presidential Candidacy

This essay first appeared in the *Washington Post* on
April 10, 1983.

The fundamental relationship between blacks and the
Democratic party must be renegotiated. Blacks and the Democratic
party must either reaffirm a covenant as being in their mutual best
interest, or blacks must find new ways to determine their destiny. One
indication of current black dissatisfaction is that all across the nation
grass-roots and top black political, church, business, and community
leaders are discussing the proposition of making the institutional—as
distinguished from merely a personal—political move of running a
black presidential candidate in the 1984 Democratic primaries.

In part, this is in response to the Democratic party taking the black
vote for granted and the Republican party writing it off. For Democrats,
race is increasingly becoming a litmus test and the central threat to the
viability of the party. Black Democrats have won primaries in South
Carolina, North Carolina, Mississippi, California, and Chicago, yet significant numbers of white Democratic leaders and voters are choosing to
support white Republicans over black Democrats. If black people and
their leaders support Democrats without regard to race, but others
cannot reciprocate, then the character and viability of the party must be
called into question.

With regard to a black presidential candidacy, there are four critical
questions to be considered. Why run? What would such a candidacy
require? What would be the advantages? What are the arguments
against such a candidacy?

Why Run?

Blacks have their backs against the wall and are increasingly distressed by the erosion of past gains and the rapidly deteriorating conditions within black and poor communities. As black leaders have attempted to remedy these problems through the Democratic party—to which black voters have been the most loyal and disciplined group—too often they have been ignored or treated with disrespect. Mounting a serious presidential candidacy is one way of insisting that black leaders play significant roles and help shape policy and programs for the party.

Second, given the coalitions that are possible, a black candidate could win the nomination and be elected. Currently, none of the announced or anticipated candidates is exciting to the black community, and Democrats need more than an anti-Reagan program to stimulate massive interest and broad-based participation. None of the current candidates is moving in ways that would bring about this kind of involvement, create the needed coalition, and thus provide the gains we need. In 1980, about 81 million Americans voted, but nearly 75 million "went fishing," as only 54 percent of the eligible electorate was inspired enough or felt the options were viable enough even to participate. A black candidacy could use an 18-million-eligible-black-voter base to put together a "coalition of the rejected" (the real silent majority)—including appealing to 6 million Hispanics, women, more than 500,000 Native Americans, 20 to 40 million poor whites—and an appeal to the moral decency and enlightened economic self-interest of millions of rejected white moderates, liberals, and others. It must be remembered that Hispanics, like blacks, before 1965, were denied the right to vote because of poll taxes, property taxes, literacy tests, and language barriers; and since 1965, again like blacks, they have been victimized by the new forms of denial—gerrymandering, annexation, at-large elections, and unenforced sections of the Voting Rights Act.

Third, a black should run because many of the political issues that concern blacks and other unrepresented and rejected people have been determined by the current major candidates to be politically undiscussable. In fact, the strategy advocated by Hamilton Jordan and Bert Lance is for Democratic candidates to minimize the concerns of blacks, Hispanics, women, and peace activists and give highest priority to recruiting the southern white conservative vote—the old Republican strategy for the South. Thus the current candidates are shying away from the issues of (1) full employment (e.g., along the lines of the original Humphrey-Hawkins Bill); (2) affirmative action, which has provided increased educational and employment opportunities for women, Hispanics, and blacks; (3) strong enforcement of the Voting Rights Act, including Sections 2 and 5, which has made democracy more real for everybody; (4) a renewed national commitment to a serious economic program for the poor; and (5) a new look at much of America's foreign policy, including the demand that if the United States is going to have a relationship with South Africa, we insist that it measure democracy (one person, one vote) and human rights by one yardstick. These are not issues that we can put in the stomach of any of the present Trojan horses and expect them to come out once they are inside the White House fence. We must devise our own vehicle to carry these issues to the stage when the national debates begin. We cannot ride to freedom in Pharaoh's chariot. Or, to mix analogies, all of Santa's other reindeer have had their chance to pull and lead the sleigh and present their gifts to the American people. Now it may be time for Rudolph, who has consistently pulled more weight, to have his turn.

A black candidate should run to gain political victories, but also to gain collective self-respect and recognition. Never again should blacks live and operate below their political privilege and rights.

Last, a black should run because bargainers without bases are beggars, not brokers. Primaries are the process for organizing and mobilizing interest groups. Various states (e.g., New York), labor (e.g., the AFL-CIO and the NEA), women, and other groups are currently organizing political support on behalf of their interests—both in anticipation of locking up the nomination early and in case the convention is brokered. They want their interests protected. Blacks are not adequately represented and do not have enough influence in any of these other constituencies to trust the protection of their interests to anyone else. Thus blacks and other rejected interest groups must create and provide their own protection. Therefore, in an eight-candidate field (and possibly additional "favorite son" candidacies), a successful black candidacy, in coalition with other interest groups, is achievable. Candidates run for all kinds of reasons and define their success according to their own purposes. Barry Goldwater was not elected in 1964, and George Wallace was not nominated by the Democrats in 1968, but they both "sent a message" that shifted the politics of the entire nation and laid the groundwork for Ronald Reagan's election in 1980.

To use a football analogy, we are now in the exhibition season looking at various game strategies and assessing the players on the field. During the primaries we will play the regular season, and at the convention we will conduct the Super Bowl. But, if you do not think and plan in advance, and then do not play during the regular season, you cannot participate or even get a good seat at the Super Bowl. If blacks focus all of their attention on the Super Bowl, and do little planning and do not play during the regular season (the primaries), blacks will end up basking in someone else's glory or crying in someone else's beer. It is not enough just for our conference (Democrats) to win; our team (blacks and the rejected) must also win. And for our team to win, everyone must help prepare the game plan (party policy) and be in the huddle when the plays (the platform) are called.

The Democratic party cannot make policy and write the platform without the serious involvement of blacks at every level and then ask blacks merely to sit in the stands and enthusiastically cheer the conference representative to victory (i.e., vote Democratic in the general election). Even though blacks now constitute 20 percent of the national Democratic vote, currently blacks have membership but no shared proprietorship in the party—and investors without equity reap no dividends.

What Does a Successful Black Candidacy Require?

It requires the masses, machinery, and money. A black candidate must have the ability to galvanize the masses and to define, interpret, and defend the national interest generally and the interests of black, nonwhite, poor, and rejected people specifically.

A black candidate should not move unilaterally, without broad-based, credible, and substantial institutional support from those whose interests converge with the candidacy. Around the southeast horn of the United States—Virginia, North Carolina, South Carolina, Georgia, Florida, Alabama, Mississippi, Louisiana—where the black base continues to reside, blacks still do not have even one black congressperson, their share of state representatives, and even fewer state senators. This is true mainly because of unenforced sections of the Voting Rights Act which allow the use of new forms of voter denial to succeed. Conducting state issues conferences to focus on these and other local political concerns will maximize the number of people involved, as well as broaden the base of the coalition, which in turn will maximize the benefits to be gained. By coming together and projecting an agenda that affects them, coalition members are then in a better position to pick a person who could best represent their interests. In so doing, both the presidential nominating process and the product are validated.

Finally, a black candidacy must be able to attract adequate broad-based financial support. The ability to match the spending of other candidates would not be necessary. In Chicago, Jane Byrne raised $10 million, Richard Daley raised $4 million, and Harold Washington raised less than $1 million—yet Mr. Washington defeated both of his opponents.

What Would Be the Advantages of Such a Candidacy?

One advantage is that a black candidate could win. As in the Olympics, everyone who runs has a chance to win, and everyone who runs wins something. The byproducts of a black candidacy would justify the campaign. A credible and attractive candidacy would move the issues of social justice, war and peace, hurt and healing (at home and abroad) onto the front burner of the nation's agenda. One-fourth of the total black vote is between the ages of 18 and 24. It would excite, maybe even electrify, the black, the young, the rejected, and the unrepresented masses, increasing their voter registration and political participation. For example, if black voter registration went from its current 10 million to 14 million, and black participation went from the 7 million of 1980 to 12 million in 1984, that would have major ramifications for both blacks and the Democratic party—and that does not even count increased poor white, Hispanic, youth, or other voter registration that such a candidacy would surely stimulate. A black candidacy, then, would alter the essentially negative and defensive option of the "lesser of two or seven evils" to the positive and offensive alternative of a "live" option. An increase in voter registration and political participation would have a profound impact on the status quo of the Democratic party and the nation in the general election. Eighteen million eligible and 12 million active black voters, inspired by a live option, could not be ignored.

During the debates, blacks would no longer be in the "kitchen cabinet," passing notes from the trailer to the candidates on stage, but would be on the stage arguing the nation's agenda from a different perspective. Six to ten new black congresspersons could be a byproduct. Psychologically, it might help bring to an end ideas and feelings of black inferiority and white superiority. Locally, it would enhance the power of black elected officials and delegates. It would mean positive change for blacks both in and on the media. It would change the nature of the primaries, the debates, the convention, and a new administration. Indeed, it would change the face (no pun intended) of American politics. In other words, for blacks there is more at stake than just who will be president.

What Are the Arguments Against a Black Candidacy?

One is that a black candidacy would appeal only to black voters. Not true. A black candidate who advances the issues of concern to Hispanics, women, the poor, and whites who are interested in social justice should be able to attract them as well as blacks. Blacks have had experience with running—and winning—in areas that do not have majority black populations (e.g., Tom Bradley, mayor of Los Angeles, and Alan Wheat and Ron Dellums, congressmen from Missouri and California, respectively). Clearly, these victories could only have occurred because black candidates had communitywide appeal. In addition, black leaders in other fields of endeavor have been able to attract more than just black support. In athletics, art, science, literature, and the media, blacks have pulled down curtains of resistance and operated beyond the ethnic domain. Now, in politics and trade, blacks must overcome the restraining forces and do the same.

There is no reason why a black presidential candidate who emphasizes an economy in crisis, massive unemployment, excessive concentrations of wealth, tax reform, war and peace, guns (an unprecedented $2.2 trillion in military spending) instead of butter (education, housing, health care), and labor- versus capital-intensive alternative forms of energy—just to mention a few—would not have broad appeal. These are all general concerns of national importance which happen to overlap with particular interests of blacks.

I was in Iowa recently. While there I was impressed, once the dialogue was opened, with the interest that whites showed and the willingness they had to see the direct relationship between rural white farmers and urban black consumers (i.e., what the Food Stamp program represented for both groups directly). The Food Stamp program represents money, market, and nutrition. So much of America can be tied together in this way if leadership has the intelligence, the courage, and the will to do so. Thus, beyond ethnicity, a black candidate's campaign should reflect ethics, economics, and excellence.

Another argument has been that a black candidacy would split the Democratic party and hurt the party's chances of regaining the White House in 1984. Some say a black candidacy will divide the South. Yet no one points to former Florida Governor Reubin Askew, Arkansas Senator Dale Bumpers, or South Carolina Senator Ernest Hollings—all of whom are active or potential candidates who have a southern base—and says that these campaigns are divisive. Should we not measure all of the campaigns by the same standard? How could a black candidacy that stimulated increased Democratic registration and participation be accused by Democrats of being negative? It, in fact, would be a positive net asset. The very idea of a black candidacy being divisive smacks of suggesting that blacks should be passive, that blacks "go quietly along with the program," and that they should wait and not push too hard— that that is the proper "place" for blacks in 1984. Blacks should reject all such arguments out of hand.

The argument that a black candidacy would split the progressive forces and allow a candidate less sympathetic to the concerns of progressives to capture the nomination is not valid either. It is a static, not an organic, view of the possible political options. It assumes that those who have been sympathetic in the past will remain so and that, given the option of a broader political base to choose from, other candidates would not or could not grow and move to capture a large progressive political bloc of voters. And at this point all of the current and speculated candidates are ignoring the concerns of blacks, women, Hispanics, peace activists, and the poor.

To illustrate the point, Lyndon Johnson's record was more conservative than John Kennedy's, but when presented with new political options, he was capable of growing. On the other hand, in Chicago the two politicians in the Democratic party who are considered the most progressive, Walter Mondale and Edward Kennedy, not only failed to endorse and work for the most progressive live option, Harold Washington, but endorsed and worked for his opponents. Even more than that, their contempt, disrespect, or disconnection from blacks and Hispanics was so great that they came into a city that is 42 percent black and 15 percent Hispanic in a local primary election without even talking with or consulting the three black congresspersons; State Comptroller Roland Burris, the largest vote-getter in the state in the November election; Richard Hatcher (in neighboring Gary, Indiana), the vice-chairperson and highest-ranking black at the Democratic National Committee (DNC); and local or national black and Hispanic indigenous leadership. Even now, after all of these abuses and a long train of grievances, Charles Manatt, chairman of the DNC, has not even sought to convene a meeting with black leadership or potential candidates to discuss the concerns.

Blacks, Hispanics, and the poor have always been told that they should not ask others to do for them what they can do for themselves. Thus it would be illogical to argue that they should do everything for themselves except when it comes to running for president. Then at that point others say, "We'll do that for you." To that logic, increasing numbers of people are saying, "No thanks." Before 1965, when blacks and Hispanics had no political straps or boots, the suggestion to pick yourself up by your own bootstraps was cruel. But now that blacks and Hispanics have 24 million potential political boots and straps (with feet in them), more and more people are saying that they should simply lace them up and—for the betterment not only of their interests but for the enrichment of the entire nation—run for themselves.

HUMAN RIGHTS
ADVOCATE

"We must measure human rights by one yardstick.
We can't define democracy as majority rule in
North America and as minority rule in South
Africa. We can't impose economic sanctions in
Poland because of martial law and then become
South Africa's number-one trading partner. We just
want the game played by one set of rules."

Measuring Human Rights
by One Yardstick

This essay first appeared as a Universal Press Syndicate
newspaper column on January 3, 1982.

The recent events in Poland have understandably
moved President Reagan, Pope John Paul II, the press, the AFL-CIO, and
all persons concerned with human rights. There is obvious worldwide
sympathy for Solidarity and the Polish people as they fight for democratic reforms and freedom in their society. The imposition of martial
law by the Polish government demonstrates the depth of the Polish
social and political crisis.

Not only have there been moral and political statements in support of
Solidarity and the Polish people, but actions have been taken by each of
these persons or institutions to aid the Polish people. President Reagan
imposed a series of economic sanctions on Poland and welcomed the
defection of the Polish ambassador. Pope John Paul II sent two special
ambassadors to Poland and expressed an interest in going there himself.
The AFL-CIO has sent financial aid and equipment to its fellow unionists, and the press has taken great pride in smuggling numerous tapes
and interviews out of Poland to keep those of us on the outside informed
of the situation there.

It is important, however, to step back and take a careful and more
balanced look at the way "Poland-mania" has gripped the public mind.
What immediately becomes clear is the double standard used to measure human rights. In fact, in the outcry over Poland, human rights may
not be the concern at all.

Looking at the Polish crisis more closely, one could easily conclude
that reaction to the events in Poland has more to do with our national

obsession with anti-communism than with any genuine concern for human rights. When the administration expresses the hope that it will be able to mobilize world opinion in support of its position on Poland, it is indulging in fantasy. It is fantasy because it assumes a world unaware of the hypocrisy of our human rights posture.

What do I mean? While the United States engages in moralistic protests and economic sanctions against Poland, a communist country whose government is attempting to crush a free-labor movement committed to democratic reforms, U.S. diplomacy and trade flourish with other nations whose governments have engaged daily, persistently, and systematically in human rights violations.

United States trade is flourishing with the fascist military regime in Chile, and our taxes support the repressive military junta in El Salvador. Polish diplomats and dissidents are welcomed as political refugees seeking asylum, while American military ships, under executive order, roam the high seas to intercept boats carrying Haitian refugees seeking political asylum and to turn them away from our shores without due process—a violation of human rights. Those Haitians who do reach the U.S. are held in what amount to criminal detention centers without criminal charges, another violation of human rights. Liberian political refugees— bankers, diplomats, and other former government officials—who only a few years ago were staunch allies of the United States today cannot even get a green card to work in this country.

The human rights of Palestinians, who have lived on the West Bank for generations, are violated daily by the Israeli military regime. Arab homes are demolished by army troops, students engaged in peaceful demonstrations are shot, illegal settlements on Arab territory are annexed—yet the U.S. government finances these activities with billions of dollars in economic and military aid to Israel each year.

Members of the American press have done their best to keep the outside world informed of what is going on in Poland. They have secretly filmed and written stories that were then smuggled out of Poland and which made clear the oppression and agony of the people of Poland. Yet no similar aggressiveness has been displayed in revealing conditions in Haiti, Liberia, Chile, Argentina, South Africa, or other hot spots of dramatic human rights violations, which in some instances have gone on for decades.

Even though 95 percent of Haitians and large numbers of black South Africans are Roman Catholic—Regina Mundi is the largest church in South Africa's Soweto—Pope John Paul II has not sent ambassadors to South Africa or Haiti to bring public attention to the tragic violations of human rights there.

The Polish government has attempted to crush Solidarity, the Polish free-trade union movement, and President Reagan has imposed diplomatic and economic sanctions against Poland. The South African government has attempted to crush violently the black free-trade union movement in South Africa; by contrast, the Reagan administration has drawn closer to the South African government and expanded trade relations. The United States is now the number-one trading partner of South Africa, and is the number-two foreign investor there.

Even though the exploitation of cheap labor in South Africa and Haiti helps to undercut the American worker, certainly more than conditions in Poland do, the AFL-CIO has not refused to unload ships arriving in this country from South Africa or from Haiti.

This double standard for measuring human rights is not inconsequential. It affects our national interests, for until we are consistent the United States will not have the moral authority required to influence world public opinion. The real U.S. "window of vulnerability" is not our lack of military preparedness, but the lack of a consistent human rights policy. Moral authority will only come when we determine to measure human rights by one yardstick.

Service and a New World Order

Jesse Jackson was among several religious leaders from around the world to speak at the First International Conference on Human Values in London. The conference's sponsoring patron was Prince Philip. The speech was presented April 1, 1981.

The idea, and now the reality, of an international conference to focus on human values is long overdue and thus is certainly welcomed by all sensitive people and by everyone concerned with the future and its quality. This morning the American president is in the hospital recovering from an attempted assassination. It is a raw and graphic portrayal of the need for this conference on human values. This meeting was providentially conceived and divinely inspired.

The regard that we have for human values will be reflected in our conduct. Inhumane values and disregard for human values are reflected in inhumane conduct. High regard for human values is reflected in civilized and compassionate conduct. Positive human values must be nurtured by human contact. The cultural and educational sound barriers must be broken. The veil or "the wall" must come down in order that our human feelings may meet and marry and become integrated throughout our personalities. We will not find inner peace and security until we hear the sound of the genuine in the hearts of other people. We must not be intimidated by short-term political considerations and volunteer for the prison of human isolation. Induced ignorance, born of separation, leads to fear, which leads to hate, which leads to violence, which leads to destruction. Thus the end result of this chain is the loss of human values in the human community.

We must not be afraid to grow—which involves suffering, sacrifice, and pain—to the end of restoring human values to the human community. Unearned suffering is redemptive. We must never underestimate the power of the blood of the innocent and the righteous. Such blood cannot be washed away by water and cannot be buried in the sand.

Our leaders must be challenged to see the whole world, and then they must be held accountable by the human community. President Reagan, for example, has never been to Africa, Asia, or the Arab world. We need leaders of vision to save nations and institutions from perishing. You can't teach what you don't know, and you can't lead where you don't go. We must not lead or be led by visions of fear and death, but rather we must be led by the pursuit of life and hope. People need hope more than they need help. People who keep hoping will keep hopping or moving—even against the greatest of odds.

To discuss human values out of the context of human institutions and governments is like a sperm out of the womb. In the wind, it is impotent and no longer productive. It is just a blob. Transformed people must transform nations.

My assignment is to discuss "the principle of service—human value in the community." I would like to address this issue under the rubric of "Service and a New World Order."

The Principle of Service: Foundation of a New World Order

One writer said, "Some people are born great, others achieve greatness, while still others have it thrust upon them." Actually, that's probably more true of fame than it is of greatness. Not everyone can be famous, that is, well known; but everyone can be great because greatness lies in service, and everybody can serve.

Service is ontologically grounded. It is structured into the very nature of reality itself. Need is the basis of all organization. All organizations—religious, economic, political, civic, or whatever—come into existence to address a need, and only organizations which continue to meet needs, whether the original need or a new one, survive and continue to exist. In other words, without serving need, human organizations would not even exist. Thus the only protection against genocide is to remain necessary, and service is the only thing that makes one necessary.

There is power in service. Many believe that power is the result of taking, but that's not true. The highest and purest form of power is in giving. Power taken will be taken again—by someone else. Power resulting from service cannot be lost and can only empower and enrich the giver and the receiver.

Some may say, "Now, Reverend, that service and altruism stuff is idealistic and naive. Don't you know mankind is basically selfish?" The principle of service takes humanity's selfishness and need for self-fulfillment into account. If need is the basis of social organization, and serving that need is power, it is also true that self-interest is the sustaining force. Even Jesus recognized this trinity when he said, "Love your neighbor as yourself." Love is the most basic human need. To serve your neighbor (in the spirit of love) is to love your neighbor. And it is impossible to help others without helping yourself in the process—just as it is impossible to hurt others without hurting yourself. So service is the means of loving your neighbor as you love yourself. The divine law of reciprocity is structured into reality itself.

The principle of service, then, doesn't deny the needs of self and ego and does not deny the need for power; rather it affirms their fulfillment in the highest and best manner. When Jesus said, "Deny yourself," he did not mean, primarily, to deny yourself "things" (although this may be a byproduct) or to repress or sublimate your ego. He meant that we should deny the self that leads to selfishness, and the only way to avoid selfishness is to engage in service to others in the spirit of love.

Everybody can and ought to consciously adopt a life style of service. Serving others implies strength helping weakness. But because that is the case, service can be paternalistic, chauvinistic, degrading, and used as a means of power to control other people. It need not be, but it can be. For those tempted by such evils, we need only remind ourselves that all of us have strengths and weaknesses. None of us is whole. All of us can serve, but all of us need service. All of us are crippled or handicapped in some way. Some of us are physically and mentally handicapped, while others of us are handicapped by racial, sexual, cultural, caste, or class meanness, fear, or ignorance. All of us need to use our strengths to heal and mend the weaknesses and infirmities of others and to be healed by the strengths of others.

Last, in some quarters, service has been given a bad name and brings with it a bad reputation. Colonialism and racism have confused the principle of *service* with the principle of *servitude*. The call for the free expression of servanthood must be affirmed. The chains of involuntary servitude must be rejected, resisted, and overthrown. There is an ethical mandate to be of service, but, with the same fortitude, don't be servile.

Opportunities for Service: Overcoming Obstacles to a New World Order

The principle of service is the foundation, the starting point, upon which everything else is built. But there are obstacles to a new world order which provide us with some of the areas and opportunities for service.

Historic and continued racism, colonialism, and neo-colonialism are obstacles to a new world order. The pathology of racism has been in the past and remains today the chief impediment in our striving for a more just and humane world in which to live. Racism, a philosophy of superiority based on skin color, is untrue scientifically, immoral theologically, unhealthy psychologically, and unworkable economically and politically for very much longer.

It may be uncomfortable to both say and hear, but racism as a pseudoscientific world outlook was theologically and philosophically systematically originated, organized, and propagated from the leading religious and educational institutions in the Western world in England, Germany, and the United States.

In America, and in the Western world generally, racism and colonialism have sapped our spirits and absorbed valuable energy. They have brought tensions and mistrust. As we meet today, two of the most dominant issues in the United States and around the world are the two missing and twenty murdered black children in Atlanta and the hanging—nineteenth-century Ku Klux Klan–style—of a nineteen-year-old black boy in Mobile, Alabama. In England today, laws to exclude nonwhites and the New Cross March—which is really a symbol of long-standing and underlying racial tensions and mistrust—are some of the most dominant issues here.

Racism makes some feel superior and others inferior. Racism has brought negative publicity and images upon us. Racism has divided families, communities, nations, and our concept of justice. Racism has split religious institutions and distorts the image of God. Racism has allowed politicians to exploit our emotions for their short-term political gain but at a long-term loss to their constituencies, their nations, and the world. Racism has stripped our political and economic leaders of moral authority, and now they cannot challenge a young generation who themselves too often have become alienated, estranged, and even nihilistic in their approach to life and the world.

Racism is a disease of the soul. Racism has blinded Europe, North America, and most of the "white Western world," and has left moral cataracts and scar tissue on our world eyes. Thus our vision of a new world order is blurred, unclear, and racist. Racism is fundamentally a moral problem, a problem of human values, running from our minds to our local communities and to our international community. Racism as a cultural resource and sinful habit doesn't have much value as a medium of foreign exchange. A conference such as this allows us to see such human values questions a little clearer. The silence of the religious leadership in the Western world on this concern is a form of betrayal, and, if we don't speak, "the very stones would cry out" (Luke 19:40).

Another obstacle to a new world order which provides an opportunity for service is the question of war and peace. The world currently is spending approximately $550 billion a year to kill and maim and at the same time is cutting back on money and services to bind up and heal. We're killing the healing process, when we need to be healing the killing process with disarmament and nonviolence. The United States is discussing development of mobile missiles and a neutron bomb that kills people but leaves buildings intact at the same time that nearly ten million of its people are unemployed and another ten million are underemployed and over fifty million people—almost as many people as there are in Great Britain and nearly one-fourth of America—are living in or hovering around the official poverty mark by our standards.

There must be a stop to the rapidly escalating arms race and the development and deployment of nuclear weapons. The goal must be a de-escalation of the arms race and, ultimately, disarmament. The vast expenditure of funds on arms is immoral, it escalates rather than reduces political tensions, and it distorts national economies and the world economy in a way that is ultimately economically contradictory and in the long-term will not work.

Holy Scripture tells us that "Where your treasure is, there will your heart be also" (Matt. 6:21). Currently too much of the world's treasure is going for arms when it should be going to help create a new world order. Worldwide, we are spending more money on arms than the gross national product of all the countries on the African continent and the Middle East combined. Again this is fundamentally a human values question. For either we will learn to live together as brothers and sisters or we shall surely die apart as fools. The issue is coexistence or nonexistence. There is no coexistence when at any given moment someone can throw a match in a loaded powderkeg and destroy us all.

Economic disparities between the white and non-white world, between the rich and the poor, between the North and the South are at their core human values and moral questions. Who are the wretched of the earth?* They are the nearly 70 percent of the world without safe water. They are the 450 million who are afflicted by schistosomiasis and filariasis, the leading causes of blindness. They are the more than two billion human beings—54 percent of humanity—who live in countries where the per capita gross national product (GNP) in 1973 was under $200. The poorest among them, 30 percent of the world's population, have just 3 percent of its income.

They are the citizens of countries that have been falling behind the

*The section that follows draws upon Michael Harrington's research in *The Vast Majority* (New York: Simon & Schuster, 1979).

economic levels of the West during the past four centuries. More recently, between 1952 and 1972, the GNP of the economically advanced
nations increased from $1.25 trillion to $3.07 trillion. That increment of
$1.82 trillion was three and a half times the aggregate product of the
underdeveloped world in 1972, which was $520 billion. Using constant
(1973) dollars, the rich lands saw their per capita income move from
$2,000 to $4,000, while that of the poor countries went from $125 to
$300. The major Western economic powers have two-thirds of the
globe's income but only 20 percent of its population. The underdeveloped nations, with more than 50 percent of the people, have less
than 13 percent of the income.

The poorest of the poor—those countries with less than $150 per
capita GNP in the early seventies—contain about 1.1 billion people.
More than 915 million are found in Asia; another 170 million in Africa;
about 8 million in the Middle East; and 6 million in the Caribbean. And
this does not include China, with an estimated per capita GNP of just
above $170 in 1973 and its population of over 800 million people. Until
we begin to serve in this area, a new world order will simply remain a
distant dream and an ideal.

Another obstacle to the creation of a new world order is in the area of
educational communications. The news media—newspapers, radio,
television, and movies—have replaced the religious institution, the
home, and the school as the essential educators of our day. The news
media have become the primary transmitters of information, folkways,
mores, and cultural values. In many ways they have the most fundamental power of all, because they have the power of appraisal, that is,
the power to determine priorities and establish what or who is
important.

But how have the mass media portrayed the nonwhite, non-English-
speaking, and non-Christian world? Fundamentally, they have ap-
praised us in four ways:

• We are projected as being more violent than we are. We are projected as robbers, thugs, and rioters rather than as victims of reduced
options. We are projected as terrorists rather than seen as trapped people
who are victimized daily by institutional violence and who have had all
other avenues of redressing our grievances stymied or cut-off.

• We are projected as less intelligent than we are.

• We are projected as less hard-working than we are. We work, most
of us, every day, at the most menial, dirty, and low-paying jobs. We are
not lazy and shiftless and undependable. In fact, if we were to walk
away from our jobs today, the world would come to a halt.

• We are projected as less universal than we are. There is an attempt to keep us and our minds locked up in a ghetto or barrio, when, in fact, we are the most universal of citizens.

Thus racism, war and peace, economic and educational equity and parity, and educational communications all provide us with opportunities for service in overcoming obstacles to a new world order. Each of these concerns is fundamentally a question of human values.

The Method of Service: The Possibility of a New World Order

The possibility of a new world order has two dimensions to it. On one side is the question of external opportunity. External obstacles to opportunity are what we have just finished discussing. That is a valid concern, and we must keep an aggressive focus on these and other issues which limit human opportunity. But there's another dimension to the struggle that oftentimes those concerned with the opportunity side of the ledger don't like to deal with. The internal dimension is equally fundamental. For if the doors of opportunity swing wide open but we are too drunk or high or apathetic or unprepared to take advantage of them, we will have simply gained the whole world but lost our own soul.

What the oppressed and so-called wretched of the earth have sustained themselves with over the last several centuries has been our fundamental sense of religion and faith. We have not had political power or economic power or military might; our strength has come from the inner resources of our soul. We fundamentally believe that might is not right; right is might. Our religious belief has convinced us, through experience, that the arc of the universe is long, but it bends toward justice.

Some call this religious dimension—this X factor—God; some call it Yahweh or Elohim; some call it Allah; some just call it a mighty force; while for others the essence is too great to name or even contemplate. But it's real. This religious factor has sustained our hope, our faith, our trust, and our sense of meaning even when the night was long. It has kept us humble and patient when those all around us were arrogant and impatient. God may not have given us all that we wanted, but he's given us all that we've needed, in time, and he gave it on time. As we struggle for a new world order, we must never lose our sense of religion, the sense of our ultimate importance in the scheme of things.

Our sense of spirituality and our internal religious depth must be matched with strong moral character. The death of ethics is the sabotage of excellence. The renewed focus on racial identity and pride, which we must affirm, is not enough. We must not only be ethnic, we must be ethical and efficient and enduring and excellent. We can settle for nothing less than morally excellent conduct and efficient economic performance. *Nobody has earned the right to do less than their best.*

We have the massive challenge before us—perhaps the challenge of this decade—to measure human values by one yardstick. When we pray and say "Our Father," "our" must cover the entire human family. It must cover all of God's children. When we say "Our Father," the human family cannot be described with an arc but rather with a circle that encompasses the entire human family. Our Father must include the children of Crossroads in South Africa, Palestinians in the refugee camps, blacks in America's ghettos, aborigines in Australia, the boat people from Southeast Asia and Haiti, and the malnourished in Bangladesh.

The fact of recognizing these rejected stones of previous generations, who are now the cornerstones of this generation, constitutes for many in the ruling class a state of cultural shock that has paralyzed the most developed minds of Western civilization. It has de-certified their private education and left them dizzy, staggering like a drunken man. They resist a world in which everybody is somebody. Being driven into an uncertain future against their will, they are being pushed forward but are reaching back, grasping for a relationship with the past that is nonnegotiable. We can't go backward.

We must struggle with developed and made-up minds. There is nothing more powerful in all the world than a developed and made-up mind. As this process of a new world order is unfolding, there has been a radical redistribution of economic and political power, but more importantly there has been a radical redistribution of self-determination. Africans, black Americans, Arabs, brown-skinned people from Mexico, Central, and South America—all of us have changed our minds in this slave-slavemaster relationship. Slavemasters never change their minds. I've never met or known any retired slavemasters. They never get tired of being master. Only when the slaves change their minds does the relationship change. Tarzan—as the prototype of the white man and the African stereotype—may not have changed his mind, but Nkrumah, Lumumba, Mugabe, Machel, Bishop Tutu, and the natives have changed their minds.

Politically and economically, the Western world is shaking because its foundation is crumbling. The Western pilot may change with the various elections, but it is not merely the pilot that is in trouble—it is the ship. Raging winds and fierce waters upon which the ship must sail are the bases for the turbulence. The issue is not the pilot, it's the ship. The Western crisis can't be controlled by the ship or ignored by the pilot.

Western civilization was built on cheap labor, cheap raw materials, cheap energy, and race exploitation. Reactionaries long for an ancient place and time—they will seek mastery, not justice. Their fervor for yesterday is not the answer; it is a sign of panic. In the midst of their economic panic they're also experiencing cultural shock because the people they have to turn to and deal with are people of color and are from different cultural traditions.

The world today is one-half Asian, one-eighth African, and is depending on the Middle East to energize it. The new world order recognizes that most people in the world are neither white, Christian, English-speaking, nor rich. They are poor, black, brown, and yellow, and they yearn to be free.

In the process of the redistribution of human values, we must learn to live together in mutual respect. North America and Europe must now do a hard thing. They must make the psychological adjustment from being superior over to being equivalent with and sometimes dependent upon. The world is interrelated, and its people are interdependent. Independence is an illusion, and isolation is suicidal. The Western mind must do something it has not had to do in the last four hundred years— think in creative new ways, use ingenuity, be patient, respect other people, respect nonwhite people, and regain and operate with moral authority, not merely economic, political, and military power.

Human rights for all human beings is the rallying cry. The human rights and the civil liberties of those struggling for more humane and just societies—in South Africa, Argentina, Chile, Brazil, El Salvador, or wherever in the world—must be protected and defended. The attempt by the South African government to take the passport and travel visa of Bishop Desmond Tutu, the chairman of the South African Council of Churches, must be met with worldwide opposition and protest.

Freedom of the press must be defended, but fairness in the press must constantly be demanded. Human rights, civil liberties, and a free but fair press must be defended against the onslaughts of the extreme right or the extreme left.

Our Challenge of Service

This is our challenge of service. This is our moral obligation to human values. Service is the foundation of the new world order. Opportunities for service abound in removing obstacles to a new world order, and we must struggle against internal deterrents and with internal strength if we are to realize the possibility of a new world order.

This generation has the opportunity to set the world on a new course of racial and cultural reconciliation and peace through reversing the arms race and ultimately through total disarmament. It has the challenge and the opportunity to bring greater economic and educational equity and parity into the world. It has this opportunity if it maintains a sense of passion for knowledge, science, religion, and human values. We can move the world in the direction of fulfilling some of its loftiest dreams, ideals, and prayers. We have the natural resources beneath the soil and in the universe, the growing human knowledge of our minds, and the technological know-how to reach and achieve goals beyond the wildest dreams of any generation that ever lived.

But we must know, especially the young, that in order for change to take place, effort must exceed opportunity. What does it matter if the doors of opportunity swing wide open if we're too drunk or high to walk through them? What does it matter if we have new books or old books if we have lost the motivation to open either? What does it matter if we have new ideas but are afraid to employ them? What does it matter if we have the opportunity to love each other if we're afraid of each other?

Those of us who are behind must get up earlier, we must work harder, we must be more determined, more humane, more sober, more sane, and more sensitive. The victim is not responsible for being down, but he or she must be responsible for getting up.

We must know and not violate the laws of development. There must be changeless values in these changing times. The laws of convenience lead to collapse, but the laws of sacrifice lead to greatness. When the world says, "You can't," you must say, "I can." When the world says, "You won't," you must say, "But I will." When the world says, "Perhaps," you should say, "I must."

Dietrich Bonhoeffer was right when he said, "To live is to suffer; but to survive is to find meaning in the suffering." We must not avoid suffering for a righteous cause. Suffering breeds character, character breeds faith, and in the end faith will not disappoint.

We must fight for social change—economic and political equity and parity—but we must also fight for a revolution in moral values and in the quality of life.

We gain life when we give life. We increase value with values.

I leave you with this thought. The spirit that this generation needs can be found in the words of a song that black children were singing in Crossroads, South Africa, when I visited there a year and a half ago. Those children, in the very pit of exploitation—no bathroom, no running water, no right to vote, no political protection, no judicial regard—with nothing but their hope and faith in God were singing, "Let us remain alive and alert as a nation." The spirit of that song must apply to our world. They were saying, in effect, that just because you are forcing us to live in the slums does not mean that you can force the slums to live in us. With character and humane values we will rise above our circumstances.

So run on and don't get weary, fight on and don't faint. I'm not unmindful of our suffering and the tears of pain still being shed. But hold on and don't give up. Weeping may endure for a night, but joy, joy, joy, for the faithful, is coming in the morning.

Thank you very much, and God bless you.

Brown
Twenty-five Years Later

This essay first appeared in the *New York Daily News* on May 17, 1979, the twenty-fifth anniversary of the date the Supreme Court handed down its decision in *Brown v. Board of Education*, which called for desegregation of the nation's schools.

May 17, 1979, marks the twenty-fifth anniversary of the *Brown v. Board of Education of Topeka* Supreme Court decision. Unquestionably, the 1954 *Brown* decision was the most significant Supreme Court decision for black progress in the nation's history. It was the first decision to establish equality under the law. For nearly 350 years, black people had operated with no constitutional or legal protection. Belatedly, blacks were granted three-fifths constitutional status, only to have the Supreme Court, in the *Dred Scott* case, declare that blacks "had no rights which a white man must respect."

In 1896, in the *Plessy v. Ferguson* case, the Supreme Court legally brought to an end the period of the First Reconstruction by establishing the "separate but equal" principle, which became the basis for the entire Jim Crow apartheid system in the South. The issue in *Plessy* was transportation, but the principle spread to every facet of American life. *Brown*, of course, overturned that principle and held that "separate but equal" was inherently unequal.

"*Inherently* unequal" meant, philosophically, that if two systems were truly equal, there would be no need to keep them separate; and through historical experience, it was clear that if they were separate they would not be equal. So "inherent" referred to philosophical and practical contradictions, not the inherent superiority or inferiority of one system over and against another.

87

Although the issue in *Brown* was education, the legal principle became the basis for all of the civil rights laws of the 1960s (the 1964 Civil Rights Act, the 1965 Voting Rights Act, the 1968 Open Housing Act), and the basis for affirmative action, business set-asides, and affirmative marketing in housing in the 1970s.

Noted historian John Hope Franklin indicated recently that many, if not most, of those involved in preparing for the case fully expected (rather innocently) that segregation would be a thing of the past within five years of the decision. But where are we twenty-five years later, and what must be done now to achieve equality?

We now know several things and have learned still others in the intervening years. We know that the struggle to desegregate our schools has, fundamentally, shifted from the South to the North (e.g., Boston, Chicago, Los Angeles). We know that the fundamental issue no longer is segregated schools but segregated school systems. We know that although the law has changed, America's will has not, and that the same forces that were in charge of segregation are now in charge of desegregation.

White male leadership is still essentially morally bankrupt, having neither the will nor the insight to alter or abolish this crisis in the American culture. White America still feels that it has everything to lose and nothing to gain, and blacks and browns have everything to gain and nothing to lose in desegregation, rather than seeing the advantages of exposing all of our children to cultural diversity in their formative years. Contrary to the warnings of the Kerner Commission eleven years ago, America is moving, educationally, not toward two societies, separate and unequal, but toward three: a suburban school system essentially built on class; a private (largely church-supported) school system essentially built on race; and an inner-city public school system essentially built on rejection and alienation.

The Supreme Court has shifted the burden from proving "effect" to proving "intent." The Congress, especially in the Eagleton-Biden Amendment, has crippled the executive branch's ability to effectively enforce desegregation, and, even where it could act, the executive branch has moved timidly, if at all.

The nation's agenda for desegregating the nation's schools today should be: (1) to aggressively enforce the present law; (2) to desegregate the power; and (3) to complete the task of changing people's hearts and feelings, which will alter their behavior and actions. As the nation's custodians decry the spread of lawlessness, they still do not seem to understand that lawlessness is contagious, and so long as established leadership either evades, ignores, or perverts the law, they become the role models and create the climate for lawlessness throughout the other levels of our social order.

In fairness, there has been some small bit of progress, but we must continue to be vigilant and fight the barriers to opportunity. On the other side of the issue, because there is a dialectic involved, blacks and browns must have the will to take advantage of opportunities that are available and maintain the urge to excel. Blacks and browns still have to perform in a manner superior to whites just to be considered equal. And the only protection against genocide is to remain necessary. Thus our young people must avoid the pitfalls and diversions that would make them unnecessary and keep them ignorant and enslaved—mass-media diversion, sexual promiscuity, drugs, violence, and vandalism.

In twenty-five years, our fundamental goal has not changed. It still is equity and parity—our fair share. The particular target has shifted from civil (citizenship) rights to silver (economic) rights within the context of a broader human rights struggle. Increasingly, the struggle will not be simply around issues that are moral (right and wrong) but around issues that are moral, legal, political, and economic at the same time.

The nation's resistance to equity and parity has intensified. Progress must be made—it is in our national interest—but it will have to be made against a headwind. Just as the issues have become more sophisticated, the means for dealing with them must be just as sophisticated. We must now use moral persuasion, education, litigation, economic development, direct action, political and consumer power to achieve self-determination.

The challenge twenty-five years ago was to secure these rights and broaden the base of opportunity. The challenge twenty-five years later is to fulfill these rights through a determined attitude and a superior effort. Racial demagogues fighting to keep our children alienated from one another are enemies to education and a threat to domestic tranquility and our national security. The absence of the moral influence of the church (still the most segregated institution in America) is appalling. In spite of these obstacles, hope and optimism must reign over negativism, pessimism, and cynicism if we are to overcome. Present massive detachment must be replaced by massive involvement, because effort must exceed opportunity for change to occur.

As people seek to assess and measure the last twenty-five years of progress—with the perversion of the real issues (e.g., in *Bakke*, *Weber*, and the Sears suit) through the use of emotional code words like "reverse discrimination" and "preferential treatment," and an abundance of black athletes and some entertainers on television giving the false impression of great progress for the masses of black people (perceived, falsely, to be at the expense of whites)—the facts are different.

There is 1 white attorney for every 680 whites, 1 black attorney for every 4,000 blacks; 1 white physician for every 649 whites, 1 black physician for every 5,000 blacks; 1 white dentist for every 1,900 whites, 1 black dentist for every 8,400 blacks. Less than 1 percent of all engineers are black. Blacks make up less than 1 percent of all practicing chemists. Blacks still comprise less than 1 percent of all the public elected and appointed officials in the nation. On May 17, 1979, twenty-five years later, there is still no national commitment to close these gaps or to achieve equity and parity, which was the intent of the law in the first place.

A renewed commitment to a just society must now be made by all. In the 1960s blacks used moral persuasion and political empowerment as a way of defeating Southern apartheid. In the 1980s a coalition of human rights activists must emerge in order to save all of us from the ravages of disease, ignorance, poverty, and war.

So we must now put forth an agenda of reconciliation between the races. We must make developed minds and strengthened characters a priority in our values, our budgets, and our politics. We must secure full voter registration, education, and political participation, in contrast to withdrawing or escaping (especially for blacks, browns, and the nation's youth). We must struggle through disciplined political and economic leverage, plus creative direct action, to put America back to work. And we must create alternative renewable energy resources and technology that will allow for continued economic stability and progress in a safe and healthful environment.

This is a workable agenda. It is one that we can do, ought to do, and must do. It is the imperative of now.

It's Not the Bus—
It's Us

This is a compilation and condensation of three essays on busing, one of which appeared in the *New York Times* on March 8, 1982, the other two being Jackson's Universal Press Syndicate columns of December 7, 1980, and December 28, 1980. The basic article was written in response to a 57–37 Senate vote in late February 1982 to bar federal courts from ordering the busing of children for racial reasons more than five miles from home or ordering children to travel by bus longer than fifteen minutes.

✗**A**fter a period of dormancy, busing is back in the news again. Political opportunists in the Senate want to turn the Supreme Court's school-desegregation decision in *Brown v. Board of Education* into an Indian treaty—a law on the books, but unenforceable.

✗The Senate has voted, 57 to 37, to bar federal courts from ordering, for racial reasons, the busing of children more than five miles from home or ordering children to travel by bus longer than fifteen minutes. The bill, on which the House must also vote, would allow the Justice Department to ask the courts to overturn existing desegregation plans that require busing in violation of these two new guidelines.

It was not just Republicans who voted for the bill. There is emerging a conspiracy between Democrats and Republicans and between the executive and legislative branches to take away federal legal protections for which thousands of people, black and white, have struggled and died. First, the executive branch granted tax-exempt status to private schools that practice racial discrimination—a snafu from which it is still trying to extricate itself. Next, the legislative branch attempts to pass laws ensuring that segregation in publicly supported schools will continue.

At the same time, a recently completed two-year study of medium-sized cities by Catholic University's Center for National Policy Review indicated that busing works to desegregate not only schools but housing patterns as well. Indeed, Diana Pearce, author of the study, concluded, "If we have metropolitan school desegregation, we will have housing integration, and we will see the end of busing."

Why should busing be such a potent issue? The Senate did not propose ending all busing, only busing for desegregation. If it had outlawed all busing, education would have halted. Riding the bus to school is an American institution. Handicapped children ride buses so they can receive adequate schooling. Rural children ride buses so they can enjoy the advantages of consolidated schools. Private schools bus their students. In fact, 55 percent of the children in America's public schools ride buses every day.

But it isn't this kind of busing that has people upset. It's the 3.6 percent of American public-school students who are bused because the schools are illegally segregated. Such a schizophrenic approach to busing leads me to conclude that *it's not the bus—it's us* (black people). Riding the bus to school is all right as long as it isn't to desegregate the schools.

The attacks on busing are diversionary. The central issue is the legal obligation to provide equal educational opportunity in a pluralistic society. The issue is not transportation, it's race relations and equal protection under the law.

Many people say they favor neighborhood schools. But do they fight for open housing? As the recent study indicates, busing can help break down segregated housing patterns and eventually make busing unnecessary. But most black children have never had neighborhood schools. When I was growing up, we had to go across town or out in the country to school. We walked to school, hitched a ride with some friends, or bought tickets and rode the local buses. White children didn't ride those buses; they always rode yellow school buses. In fact, the buses we rode took us past white schools located close to us (neighborhood schools) to all-black, segregated schools.

Others argue that they don't like the forced nature of the busing. But children are "forced" by law to attend school until they are 16, and most of the 55 percent of public-school children who ride buses daily are "forced" to ride them. Yet this causes no outcry. It's not the bus—it's us.

But riding buses is dangerous, people say. In fact, walking to school is three times more dangerous. Isn't busing doomed to fail because it produces so much white flight that desegregating the schools will be impossible? White flight existed before busing, and, if busing ends, white flight will still exist because most of it is related to the flight of industry (and thus jobs) from our cities.

Busing is a code word for racism and rejection. If those sounding the battle cry and leading anti-busing rallies and marches were also aggressively supporting open housing, many would feel differently. But most of those in Congress leading the charge against busing also have long records of opposing human rights issues and programs: open housing, voting rights for minorities, affirmative action, the Equal Rights Amendment (ERA), and the minimum wage.

Recently a new twist has been added, however. Some say that not only are whites against busing, but that blacks are, too. True, some blacks oppose busing, but not for racial reasons. Blacks sometimes are against busing because all decisions about desegregation are being made for them, not with and by them. Students, teachers, and administrators have been desegregated, but not power. Now, an all-white Senate is making decisions that affect blacks' educational opportunity. When power is not desegregated, black children, parents, and educators have no way of protecting themselves or redressing grievances.

What grievances? As documented by Nancy L. Arnez, chairperson of the Department of Educational Leadership and Community Services at Howard University, desegregation in a power vacuum has had the following disastrous consequences for the black community:

1. The loss of teaching and administrative jobs by blacks through dismissals and demotions.

2. The loss of millions of dollars in projected earned income.

3. The loss of racial role models, heroes, and authority figures for black children.

4. The loss by black children of cherished school symbols, colors, emblems, and names of schools when their schools are closed and they are shifted to white schools.

5. In the new setting, subjection to resegregated classes and buses and exclusion from extracurricular activities.

6. A disproportionate number of black students suspended, expelled, and pushed out of school.

7. Exposure of black children to hostile attitudes and behavior by white teachers and parents.

8. Forced one-way busing policies and the uprooting of black children for placement in hostile school environments without any support systems.

9. Misclassification of blacks into special-education classes and tracking systems.

10. Unfair disciplinary practices and arbitrary school rules and regulations.

11. Ignorance of black learning styles, culture, and social, educational, and psychological needs.

These are entirely different reasons than the ones whites give. The Senate, the president, and the American people should not misinterpret black opposition to busing. It is not opposition to desegregated education. It does not mean blacks are willing to bargain away their constitutional rights just because busing is unpopular. Justice and equal opportunity for blacks in America never have been popular. That is why we need the protection of the law. The Senate and the president, rather than trying to figure out ways to circumvent morally sound and just laws, should concentrate instead on upholding and enforcing them.

So much attention has been put on busing that many have lost sight of the alternatives. While there are alternatives to busing, there is no alternative to desegregating our nation's schools. Desegregation is the law of the land and has been since the 1954 *Brown* decision. That decision said: "We conclude that, in the field of public education, the doctrine of 'separate but equal' has no place. Separate educational facilities are inherently unequal."

"Inherently" unequal because, philosophically, if educational facilities and opportunities were truly equal there would be no need for them to be separate (a logical contradiction); and if they are separate, we are assured through historical experience that they will not be equal (a practical contradiction).

Apart from the technical methods for achieving desegregation, which we shall discuss shortly, other human factors are necessary to achieve a successfully unified school system and equality of opportunity. Community participation is essential if those affected by desegregation are to be and feel a part of the process. Community resistance or support will be increased or decreased in proportion to how involved and informed a community is.

Leadership is also critical. Where the political, business, civic, religious, and educational leadership has exerted strong moral and creative leadership, desegregation has tended to proceed in a healthy and orderly fashion. Where it has not, demagogues have tended to fill the leadership vacuum, polarizing the community and making the desegregation process long and painful for all involved.

Beyond these human factors, there are various techniques for achieving desegregation:

1. *Boundary Changes.* In most communities the simple procedure of redrawing school boundaries—since they most often have been drawn

to perpetuate segregation—both enhances desegregation and allows people to stay in their general neighborhood.

2. *Feeder Patterns.* The attendance areas (particularly for students going from grade school to high school) can be arranged so as to "feed" students into schools with desegregation in mind.

3. *Pairing.* Two schools of varied racial groups close to each other are "paired" according to grade level (e.g., grades kindergarten through four at one school and grades five through eight at the other).

4. *Changes in Grade Span.* The range of grade spans (K through eight, nine through twelve) are rather arbitrary. The broader the range of grade span within a school the easier it is to fill that school with children from the immediate neighborhood because of segregated housing patterns, thus perpetuating segregation. Narrowing the grade span at particular schools (e.g., third and fourth grades only) necessitates drawing from a larger geographical area, thus allowing desegregation to be achieved more easily.

5. *Magnet Schools and Career Academies.* While "special schools" are a way of attracting students of all races, they tend to attract the above-average students. The average student probably has more to gain from an integrated education and thus should not be denied equal opportunity by limiting the desegregation process to the status of a fringe benefit within the public-school system.

6. *New Facilities.* Sites for new schools can be chosen to maximize the goal of desegregation.

7. *Metropolitan Desegregation.* It is no longer a question of "segregated schools" that must be desegregated but entire "segregated school systems." Only metropolitanwide (sometimes called "cross-district") desegregation addresses itself to this problem.

While busing, even as a last resort, continues to receive the lion's share of attention, these other effective means of complying with the law are available. While busing must remain a tool, along with the other techniques, for desegregating the schools, we should not lose sight of the fact that the most fundamental factor in desegregating the nation's schools is whether the nation is convinced of the moral rightness of desegregation, and thus is committed to creating the political will to insist upon equal educational opportunities for all of our children.

In Search of a New Focus and a New Vision

Jackson gave this speech at the conclusion of a march from the White House to the Capitol on May 17, 1980, the twenty-sixth anniversary of the *Brown* decision. The purpose of the march was to put pressure on the Carter administration to address the problem of "stagflation"—high inflation coupled with high unemployment. The march was the culmination of six months of political activity concurrent with the 1980 presidential primaries, attempting to get the candidates to focus on jobs, peace, and justice.

We come today in search of a new focus, a new vision. The national vision is blurred. We must find a better way.

We come as a coalition of church and labor, multiethnic, poor, and concerned people. A coalition that is born of necessity and desperation. Today's action is a signal of a spring and summer offensive for social change and social justice. We have to make the rejected visible. We have come to touch the conscience of the nation.

We have marched today from the White House to the Capitol, and forty cities are marching concurrently with us. Our protest will grow. The prevailing order has conspired and shifted to dangerous reactionary and inhumane conservatism. We will march in targeted districts; we will have job and hunger hearings in targeted districts. We will have voter registration in targeted districts. Eighty congressional districts have 15 percent or more black voters. We will lobby in targeted districts. We will engage in selective patronage boycotts against corporations that refuse affirmative action programs. We will struggle to survive. We will prevail.

In this jungle we have more than switches. We have strategic weapons:
the vote, consumer dollars, marching feet, and made-up minds. There is
agony in the land. But there is power in a made-up mind.

Today we are determined to make the black, the brown, the poor, and
the rejected visible. Again today we gather to redress our grievances
against government and private industry policies that are adversely
affecting the masses of our people. There is anxiety and fear throughout
the land. People are groping in darkness and despair. People turning
upon themselves, trying to escape the reality of a living nightmare.
Some are turning against their brothers and sisters (fratricide); some are
turning against their neighbors (homicide); some are turning against
themselves (suicide); others are slowly dying in prisons and on street
corners with assassinated dreams, with a future ranging from reduced
options to no options. People are victims of government policies and
reactionary interpretations of laws that make it more likely that they will
be victims of welfare and incarceration rather than beneficiaries of
employment and education.

For those of us who have gathered, sending messages to Washington
has not worked. We have come today to bring that message and to serve
notice that there is widespread desperation in the land. We seek a better
way. As we challenge the blurred vision, we are clear. We want change,
here and now. Pain is not localized and narrowly focused, and neither is
our protest. The executive, legislative, and judicial branches of government, private industry, organized labor, and the mass media each have
played their roles in locking the black, brown, and the poor behind the
veil and ignoring our anguish. The president and Congress must tackle
the giants of industry. Congress must enact sufficient laws to reduce the
flight of capital abroad and stimulate the flow of capital at home.

Surely the national leadership knows that there will be no balance-of-
budget until there is balance-of-trade, and there will be no balance-of-
trade until we become competitive again in the world market. Our
nation is suffering from a double economic hemorrhage. On the one
hand, because of antiquated equipment and inferior management, we
have lost our edge in automotive and steel production and in electronic,
rubber, and textile production. We also have become energy dependent,
mainly because special interests have been allowed to operate against
our national interest. On the other hand, the flight of capital involves a
loss of $150 billion annually from the United States economy, last year
forcing American workers to compete with the slave wages of workers
under totalitarian regimes. The president and Congress must tackle the
giants.

To balance the budget by threatening public service jobs and hospital
care and aid to the elderly is to become a militant, holding the poor as

hostages. We don't want an ayatollah. We want the president to tackle the giants. Making demands upon the poor that they cannot refuse is not discipline, it is punishment. To tackle our trade deficit and our industrial inefficiency is to stop the blood that is gushing from our economic jugular vein. To balance the budget by threatening social services is to put a tourniquet on the little finger. The economic impact of balancing the budget was less than one-half of 1 percent. It is immoral, and it makes no economic sense. The rich will not sacrifice for the country, and the poor are being sacrificed for the country. We deserve better leadership or new leadership.

Our suffering is not voluntary. This is not sacrifice; it is involuntary. This is punishment. It would be narrow-sighted only to focus on the executive branch. After all, we elected a president, not a king.

On this very hill are the butchers of our dreams. The idea of a balanced budget was born on this hill. We must know who the chairpersons of significant committees are and what their powers are. For example, we must know that the Senate Budget Committee is headed by Senator Ernest Hollings of South Carolina; we must know that Robert Giamo of Connecticut is the chairman of the House Budget Committee. We must understand the budget cycle so that we can exert pressure at the proper place at the proper time. We must reward or retire these gentlemen according to their deeds.

When the balance-the-budget hysteria or the Proposition 13 mania struck Washington, the president proposed to cut 50,000 jobs; the Senate proposed 200,000 community service cuts, eliminating Title 6 of the Comprehensive Employment Training Act (CETA), and proposed to add $7 billion to the military budget during peacetime. They are smoking pipes with gunpowder in them. We must not let these killers of a dream go unnoticed again or remain acceptable any longer.

As we broaden our view, the Supreme Court, which ruled in favor of Bakke last year, thus altering affirmative action and negating creative justice, has surpassed the insensitivity of that decision with the *Mobile* decision. This decision, which renders constitutional at-large districts, will virtually wipe out every black board-of-education member, city council member, and state legislator in the nation. It is the most racist Supreme Court decision of the twentieth century and fundamentally undercuts much of the impact of the Supreme Court's 1954 decision in *Brown.*

As we broaden our view, let us not forget the media with its appraisal power. Of the top 134 network executives, only 2 are black. Of the 1,769 daily newspapers, only 6 have blacks in executive management positions. As a result of media insensitivity, we are projected as impotent when we are important, and projected as liabilities when we are in fact assets. The media constantly engages in five aggressive acts against the black and brown community. We are projected as (1) less intelligent than we are; (2) less hard-working than we are; (3) more violent than we are; (4) less patriotic than we are; and (5) less universal than we are. They do not call Senator Kennedy "white senator" or the president "white president" because their skin color is self-evident. When they refer to us as "black leaders," they are not describing our skin color, which is self-evident. They are defining our domain. We must reject this racist aggression, for when people can define you, they can confine you. The world is our stage. We are not slaves of the ghetto; we are citizens of the world.

When one looks at the executive, judicial, legislative, media, and corporate leadership, it is clear that there is a leadership crisis in the nation. It is clear that our national vision is blurred, and we must find a better way. If history is instructive, and it is, it will tell us that the vision to save the nation will not come from the palace, it will come from the stable—the salt of the earth. The vision that we seek will not come from the White House or the state house but from your house and my house. We must find a new focus.

An example sums up for me the comprehensive vision we must have. Last year when the DC-10 crashed in Chicago, as people viewed the charred remains of the people and the wreckage, the first analysis dealt with the state of the pilots. Were they alert? Were they sober? Were they qualified? The second inquiry was about the condition of the plane. As they analyzed the plane, they checked the engine, the radar equipment, the fuselage, and the wings in great detail until they found a weakness in the bolts or the engine mounts. A superficial analysis would have been pilot error. An independent analysis reveals that the present harassment in this nation is more than pilot-(president-)deep. The entire structure is faulty, and a major redefinition of the nation and its purpose is in order.

Today we demand a broader focus and a new focus. We must focus on summer jobs not merely summer games. We must focus not merely on the fifty hostages in Iran but the seven million unemployed hostages in this nation and the five hundred thousand American prisoners who are mostly political prisoners, who cost us an annual average of $17,310. If one goes to any state university for four years, it would cost less than $20,000. If one goes to any state or federal penitentiary, it would cost between $60,000 and $130,000. Employment and education are cheaper than welfare and incarceration.

We demand a new focus. The young who are the victims must fight for change. They must be sober, sane, and sensitive. They must combine direct action with political action. We must register the 3.1 million graduating high-school students. They must come across the stage with a diploma in one hand, symbolizing knowledge and wisdom, and a voter registration card in the other, symbolizing power and responsibility. Then in the fall, institutions of higher learning must register their 11.2 million students to vote when they register for classes. This generation can determine the course of this nation.

Black colleges must be seen as institutions of necessity to be cherished. They produce 40 percent of all black college graduates. They have developed a specialty in transforming rejected stones into cornerstones, in giving life and nutrition to dry bones. They deserve 50 percent of Title III funds and $100 million in research.

We must find a new focus. We must do it as a coalition. The blacks, browns, women, and the locked-out will either fight together, creating an expanding, healthy economy, or fight each other over a sick economy. In the short run, we must reject the balance-the-budget hysteria. In the short run, we must shift from a policy of *economic strangulation* to a policy of *economic stimulation* in the public sector. The poor must be equipped to fight inflation. Jobs are the best equipment. We reject fighting inflation with unemployment. After all, unemployment is inflationary. For every additional 1 percent increase in unemployment, one million more people are without work, and the cost is $30 billion.

Our first priority is jobs in the private sector, which is collapsing through no fault of poor people. Our second priority is public-service jobs. If they fail, in desperation we will accept welfare, unemployment insurance, or subsidies, but we want to work. We want to rebuild the central cities. We want to clean the sewers, pave the roads, build mass transit, build schools, teach children, build houses, and provide services for people who cannot help themselves.

We want to work. We want an economic stimulus package of $25 billion. Three years ago, the economic stimulus package of $20 billion reduced unemployment from 9 percent to 6 percent in a fifteen-month period.

We want a new focus. The unpatriotic despotism of private industry has taken the sweat and money of the American laborer. Undercutting U.S. labor in the world market must stop. The new focus that we seek is not a pipe dream. We will work for it. We will accomplish it. We will march and make the poor visible. We will challenge every official to be accountable to the people.

The humanity of women must be affirmed. Women are first-class people. We must reject their second-class status. Justice is indivisible.

We start with the simple premise—human rights for human beings. No longer will we accept superior rights for some and inferior rights for others, but equal rights for all. Justice must be measured by one yardstick. We must demand sameness of respect though we may not have oneness of roles. Roles may differ by culture and choice, but equal protection is a matter of law. This is called simple justice. Our judicial system, which enunciates our society's laws, must catch up with natural law. Simple justice is a threat to the hardened arteries of the status quo which cling to the past by habit, culture, ignorance, superstition, economic exploitation, or a combination of them.

We as a people must affirm the personhood of our mothers and sisters, our aunts and daughters. Any man who would condemn his mother or wife or sister to the eternal damnation of second-class status must examine himself. And any woman who would volunteer for such a status likewise needs examination.

We in America are just 4 percent of the world. We need everybody in the race for productivity. All minds must be used at optimum speed for us to survive. We must be concerned about foreign policy. We came here on a foreign policy. Foreign policy is domestic policy.

As for the boat people, we must remain humane and sensitive to boat people. After all, we were the original boat people. We didn't come here on an airlift. We did not come as immigrants looking for a thrill, but rather as slaves against our will; but we were on boats. Even as we open our arms, we must not die unarmed with the truth in an undeclared cold war with communism. Line up the boats, first come, first served: Africans, Pilgrims, Haitians, Cubans, Indochinese. Do not allow racism to weaken our credibility as we wrestle with the growing crisis of the immigration policy.

Affirm the humanity of the Haitian refugees. Don't lock them out on some false distinction between economic and political refugees. The Statue of Liberty says, "Give me your tired, your poor, your huddled masses. . . ." We will no longer grant the State Department immunity from major protest and accountability.

We must have a new vision. We must gain the inner strength to rise above our circumstances. We must focus on conditions, not merely candidates. Ultimately our struggle is a struggle to change the character of our nation and thus to enable us to be leaders and servants in the world. We can render service without being servile. We must struggle for a new character that has ethical content. We must categorically reject racism.

If racism merely takes off pants and puts on a dress, nothing fundamental in the character of our nation has changed. If hatred and tyranny merely change color, nothing essential has changed. We must fight for a new character with ethical content.

Racism is unproductive economically.

Racism is unhealthy and sick psychologically.

Racism is immoral theologically.

Racism has destroyed the image of God.

Racism has split religion.

Racism has made us less credible as a people.

We must reject racism.

Sexism is intellectually unreasonable. It is psychologically painful to the oppressed. It will be the basis of political obituaries for those who don't understand it.

We must have a new vision, a character with ethical content. We cannot equate shack-ups with marriages. We cannot equate foul speech with free speech. We cannot fight to lower the liquor-drinking age. We cannot use gambling and chance as a substitute for a sound economy with choice. We must move beyond the political to the prophetic realm. We who care must represent the new people.

When the storms of life rage and our enemies mount against us, we must use willpower and cope with, and not pill power and cop out. We must know that we will win the proposition of human rights for human beings everywhere because it is right, and it is God's will.

Hold your heads high!

Just because it rains, we don't have to drown!

Hold your heads high!

When it's dark out, the stars can be seen most clearly.

Hold your heads high!

We are victims of *second-class* treatment, but we are *first-class* people.

God has space for us, a time and place for us!

God has purpose for us!

Through it all, we've learned to trust in him! Our burden is heavy, our suffering is great. But God is the source of energy.

He didn't bring us this far to leave us!

To that end, we are willing to suffer, for we know that unearned suffering is redemptive. Suffering breeds character, character breeds faith, and in the end faith will not disappoint.

Let us march on until victory is won!

Overcoming New Forms
of Denial

Jackson gave this speech as the commencement
address at the University of Massachusetts Medical
School, Worcester, Massachusetts, on May 24, 1981.

To Chancellor and Dean, Dr. Robert E. Tranquada; to
the distinguished faculty and staff of the Medical School of the University of Massachusetts; to the honored civic, business, and political leaders in Worcester; to the families and friends of students; to the graduates who have paid the price of sacrifice, discipline, and study; and to all who are present to participate on this happy and joyous occasion of celebration, I want to thank you for your very kind introduction and greeting.

Goals are necessary for individual and national development. Decades become convenient categories for measuring development (or the lack of development) and for projecting goals to be achieved. Today I want to speak on the subject, "Overcoming New Forms of Denial." First, I want to remind us of the past, the old forms of denial. Second, I want us to face and discuss the new forms of denial; and last, I want to rally us to overcome all forms of denial in the pursuit of liberating the human body and spirit.

Before getting into the body of my remarks, I think it is important briefly to discuss the times in which we live. As a preacher I often say to a congregation that a text without a context is a pretext.

The first characteristic of our society, indeed of most of the Western world, is that it is a civilization in moral and spiritual crisis. This crisis has a personal and internal dimension (seen in such things as abusing oneself with alcohol and drugs, engaging in sex without love, making unwanted babies, committing violent acts or suicide), which too often is being exploited by both religious and secular charlatans, usually from a conservative religious and political school of thought. It also has a societal or structural dimension (seen in such things as sexism, militarism, racism, and economic exploitation), which often is exploited by religious and secular liberals. The two sides often talk past each other, and, while they may share many of the same values—both personally and socially—reconciliation often seems difficult and nearly impossible. But the fact remains, whether we are doctors, lawyers, businesspersons, or preachers, until we see people and the society from a holistic perspective—which includes taking seriously moral values and spiritual renewal—we will continually deal with effects and never with causes, and we will never be able to plumb the depths of individual and societal life.

A second characteristic troubling our times which is blatantly obvious to everyone is that our civilization is in economic crisis. Double-digit inflation—whose origin was an ill-conceived and immoral war in Vietnam, but which is fed and perpetuated by financial greed—has devastated the purchasing power of Americans, and nowhere are the problems and contradictions of our economic crisis more apparent than in the medical field. The Nixon, Ford, Carter, and Reagan administrations have, in varying degrees, used or are proposing to use unemployment as the way to combat inflation. So stagflation, with its accompanying budget deficits, a nearly trillion-dollar national debt, and an increased personal and social dependency syndrome, has characterized the 1970s.

The economic crisis has simply heightened and brought out in the open the underlying racial crisis that is so pervasive in our society. Racism is still the number-one threat to domestic tranquility and continues to distort our foreign policy as well. Racism, a philosophy and set of beliefs, actions, and institutional arrangements based on the superiority of one skin color over another, is untrue scientifically, immoral theologically, unhealthy psychologically, and unworkable economically and politically for very much longer. Increasingly it's becoming too costly and too dangerous.

There has been a lot of concern, and rightly so, about the Miami disturbances, the Greensboro massacre, the attempted assassination of Vernon Jordan, the brutal slayings in Buffalo, and the missing and murdered children in Atlanta. But even more dangerous is the general anti-black meanness mania that is gripping virtually every segment and institution in our society. There may or may not be a physical conspiracy to kill black people, but there certainly is a cultural conspiracy to kill us. Whether physically, politically, economically, psychologically, or spiritually, the personality of the culture is anti-black. It is no less true in the medical area. Under the current supply-side proposals of the Reagan administration, black wealth and health providers (doctors) will decline, and black patients and health consumers will increase.

A Reminder: Old Forms of Resistance

This anti-black personality of the American culture is nothing new, and neither is its denial of the depth and dimensions of the problem. America has never acknowledged the uniqueness of the experience of blacks in this country. We were the only people brought here against our will, rather than as immigrants seeking a thrill or a new way of life. No other group endured 250 years of slavery and was characterized in the Constitution as three-fifths human. No other group endured 100 years of illegal apartheid, and no other group endures to this very hour the degree of daily denial, indignity, and discrimination that is heaped on black people. The old forms of denial were, relatively speaking, simple. They were clear-cut laws of denial and rejection: slavery; the extermination of the Native American; the expropriation of life and land through terrorism, downward land assessment, and eminent domain; the annexation of Hispanics against their will; and the raw exploitation of workers by private businesses where workers were forced to work long, dirty, and dangerous hours for slave wages. This was the period when the very laws were stacked against us. No thought was given to training those to heal whom the Constitution declared to be only three-fifths human. Medical education was not for those "who had no laws which a white man must respect." For black people, then, there was no legal protection under the law, much less equal protection under the law.

The struggle that has dominated the over three and a half centuries of our presence on this continent has been one to gain first the recognition of the law and then equal protection under the law. Thus we fought for the Thirteenth, Fourteenth, and Fifteenth Amendments to the Constitution, a struggle which we championed—but all benefited. That is why, in this century, we have continued to fight for the 1954 *Brown* decision, ending the "separate but equal" legal principle and providing for equal educational opportunity by law. It is why we fought for the 1964 Civil Rights Act, providing us equal access to public accommodations; the 1965 Voting Rights Act, assuring us by law of our right to vote—which must be fought for again and renewed in 1982; and it is the reason we fought for a 1968 Open Housing Act—*to provide equal protection under the law.*

As we struggled, and won, equal protection under the law, a new dimension of the problem began to manifest itself. The historic struggle had been a horizontal one, seeking access to areas where we formerly, by law, had been locked out. But the struggle shifted from an essentially horizontal one to an essentially vertical one. Upward mobility, not just access, became the key. It was a shift from equal protection under the law to equal protection within the law. In many instances we were legislated in but "regulated" or "costed" out. What real difference does it make to have the right to live in any neighborhood but not have the money to pay the house note? What is the fundamental difference in having the right under law to enroll in any medical school but not have the ability to pay the tuition? When the shift from citizenship rights to economic rights, from access to equality, began to take place, some of our former allies, rather than making the adjustment and growing into the new dimensions of the struggle, chose instead to become our adversaries.

There has been a lot of controversy around desegregating the nation's schools, busing, affirmative action, and minimum quotas, but most people have missed the crux of the matter. The fundamental problem is fairly simple. The same people who were in charge of segregation are now in charge of desegregation. We have shifted teachers and principals and children and some money, but we have not shifted power. The power—which schools get closed, who gets bused and where, who gets admitted to law and medical school and for what reasons—the power to plan, to decide, to appraise, and to define is still fundamentally in the same old hands. Until we learn to share power within our various institutions, not merely grant access paternalistically, our progress toward racial reconciliation will continue to be at a snail's pace.

A Reality: New Forms of Denial

We have experienced a similar period in our nation's history. The First Reconstruction, for a decade, was filled with hope and promise, but in the Hayes-Tilden Compromise of 1877, when faced with a choice of moving forward or going backward, our nation chose to go backward. Hayes cut a deal with the South to win the election, and the legal and military protection blacks had enjoyed from the federal troops was withdrawn. Psychologically, both then and now, the nation's mental state could best be characterized as paranoid schizophrenia. Race now, just as it did then, has split the American psyche, and the nation chose to turn backward in fear rather than move forward with courage.

Under Mr. Reagan, who launched his "states' rights" campaign in Philadelphia, Mississippi, where three civil rights workers lost their lives in 1964, we are again seeing an attempt to withdraw federal protection from black, brown, and poor people. The war on poverty has now become a war against the poor. The name has changed, but the game remains the same. Old forms of resistance have simply become new forms of denial.

STRAIGHT FROM THE HEART

One of the keys to the new forms of denial is the power of appraisal and definition. If people can define you, they can confine you. There is a concerted effort now to reappraise the definition of "acceptable unemployment." If full employment is defined as 3 percent, but the nation has 7.5 percent unemployment, then the government is forced to do something about that which is morally and socially unacceptable. But if full employment can be defined as 6 percent, then it becomes a troublesome, but not a morally and politically outrageous, situation, and the politicians need not get too concerned or do anything.

The same thing is true of medical care. If health care can be defined as a privilege—as the Reagan administration proposes—rather than as a human right, then health care can be sold in the marketplace alongside cars, television sets, and stereos. We in the human rights community must argue, march, and fight to make health care a human right universally available to all based on need rather than a privilege available to some based on their ability to pay. And a medical education must not be denied for any reason to anyone who has the interest, aptitude, discipline, and desire to serve and bind up the wounds or prevent wounds to their fellow human beings.

We must also redefine the scope of medical concern. We still mainly prepare doctors to treat effects after the fact rather than deal with conditions in a preventive way. We not only need medical specialists but medical generalists who can deal with the whole person and who are politically aware and active. The American Medical Association is politically aware and active, but too often it is less concerned with patients, especially the poor, than with its own economic self-interest.

The Supreme Court, the Congress, and the executive branches of government are all party to the new forms of denial to black and poor people. The Supreme Court is increasingly shifting the burden of proof in discrimination cases from "effect" to "intent." Senator Orrin Hatch says he will push for a constitutional amendment outlawing affirmative action, and the Heritage Foundation, with which Ed Meese is closely associated, is recommending that the federal government even stop gathering data by race, sex, or ethnic origin. Many so-called liberals now oppose affirmative action. The *Bakke* case, you will remember, was a case involving the admission of blacks, nonwhites, and women to medical school.

Much of the controversy surrounding affirmative action over the last decade centered on several myths. Probably the most critical myths were that affirmative action was really "discrimination in reverse" and that blacks were "gaining at white expense."

The facts continue to dispute the myths, however. A report by the Illinois Board of Higher Education documents the discouraging record in that state. The percentage of black students in Illinois medical and dental schools has actually decreased since 1970. While blacks constitute 12.8 percent of the state's population, of the 762 first-year medical students in 1970, only 34, or 4.5 percent, were black. By 1980, the percentage had fallen to 4.4 percent (53 blacks out of 1207 first-year medical students). In dental schools the record was even worse, as the percentage of black enrollment in Illinois dental schools decreased from 3.3 percent to 2 percent in the last ten years.

A similar picture emerges on the national scene. According to the Association of American Medical Colleges, enrollment in the nation's 126 medical schools this fall reached an all-time high of 65,189 students, 1,400 more than last year. This year's entering class of 17,186 was the largest ever. Overall, 55,434 students (85 percent) are white; 3,708 (5.7 percent) are black; 2,761 (4.2 percent) are Hispanic; 1,924 (3 percent) are Asian-American; 221 (0.3 percent) are Native Americans; and 1,086 (1.7 percent) are foreign.

Enrollment in medical schools jumped by nearly 10,000 in the last five years. White enrollment grew by nearly 7,000, while the number of Hispanic and Asian-American students nearly doubled. While resistance to affirmative action and the myths surrounding affirmative action have mainly focused on blacks, the number of blacks in medical schools grew slightly from 3,456 in 1975 to 3,708 this year (a net gain of 252 in five years), but the percentage actually fell from 6.2 percent to 5.7 percent. Three black medical schools—Meharry, Howard, and Morehouse—still produce 85 percent of the black doctors in this country with less money and facilities than their 123 white counterparts.

This is consistent with the facts covering the first part of the decade. There were 9,571 whites and 282 minorities who entered U.S. medical schools in 1968, the last year before affirmative action programs began to get under way. In 1976, there were 14,213 white and 1,400 minority first-year medical students. Thus the number of "white places" did not remain constant but actually rose by 49 percent. Thus white access to medical training was not diminished but actually was substantially increased during the affirmative action years.

In short, the reality has been and continues to be contrary to the myth that affirmative action is allowing blacks to make progress at white expense. While some may choose to use America's economic crisis as an occasion to use blacks as scapegoats by attacking affirmative action, those concerned with dealing with reality would do well to keep the facts in mind.

The Reagan administration is attacking health care and health education for black, brown, and poor people from many angles. The shifting of monies from meeting human needs to the military will make the black and poor, but also the nation as a whole, less healthy. New attacks on the poor, especially the working poor, such as ending or cutting back on monies for child nutrition programs, food stamps, prenatal care, public hospitals, health clinics, and more, will directly impact negatively on the health of the poor and the nation's health.

The rapid rise in tuition to medical schools—now in the $10,000–12,000 per year bracket in many schools—and the federal cutbacks to medical schools and grants and loans to students desiring a medical education will make it more difficult for blacks and other nonwhites to get into and stay in medical school. The increased debt will tend to frighten most poor people away from seeking a medical education. And even for those who succeed in getting through under these conditions, the financial burden of paying back $30,000–40,000 upon completion of medical school almost forces doctors to take the most lucrative offer or opportunity rather than serve in the areas of greatest need. In the future, if this trend continues, a medical education will become the province of the very well-to-do. Cuts or the threat of cuts in the National Science Foundation, the National Health Service Corps Scholarship Program (which is composed of about 25 percent minorities), the Health Careers Program designed to interest more high-school students in the medical professions, even fewer finances for the already underfinanced black hospitals, public health clinics, and teaching hospitals—all foretell disaster for the health care and education of black and poor people.

So fundamentally the Reagan administration is hitting the medical and medical education needs of the poor from four angles: (1) the Reagan administration is attacking the early childhood nutritional needs and similar preventive programs, thus stunting our growth at the very start; (2) the other environmental factors which contribute to ill-health will increase because of the economic and social policies of his adminis-tration—accidents, homicides, exposure to toxins, overcrowded and poor housing, etc.; (3) they are proposing to siphon off public funds for private use through tuition tax credits or a voucher system, which will negatively impact the preparation of the masses of the poor for a medical education; and (4) by opposing affirmative action the Reagan adminis-tration opposes our upward mobility, our ability to grow. Under these conditions, the just and the merciful will go to the suites and the streets with us, not to the courts against us. And the challenge to the victims is to use their genius to make the best of a bad situation.

As I mentioned earlier, the challenge to doctors in the 1980s is not merely to become medical specialists but politically aware and active generalists as well. Health care is a worldwide need. Who are the medically wretched of the earth?* They are the nearly 70 percent of the world without safe water. They are the 450 million who are afflicted by schistosomiasis and filariasis, the leading causes of blindness. They are the more than two billion human beings—54 percent of humanity—who live in countries where the per capita gross national product (GNP) in 1973 was under $200. The poorest among them, 30 percent of the world's population, have 3 percent of its income.

They are the citizens of countries that have been falling behind the economic levels of the West during the past four centuries. More recently, between 1952 and 1972, the GNP of the economically advanced nations increased from $1.25 trillion to $3.07 trillion. That increment of $1.82 trillion was three and a half times the aggregate product of the underdeveloped world in 1972, which was $520 billion. Using constant (1973) dollars, the rich lands saw their per capita income move from $2,000 to $4,000, while that of the poor countries went from $125 to $300. The major Western economic powers have two-thirds of the globe's income but only 20 percent of its population; the underdeveloped nations, with more than 50 percent of the people, have less than 13 percent of the income.

The poorest of the poor—those countries with less than $150 per capita GNP in the early seventies—contain about 1.1 billion people. More than 915 million are found in Asia; another 170 million in Africa; about 8 million in the Middle East; and 6 million in the Caribbean. And this does not include China, with an estimated per capita GNP of just above $170 in 1973, and its population of over 800 million people. Until we begin to serve and bring preventive and immediate health care to these areas, world health will simply remain a distant dream and an ideal.

A Rally: Overcoming the Old and the New on the Road to Liberation

It is not enough just to recognize the various crises, including the health crisis, confronting our nation. We must rally to do something about them. We must rally our will and conscience to change these conditions. And we must rally public, economic, and political support. It's not enough just to analyze our condition, because we can become victimized by a paralysis of analysis. It's not enough just to rebel; we must reform. Proposition 13 represented a tax rebellion, but it didn't represent tax reform. Electing Ronald Reagan represented political rebellion, but it didn't represent political reform. In fact, it represented a dramatic step backward.

*The section that follows draws upon Michael Harrington's research in *The Vast Majority* (New York: Simon & Schuster, 1979).

If our rebellion is to lead to reform, we must build a coalition of humane, concerned, and committed people. We cannot align ourselves purely along racial, ethnic, religious, economic, and ideological lines. Rather, we must share a common commitment to justice and human rights for all human beings.

We must rally behind health-care legislation. We must look carefully and continue to press for the passage of the Kennedy-Corman National Health Insurance package, and we should not dismiss out of hand the Dellums bill for a National Health Service. I'm not hung up on the form as long as it provides effective and universal health care and is financially available to all who need it.

In conclusion, let me say this. You who graduate today must bring skills and values to the table. We must fight for social change—economic and political equity and parity—but we must also fight for a revolution in moral values and in the quality of life.

We need doctors, but doctors who are concerned with public health, not just personal wealth.

I leave you with this thought today. The spirit that this generation needs is to be found in the words of a song that the black children in a place called Crossroads in South Africa were singing when I visited there a year and a half ago. Those children, in the very pit of exploitation—no bathroom, no running water, no right to vote, no political protection, no judicial regard—with nothing but their hope and faith in God, were singing, "Let us remain alive and alert as a nation." The spirit of that song must apply to our world as well. With character and humane values we will rise above our circumstances.

So all of us must run on and not get weary, fight and not get faint. Those who would see justice must hold on and not give up. Joy is coming in the morning.

Thank you very much. Happy graduation, and God bless you all.

PREACHER

"Today we can make a choice. We can choose to live and not to destroy. We can choose life over death, help over hate, reason over race, and character over color. This day the God that we serve—if we will just trust him in all our ways—will still raise us from the guttermost to the uttermost. He will raise all of us from disgrace to amazing grace."

Our Spiritual and
Prayer Roots

For nearly two decades, Operation PUSH (and its
predecessor, the Southern Christian Leadership
Conference's Operation Breadbasket) has sponsored a
weekly Saturday Morning Community Forum in its
2000–seat auditorium at its national headquarters in
Chicago. Issues of local, state, and national concern are
addressed by national and international religious,
political, and business leaders. Jackson gave this
sermon there February 26, 1977.

As we salute Black History Month, I want to spend a
few minutes talking about "Our Spiritual and Prayer Roots." I've had
many invitations over the course of the last few months to speak at
various schools and universities around the nation. Invariably, they
want me to speak about the "fruits," although they keep saying "roots."

Reverend, they say, speak of our political history. Well, we had lieutenant governors in the last century. We had congressmen in the last
century. We've had great politicians like P. B. S. Pinchback and Adam
Clayton Powell, Shirley Chisholm, and Barbara Jordan—but our political exploits are the *fruits* of our history.

Reverend, speak to us of business. We've had and still have great
economic institutions and great personalities: George Johnson, Madam
C. J. Walker, John Johnson, and other men and women around which
our economic development has occurred. But our economic development is not the root of our existence, it's one of the fruits of our
existence.

People ask me to speak of our educational development and our great educators. You can name Mordecai Johnson and Benjamin E. Mays and a long list of great college presidents; George Washington Carver and other inventors and scientists. But there was a time when it was illegal for us to learn how to read and write. Our having access to education and educational institutions was a part of the later development of our community. Our educational institutions are the fruits of our labor.

And we've had great entertainers: Bojangles Robinson, Sammy Davis, Harry Belafonte, Ella Fitzgerald, Oscar Peterson, and Sidney Poitier. Down through the years we've had great athletes. Not only O. J. Simpson and Gale Sayers but Joe Louis, Ralph Metcalfe, Jesse Owens, and Jack Johnson. Down through the years we've had our share of great athletes and great entertainers, but I want to argue today that these are the *fruits* of our tradition. Life, however, is in the *roots* of a tradition.

They have been able to lift up our fruits, use them in their best days, get the sweetness out of them and then throw them to the ground, let them rot and then walk over them and turn what once were sweet apples into sour cider. I look at a man of the stature of Joe Louis opening doors at Caesar's Palace. He once was a great fruit. Now they trample upon him and look at him as if he's a thing. I look at the role that Jackie Robinson played in helping to make baseball the game that it is today. Yet the commissioner of baseball has not been able to come up with one award in the name of Jackie Robinson. We look at the coaching staffs of great basketball and great football teams and we look at the scarce number of blacks in the front office. They've always had a way of taking the best of us and ignoring the rest of us, turning our grapes into raisins and letting them become bitter.

How did we survive? Whether through politics, through business, through school, through entertainment, through ball fields—I argue that it was the church. That's where our roots are.

Let's argue the case a minute. The black church sustains blacks collectively by giving us a reason to live amid adversity and oppression. It was the black church that said that the storm will pass over, that there is a brighter day ahead. It takes us back to the origins of African religion. Before they knew there was a Muhammed or a Jesus, they knew there was a God who made the sun to shine and the moon to glow. Their customs are older than written or recorded history. Great African religions did not debate theology; they assumed that any reasonable person knew that there was a God who was creator and that people were the creatures. So they worshiped every manifestation of God—not because they were heathens. They worshiped God's sun, they worshiped his moon, they worshiped his rain, they worshiped his soil, they worshiped animals—they worshiped every manifestation. So no slavemaster taught us how to worship God. There are roots that run deeper than the mind of the slave or the slavemaster.

The church gave us a *why* for living. One writer said if you can endure the *how* of living because you know the *why* of living, you have a reason for living. You can get up early in the morning, you can work without wages—if you just have a reason to do it.

Second, the black church became the first institution to preach and practice collective self-reliance. The earliest rudiments of economic mutual development came from the black church. Bishop Richard Allen, founder of the A.M.E. Church, and Absalom Jones, the first black Episcopal priest in the nation, formed the first officially established black church. Most black insurance companies started in the basement of some church. No churches started in the basements of insurance companies; the insurance companies started in the basements of black churches. And that's why, black banks and black insurance companies, when our black churches come to you, don't look down on them, for if you do you're looking down on your momma and your daddy. You're looking down on your founder, on your creator, on your base. No creature is ever greater than its creator.

Third, the earliest black educational institutions were formed by the black church, were sheltered in black churches. We talk about the underground railroad. Well, the black church was the railway station. In the 1850s, before the Emancipation Proclamation, Wilberforce University was founded by Bishop Daniel Alexander Payne, acting under the authority of the A.M.E. Church. At the end of the Civil War, predominantly white denominations organized black churches and black schools in conjunction with the black church. As late as fifty years ago, many parishes in Louisiana still had no public schools for black children. Black churches organized boarding schools for high school to develop the minds of our children. You cannot compare the record of Harvard and Yale with Benedict, Allen, Morris Brown, Morehouse, Payne, and Wilberforce. All are products of the black church—our roots.

Fourth, our earliest move for political emancipation was by the black church. Let us not forget that Nat Turner was Reverend Nathaniel Turner. Let us not forget that when they had the lynching confrontation in South Carolina challenging Denmark Vesey, they also put the A.M.E. Church out of South Carolina for twenty-five years. That was because the base of Denmark Vesey's activity was that church.

Fifth, black church leaders played an active role in the formation of our civil rights struggle. When Rosa Parks had a toe ache, she didn't go to a podiatrist—she went to the black church. When her feet were hurting, she didn't go to the emergency room of the hospital because something deeper than her toe was hurting. Her pride was hurting. Her sense of existence was crushed, and she went to the church. There she found a waiting ear in a prophet named Martin Luther King, Jr. So if a Montgomery bus boycott was organized, it was organized out of the black church. There was a march from Selma to Montgomery; it started at Browns Chapel A.M.E. Church, and it marched to Montgomery, Alabama. It was no accident today that we have as leader of OIC Reverend Leon Sullivan; as head of NAACP Reverend Benjamin Hooks; as head of SCLC Reverend Ralph Abernathy; as UN Ambassador Reverend Andrew Young. There is a tradition of humanity and courage that emerges from our roots, and that is why this generation must appreciate the roots that brought us through.

Last, there's a prayer tradition that emerges from the black church. My grandmother doesn't have any money, doesn't know anything about a balance sheet, but she knows the worth of prayer. My grandmother doesn't have any education, she can't read or write, but she's never lost. She knows the worth of prayer. She's never taken a course on nutrition at the university and can't read the directions of Betty Crocker, but she's a chemist in the kitchen. She knows the worth of prayer. To the world she has no name, and she has no face, but she feels that she has cosmic importance because there's a God she communicates with in the heavens who is eternal. And so she knows that every boss is temporary, that every rainy day is temporary, that every hardship is temporary. She used to tell me, "Son, every goodbye ain't gone. Just hold on; there's joy coming in the morning." I used to wonder how she made it. I went back and got one of those old prayers they used to pray down in Long Branch Baptist Church. I don't know whether or not you can read all six hundred pages of *Roots* or not. I hope you understand Kunta Kinte. I hope you understand some of the African terminology, but there's a tradition that we've kept that hasn't been on NBC or CBS or ABC, and UPI and AP haven't picked it up. These are our roots, and they run underground today.

I thank Thee, Lord, for sparing me this morning, for the blood running warm in my veins, for the activity of my limbs and the use of my tongue. I thank Thee, Lord, for raiment and for food, and, above all, I thank Thee for the gift of Thy darling Son, Jesus, who came all the way from heaven down to this low ground of sorrow, who died upon the cross that "whosoever believeth upon him should not perish but have everlasting life." Our Lord, our Heavenly Master, we ask Thee to teach us and guide us in the way we know not. Give us more faith and a better understanding and a closer walk to Thy bleeding side. I have a faith to believe, Lord, that you are the same God that was in the days that are past and gone. Thou heard Elijah pray in the cleft of the mountain; Thou heard Paul and Silas in jail; Thou heard the three Hebrew children in the fiery furnace. I have a faith to believe that you once heard me pray when I was laying and lugging around the gates of hell with no eye to pity me and no arm to save me. Thou reached down your long arm of protection, snatched my soul from the midst of eternal burning. Thou placed a new song in my mouth. Thou told me to go and you would go with me, to open my mouth and you would speak for me. For that cause, Lord, we call upon you this hour. And we call upon Thee; we ask you don't go back to glory, neither turn a deaf ear to our call, but turn down the kindness of a listening ear. Catch our moan and our groan, and take them home with you in the high heavens. We plead bold one thing more, oh Lord, if it is Thy glorious will, I pray to Thee, O Lord, our Heavenly Master. We ask Thee to search our hearts, tie the reins of our mind, and if Thou see anything laying and lugging around our hearts that not your right hand planteth and neither is pleasing to Thy sight, we ask Thee to remove it by the brightness of your coming; cast it into the sea of forgiveness, where it will never rise up against us in this world, neither condemn us at the bar of judgment, if it's Thy will. Oh God, our Heavenly Father, we ask Thee to make us a better servant in the future than we have been in the past. We thank Thee, our Heavenly Father; won't you have mercy. Please remember the sick and the afflicted, the poor and those in hospitals, bodies racked with pain, scorched with parch and fever. Have mercy on them, if it's Thy glorious will.

This is our tradition; these are our roots. "Come by here, my Lord," somebody said, "come by here." Not songs with complicated lines but songs that the salt of the earth can sing. Not only "Lord, come by here," but I got a mother down in Georgia and I want you to go by there, oh Lord, won't you come by here. I heard somebody else say, well, Lord, I'm gonna wait. I'm gonna wait 'cause I can't do nothing 'til you come. I'm gonna hold on to your unchanging hand. Then long before they knew about Jesus, in the Old Testament, they say we know you can part the waters and you can come to us in the midnight hour. The church has been our rock in a weary place. The church has been our foundation in ages past.

My daddy was without an education, wasn't a politician, couldn't vote, nobody knew his name—but he came back one day and said somebody had laid his hands on him. He said, I went to church today and the preacher recognized me, and now I'm a Trustee. Honey, I got an extra key; I can open the church when I want to. You know, I went down to the bank today for the first time, and I put my name on the check, and our church got a bank account. Next week I'm going down to Columbia to the state convention as a delegate, and I'll meet other folk from all across the world. The church.

Before Aretha Franklin was on the stage, she was in the pulpit.

Nobody from Columbia records wanted to hear her sing. But somebody in that church said, Sing on, my child.

You can cut off my limbs, you can blow away my leaves. If the wind blows, you can bend my trunk. You can even cut it down. But don't bother my roots. My roots run underground, and they get watered deeper than the eye can see or the air can hear. Lord, protect my roots. Wilt not Thou revive us again? Wilt not Thou revive us again that we might find joy in Thee?

My daddy was fired, my mother was sick and couldn't work, and it was about Christmas time. We were supposed to go to church and exchange gifts. Momma and Daddy were inclined not to go because we didn't have any gifts to share. Daddy was downhearted; his pride was hurt. Momma said, Well, Honey, both of us are in the choir. We can give our voices to the Lord. Besides, these boys need to go anyhow. Maybe they can just get a piece of fruit, because, after all, Honey, it's the spirit of Christmas that really counts.

Well, there was an old man named Mr. Davis. Mr. Davis couldn't read and he couldn't write. Those days in South Carolina, black people couldn't be on welfare. Black folks didn't have any money. When they were old, they had to sit around and die. And some old, kind, benevolent lady like Miss Ida would just feed them. There were two or three people in the neighborhood who just kept big pots of vegetable soup on. When folks didn't have any food they couldn't go to the Salvation Army because they were black. They couldn't get Social Security; they couldn't get on welfare. But folks had a tradition of being kind to other folk because that was our roots. We couldn't have made it by ourselves. We came by way of helping each other. That's why when the momma and daddy had to go to work, the neighbors raised the children. All of us had to raise each other. We didn't have a neighborhood, we had a community. There's a difference between a bunch of neighbors and a bunch of hoods and a community that's made out of common unity where there's a foundation.

And so since Mr. Davis didn't have his Social Security and couldn't get on welfare, my momma used to try to help him. She had spent several months going back and forth to try to get his Social Security and finally had to get a lawyer named John Coverson—a white lawyer, a generous man who drove Mr. Davis all the way to Washington from Greenville, South Carolina, just to try to get his Social Security.

So that night we went to church. We didn't have any gifts, but there was so much spirit in the air. They were singing, and everybody was rejoicing, and the joy of it was that we had each other. Then we came back home. Momma and Daddy were walking behind, talking, and my brother and I were going down the road throwing rocks. Finally we got back down to Briar Street, and then we climbed those seventeen steps up to the door, and there were six bags of groceries there. They didn't have any name on them, and there wasn't anything written down. We said, We can't put them off the porch because there are meat and eggs here, and we don't want them to spoil. So we just set them inside the door. We weren't about to steal the groceries because that was wrong. We figured that if we stole somebody else's groceries that something bad would happen to us. We felt that if we ate somebody else's meat, it wouldn't be right. So we put the meat in the freezer and held the rest of the groceries in the corner. About three days later, Mr. Davis came by and said: Helen, sometimes I think these boys just ain't gonna be any good. Seems like they're not grateful for anything. We got these groceries here, and these big old boys won't even put the groceries up. She said, Mr. Davis, it's not the boys' fault. You see, we came home from church the other night and these groceries were on the porch. Somebody made a mistake. Mr. Davis said, I brought those groceries by here the other night. The reason there isn't any writing on them is that I can't write. But I wanted to say to you and Charlie: thank you for writing for me and helping me when I had no way out.

It is the roots. Some people doubt it, but I can't do without it. I've had too many good experiences with God to turn around now. "Somebody touched me." Somebody else said, "there's something within." Somebody else said, "beams of heaven as I go in this wilderness below." Somebody said it's "amazing grace." It's not ordinary, it's "amazing grace. How sweet the sound!" Somebody else said, "I know the Lord." This was way before the Voting Rights Act. "He heard my cry and pitied every groan. As long as I live and troubles rise, I'll hasten to his throne." "When the storm is passing over, hallelujah, hallelujah. When the storm is passing over, hallelujah."

Return to our roots. It is amazing; we couldn't read and we couldn't write, but we have been saying the same prayer everywhere. "Now I lay me down to sleep. I pray the Lord my soul to keep. If I should die before I wake, I pray the Lord my soul to take." We didn't have NBC, we didn't have CBS, we didn't have the wire services, but every time before we ate we were saying, "Lord, I thank you for the food I'm about to receive, for the nourishment of my body, for Christ, my redeemer's sake, Amen."

It is a return to our prayer tradition that will give us the power to go through a Red Sea and not have mud on our shoes, to survive a fiery furnace and not only not get burned up but not even smell like smoke. It's the power of prayer that gives old persons the power to rise above rheumatism when there isn't any liniment, to be in a lion's den and not get bit. The lions lose their appetite, and your enemies leave you alone. You turn their growl into music, and you turn their side into a pillow. "He's a mighty God; he's a mighty God, is he. He's my rock; he's my rock."

Protecting the Legacy:
The Challenge of
Dr. Martin Luther King, Jr.

This sermon was preached at Ebenezer Baptist Church in Atlanta, Dr. Martin Luther King, Jr.'s home church, on January 15, 1986. It inaugurated a week-long series of activities, sponsored by the Martin Luther King Center for Nonviolent Social Change, launching the first national celebration of Dr. King's birth date as a national holiday. In this sermon, Jackson was concerned about the trivialization and emasculation of Dr. King's legacy, portraying him as a passive dreamer rather than as the fighter for social justice that he was.

We are gathered here today in the city where Dr. King was born and in the pulpit in which he preached, where he worked for justice and human rights. We have this awesome challenge to pay tribute to his memory. The difficulty and challenge of that charge is to determine the most appropriate way to pay tribute. There are many forms of tribute, some of which are exciting and creative, some of which are irrelevant and distorting. How would Dr. King wish us to pay tribute? must be the question that is answered.

When another group was wrestling with the same subject—how you celebrate a holy day—Micah said: "O man, He has showed you what is good. Do justice, love mercy, and walk humbly before thy God."

I could not help but stop by the basement of this church on the way to the pulpit, for I was privileged to be with a small band of warriors, apostles, and disciples on January 15, 1968, the last birthday Dr. King was alive. He showed us on that day how to celebrate his birthday by the way he celebrated his own birthday. That morning he had breakfast with his family. He had prayer at home with his family. He was a family man. He went to the basement of this church about 10 A.M., convened his staff, advisors, and supporters—Hispanics, whites, blacks, Native Americans, Asians, Jews, Protestants, and Catholics, a kind of Rainbow Coalition—and began organizing the Poor People's Campaign from Marks, Mississippi—the poorest county in America—to Washington, D.C. A most serious and sacred setting, a great and challenging mission. About 2 o'clock, someone came into the room with a birthday cake. We stopped for a moment, sliced the cake, blew out the candles, ate the cake, and kept on organizing the Poor People's Campaign. That's how he celebrated his own birthday.

Birthday celebrations must be appropriate to the person whose birthday it is. That's why when people have Christmas parties at which Christ would not be welcome, it's a fundamental violation. If you want to have liquor at your birthday party or sniff cocaine at your birthday party or engage in all kinds of vile conduct, then do it at your own birthday party in your own name. If you want to force gifts as political payoffs to maintain superficial friendships, then do it in your own name at your own birthday party. But you should not snatch out the lights on Jesus' birthday party. You should not undercut the sacredness of it and impose your own commercialism on his birthday party. Dr. King is a special kind of person who established how he wanted his birthday celebrated. You might recall that his request was basic: "Just say I tried to help somebody." His motivation was just as basic: "I just want to do God's will."

In life he called himself "a drum major for justice," and those of us who marched with him can attest to that fact. In death, however, he is being projected as a "dreamer" who dreamed of America as it ought to be and not as it is or was. The media portray him as a nonthreatening dreamer, but he projected himself as a drum major for justice. His mission was "to disturb the comfortable and comfort the disturbed." The media want to focus on children and status-quo politicians rather than his SCLC staff and fellow warriors—Dr. Abernathy, C. T. Vivian, Dorothy Cotton, Fred Shuttlesworth, Hosea Williams, James Bevel, James Orange, Wyatt T. Walker, and many others. He was not a pied piper, a kind of free-spirited man, walking alone with a dove in one ear and the American flag in the other, operating five feet above reality. He was a drum major with a major band of apostles and disciples behind him.

I speak today as an eyewitness. We must resist this weak and anemic memory of a great man, for this is the strategy of the enemy and of those who do not know any better. To think of Dr. King only as a dreamer is to do injustice to his memory and to the dream itself. The so-called "I Have a Dream" speech in Washington on August 28, 1963, was not a speech about dreams and dreaming; it was a speech describing nightmare conditions. He said that we have paid our dues and have been given a promissory note, only to find out that it has bounced and come back marked "insufficient funds." The premise and substance of that speech was about social and economic justice. The motivational and inspirational conclusion was that Dr. King had a dream about a new day, about new possibilities. In a similar way, don't confuse the substance of my remarks today with how I may end this address.

Why is it that, even though Dr. King was perhaps the greatest Christian practitioner of applied theology of our era, Mr. Reagan cannot honor his memory without qualification—implying he was a communist agent instead of a prophet in the Judeo-Christian tradition? The U.S. government honors him today, but some of us remember that it was this same government that tailed him and trailed him, that engaged in character assassination. It was the same government of FBI Director J. Edgar Hoover. It was the same government of Robert Kennedy who wiretapped his phone. It was the same government who is still at least implicated because the jury is out on the direct involvement in his assassination. Why is it that so many politicians today want to emphasize that Dr. King was a dreamer? It is because they want us to believe that his dreams have become reality and that, therefore, we should celebrate rather than continue to fight on January 20.

There is the struggle today to preserve the substance and the integrity of Dr. King's legacy. Some people today want to project him as a dreamer because they wish us to remember him as an idealist detached from reality, when in fact he was a realist with high ideals. He had one foot in Montgomery and another in the New Jerusalem (high ideals), one foot in Birmingham and another in the New Jerusalem, one foot in Selma and another in the New Jerusalem. Realism with high ideals, not idealism without reality. When we know this, we honor his memory concretely. We honored him today as we marched five hundred people on the Justice Department. Attorney General Meese would not see us; he locked the door of Justice. We left our demands on the door. We then fed five hundred people and registered more than six hundred to vote.

How do you celebrate his birthday? You knock on the door of Justice; you feed the hungry; you empower the locked-out. To be authentic and in his spirit, January 15–20 must be the period of highest voter registration, the biggest boycotts, the most resistance, the most direct action, the most companies confronted who will not hire or promote, the most anti-apartheid activity. We should not play cozy with those who kill in South Africa, the Philippines, and Central America. We must fight against violence and terrorism everywhere and measure human rights by one yardstick.

Dr. King was not assassinated for dreaming but for acting and challenging the government, just as Jesus was crucified not for the Sermon on the Mount but because he led people to question the legitimacy of Herod and the Pharisees. Dr. King made us question the legitimacy of the American government's policies, and thus the wrath of that government came down on him. Conservatives have tried to change Jesus into a reactionary. They focus on the harmless baby wrapped in swaddling clothes and on the crucified Christ, dying and dripping in blood. Both times—when he was a baby and couldn't talk and when he was on the cross and couldn't walk—they love him. But when he was walking and talking, kicking tables in the temple and saying "feed the hungry," they reject him. In life he drove the moneychangers from the temple; he challenged the ritual over the reality of the Pharisees; and he elevated the common people. He measured wealth not by the size of their corporations but by their character.

Thus in life Jesus was rejected by the innkeeper and hunted by Herod. The innkeeper would gladly have accepted Jesus if he had known that he was going to attract all that business to Bethlehem. He would have given Mary and Joseph a complimentary room. If Herod had known that this was only about Santa Claus coming once a year to give annual joy and merriment to cover up the daily sorrow, Herod would have welcomed him. But Herod could not accept Jesus because his existence was a threat to him. Jesus was out to change things. His doctrine was not love without responsibility.

Dr. Martin Luther King, Jr., was a Tillichian scholar of applied social ethics. Thus he saw love, power, and justice as intertwined. He taught us that peace was not the absence of noise but the presence of justice. There will be no peace where there is no justice. He argued that love without power is anemic and weak and that power without love is crude and insensitive. Love acts and behaves. In the same way, Dr. King's life threatened the political establishment. He demanded an end to U.S. apartheid. He demanded the dismantling of that system through the civil rights laws. He challenged a popular president over the Vietnam War.

If we say that Dr. King was a dreamer, then we must define "dreamer" and realize the kind of dreamer he was. There are all types of dreamers. There are *daydreamers* who have idle fantasies. You see them walking through the park. There are *mystics* whose dreams are otherworldly. There are *visionaries* who see the world of the future as it can be. Then there are those who, like Joseph in Egypt, *see through nightmares* the world as it will be unless people heed the warnings. Such a person is a special type of visionary—a prophet. Dr. King was such a dreamer—a visionary and prophet who could interpret the dreams and the nightmares of America's future, but he also had a vision. He made it very clear that there is nothing more powerful in the world than to be morally right, in contrast to having military might. A materialistic and militaristic people find it very hard to hear Dr. King in the spirit.

That's important in this interpretation. I am reminded that when Mary found out she was pregnant and could not explain her pregnancy—because she had not been with a man, and because she was young, unmarried, and in agony—she ran to her cousin, Elizabeth (see Luke 1:39–56). When she got to Elizabeth's house, before Elizabeth even saw her—Mary was just conceiving, she wasn't even showing her pregnancy—Elizabeth heard Mary's voice and said, "Something unusual is going on. You know, that's the Lord in your belly. And, I tell you, I feel honored that you would even come to my house. What have I done to deserve this?" I contrast that with the innkeeper, because this man saw Mary at nine months, in labor. Elizabeth in the spirit could hear with her spiritual ear what the innkeeper couldn't see with his physical eye.

To deal with Dr. King, you must hear with the spiritual ear to know that beneath that which you see and read there is another message. He said to America, you don't believe it, but might is not right; right is might. They dismissed him as an idle dreamer who was naive and didn't understand the facts of life. He was just a preacher. He didn't understand big things. Just a preacher. Never sat at the U.N. Just a preacher. No degree in foreign policy. Just a preacher. Never managed a U.N. or military budget. Just a preacher. He understands some things, but this is the big picture: might is right.

Last week President Reagan called for a boycott on terrorism in Libya. He was right to call for a fight against terrorism. All of us must be against terrorism everywhere in the world. But I wonder why no one responded? President Reagan has power over the world's largest economy. He has the power to push a button and destroy the world forty times over. He is considered the single most powerful man in the world. He has might. But when you stand before the U.N. and don't mention South Africa; when you stand before the U.S. Congress in joint session after Geneva and never mention South Africa, where our folk are dying before, during, and after his address; when you support state terrorism in South Africa and practice state terrorism in Central America, by the time you get to the Middle East you have lost your moral authority. You are not believable.

Dr. King's power was not in standing armies, in marines, in air-force jets, or in big dollars. He heard a song go this way, "If I'm right, he'll fight your battle." Dr. King had a power that is available to all of us: he was right. Rosa Parks had nothing else but right. The students in Greensboro, handcuffed, trying to get a hamburger, had nothing else but right. The

Freedom Riders had nothing else but right. John Lewis and Hosea Williams, going across that bridge in Selma, had nothing else but right. Martin Luther King, Jr., speaking against the Vietnam War, had nothing but right. There is nothing as a strategy more powerful in the world than to be right.

Dr. King had moral authority. That's what my grandmother has. When she says "shut up," you get quiet, not because she can smack you or hurt you, but because she's right and she loves you. She has power and love and justice. She's right. In order to have moral authority, the gap between your words and your actions must close. John said, when he saw the Master, it was like the Word becoming flesh and dwelling among us. Dr. King foresaw with that kind of dreaming that the Vietnam War would wreck the economy, would wreck homes and lives. He foresaw that the Middle East crisis would only worsen so long as there was a no-talk confrontational policy. In our own country, he foresaw that if adults were living double standards, they would lose control over their youth. Thus we have babies making babies, self-destruction, and widespread dope addiction.

Like Joseph, Dr. King could interpret dreams and nightmares, but he also had a vision. Now here is the challenge to our government. While Pharaoh had the good sense to give the job of staving off the famine to the man who interpreted the nightmares, our leaders denied Martin that opportunity. Pharaoh did not care that Joseph was a foreigner, that he was a Jew, that he was young, that he was in jail accused of trying to rape Pharaoh's wife. When Pharaoh started having these nightmares and learned that Joseph could interpret them, he went past all of that— not just to steal Joseph's ideas—but to put him in a position of power and authority. Joseph was therefore able to save the economy, his own family, and Egypt. America couldn't get past race long enough to appreciate the prophetic truths of Dr. King. So, as opposed to bringing him in and hearing his voice, they locked him out. The result is that today we have Dr. King's memory, but we missed the opportunity then to benefit from his wisdom.

If Dr. King were alive and here today, he would be surprised that some of those who marched with him in life would be marching against him today. There were allies in the Freedom Movement who left us in the Justice Movement. I see our history in stages. In the fifties and sixties, we were locked out. Then we passed laws in 1964, 1965, and 1968 so that we could move in. From "out" to "in" was the Freedom Movement, but the goal was always social and economic justice. The Freedom Movement shifted gears and went from moving in to moving up. When we turned and started going up, we lost a lot of allies. We said, we're not objects of pity. We don't want welfare, we want our share. We don't want generosity, we want reciprocity. We don't want aid, we want trade. There was a shift in the struggle and a shift in allies. One stage locked out; another stage moved in; another stage moved up. The goal is our share.

Dr. King talked about "creative justice." I have five children. I do not treat them equally; I treat them adequately. They require different things. So you have "creative justice." You can't play by the traditional rules if one child is maimed and crippled and hurt. Preferential treatment for white males was the law. For 250 years slavery was the law. For 100 years, segregation was the law. De facto discrimination even today is the law of the culture. So we have several stages. In one stage, the law said don't discriminate, so we had regulations outlawing discrimination. But that wasn't enough, so there was affirmative action, where you go out of your way to stop discrimination. You advertise and you recruit. But that wasn't enough. We then had to measure what you did, so you had goals and timetables. How are we doing? That's where yesterday ended. A headline in the *Washington Post* the other day indicated that the Reagan administration did not want to count the number of minority businesses any longer. In other words, if the truth sets you free, then denying the truth keeps you in captivity. And then today they said that the Reagan-Bush-Meese apparatus wants to unravel the executive order for affirmative action written by Lyndon Johnson. But they felt they should not do it this week, between January 15 and 20, because America is aroused this week. So on January 21 they expect us to fall asleep again.

There are four stages. Stage one: don't discriminate in the laws and regulations. Stage two is affirmative action: advertise and recruit. Stage three is measure: goals and timetables. Stage four: if that fails, minimum quotas. We should impose quotas as a last resort when everything else has failed. Affirmative action is equal opportunity. It is not reverse discrimination. It is not preferential treatment. It is not for blacks; it's for women and blacks, Hispanics, Asians, Native Americans—the locked-out. It does not require you to hire unqualified people; that's illegal. It has not taken white male jobs. Steel, electronics, rubber, textiles—those jobs didn't go to Watts or Harlem, they went to South Africa, Taiwan, South Korea, and slave-labor markets. Affirmative action does require you to include qualified blacks, Hispanics, women, Asians, and Native Americans in the pool. We don't want any unqualified airline pilots. Affirmative action, with goals and timetables, does require you to measure your progress—or the lack of it. Affirmative action with minimum quotas does require you to enforce the law. Democracy does not guarantee success, but it does guarantee opportunity. That's why it is time for challenges and changes and new strategies.

Jesus, in his profundity, did not mince his words about a mean political ruler. He said, "Go tell the fox." In other words, Jesus called a spade a spade. That was real prophetic integrity. Nathan looked at David. Everybody was bowing and scraping because David was in charge, was popular, talented, had a harem of women, and everybody was writing big articles about him, snapping pictures, and all of that. Nathan walked right up and said, Mighty glad to see you, brother David. Well, glad to see you, Nathan. You know, I was just thinking. The other day I saw a man with a sheep farm and lots of sheep all over the meadows. David said, Yeah. Now another man had a little baby lamb, and you know what that first man did? David asked, What? You know, that man left all those mature sheep, all that wealth and wool, and went over the fence, got that man's baby lamb, and got that man killed. David said, That's terrible. Nathan said, I'm talking about you. With all of these women, all of this wealth, all of this pleasure, and here is one man with one woman, and yet you take his woman and get him killed. It's you I'm talking about. Now that's real prophetic stuff.

Dr. King came back from getting the Nobel Peace Prize, and he was at a reception in the East Wing of the White House. Lyndon Johnson was saying Dr. King's so great, he's such a nice guy, and all that. Dr. King said, Yes, but what about the Voting Rights Act? Now Johnson was popular at that time, and everything was going right, but Dr. King was concerned about the right to vote. Johnson said, Now, Martin, you know I'm your friend, and you know I'm with you. I'm liberal. But the Congress is too conservative. Dr. King said, Right. I'm leaving. Johnson asked, Where are you going? To Selma. Dr. King didn't play with Pharaoh; he called his hand.

Today President Reagan went to an elementary school in Washington, held up little black children in his hands, with onions under his eyes so he would look tearful, pitiful, and solemn. He said he was doing this in the name of Dr. Martin Luther King, Jr., and the sweet land of liberty. The same man didn't support the boycott in Montgomery; he was old enough. The same man didn't support the sit-ins in Greensboro; he was old enough. The same man didn't support the Freedom Rides. The same man didn't support the march from Selma to Montgomery. The same man right now implies that Dr. King was a communist. The same man who didn't respect him in life is now trying to unravel every accomplishment in death, including the holiday. And now he holds up an innocent child, exploits that baby's tender emotions because the baby feels good about being in the presence of the president. Is there redemption for him? Well, yes. But redemption comes through seeking redemption and a change in behavior. Are you saying that Reagan shouldn't honor Dr. King's birthday? Yes, I say he should honor it; he shouldn't dishonor it. The front page of the *Washington Post* today says he is contemplating waiting to overturn Johnson's executive order on affirmative action until after the holiday because it would be bad publicity. How can Reagan honor Dr. King? Today should be the day of his national civil rights address. This day he should tell those children, as president, I will fight to guarantee you a breakfast and a lunch program. That's how you honor him. I guarantee you an education. Under Reagan there are more blacks graduating from high school and fewer going to college. I guarantee you an affordable house. I guarantee you jobs, peace, and justice in your day. I guarantee you support for affirmative action. I support Dr. King's initiatives. And yet the press will give him a free ride and project him as a kindly old man. George Bush went to New Hampshire a few weeks ago to attend the funeral of a man that he didn't like and who didn't like him.* It was in the paper. Why would George Bush go to New Hampshire in an air force jet, Secret Service, looking like he's sad at the funeral of a man who didn't like him and whom he didn't like? He was out there hustling votes at the man's funeral. The press gave him a fit. Those same standards must apply to Reagan.

Dr. King still challenges Reagan and this culture. He is still saying that right is might. If you don't believe that that's a challenge, look at all the popularity polls of Reagan, at all his power. They say he's a great president, elected twice. He has all power in his hand. He can fly in Air Force One. He is connected with the world and can call Gorbachev directly. He can make or break an economy. He can overthrow nations. He can sneeze and the nation will catch a cold. He has all this power, he has all this might. And this lowly preacher had none of that. He just had right. What's my point? With all of Reagan's power, with all the king's horses and all the king's men, even America will never have a national holiday named after Ronald Reagan.

And so I close on this note. We celebrate Dr. King's birthday as he celebrated his own birthday—at home with his family, praying, eating, and sharing. As he celebrated his own birthday—in the basement of his church, organizing the poor people of our nation. As he celebrated his own birthday—organizing creative tension. As he celebrated his own birthday—disturbing the comfortable and comforting the disturbed.

He left us from the mountaintop. At the mountaintop is the crucifixion. On top of Calvary is the crucifixion. But beyond Calvary is the resurrection where the stone is rolled away. He foresaw loneliness and difficult days ahead. But he left us with two things. He didn't leave us any guns. He didn't leave us any money. He didn't leave us a standing

*William Loeb, owner and publisher of the Manchester, N.H., *Union Leader*. Loeb had always attacked Bush as being too moderate.

army. He left us with just two things. One was a charge, and the other was a promise.

A charge to heal the nation—humane priorities at home and human rights abroad. Measure human rights by one yardstick all over the world.

A charge to our youth. Say no to drugs. Say no to liquor. Say no to babies making babies. Say no to violence. A charge to our youth. Don't watch five hours of TV a night, choosing entertainment over education.

A charge to fight for affordable housing and health care, to fight against old people dying in the dark and the cold, eating cat and dog food.

A charge to support women, infants, and children.

A charge to measure leadership not by following opinion polls but by molding opinion.

A charge to measure character by how you treat the least of these.

A charge to have regard for the baby rejected by the innkeeper and living in the stable behind the hotel. Red, yellow, black, brown, and white—we're all precious in God's sight. A charge to look beyond the race of the matter. There are forty-one million people in poverty; twenty-nine million are white. The poor are mostly white, female, and young, and most of them work; they're not on welfare. According to Harvard's Dr. J. Larry Brown, hunger hurts. When a baby cries at midnight because it went to bed supperless, it doesn't cry in race; it doesn't cry in sex; it doesn't cry in religion; it cries in pain.

A charge to shake the foundations and reshape the priorities.

A charge to keep and a God to glorify.

But Dr. King gave us another weapon. He gave us a promise. He said, I may not get there, but I promise you you'll get there one day, one glad morning. I don't know what morning it will be, but one glad morning the wicked will cease from troubling, and the weary will be at rest. I may not get there, but I promise you there's a new city whose builder and maker is God. I know that you're going to cry sometime; you're going to hurt sometime; you're going to be lonesome sometime. Weeping may endure for a night, but if you hold on and hold out, joy is coming in the morning. I promise you the road will not be easy, but I didn't bring you this far to leave you now. I promise you, yea, though you walk through the valley of the shadow of death, you should fear no evil, for the Lord is with you. It gets dark every now and then, but the Lord is my light and my salvation. Whom shall I fear? The Lord is the strength of my life.

He left us a promise. If my people, who are called by my name, will humble themselves and pray and seek my face, then you will hear from heaven, and I'll give back your land.

Binding Up the Wounds

In a conversation with a *Washington Post* reporter that both parties agreed was private and off-the-record, Jackson referred to Jews and New York City as "Hymies" and "Hymietown," respectively. The reporter later unilaterally decided to put this private conversation on the record. After being questioned by reporters for a week and neither confirming nor denying the comments, in this sermon—given at Temple Adath Yeshurun in Manchester, New Hampshire, on February 26, 1984, two days before the New Hampshire presidential primary—Jackson for the first time admitted having used the terms.

There is a story in the Bible about Jacob wrestling with an angel. It dealt with the great dilemma of the conflict between Jacob's inner and outer selves. The inner self yearning to be free, the outer self negotiating with the politics of his day. Ultimately the inner self prevailed. After wrestling with the dilemma, Jacob lost the rhythm of his step. He came up lame, but the freedom of his soul was restored, and thus he is worthy of recognition in the holy writ.

There are temptations before us to do that which is popular or expedient, because all humanity yearns for acceptance in the face of so much rejection. There is a temptation to be political, because in the face of competition we want to win. There is, however, another obligation—to be prophetic, to do that which is right and moral even if it is politically inexpedient and even if you lose. For even if we should gain the whole world, but lose our souls, we would have nothing.

Apart from the politics of the day and the give and take of combat, our irreducible essence must be our integrity. *That* is nonnegotiable; that, water cannot drown; that, fire cannot burn; that, politics will not compromise.

The delay in coming to this temple today must be seen from several perspectives. There is a statement of relief in the scripture that says "I was glad when they said unto me, let us go into the house of the Lord." When I listened to the late Rabbi Abraham Heschel, and when I listened to the late Dr. Howard Thurman preach in the temple, I felt welcome. When I spoke in Skokie when the Nazis threatened to march on Skokie and I stood there with my family and Rabbi Marx, I felt welcome.

Since I returned from my first trip to the Middle East in 1979, there has been so much pain, anxiety, and hostility that I have not felt welcome.* Therefore in my campaign I have sought to find another way to ease the pain and to open a path to reconciliation. I have offered my campaign as a vehicle to dialogue, to bring blacks and Hispanics and Jews and Arabs together—to become reunited as children of Abraham.

When, therefore, press reports were circulated, brewing up the storm about the word "Hymie," I was deeply disturbed. I watched as the word expanded into paragraphs and then into chapters. At first I was shocked and astonished at the press's interest in this ethnic characterization made in private conversations, apparently overheard by a reporter. I was equally interested that the newspaper saw fit to insert it in line 35 of a story, the propriety of which has been questioned even by the newspaper's own ombudsman. What concerns me now is that something so small has become so large that it threatens the fabric of relations that have been long in the making and that must be protected.

In part, I am to blame, and for that I am deeply distressed. Like Jacob, for a week my inner and outer selves have wrestled. I have been confronted by conflicting moral challenges. When confronted with the charge, I hesitated, for to say "Yes, I had said that," I feared would have thrown up an insurmountable obstacle to my efforts to keep open the much-needed path to dialogue. To have said "No" would have compromised my essence, my moral integrity and authority.

Even as I affirm to you that the term was used in a private conversation, the context and spirit of the remark must be appreciated. In private talk we sometimes let our guard down and become thoughtless. It was not in the spirit of meanness, but an off-color remark having no bearing

*In November of 1979 Jackson went to Israel, Jordan, Egypt, Syria, and Lebanon. Israeli Prime Minister Menachim Begin refused to meet with him, but he did meet with Jerusalem Mayor Teddy Kolleck; Egyptian President Anwar Sadat; Syrian President Hafez Assad; and Yassir Arafat, chairman of the Palestine Liberation Organization (PLO). His meeting with Arafat was resented by many American Jewish leaders.

on religion or politics. I deny and I do not recall ever making such a statement in any context that would be remotely construed as being either anti-Semitic or anti-Israel. However innocent and unattended, it was insensitive and wrong. Those of us who would lead must make the sacrifice of living in a fishbowl and leading by example. A moral leader must be tough enough to fight, compassionate enough to cry, human enough to err, humble enough to admit it. We must forgive each other, redeem each other, regroup, and move on. To err is human, to forgive is divine.

However, I categorically deny that this in any way reflects my basic or overall attitude toward Jews or Israel. I categorically deny allegations that I am either anti-Semitic or anti-Israel or that there is anything in my personal attitude or my public career, behavior, or record that lends itself to that interpretation. In fact, the record is the exact opposite. I have offered and offer my candidacy to you to assure the proper cultivation of dialogue and relationships among blacks and Jews and Arabs and other Americans. The healing within this Rainbow Coalition must take place because the world is at stake. We will either learn to live together as brothers and sisters, or we shall die apart as fools.

Barbara Walters, at the League of Women Voters debate, also asked about two other alleged statements attributed to me. One, that "I am sick and tired of hearing about the Holocaust," and, two, that I equated Israel with the PLO. I categorically deny making the "Holocaust" statement. The origin of the alleged quote is *Newsweek* magazine. In 1979 they quoted Phil Blazer, editor of *Israel Today* magazine, as saying that this is what I said. The reason this alleged quotation keeps coming up is that the head of the B'nai Brith Anti-Defamation League, Nathan Perlmutter, has circulated a nineteen-page single-spaced memo to a wide range of reporters and opinion makers in an attempt to discredit, disrupt, and destroy my campaign.

The context of the alleged, but false, quotation was a visit I made to the Vad Yashem Museum in Israel. After visiting the museum and being moved by what I saw, I expressed my genuine sadness and said that it was tragic and should never again be allowed to happen. Because I refused to say that it was "unique"—I know the history of black Americans, Armenians, Native Americans, and others—Mr. Blazer was upset and gave this false quotation to a reporter.

The allegation about my equating the PLO and Israel must also be seen in context. Israel constantly refers to the military arm of the PLO as "terrorists" and to its own military arm as "soldiers." The PLO refers to its military arm as "soldiers" and to Israel's military arm as "imperialists." In war both sides see their own military as soldiers fighting a just cause while they attempt to dehumanize the enemy. My point is,

STRAIGHT FROM THE HEART

whether a PLO soldier plants a bomb in a garbage can or an Israeli soldier drops a bomb from an airplane, the bottom line is the same— death all around. My position is that the U.S. should side with neither act but use its diplomatic and economic strength to reconcile both peoples so that the cycle of pain can end.

It is this human rights position which so antagonizes some elements in the Jewish community—although I am well aware that many Jews both in Israel and in America share our view. But among some who oppose our view there is an organized effort to destroy this campaign and this candidacy—Jews Against Jackson; Ruin, Jesse, Ruin; the Jewish Defense League (JDL) and Meir Kahane; a nineteen-page memo to key opinion makers from Nathan Perlmutter and the Anti-Defamation League; and much more.

There will be tension born of change and transition, but on matters of substance, not on matters that are trite and rhetorical.

Since my 1979 trip, I have experienced this hatred and pain. Sometimes it has been political. Sometimes it has been personal. In either case, it has resulted in the suspension of lifelong relationships—talking at each other in the press instead of with each other in person. All of this has been painful.

Sometimes it has been ugly. There have been threats against my life and the lives of my family. Threats to march on my home, newspaper ads and cartoons that were political in content but racist in intent. Even my children have suffered this pain. When my daughter was interviewed at Harvard, she was asked by a Jewish official at the university to distinguish her position on the Middle East from my own. Then she was forced to listen to a barrage of inflammatory remarks about me—at seventeen years of age.

Today we—blacks, Jews, Arabs, and all Americans—have a choice. We can take the low road of continued antagonism and mistrust, or we can turn aside all hatred and find another way.

This is the moment, like others throughout history, where our mettle is being tested. It was Nathan, a lowly prophet, who had the courage to tell David, a powerful king, that he was wrong. His mettle was being tested.

It was John F. Kennedy who admitted that he had made a mistake in the Bay of Pigs invasion. His mettle was being tested.

I feel good tonight because I know that unearned suffering is redemptive. Suffering breeds character, character breeds faith, and in the end faith will not disappoint.

My mission is to organize a Rainbow Coalition of the rejected and the disinherited. It is a glorious mission. Upon completion it will redeem the soul of the nation because it will make for harmony among Christians,

Jews, and Muslims. It will make room for the homeless. It will make room for the least of these. It will take the patches and the pieces that make up the quilt and make of them a blanket that provides security and warmth for us all.

I appeal to you today as a Jewish community in this state and in this nation to find your rightful place in this Rainbow Coalition to carry out the mission in your community that was articulated so well by the prophets of old.

I appeal today to all who have been affected by this controversy: let us go another way together. Blacks, Jews, and Arabs must dialogue together. We must learn to relate to each other right here. *This is not the Middle East. This is America.* We can begin to talk to each other at home and transport our peace across the world.

I appeal to the black community to participate in the dialogue. Integrity demands that we be honest enough to share our point of view and air our differences. But we can disagree without becoming disagreeable.

I appeal for a new covenant that binds up our wounds, that ends war, that retrieves the longings of our souls for peace and justice. Thank you very much.

From Battleground
to Common Ground
to Higher Ground

On May 13, 1983, Jackson launched Operation PUSH's "Southern Crusade" in Norfolk, Virginia. The crusade was designed to enhance voter registration, voter education, and voting rights enforcement in the South. During this period Jackson was exploring the possibilities of a presidential candidacy by himself or another black person. This speech was given before a joint session of the Alabama legislature in Montgomery on May 24, 1983. Jackson also met with Alabama Governor George Wallace, the former segregationist, at this time. Jackson's appearance here symbolized a new potential for racial reconciliation and joint political and economic development in the South.

On February 6, 1861, in this very chamber, the Confederacy was formed. Three days later it elected Jefferson Davis its first provisional president. It unified the South, but it divided the *United States* and thrust the nation's regions into war against each other— South versus North, North versus South.

The war divided the nation, the races, even families, and the separation was a source of great hurt. May 24, 1983—122 years later—your invitation to a native son of the South, the son of former slaves, to speak in these chambers is an act of reconciliation and healing. For your commitment to make the Alabama legislature a beacon of light and hope for the nation, you are to be highly commended. It is time that we leave the battlegrounds behind us and seek a common ground—and then move to higher ground.

On this historic day, when ancient barriers are coming down and new opportunities and possibilities for change are opening up, the leadership in the Alabama legislature, both black and white, deserve particular thanks. Those leaders who have assumed the responsibility for ushering in the fresh air of dialogue and communication and leaving behind the stale air of no talking, of bitterness, and of various forms of mental and physical violence—you are to be commended.

We knew this day would come. We knew this day would come because our faith has taught us that even though the road has been difficult, God didn't bring us this far to leave us. We knew this day would come because the arc of the universe is long, but it bends toward justice. We knew this day would come, not because we're lucky, but because we're blessed. Our presence here today is not accidental, it is providential—it is God's will. We serve a God who hears and answers prayer. We don't know each other as we should—and we must. We, as blacks, are projected constantly by the news media as less intelligent than we are, less hard working, less patriotic (although none of us has ever been convicted of an act of treason), less universal, and more violent.

Now that we're here together—because of God's investment in us and the stewardship that he has entrusted to us—we are obligated to give back to God a return on his investment. We must be faithful to our sworn duty. What is our duty? To defend the poor, the widows, the sick, those without parents, and the needy on every hand. To this calling and to this end, we must be faithful. Our faithfulness is all that we have with which to impress God. But if we are faithful over a few things—even the least of these—God will promote and elevate us and make us rulers over many. God has written laws into the very structure of the universe, and one of these laws is that it is impossible to help someone else without helping yourself in the process. And by the same token, it is impossible to hurt someone else without hurting yourself at the same time. We must defend the poor. Beyond ethnic reconciliation, there must be sound ethical conduct and a keen economic vision.

Too much of our nation is bogged down in cynicism, pessimism, negativism, and despair. Our external problems are great, but we must not let them break our spirit. As leaders of this state and nation, and for the good of our people, we must revive the spirit of hope and optimism in our people. We are obligated to spread miracles and possibility, not misery and despair. We must lead and show our people a way out. We must provide a plan and chart a course. We must navigate this journey from needs to fulfillment. How do we do it?

First, we must have a feeling that "I am somebody." A strong sense of self-reliance, self-respect, and the right to self-determination must light our pathway. Nobody will save us for us but us. I believe that the lack of self-esteem—the feeling that "I" don't count, that "I" can't make a difference—is one of the most important issues of our day. I always begin my speeches to students with a chant entitled, "I Am Somebody." The "I Am Somebody" litany is designed to say to all of us, I may be poor, uneducated, unskilled, prematurely pregnant, on drugs, or victimized by racism—whether black, brown, red, yellow, or white—but I still count. I am somebody! I must be respected, protected, and never neglected, because I am important and valuable to myself and others. I am a unique and significant person with hopes, dreams, and aspirations that must be encouraged and developed rather than crushed or ignored. The acceptance, in word and deed, of this idea, this premise, this feeling, is the first step to achieving a brighter future for millions of our children and our society. People who feel good about themselves will care about and help other people.

In education, we are confronted with collapse. But analysis is not enough; we must show a way out. The crisis is dialectical. On the one hand, we must demand equal opportunity, but on the other we must demand superior effort. If our students watch five hours of television every day and study for only two hours—choosing entertainment over education—we cannot move from mediocrity to excellence. Our students must be convinced that if they can conceive it and believe it, they can achieve it. They must know that it is not their aptitude but their attitude that will determine their altitude, with a little intestinal fortitude. We cannot become so preoccupied with the five Bs—budgets, buildings, blacks, browns, and busing—that we forget about the five As—getting our students' *attention*, their *attendance*, changing the *atmosphere* around education, and affecting their *attitude*, which will result in *achievement*. We must keep the As and Bs in balance and in perspective. It does not really matter if the doors of opportunity swing wide open if our students are too drunk to stagger through them. It doesn't really matter if a teacher has a Ph.D. or "no-D" if our students don't show up for class. It doesn't really matter if the teacher is black or white if our students are antisocial toward both.

In many ways we live in an economic jungle, but we have sharp tools to cut through the vines—minds, votes, dollars, and each other. Too often, however, we have focused on the minor and lost sight of the major. We have put too much of our focus on the schoolyard and lost sight of the shipyard. Integration in the schoolyard *does not* threaten America—in fact it will help us—but unfair trade and slave-labor competition in the shipyard *does* threaten us.

On May 13, in Norfolk, Virginia, we marched ten thousand people on city hall to protest an attempt to resegregate the schools. But if those ten thousand people had marched, instead, to the shipyard in Portsmouth, they would have seen Honda and Toyota, Suzuki and Yamaha, Sony and Panasonic and Nikon being unloaded at the docks and replacing Buick and Chrysler, Harley Davidson, Zenith, Motorola, and Kodak in the American marketplace. The schoolyard—social policy—is not our problem; indeed, it is our solution. The shipyard—economic policy—is where we must focus our attention. And if we turn *to* each other and not *on* each other, nothing and nobody can stop us from achieving our place in the sun.

Our presence here today is an expression of the genius of our democracy. Historically, women, and, until twenty years ago, blacks, Hispanics, youth, and poor whites, were locked out of the system. The methods of poll taxes, literacy tests, grandfather clauses, and violence denied people the right to vote. But twenty years later, we've made a transition within the law. Democracy is making room for all of us. Now we need not explode through riots nor implode through drugs. We can use the potent weapon of the vote in this democracy to bring about change.

The triumph within our democracy is that we can change the nation's course through elections and not through revolution. The great sin in a democracy is detachment and noninvolvement. Democracy guarantees participation—not domination. Democracy guarantees opportunity— not success. Democracy guarantees one's personal choice—not a perfect choice. Democracy guarantees the right to choose—not the right to win. All of us must exercise our right to choose. We must play the game by one set of rules and be mutually supportive. One key must fit every door in the democracy. Thus we should not be legislated in by the federal government and then regulated out by the states and the political forces who want to change the rules to make it more difficult for us to win. Rules like changing state primaries to caucuses. Rules like 20-percent thresholds. Rules like winner-take-all and winner-take-more. But our journey from hate to healing, from slave ship to championship, will not be complete until we, without restraint based on race, sex, or religion, can go from our house to the state house to the court house to the White House. We must be allowed to suffer and serve at every level of our nation.

The search is for common ground. We now have the opportunity to choose a new vision, a new course, and a new coalition. We must focus more on the shipyard and less on the schoolyard. A multicultural educational system does not threaten our way of life—in fact, it is therapy for our way of life. But unfair competition between the American worker and corporate robots and American business going to cheap labor markets abroad, replacing American workers, is a threat. There has been a collapse in auto, steel, electronics, rubber, and textiles because of corporate greed, mismanagement, and new world competition.

When I was a little boy growing up in Greenville, South Carolina, we used to go downtown to a store on the corner. And there was this dog listening to his master's voice. There is a lot more advertising on television now than then, but I've not seen that dog on television lately listening to his master's voice. I did a little research. I found that it was an English-trained dog, but his master is now speaking German and Japanese.

It is not enough for the rejected to go from protest to politics; we must go from protest to politics to parity. *Parity*, not merely participation, is the new watchword. Affirmative action, to offset negative action, is democracy's commitment to equal opportunity. Affirmative action is necessary because 90 percent of the $25,000–plus jobs still belong to white males—which reflects the distribution of neither genius nor merit. But even affirmative action in the context of plant removals and new international competition must take on new meaning. White male workers are not losing their jobs through affirmative action to blacks, Hispanics, and women. American workers—white, black, and Hispanic, male and female, young and old—are losing their jobs because corporate America is shipping capital and jobs to cheap labor markets abroad—Taiwan, South Korea, and South Africa.

If a young man wooed your daughter, promised her love, and received affection in return, married her, together they had a family and provided each other with economic and emotional security, you would proudly claim him as your son-in-law. But, if one day he suddenly left her with nothing because he was attracted to another lover, you would consider him an outlaw not an in-law.

Yet this is exactly what corporate America has done to communities all across America. They courted cities, received tax breaks and consumer dollars, and promised jobs, taxes, and economic stability in return. Then one day they just packed up and left the community high and dry. These corporate outlaws and rapists must be challenged and their behavior rehabilitated and redirected. Affirmative action must be expanded and redefined to include affirming the American worker and his or her community and prohibiting American corporations from engaging in such negative action at home and abroad.

A new public policy will set this nation on a course of reindustrialization, reeducating and retraining our work force. "Put America back to work" must become the rallying cry of the American people. This administration gave corporate America a three-year $750 billion tax break, an investment made by the American taxpayer. We thought we were getting a reindustrialization program, a growth program, a jobs program. Instead, American industry used this money to replace people with machines, to grow through diversification and record mergers, and to leave the American labor market for cheap international labor markets, usually under totalitarian regimes. For this $750 billion investment, a new public policy must demand returns to the investors, to the American people. Those companies who do must be granted "favored corporate status." If the government does not assume a responsible position and a responsibility for *all* of the American people, and corporate America will not, then the people suffer in total rejection.

Our national security is being threatened from within because of a shaky and unjust distribution of our economic wealth and by waste, fraud, and abuse in the military. We must have tax reform that is fair to all. And nobody should question any American's, but especially black America's, commitment to providing for a strong national defense. We were the first to die in the American Revolutionary War. Never in the history of the nation has any black person ever been convicted of treason. We volunteer disproportionately for the armed services and die disproportionately in military service to our country. As we meet this afternoon, Lt. Robert Goodman languishes as a Syrian prisoner of war after being shot down over Lebanon. We sacrifice the most, yet we have the least rank in the armed services.

But a new course must define national security in broader terms than just military might. We need a strong national defense; that is the first duty of government. But waste, fraud, and abuse resulting in $750 billion in military cost overruns add nothing to our national defense. And a sick, illiterate, ill-housed, malnourished, unemployed people is more of a threat to our nation's security than a mythical Russian bear coming through an imaginary window of vulnerability.

The $750 billion in cost overruns has nothing to do with defense or with the morale of our soldiers. Over the next five years, each state could receive $15 billion from the projected cost overruns of the military budget alone. Speaking of birds, if hawks support a $1.6 trillion military budget, and doves support less than that, what kind of bird (besides a dodo bird) supports the cost overruns which benefit neither national defense, military personnel, nor the state? It simply lines a few individuals' and a few corporations' pocketbooks.

We must choose a higher ground. There is enough wealth in the nation to make education and reeducation available to all based on the will and ability to learn. There is enough wealth in this country to make quality health care available to those who are sick and need to get well. We must remove the remaining barriers to full political participation—dual registration, second primaries, gerrymandering, annexation, at-large elections, and inaccessible registrars. The most natural allies—the have-somes, the have-littles, and the have-nots, both black and white—

must come together and fight for change, fight for a new public policy and a humane course.

As leaders, we must remove the cataracts of race from the eyes of our people and lift them out of poverty, ignorance, disease, and fear. We must lift the boats that are stuck on the bottom. We must not blind them with prayer clauses, drape them in flags, and give them hot feelings of false racial pride when they remain hungry, ignorant, and diseased in the wealthiest nation in the history of the world. If our people can learn to play together on the ball field and die together on the battlefield, then we can teach them the value of turning to each other to improve their economic and social conditions, rather than turning on each other in racial and economic hostility.

Right here in this legislature, we must elevate people from the battleground, find a common ground, and then move on to a higher ground. Your "common ground" and "higher ground" cooperation on the Alabama redistricting map is a sign that you are prepared to do just that. You have made more progress in fair and equitable representation than the state legislatures of New York and New Jersey in that regard. For that you are to be commended.

The South need not remain the poorest region of the nation. If we disallow others to rob and rape us economically—and stop bruising each other economically and psychologically—the South can rise again. But in its rising, it will be a New South—a South where the sons and daughters of former slaves and former slavemasters sit around a common table of humanity and drink from the cup of mercy and justice. We must forgive each other, redeem each other, regroup, and move to higher ground. The rejected stones can become the cornerstones of a new progressive coalition in America who will help to reshape a new domestic and world order. Blacks and whites, rich and poor, young and old, male and female must be prepared to share power and responsibility.

What do we recommend?

1. We must make democracy real and accessible for everyone. Thus we need a bill that will deputize registrars and make them available to everyone in every precinct in the state of Alabama. Each year thousands of high-school seniors are graduating. They should come across the stage at graduation time with a diploma in one hand, symbolizing knowledge and wisdom, and a voter registration card in the other, symbolizing power and responsibility.

2. There must be a continuing commitment to share power and responsibility. We can no longer just accept integrated voting and continue to practice segregated slate making. Blacks must be allowed to become part of the state ticket—and be supported by the rest of the

party. We must be slated for governor, lieutenant governor, U.S. senator, and congressperson. Everyone who has something to contribute must be respected and included—and we will all benefit. We must end the new forms of denial—gerrymandering, annexation, and at-large schemes. The way to phase out welfare is to phase in our share—of employment, executives, professionals, and trade—at every level of government, coroner to Congress. Let us share.

3. Private industry in the state and nation must be seen as development banks for the underdeveloped. The restraint of private trade must stop. Five of every six jobs in this country are in the private sector. We are seeking trade, not aid; parity, not charity; economic reciprocity, not social generosity. We want economic independence, not social dependence. Such an approach will allow the developed to grow and the underdeveloped to develop. It is a plus for all of us. The procurement budget of the state must be shared by every region and race.

4. The black college must be preserved at all cost. The black college has developed a specialty. It specializes in reaching the so-called unreachable, the so-called unteachable, and gives hope to the rejected. It serves our community and nation well and must continue to receive support. Indeed, it must receive increased support. These schools have taken the rejected stones and turned them into the cornerstones of a new social and economic order.

5. Last, this legislature must assume a national responsibility. I hope you will hold hearings on the number of jobs lost from the import-export imbalance. After your state hearings, Governor Wallace, with whom we met yesterday, could use his considerable influence to convene the governors of the southern region—ten southern governors—in an economic summit conference on imports and exports. Ten southern states could use the $150 billion in their share of the military budget cost overruns. These ten states could demand economic accountability from corporations that receive investment from the taxpayer.

Today, this is a marvelous place from which to speak. A place where Jefferson Davis stood, where Martin Luther King, Jr., should have stood. But this has been a marvelous day. We serve a merciful God who keeps on giving us chances to make a difference.

Not too far from here a prophet, Martin Luther King, Jr., stood. And perhaps he was too close for you to see; or perhaps he was too far away for you to hear; or perhaps the prophet remains without honor in his own hometown. But he did say that one day we would learn to live together as brothers and sisters or we would surely die apart as fools. There is a higher ground. There is a higher ground.

Many years ago, Charles Wesley wrote:

A charge to keep I have,
    A God to glorify.
A never dying soul to save,
    And fit it for the sky.
To serve the present age,
    My calling to fulfill;
O may it all my power engage
    To do my master's will.

Today we can make a choice. We can choose to live and not to destroy. We can choose life over death, help over hate, reason over race, and character over color. People of the world, this day Alabama can move from battleground to common ground to higher ground. This day the God that we serve—if we will just trust him in all of our ways—will still open the Red Sea; he'll still lock the lion's jaw; he'll still save us from the fiery furnace; he'll still make our enemies leave us alone; he'll still make the lion lie down with the lamb; he'll still make easy our way; he'll still make crooked roads straight; he'll still raise us; he'll still raise us from the guttermost to the uttermost; if we will but trust him. He will raise all of us from disgrace to amazing grace.

God bless you, and thank you very much.

Religious Liberty:
Civil Disobedience, Conscience,
and Survival

Jackson presented this speech to a Bicentennial
Conference on Religious Liberty in Philadelphia on
April 27, 1976.

I am honored and privileged to be a part of this religious celebration. I am concerned that we in this conference, at this moment in history, attempt to address ourselves in the most profound ways that we can to organize to make a difference in this world. I want to speak about "Religious Liberty: Civil Disobedience, Conscience, and Survival."

When engaging in civil disobedience, the weight of proof is almost always on the individual, for the state is a mass of individuals and a more constant and responsible entity. The impersonal nature of the state deprives it ultimately of feelings and thus reduces persons to cogs in a wheel. The state at best is capable of justice but not love—though a totally sharp line need not be drawn. Primarily, though, we need a balance of *power.*

The state at its best serves God-like functions—it distributes justice and mercy, goods and services; protects and shields; produces and provides. Seldom is the state at its best, and usually it is capable of being dispassionate, impersonal, and tyrannical. Most people would rather switch than fight.

But the cross—the high hill of conscientious objection—stands between life and death, fear and courage, freedom and slavery, mortality and immortality. Thus when Christians choose the way of the cross— the way of integrity, involvement, and intelligence (the way of "not my will, but thine," the way of a higher calling)—they take a cross from around their necks and put it on their backs and move from admiring Jesus to following him. Thus they accept the freedom and assume the responsibility of conscience.

Conscience is the pursuit of higher law, the authority to discern just law from unjust law. A just law is a law made for one group and when applied is acceptable to all. It is a just law because it has universal character. An unjust law is made by one group for its advantage but does not offer the same services or options to others.

The sense to discern and the freedom to choose obligates one to bear the cross or pay the penalty until a crucifixion is transformed into a resurrection.

The divine authority by which you speak must help you bear the weight of raising the general consciousness to your level of perception— e.g., Mahatma Gandhi in India; Dr. Martin Luther King, Jr., in his civil rights struggles; Jesus Christ on Calvary—all the result of civil disobedience.

Unearned suffering is redemptive, and truth ultimately prevails. A judgment has to be made. There must be a moral relationship between the people and the issues raised. The means by which they live must be consistent with the ends for which they live.

The appointments of government may lead to rebellion for selfish reasons, but the anointment of God may lead to authentic civil disobedience or objection to the state. The laws of convenience lead to collapse, but the laws of sacrifice lead to greatness.

Proverbs 30:7–9 reminds us to seek this sense of balance and responsibility. The writer says, Two things I require—don't give me too much or I'll ask "who is God?"; but don't give me too little or I'll steal and defame your name.

I conscientiously object to spending all my time discussing conscience and civil disobedience while our movement for liberation has been slowed down by blurred vision and an ethical collapse. Thus I want to expand my remarks to include the present stage of our struggle and what we must do concretely to overcome the present state of spiritual decadence and despair.

The handwriting on the wall of history requires a serious, scientific, and sober assessment of these times. First, we must actually assess and then meet the demands of these particular times.

The first major period for us as a people on these North American shores was a period of "no government." We were denied citizenship rights. It was illegal for us to own land; illegal for us to marry; illegal for us to be educated; illegal for us to vote. Constitutionally, we were considered three-fifths human. We were in a period of "no government," slavery, or colonialism.

The next stage we call "semi-government" or neocolonialism. This was a period in which we had more rights, but inasmuch as we did not have all of our rights, this period, too, was insufficient.

Politically, we always had to choose between two evils. If one dared to smile, we called that person "liberal." If one snarled, we called that person "conservative." But both belonged to the same church, the same country club, and were educated together. However, a smile was so much more pleasing than a whiplash! We gave our support to the coalition.

In the period of "no government," only our brawn or our muscle was considered valuable. In "semi-government," most of our brawn and only a little of our brain was considered necessary. We were able to participate and benefit only to the extent that it was to the advantage and self-interest of our partner in the coalition. Thus we were pawns rather than partners in a power struggle. We played ball, but they coached and owned the team. We went to school, but they ran the administration. We lived in the cities, but they ran the government. We read the books, but they wrote them. This period of "semi-government" was a period of tremendous contrast with slavery, yet it left us undeveloped and underdeveloped because it did not demand of many of us the sense of responsibility and use of mind that free people must have.

As a result of our marching feet and the creative and courageous leadership of Dr. Martin Luther King, Jr., we acquired a Public Accommodations Bill in 1964 and a Voting Rights Bill in 1965. Once these rights were gained, however, our yearning for freedom was translated into a yearning for power. The fiery flames of Watts and Newark were such symbols. The cries of Black Power and the ballot in our hands began to burn away the clouds of inferiority and semifreedom. We were ushered into a new period called "self-government." This is, by far, the most challenging period. It requires of us the full use of our minds and bodies, our wits and intuition, our feelings and our spirituality. The sum total of our being will be required to hold this mountain and to man this fort.

Self-government, this awesome new responsibility, demands the pursuit of excellence in every facet of life as the only protection from extinction or a return to slavery. Our only protection against genocide is to remain necessary. This yearning for self-government required our putting together several steps by which we measure where we are.

First, we had to identify the oppressor. We identified it as the ideology of racism prevalent in every facet, in every institution, of American life—home, church, school, labor, and management.

Second, we had to accept the challenge of finding ways to stop the oppressor. Thus we had to struggle. We had to hang. We had to march. We had to go to court. We had to pray. We had to do all of this and more.

Third, we had to replace the oppressor. We did it fundamentally through the electoral process. In Washington, D.C., today, we have a black mayor, a predominantly black city council, a black school superintendent, a black congressman, and virtually an all-black city. There we reside in the belly of the whale, just ten years after the Voting Rights Bill. In a mere ten years, on one level, amazing political progress has been made.

When we went to Selma in 1965, we had only three black congressmen. Today we have seventeen congresspersons. We went there with two million registered black voters. Today we have eight million. We went there with no black mayors. Today we have 130. We went there with four hundred black elected and appointed officials; today we have slightly over four thousand—including two lieutenant governors and a U.S. senator.

There is significance in this growth as a direct action movement begins to use the political lever, for it means that we can no longer be discounted, can no longer be publically insulted—unless someone is willing to pay a severe penalty of defeat or political extinction. In 1960 Kennedy beat Nixon by 118,000 votes. It was an enthusiastic black vote—because he helped get Dr. King out of jail in Albany, Georgia— that made the difference. In 1968 Nixon beat Humphrey by 550,000 votes. It was an unenthusiastic black vote that meant the difference. Dr. King had been assassinated. Robert Kennedy had been assassinated. The war was still raging in Vietnam. In our frustration, we threw away more than a million and a half votes in a futile effort in the California Freedom party.* The point is, the difference between the winning of Nixon and the losing of Humphrey was the lack of an enthusiastic black vote.

Thus between 1960 and 1968, two presidents won by less than seven hundred thousand votes. Now what does our seven million votes mean? It really means that hands that picked cotton in 1966 can pick presidents in 1976. Thus our options in some measure have changed. On the other hand, just as there are eight million black registered voters, there are eight million unregistered. Just as there was a hopeful and progressive spirit that brought in a relative political and material prosperity, there is a measure of decadence and despair threatening to slow down that Freedom Train.

Lest we forget, no candidate can ignore us now. In 1972, we were 25.7

---

*An independent party on the California ballot in 1968 composed of peace and civil rights activists who were disaffected with the Democratic party.

percent of the national Democratic vote. Prior to Mr. Carter's "slip of the lip" earlier this year,* there was some notion that the black vote could be ignored. After all, there is not much evidence that blacks will go Republican en masse. The black vote is so dominant now in the Democratic party that we can defeat this party: (1) by going Republican; (2) by staying home because of a lack of enthusiasm; or (3) supporting a third-party effort. Thus we cannot be ignored. With this strategic position, no one can say we are impotent. In fact, all must say that we are important. With such a strategic position increasing our chances of self-determination, we must be more effective, more just, and provide more service than the previous stages of no government and semi-government. That is the responsibility of self-government.

If we do not, the fourth stage will set in—the period of counterrevolution and backlash. A loss of confidence will follow. We must assess these times. My basic premise is that nobody will save us for us but us. Self-control precedes community control. We must love ourselves properly before we can love others adequately—but we must know the power of love.

For most of us, this adjustment to self-government requires putting new demands on ourselves and on each other. We must not fear the change we seek. If I might give you an example: you must use one strategy going up the mountain, but another strategy is required to stay on the mountain. There once was a long trip from Egypt to Canaan. It only required courage to overcome fear—to identify the oppressor by ethnicity and leave Egypt. But to stay in Canaan required more than ethnicity. It required ethics, internal moral discipline, economics, and education. Pharaoh never assumed the responsibility for the development of the escapees or the refugees. That is as true today as it was then. Thus I contend, nobody will save us for us but us.

Let us view self-government. In self-government we have the mayor of our choice; our own school principals; our own superintendent of schools; and yet our most precious commodity—the lives of our children—are found weighing in the balance. To save them is our tremendous work. To create a posterity for which all of us can be justly proud is our high calling. The crisis in which we find our children and ourselves is so national, so nasty, and so dangerous that all of us must be involved. It is everybody's assignment.

We can't escape our responsibility through dope, alcohol, sex, philosophy, or religion. We must be involved. Parents, life begins in the bedroom, it is developed in the classroom, and it is directed from the

*During his campaign, Carter more than once spoke approvingly about preserving the "ethnic purity" of neighborhoods. Many interpreted this as racially insensitive and as an appeal to white voters.

board room. If, when the physical umbilical cord is cut, the spiritual umbilical cord is not connected, we have failed in the bedroom, the classroom will become a detention center, and as a result there never will be power in the board room. All of us must give the best of what each has to offer to this struggle. Parents must supply the spiritual nutrients that no government can offer—motivation, care, discipline, chastisement, and love.

Children must be involved in their own destiny. Children cannot play the game "you can teach me if you can catch me." Our children must assume their responsibility as well. They must put forth effort, practice, time, and belief in education as well as have the will to learn.

Teachers must engage in rigorous preparation, inspiration, dedication, and the best of instruction. The principal must be the moral authority who demands discipline which results in development. Administrators must justify an adequate budget, set policy, and interpret the system. The media must reward achievement, and the preacher must see education as God's will—as part of our moral responsibility. All must be involved.

Our theme is "PUSH for Excellence." We know we are in a desert, but the challenge is to make flowers bloom in the desert. Parents must hew a firm foundation out of the soil and the rock. They must become copartners with professional educators as architects and designers to build a new creation.

There are economic factors contributing to this crisis. There is a national epidemic of failure in our public schools along with an ethical collapse in our civilization. There is the lack of an effective national urban policy, evidence of racism, and the frequent disruptions caused by the struggle against inequities. But there are also noneconomic factors contributing to this crisis that cannot be explained away simply by poverty, except the most destitute.

Our problem is that we are living in a state of political decadence. The sum total of a lot of individual decadence has set a political climate. Thus what once was a solid foundation where people took little and did much now is an acid base, and nothing grows in acid—neither children, nor houses, nor dreams. We must change our attitudinal disposition toward life, toward education, and toward religion. The change must come from the bottom up. No psychological godfather is going to wake us up one night and save us from this nightmare. No Savior will ascend to the throne in the White House. Nobody will save us for us but us.

Ultimately, the only way to stop drugs from flowing in the schools is for children's arms and nasal cavities to cease being a market. This student participation in the drug traffic represents a breakdown in morally sound conduct and rational behavior. My visits to schools around the nation reveal that there is a breakdown in moral authority, discipline, and thus development. I distinguish moral authority from legal and/or tyrannical authority.

Our organization PUSH has as its symbol a pyramid. The left side of the pyramid represents economic generation, the right side spiritual regeneration, and the base represents discipline. With regard to economic generation, our emphasis is on both private and public economic policy. We want houses and jobs. We want the traditional material goals. We want community control, but we know that neither man nor woman can live by bread alone. There is another longing, a need for spiritual regeneration which emphasizes self-control. Discipline, however, is at the base of economic generation and spiritual regeneration.

We know that personal will and sound values are essential to human progress. Even the absence of racism is not the presence of justice. The absence of Wallace doesn't necessarily mean the presence of a good candidate. The death of ethics is the sabotage of excellence. The aftermath of our rebellion, like the afterbirth material which follows the birth of a child, must be removed from both the mother and child—lest the germs kill them both. This, too, is true in the aftermath of a successful rebellion. There are remains which must be cleaned up and removed in order for the true purpose of the revolution to be fulfilled.

Extremes have begun to set in. Confusion too often is the result. Many stopped being servile, which was legitimate; but now they don't even want to be of service—and that's illegitimate. The general rebellion against all authority must stop. We must be sober enough to be discriminating. We must distinguish between that which must be revered from that which must be rebelled against in order that our action might have meaning. There is a difference between being mean and being meaningful. Many rightfully stopped working for nothing, but some do not see the value of working for something. Work is important. Beyond wages, however, character formation, identity, self-esteem, self-fulfillment, and mental stability are all associated with work and achievement. The servant is worthy of his hire, and the job must afford the worker wages, but we must work. When we are deprived of a job, we lose more than money. We rebelled against tyrannical authority, but now we are rebelling against all authority—parental, educational, moral, and religious. That is unsound.

The value of God-consciousness as a part of the cosmic hierarchy has been slowly removed from the experience of this generation of young people. Thus some of the sickness that we see manifesting itself is the product of a publicly godless generation.

Most of us still live in a three-tiered cosmos: there is God's domain, the human domain, and land—a material domain. When we remove God from his domain and engage in the cosmic domain as though we're

STRAIGHT FROM THE HEART

self-sufficient, then human beings project themselves into God's domain and play God. People can only *play* God; they can't *be* God. They can put their names on buildings and highways or try to buy or build immortality through some tangible material means. They can fly higher than birds and swim deeper than fish. They can play God for a minute in history. But when human beings play God, then land and materialism rise up and are valued at the level where man and woman, boy and girl used to be. As a result, we now respect and revere cars and rings like we used to respect boys and girls. The tragedy of that disruption of the cosmos is that God is not really moved. It's just an illusion. The problem is that people move and change, and their illusion never stays. Thus they have no foundation, and without a foundation there is a bottomless pit of degradation.

If children will not give deference to God—the origin, the Creator of creation—ultimately, those children will not give deference to their parents, their teachers, their brothers, or their sisters. If we will not accept God as Father, there is no basis for accepting each other as brothers and sisters. God must have his domain. In our schools, when prayer came out, pistols went in. When hope came out, dope went in. Choose the God of your choice, but don't play games with the Creator. You can change his name, but not his claim. He's God anyhow.

It is fully clear to me that the death of ethics is the sabotage of excellence. What difference does it make if a teacher gives a child homework if the parent does not make the child stay home to do the work? What difference does it make if children have a new book or an old book if they never open either? What does it matter if children's classmates are black or white if they are antisocial toward both?

There is still something basic (not conservative) about reading, writing, counting, preparation, rhythm, repetition, trial, and error. We still must learn the theory, practice the theory, and eventually become masters! These steps to greatness are the same for singers, dancers, preachers, actors, ball players, conservatives, and liberals. The note of greatness is the same key on the universal keyboard. There is no shortcut to greatness. The controversies over busing, desegregation, budget, equal representation all have to do with adult power struggles—and very legitimate power struggles. But more basic than that in all schools is the presupposition that there is a *will* to learn and an *urge for excellence*. When that spiritual quality dies, a new school building is no compensation.

On the present acid base, where in too many instances the desire to be somebody has died, racism can't kill us because cynicism gets us first. We're experiencing a situation where death has changed its name from

Southern rope to Northern dope. Genocide can't get us because homicide, fratricide, and suicide already have.

With this present acid base, other judgments are premature. How can we judge teachers when they do not even have the climate in which to practice their trade? To judge some of our teachers in this atmosphere of guns, knives, threats, and violence is like sending Hank Aaron to bat with a popsicle stick or Muhammad Ali into the ring with one glove on and his other hand tied behind his back. Until the rules are set straight and the axis is put back in place, everything else is logically out of order.

What do we do? Do we play in a corner and evolve a theology of self-love, self-beautification, and self-preoccupation? Do we go off into our little cubbyhole and start playing and eating grass and apples? Whether we're shouting or being quiet, we cannot remain theologically sound and stay detached from the real problems of this world. We contend that we must organize on a school-by-school basis, citywide councils of students for discipline and against drugs, racism, and violence. We must give them the option to come forward. We cannot do that if we are detached from them. We must also organize citywide councils of educators for discipline and against racism, drugs, and violence—as well as preachers, parents, communicators, and others. Our publicly licensed radio must stop the glorification of mass decadence. When in Rome, we cannot act as Romans. We must transform Rome.

We must stop the institutional undercutting of exaggerated doubt about educational pursuits in our children's minds. Some ministers naively do this by suggesting: "Get all the education you want, but get Jesus"—as if there were some conflict there! On the other side, some educators say: "Shout and be as righteous as you please, but you better learn how to read and write." The fact of the matter is: Preachers need to go to school; teachers need to go to church; and parents and children need to do both. The institutional undercutting needs to stop.

At night, it is not enough to tell ABC, CBS, and NBC, "Don't put violence on my television." Parents must be home to turn the television off, whether it is violent or nonviolent. We can't keep passing the buck on everything. We should stop sending report cards home by the children. Parents ought to come to school to pick them up. That is their responsibility. They must get involved en masse.

I was on a program with Dr. Robert Schuller some months ago. He said, "Reverend, you came from a segregated South Carolina, took abuse and humiliation, and went to jail. Why aren't you bitter toward Southern white people? They discriminated against you." I said, "Because I assumed there was something wrong with them, that they were sick. I would not allow them to punish my body *and* my soul. Even in punishment, I had the option of how I would respond to pain. I know it is not your aptitude but your attitude that determines your altitude, with a little intestinal fortitude. No matter what yesterday's strife, today is still the first day of the rest of your life. If you bring all of the burdens, aches, and agonies of history on today's shoulder, you'll be too weighted down to walk into the future even if the doors are wide open. We rehearse and rehearse history until we carefully bear all the burdens of yesterday's wars and lose the capacity to forgive and redeem because we've got too much trash on our shoulders."

Someone said: "What was the high experience for you in education? Was it elementary school or high school? Was it the University of Illinois, North Carolina A & T, or the University of Chicago Graduate School? Where was it?" As I reflect, it was the first day I started school. My mother took me to school and told Miss Georgeanna Robinson, "This is my boy. I want you to help me develop him. He gets out of hand every now and then; therefore you might have to chastise him. If you do, send a note home, and he'd better bring it. If I don't see you at the PTA because I work at night, I'll see you at church on Sunday." For you see, Miss Robinson taught public school Monday through Friday, but she taught Sunday school on Sunday. She realized that there was a relationship between intellectual and character development. She took me down to Mr. Graham's office to reinforce the discipline. They disciplined me to teach me how to discipline myself.

With the home (not the house, but the home—we never did have a house made of brick and mortar, but we had a home made of love and prayer and some other kinds of things you can't record on paper), church, and school—I was trapped in a love triangle into which not even segregation and barbarism could break. There is the ability to be in the fiery furnace and escape unburned, with not even the smell of smoke—if one has religious immunity, not escapism.

Our public schools have become too informal. There is not the resilience that must exist there. We must have new definitions of men and women. Too many of our young men think they are men if they kill somebody—as opposed to being a man because they heal somebody. We've never struggled to teach nonviolence in the schools.

Many think they are men because they can make a baby, not because they can raise a baby. Many girls stoop to the distortion of abortion because they are not educated to appreciate life. They walk as hunks of sex, and boys fall for the bait, and then both, out of passion, panic. We fail to deal with the ramification of the devaluation of human life. Some even suggest that having babies is a woman's role. Women can't make babies by themselves, nor can men—though they can be irresponsible when they've planted the seed. Life must be maintained as the highest value in this cosmic order, and when abortion chairs and convenience become more basic than children, even the religious objectors become extensions of the decadence.

We exaggerate the importance of the time from conception to birth— nine months. No man can become pregnant. No man can have a baby. Most probably couldn't stand the pain. Our great contribution as men really begins at birth, not at conception. But functional definitions of manhood and womanhood are so messed up that there is no appropriate imagery from birth up to age eighteen—where the real struggle is. The real struggle begins there, because that's where the failures are.

I went to a horse race one time down in Miami, Florida. I was down there with Reverend Jones and some other ministers at a conference. I don't know how I ended up at a horse race except I'd heard about Hialeah, and the Bible said "Go ye into all the world." I figured Hialeah was part of the world, so I went there that afternoon to do a little basic observation. While there I was telling some of my friends, "I've never been to a race before." Like a preacher, I'm always searching for a sermon in everything.

I noticed they had lines in front of little cages—$2 windows, $5 windows, $10, and on up to the $100 window. At the $2 window, there was a long—*long*—line of people. The $100 window had just a few people. The people who were buying the $2 tickets all had hot dogs, peanuts, and beer and were talking very loud. The food they had in their hands cost more than the ticket. They were determined to make money at the track. They were eating hot dogs, drinking beer, chewing peanuts, and talking loud. The people at the $100 window were not talking loud. Some of them had cigars in their mouths and binoculars around their necks.

Finally someone said, "It's time for the race to start!" The people with the $2 tickets kept drinking beer, eating hot dogs, chewing peanuts, and talking loud. Those with the $100 tickets went over near the starting gate. They went as close as the ushers would allow them. The race was about to start. The people with the $100 tickets took their binoculars out to make certain their horse was not lame and nothing funny happened at the starting gate.

But the people with the $2 tickets were up in the stands by this time— eating hot dogs, drinking beer, chewing peanuts, and talking loud. Then the race started, and the horses were off and running. The people with the $100 tickets were up on their tiptoes, nervously looking at their horses racing down the track. The people with the $2 tickets continued eating hot dogs, drinking beer, chewing peanuts, and talking loud.

The horses made the first turn—and the people with the $100 tickets looked as far as their binoculars could see. Finally, you couldn't see because of the hedges. They stood there looking nervous. But the people with the $2 tickets were eating hot dogs, drinking beer, chewing peanuts, and talking loud.

When the horses came down the final stretch they were very close together. The top four money winners began to emerge because the jockeys who had been riding the horses all the way got low and close and tightened up the bridle with the left hand, using the stick on the horse's butt as they came down the straightaway. Those who had been eating hot dogs, drinking beer, chewing peanuts, and talking loud came rushing past the gate, trying to knock over the usher, cussing and raising hell, trying to find out where their tickets were, and trying to snap pictures at the end.

No matter what the state of affairs of political and economic war and peace are, as long as the masses of the people are being avoided by those of us who assume we control the truth, so long as the masses are allowed to sit in the stands eating hot dogs, drinking beer, chewing peanuts, and talking loud, no real progress is going to be made.

It reminds me of school. In September only a few parents are there with their children as they start to school. Most parents only come at graduation time, rudely knocking each other over, knocking the teachers over, taking pictures, looking at their little incomplete, half-developed, immoral, sweet little child. Killer, robber, racist—graduates with no information because while the work was going on they were sitting around.

Nobody will save us for us but us. Whether we conscientiously cooperate or conscientiously resist, unless that acid is dried up and turned to rock, no one can survive. We *can* survive because we serve a mighty God. We *can* survive because we can overcome our cynicism and our negativism, but our analysis must be accurate and sound. Our diagnosis must be true, even if it indicts us, if our future is to be any different.

COMFORTER

"We live as if life is certain and death is uncertain. But death is certain! Death is another one of God's promises. It challenges our immaturity and makes us face the responsibility to live on in spite of. Death bids us be prepared. Weeping may endure for a night, but joy cometh in the morning."

Genius and Master of Music: Eulogy for Donny Hathaway

Donny Hathaway was born in Chicago on October 1, 1945, and grew up in St. Louis. He was a well-known gospel singer when he was but three years old. In addition to writing and performing his own music, he served as arranger, composer, performer, and producer for artists such as Curtis Mayfield and the Impressions, Roberta Flack, Jerry Butler, the Staple Singers, and Woody Herman. Hathaway plunged to his death from the window of a New York City hotel under unknown circumstances. Jackson preached this eulogy on January 21, 1979.

There is an eternal and universal struggle between life and death. Death and despair have brought us to this place. Life and hope will take us away from this place. Life has both mystery and meaning. It is our duty today to interpret and to inspire. We seek the truth as our key to understanding and liberation. We are taught that the truth will make us free.

Tragedy has the master key to everybody's house. Death brings to everybody's door a telegram that must be signed. As we grow older, our black hair becomes gray; what was hair becomes bald; our smooth skin becomes wrinkled; our telephone books become obituary columns. These are signs that we are here but a few days, and they are filled with trouble.

We live as if death is uncertain and life is certain. But it is life that is uncertain. Death is certain. Death creates unplanned family reunions. Death makes us humble and accountable. Death deflates our arrogance.

Death reminds us of our finitude, of how limited we are. Death makes us reach for a rock that is higher and a force that is mightier. Death sends us on a search for the God that we take for granted.

There is democracy in death. All of us must come this way. Death is a part of life. It offers us one of life's lessons for which we must prepare and be aware. Those of us who remain still have a chance to get our house in order.

There is no trauma to the living greater than the death of a loved one. A piece of us is torn open. Our love is exposed. Nature moves us to cry and express ourselves. Death is the boundary of our existence. It is the wall that all of us must come to. It separates this life from the next life. Death is too high to go over, too low to go under, and too wide to go around.

Life is the latitude we have before the wall of death. Life is our freedom. Life is our option. In life's freedom, we have the option to choose the high road or the low road, to be loving or hateful, to be mediocre or excellent.

Everyone cannot be famous, that is, well known. But everyone can be great—for everyone can serve. Service is the basis of our greatness; the reason why there is such national interest in this occasion today.

Donny Hathaway, one of the authentic geniuses of our day, was both famous and great. By some route, all of us will walk down roads that lead to this point—a final community celebration. Some come by homicide, some by suicide, some by fratricide, some by genocide, some by accident. But the bottom line is that we all come to this point.

I am not preoccupied with how Donny died. Based upon the information that I have been able to gather from the people who were with him to the very end—people in whom I have trust and confidence and a group of people with whom I'm intimately acquainted—the death of Donny appears to be neither suicide nor homicide but rather an accident. Donny died with his coat and scarf and cap on. It is not likely that one would go through the effort to be fully attired just to jump out of a window. On several occasions, Donny would sing in his room all night, and some hotels put him out, and so he learned to open the window and sing to the wind as a way of not disturbing the guests. Because of a driving compulsion to preach the gospel, Donny would often go out on the ledge at night and preach as a way of realizing the joy of his salvation.

How he died cannot consume our time, but rather how he lived and what he contributed. His legacy is music. The genius of Hathaway. That he was born, lived, and lives on through music stand as indisputable facts without contradiction. This man, this genius, had a rare combination of soul and science, beat and balance.

When an old man dies, I often feel that his time has come. He has had his chance. Whether he squandered his life or used it well, he had his chance. But when a young man dies I often feel that he has been cheated and robbed of what he might have contributed to humanity. And yet, when Job asked God why so many terrible things had to happen to him, he got no satisfactory answer. God asked, Job, who are you to quibble with the Almighty? But, God, I may choose to ask, "Why is Donny dead at 33? Life has gone. You've taken a genius. What can we do?"

Only three things. First, we can console the bereaved family and friends who are left. This we must do, for grief is like a heavy load. When shared, it is easier to bear. Friends everywhere want to help carry this heavy load.

Second, we can exhort the living to an emulation of the virtures of the deceased, and it might well be that Donny will influence our lives in death even more than he did in life. We must remember that time is a great element in the solution of all problems.

Third, we can trust God and rely on our faith. When the philosophers have philosophized and the theologians have theologized and the poets have framed their verse, we are all driven to rely on the everlasting arms of Almighty God.

This is why I believe in immortality. There must be a place somewhere where Donny can fulfill his dreams. I continue to use the term "genius." I do not use this word lightly or inadvisedly. There are three basic characteristics of a genius:

1. *Prodigy.* Mozart, at four years of age, could tell when violins were out of tune. From ages six to fifteen, he was on tour across Europe playing clavier, organ, and violin. In terms of prodigy, Donny Pitts, known to us as Donny Hathaway, at age three, was touted as the world's youngest gospel singer accompanied by his own instrument.

Donny was considered by Howard University School of Music as one of the two greatest natural talents that had matriculated there (Andre Watts, the classical pianist, the other). They could not teach Donny but could only expose him to new musical avenues.

Donny did not listen to popular music or rhythm and blues until he was at Howard University at age eighteen.

2. Geniuses are *prolific.* Schubert, like Mozart, was one of the fastest writers in musical history. He could conceive a whole work in his head and write it down in a very short period. Donny was prolific. Donny was able to create original compositions in classical, pop, jazz, rhythm and blues, big band, instrumentals, and gospel music.

Donny composed, conducted, and scored a major studio movie, *Come Back, Charleston Blue,* after substituting for Quincy Jones, despite never having done such before. He completed it all in just two weeks. He reduced the chart to detailed mathematics and commented that it was simple deduction. Donny wrote two symphonies in 1973. When Kenya was born, he wrote a symphony in thirty days.

3. *Conflict.* Because of being absorbed in their art, geniuses find themselves in conflict with the world and with themselves. For example, Mozart's biographer says of him, "For just as this rare being early became man so far as his art was concerned, he always remained, as the impartial observer must say of him, in almost all other instances, a child. He never learned to rule himself for domestic order, for sensible management of money, for moderation and wise choice and pleasures. He had no feeling. He always needed a guiding hand. The last ten years of Mozart's life were full of stress and creativity. He felt that his new life in Vienna was against his father's wishes."

Donny also knew conflict and felt in conflict. Because of his childhood, he constantly felt guilt about commercial music. The conflict is best established by "Thank You, Master, for My Soul" on his first album and "I Love the Lord" on his last complete album, where he took a gospel chart and performed it classically. In addition, he was tormented by whether his music was good for God and race.

Geniuses often die young. They get there quicker. Their impact penetrates. It is deeper. Bright lights burn more quickly. It is said that candles that burn at both ends are consumed more quickly. One observer exclaimed, "But, oh, what a beautiful light."

Mozart died at 36 years of age of a kidney disease. Chopin died at 39 of typhoid fever. Mendelssohn at 38. Bellini at 34. Schubert at 31. Dr. King at 39. Jesus at 33. King Tut as a teenager. Donny Hathaway at 33.

Genius can never be explained rationally.

● No one side of town or race or sex or period in history has a monopoly on genius.

● Genius is set aside for some divine purpose. The potential sometimes is realized or actualized and sometimes not, but it always is special.

● Genius is an act of grace, unmerited favor from God.

Music is often the medium for the message of the genius. To reach into outer space and pull the definite out of indefiniteness, requires genius. To pull something out of seeming nothingness. To orchestrate the discordant sounds of the universe into the science of a song. To unfold silence into a symphony is genius.

Donny pulled a message out of this mess age and gave us a mind massage in this mass age.

Five years ago, Donny suffered what is called, in psychological language, a nervous breakdown. After a musical bomb exploded and detonated in Donny's mind, the psychologists told Attorney Franklin, Donny's confidant and friend, that Donny heard eight versions of a song simultaneously, from classical to blues to gospel. From the most complex to the most simple—simultaneously. Donny had empires in his brains. A genius, I tell you.

Donny was a minister and a master of music. The sounds he heard were bigger than labels (plus pop, jazz, rock, gospel, and so forth). He embodied and projected the varied experiences of a people through the medium of music. A genius who remained loyal to his roots, even in the midst of root rejection and misunderstanding, he dared to break out of the box. He never snapped the umbilical cord from his roots. He sang the Lord's song in a strange land. He sang and wrote music of redemption. He sang of *agape*, God's love. He sang of *eros*, romance. He sang of *philia*, the love between brothers and sisters.

Those limited by labels missed the genius of Hathaway. One writer said, and I believe it, "that to live, love, and give 'tis but a greater thing." That is to open the heart and let it sing.

Extension of a Man, an album recorded by Donny, may well be the consummate album conveying the black experience musically. Listen closely to the best of "Come, Little Children," recorded in 1973, and you will hear the pulsation of disco. It was perhaps the first disco record before the international craze began. In "I Know the Lord, He Heard My Cry," Donny took the basic black testimony and life affirmation of the most rejected blacks and gave to that song of hope strings and tuba and harp and psalter and percussions—it is worship.

Donny, the genius, a man with a mind at work. During the last few years, Donny's closest friends, Roberta, Stevie, and David, would often speak of the voices that Donny was hearing. Donny himself spoke to me about the voices. Just last Saturday, Donny had been practicing and rehearsing on his latest album, and he stopped; he heard voices. In Donny, there was inner conflict. He was not just on the edge Saturday night. Like every genius, Donny lived on the cutting edge, just a mere step away from another stratosphere. He heard the voices of the people. He heard the voice of Jesus. He heard voices without name or identity. He heard voices. His soul was at war, in tension.

He had a high-frequency channel with a receptive antenna. He was often on FM when most of us were on AM. Or sometimes on UHF while others were on VHF. Sometimes he heard both channels at the same time, and then there were times when a third channel, new birth, was about to come through. He lived his life on the edge.

There are pictures in this room right now that you cannot see. There are voices in this room that you cannot hear. If you had the antenna of a radio or a TV to receive these sound and picture waves, you'd experience them as you do when you are listening to a radio or watching a TV. Or perhaps, if you had the mind of Donny, you could do the same. Many of us have low antennas and weak receivers, and so we don't live on the edge, and we don't die early and in tragedy, but our long lives, like Methuselah, are nothing but a journey in space occupation that means nothing. Donny was on the edge in a constant state of tension. Tension between the sacred and the secular. Tension between the temporary and the eternal. Tension between nature and destiny. Tension between his background and his foreground. Tension between the defense of music business and the offense of music creativity. Tension between commercial music and pure music. Thus he often marched to the beat of a different drummer on the brink, at the ledge, on the edge.

And so, today, the song ends, but the melody lingers on. In our lives, we know sunrise, a period of birth. We know noon, a period of highest fruition. And we know sunset, the period of death. So long as we can stay in the rhythm of this predictable groove, we feel comfortable. But every now and then the sun is eclipsed at high noon, and there is no sunset. God intercedes, uses his power to make a unilateral entry into the universe to declare himself and make his presence felt. If he will interrupt the flow of nature and the universe to declare himself unto all of time and eternity, he surely will break into the universe to embrace one of his own when his mission has been realized.

Donny was a star in the classic sense of the word. One of God's very own in the religious sense of the word. A real star. When we look at the attributes of a star, we see Donny. A star has an orbit. A star has gravity. A star is bright. To see a star fully, you need special instruments. A star is luminous; it gives off light. A star guides. A star has the attributes of nova, that is, it becomes very brilliant in a very short time. Stars have two kinds of clouds around them: (1) bright nebula, that is, clouds found around stars which reflect it and give off additional brilliance, and (2) dark nebula, dark clouds that do not glow but obscure the celestial objects beyond them. And in the absence of stars, when they have burned out, there are black holes in the solar system.

The presence of this star lights our fire. His absence leaves a hole. But his message is clear and is left with the ages.

In a few days, no doubt, the records will begin to come off the press. *The Best of Hathaway.* I don't know what the arrangement will be, but I'm clear about what Donny's message would be to us today.

I hear Donny saying to those who lived *In the Ghetto,* little ghetto boy, *You Were Made for Me.* You are *Young, Gifted, and Black.* I'm busy and burdened, but *You Ain't Heavy 'Cause You're My Brother.* I've a song for you, *Come Little Children,* don't be afraid. Realize you were made for me,

Everything Is Everything. In me, *You've Got a Friend*. *I Hear Voices*, but it's all right. They're just the *Extension of a Man*.

Come Little Children and join the magnificient sanctuary band. Listen to me: *Thank the Lord for my Soul*. Don't self-destruct by putting dope in your veins rather than hope in your brains. Come now, little children, *Where Is the Love?* I know it's difficult being a little ghetto boy. I'd give up, but *Giving Up Is So Hard to Do*. Try this therapy. Take a love song and sing it. Everywhere. Let it fill the air. Take a warm smile and wear it. You've *got* to wear it. Take a great dream and build it to the sky. Never lose it. Take a strong heart and use it 'til the day you die. Take a love song, even in a time of trouble, with broken hearts, despair, confusion, and tear-stained eyes. Sing the Lord's song. Come, ye disconsolate. *I Know the Lord; He Heard my Cry* and pitied every groan. But as long as I live and troubles rise, I'll hasten to his throne. One great morning when this life is over, with tension behind me, and confusion obliterated in the sands of time, I'll fly away.

We serve a merciful God who knows how much we can bear. A merciful God who relieves us of pain let Donny rest. A merciful God who dries our tear-stained eyes. A merciful God who will make our enemies leave us alone. An all-powerful God. He is a mind-fixer and a heart regulator. An all-powerful God who is not merely mighty, but almighty. He uses whom he chooses. He bends but never breaks. Then he calls us home to rest. All of us must come home. None is perfect but the Father. All have sinned and come short of the glory of God. Not by works, but by grace, Jesus saves. He promised that weeping may endure for a night, but joy will come in the morning. Ask the Lord at this dark hour to shine on us. Let the light from the lighthouse shine on us. Maybe not today, but one glad morning when this life is over, we will fly away to be with God, and our souls will be at rest. Donny Hathaway, the child prodigy, the genius, now belongs to the ages.

The World's Champion:
Eulogy for
Joe Louis (Barrow)

Jackson preached this eulogy for Joe Louis on April 17, 1981.

But watch thou in all things, endure afflictions, do the work of an evangelist, make full proof of thy ministry. For I am now ready to be offered, and the time of my departure is at hand. I have fought a good fight, I have finished my course, I have kept the faith" (2 Tim. 4:5–7, KJV).

Martha, at this hour, your example of love, devotion, and support is a source of comfort and challenge to us all. Very few people know, but surely God knows, that you have borne the burden in the heat of the day and held up with grace and splendor. We love you for holding up the hands of our champion when he needed you most. This is the Easter season—the season when we celebrate the death and the resurrection of Jesus the Christ. This season of pathos and passion is taking on added meaning. Joe Louis died on Palm Sunday; we celebrate his life on Good Friday. How marvelous it is to be in the rhythm of the Creator. This period has become a very fertile season for the giants.

Dr. Martin Luther King, Jr., Duke Ellington, Jesse Owens, Dr. Howard Thurman, and now Joe Louis. We also experienced the right to vote for the first time in one hundred years during this same period. And so we know crucifixion, but we also know resurrection. "Weeping may endure for a night, but joy cometh in the morning." Death, with its mighty sting, bids us: Be prepared! Death is threatening, perhaps even frightening, but it is democratic. Death has the master key to everybody's house. It brings a telegram to your door that must be signed by you.

We live as if life is certain and death is uncertain. But death is certain!

Death is another one of God's promises. It challenges our immaturity and makes us face the responsibility to live on in spite of. Death bids us to be prepared. You know not the day, the hour, the time, nor the circumstances. It is no respecter of persons. It knocks on the door for courtesy, not for permission, and it disregards all locks, combinations, and barriers.

In this natural process of living and dying, we experience sunrise, the early morning of our existence; noonday, the peak of our lives; and sunset, the evening of our lives. God let Joe see sunset—sixty-six years old, twice longer than Jesus lived. So many of our geniuses never survive sunrise. King Tut died as a teenager; the four girls bombed at the 16th Street Baptist Church; Jimmy Lee Jackson in Selma, Alabama, a challenger of the voter registration structure; Solomon Mahlanga in South Africa—so many of our geniuses had their sun eclipsed at noon. But God smiled on Joe—he experienced the sunset of life.

Our greatest consolation is that we could have lost Joe when we truly needed him. When we were in a valley and seemingly "couldn't hear nobody pray" and couldn't get a prayer through. When we were vulnerable, the stench of the Depression still in our clothes, lynching mobs threatening our existence, we were defenseless and without legal, political, economic, or military protection. But God built a fence around us. Joe was appointed the gatekeeper. What a gatekeeper! He was our Samson, our David fighting Goliath. With toughness he destroyed his enemy, yet with kindness and tenderness he soothed the wounds, revived the soul and the psyche of a people suffering under indescribable pressure and hurt. He was our balm in Gilead.

Joe Louis, our messenger of hope, defied the odds, faced a headwind, and won! History put Hitler and his theory of Aryan racial superiority on trial against Joe Louis and Jesse Owens. The jury can bring in the verdict now. The shadow of Hitler's long arm of venom has cast a dark chapter on history, but when it is dark, the stars shine most clearly. It is difficult to explain the phenomenon of Joe Louis. Joe grew to manhood in the surging currents of the corner life that made up the climate of the Detroit ghetto of his day. To place Joe against the background of his time is, by no means, sufficient to explain him. But who can explain any kind of genius?

The historical setting, the psychological mood, the temper of the age, the state of black America, and the economic and social predicament of Joe's family—all of these are important, but they themselves are not able to tell us precisely the thing that we most want to know. Why was he so different from others in the same setting? Uniqueness always escapes us as we undertake an analysis of character. Joe was great! To be famous is merely to be well known; to be great is to serve. Joe was great by virtue of his character and was made famous by virtue of his ability.

In the fullness of time, God sent Joe from the black race to represent the human race. With a combination of diplomacy, detonation, and timing, he could not be denied. Joe Louis was a hero by anointment, not by appointment. The nation did not choose its doctor and could not refuse its doctor. Against the backdrop of Jack Johnson as the first black champion and the anti-black mania that his life style created, and a Harry Wills, a ringmaster who never had the chance to fight for the title, Joe could not be denied.

All champions are not heroes; heroes are born of necessity. They must heed a need. Joe responded when we needed him—our personhood cried out for confirmation—he was the black's treasure but the world's champion. Usually, the fight is for the crown, but in Joe's case, the bigger fight was who would crown him. Everybody claimed ownership and sought identification with a hero. Authentic heroes are never in surplus.

TV nowadays has a tendency to fabricate heroes, and the supply is much greater than the demand. Thus they are situational heroes, but they do not endure. Joe was so necessary that his enemies became his footstool, yet he had so much grace he would not step on them. As in the case of Charles Lindbergh and Jesse Owens, our national ego was at stake. The ancient Israelites needed David's and Samson's role for its national confidence, its emotional security, and its divine assurance. We needed Joe. Often we tread on God-like descriptions as we describe our relationship with Joe. He was an answer to the sincere prayer of the disinherited and the dispossessed. With Joe Louis we had made it from the guttermost to the uttermost, from slaveship to championship. Joe made everybody somebody. Usually the champion rides on the shoulders of the nation and its people, but in this case the nation rode on the shoulders of its hero, Joe. He was what the Olympics were meant to be—a test of national strength, courage, and health. When Joe fought Max Schmeling, what was at stake was the confidence of a nation with a battered ego in search of resurrection and the esteem of a race of people.

In ways that presidents and potentates never could, Joe made the lion lie down with the lamb. The black, brown, and white, the rich, and the poor were together, and none was afraid. With fist and character, the predicate was laid for snatching down the cotton curtain. The shadows were lifted, and everybody got the sunshine; none remained in the shadows. We came as close as we could get with cheers and prayers. We even danced the "Joe Louis Shuffle." Our children were named after him.

I was named Jesse Louis. Others were named Joe and Louis. Girls were named Josephine and Louise. Tragically, Joe was a second-class citizen by birth but, in fact, a first-class man. He wore glory and grace with honor. The black race is envied because of Joe; the human race is enhanced and rewarded because of him. He made a nation proud of him and ashamed of itself. Even to this moment, the government's conduct toward Joe is a source of tension and shame. On January 9, 1942, he knocked out Buddy Baer at Madison Square Garden in a championship fight. He donated his entire purse to United States Navy Relief. The navy, at that time a bastion of racial segregation, was so surprised that they offered him a commission as a second lieutenant. At that time there were no blacks in the navy who held a rank higher than petty officer. The Secretary of the Navy, Frank Knox, had said publicly that as long as he was alive, the status quo would remain. Thus Joe did not think that the navy was serious with its offer, so he turned it down and enlisted in the army on January 10 in New York. Two months later, March 22, 1942, Joe fought another fight and donated the purse to the army. He fought ninety-six exhibitions, entertained more than two million troops, but ultimately was given a life sentence by the Internal Revenue Service over a tax dispute. Until the time of his death, he had not been extended mercy or forgiveness. When he tried to work, his earnings were attached. Thus he was forced out of the labor market. I hope that the generous offer of the president to honor Arlington National Cemetery by accepting Joe will extend far enough to forgive the tax debt for Joe, because he is an asset, not a liability. The paradox is that he was in debt, too. His special genius and contribution transcended money. His job was not to take us out of economic depression; that was Roosevelt's job. Joe's job was to salvage our national ego and revive our sense of work and confidence.

The only measurement for Joe is that he did do his job. He did not achieve greatness because of the presence of money, and his worth is not altered by the absence of money. It is vulgar to speak of Joe Louis and money as if money were the balancing act in his contribution. We must not succumb to the value system that forces us to measure the worth of people by a balance sheet. Such a gift as Joe must be measured in kind. Jesus died penniless. Jesus died with nails in his hands, yet he had all power in his hands. For some people, money is merely a medium of exchange. Storing it and hoarding it to leave for someone to fight over is not life's ambition. Thank God that because of Martha, Frank, and friends, Joe Louis lived above want. Joe had the best of medical care, a comfortable home, more invitations to travel around the world than he could ever honor, more clothes than he could ever wear. In the eye of many writers, money appears to be Joe's Achilles' heel. But Joe—like Jesus—was not a bargain; he was a gift. People with money felt lucky to be able to share it with Joe. His wealth did not fluctuate with the stock market.

Like Shakespeare of England and Bach of Germany, he lived on a plane above the need for personal wealth. On my side of town, we don't measure Joe by money. In one of Shakespeare's plays, the character says, "He who steals my purse, steals trash; but he who steals my good name demeans me." What God gave Joe, no interpretation can deny.

When the word came across the news that Joe was dead, my mother, nearly 60 years old, said, "Lord, have mercy. We've lost our hero . . . You and all the boys up the street have his name." After five minutes my grandmother, nearing 80 years of age, said, "We have lost all we had. We loved Joe." As a southern black man who grew up in the shadows and who was denied acceptance to the mainstream, let me declare before the world today that we loved Joe.

When Mount St. Joe Louis erupted, some ashes fell on everyone. We do not identify with the "poor old Joe" stories. His name is wonderful! For the children of 1937, who crowded around the radio and watched for the newsreel, who danced in the streets when they heard the count of "10," the announcement of a new champ was made; for those who danced on tin-top roofs, who ran in the street beating cans with sticks, fired in the air; who fell on their knees and prayed and who looked at their disenchanted bosses and suppressed their joy; for the children whose little chests expanded and broke the buttons on their shirts and who went to school the next day with new determination; they did not identify with the "poor old Joe" stories measured out by the government's meanness.

When Joe fought, something inside said, "We ought to be free!" and something on the outside said, "We can be free." Joe Louis, we love your name. To the host of witnesses gathered here, you tell the story. Let them run extra editions of the paper as they once did. Tell the people that Joe is still in the center of the ring without a challenger or a peer. Extra! Extra! Tell them Joe is too high for his critics to reach him now. You've reached another plateau. It's all right now. They can hit the street with the next edition now.

Extra! Extra! Read all about it!

Joe Louis, the pearl of the black race; the treasure of the human race.

Extra! Extra!

Our Joe wasn't dumb—he was generous. Dumb people get tricked out of their integrity. Dumb people steal, throw fights, and do other things that bring shame on themselves.

Extra! Extra!

Joe Louis, your mother's prayers were answered. The weight of the government couldn't floor you with disgrace. You're still riding the wave of Amazing Grace. Weeping may endure for a night, but day cometh.

Extra! Extra!

Joe Louis, you were there when we needed you. Let Joe rest. Call him what you want to, it doesn't matter now. Joe told Jesus it would be all right if he changed his name.

Joe Louis. He fought a good fight, he finished his course, he kept the faith.

Farewell to a Superstar and a Declaration of War: Eulogy for Don Rogers

Early in the summer of 1986, two star athletes died of cocaine overdoses—Don Rogers, a top professional football player with the Cleveland Browns, who died the morning before he was to have been married; and Len Bias, an all-American basketball player at the University of Maryland and first-round draft pick of the Boston Celtics. Jackson delivered both eulogies, developing similar themes in each. He preached this eulogy for Don Rogers on July 3, 1986.

To Don's father, Roscoe Riley; to his mother, Loretha Rogers—in her state of shock, trauma, and grief; to his brother, Reggie; to his sister, Jackie; to Don's fiancée, Leslie Nelson; to other family members, friends, loved ones, and caring community; I know that your hearts are heavy today. But I want to share with you this afternoon, as a friend and minister of the Gospel, to remind you that if you will but put your trust in God, even in your darkest hour, he is able to sustain you. If we lean on him, he will help to bear our burdens.

Even in the midst of tragedy, I am sharing with you in the spirit of Christian joy and celebration to remind you that for the Christian the tragedy of death has already been conquered by Christ's triumph over death. We serve a mighty, merciful, and loving God, and I know today that Don is at peace, having worked and served his purpose here on earth. God never makes a mistake, and in all things he works for the good with those who love and trust him.

To the family, unearned suffering is redemptive. You didn't earn this day, yet it is your cross to bear. But your suffering is not in vain. Suffering breeds character, character breeds faith, and in the end faith will not disappoint.

For the dead, this is a time to rest. For the living, this is a time to remember, to reflect, to recollect, to revive, to redeem, to rebuild and move on. The living have been given the opportunity to draw closer and to love those who remain. For the living—if we will seize the time—it is a chance to learn, a chance to lead, and a chance to liberate.

The essence of Don Rogers was the development of his God-given talent, his service to his community, and his ability to provide inspiration to our children. He taught us how to achieve, how to win, and how to lose. Even today, if we can hear and comprehend, he is still teaching the profound lessons of life—teaching natural law; teaching that you can't break the law of gravity, you can only prove it; teaching that you must live, and possibly die, with the consequences of your choices; teaching the value of the high road; teaching how to determine real friends; teaching that even the greatest among us are not perfect, and that all of us are just one step from death; teaching us that all of us have sinned and fallen short of the glory of God; teaching that the wages of sin are death.

Only the most foolish, deaf, emotionally unstable, and disabled will miss this opportunity to hear and learn from the word according to Don Rogers. He was a master teacher in life and now he has become a master teacher in death. He always had a flair for getting our attention.

The good that we do is never lost. We have lost a good man, but not his good deeds, our good memories of him, and the good that he did in life. One cloud can't block the sunshine—it can only cast shadows. Don Rogers's sunrays are longer than the shadows.

God counts up our cumulative score. You cannot judge a player by whether he made or missed his last shot. In the recent NBA play-offs, Dr. J missed the last shot, Philadelphia lost the game, and the 76ers were knocked out of the play-offs. But no one would judge Dr. J's career on the basis of his last shot.

When we look at Don Rogers's life, we must have a broader view—how consistently he played, his overall performance, his touchdown-saving tackles, his game-saving interceptions, his spectacular returns, his hard-hitting overall aggressive style of play, and the games that he won. Don was a model student, a model athlete, a model son; he had an intense love for his family; he was a UCLA all-American, a star of two Rose Bowl games, a first-round draft pick of the Cleveland Browns, and an NFL Defensive Rookie of the Year. How he LIVED, what he ACHIEVED, how he DIED—ALL are important and must be put in their proper perspective and context. Now God has called him to a higher purpose—to help get the attention of this generation and save it.

We've learned to fear the shadows of death. When we recognize the shadows, we behave accordingly. We see the Ku Klux Klan as dangerous, cowardly, life-threatening, and immoral. We associate the KKK with death, anti-Semitism, and racism. Movies don't glorify them; singers don't sing about them; little sheets and hoods are not passed around at parties. The KKK is not funny. We don't play that way.

Yet the KKK—as the shadow of death—and the rope have never killed as many of our young people as the pusher of dope. Pushers are terrorists and death messengers. Passing out a little "snow" must become as unacceptable as passing out little sheets or little ropes.

Dope is the hound of hell for this generation. The buzz, the sensation, the temporary state of ecstacy, and the, in fact, temporary brain paralysis. When drugs attack, our minds go, our morals go, our morale goes, and pretty soon the hound of hell takes our liberties and our life. It is a state of emergency.

Their moral resistance has dropped. Their ethics have collapsed. The burden of the consequences of eating the forbidden fruit has not been driven home to them. And whether they are pursuing pleasure or avoiding pain, drugs are the forbidden fruit. The war of the opiate is claiming more victims and casualties than the Civil War or World War II from our population.

Drugs are the curse of our culture. Our government is losing the supply-side struggle against drugs: (1) because of an inadequate investment in the war against drugs; and (2) because of the tremendous money made by those in the drug industry.

But more fundamental than the war on the SUPPLY of drugs is the deceptive devil—masquerading in the robe of convenience, pleasure, joy, and private fun—that has INCREASED THE DEMAND and REDUCED OUR RESISTANCE. Our minds must resist drugs. Our morals must reject drugs. The drug pusher must be seen as a terrorist, whether driven by innocence or economic gain. The natural law will not make a distinction.

Today we're in a war where the enemy is disguised as our friend. He does not have a social stigma attached to him, he shows few danger signals, he has full access to our inner circle, and he is financed by the victim. Terrorism is camouflaged as terrific. We've been infiltrated. Drugs are out-of-bounds. The painful loss of an athletic hero has forced us into a huddle. We must call time-out.

Today we declare a state of emergency. The living of our generation have been summoned to declare war on a plague. We need no draft from Washington. We must be volunteers of conscience and consciousness. Our joint chiefs of staff, civilian and military, must coordinate efforts to make of us a nation of drug war resisters.

The historic meaning, purpose, and substance of July 4th will not exist in the future if we do not fight and win this war. There is no independence without maturity, no Ms. Liberty without Mr. Justice, and no freedom without responsibility.

Often young soldiers fight wars out of blind patriotism, or out of the fear of the consequences of draft evasion, and they are unaware of the deeper meanings and higher stakes of the war. Too often the bullets of war wipe out the innocent in cross fires, as they are trapped unexpectedly and without warning or defense.

Today we are pained by another war casualty. He was a casualty in a war he didn't fully understand; a war that our government is neither totally committed to wage nor prepared to defend us against—a war that we as a people are not fully resolved to resist. The casualties are not just athletes. It is estimated that TODAY 5,000 of our relatives, friends, neighbors, and co-workers will try cocaine for the first time. An estimated 6 million people will spend $110 billion this year for the temporary thrill and escape that cocaine provides. It's war. It's war on the just and the unjust.

In the resistance to the Vietnam War, we had targets, goals, and stated demands. We marched by the tens of thousands as we fought for a new policy. But we are not as clear or as resolved against the war of the opiate. In the opium war there are more casualties, more dangers involved, and it is more widespread. Yet we are offering less resistance!

The enemy has infiltrated our ranks and is always disguised as our friend. Our superior officers—businesspersons on Wall Street, doctors, lawyers, ministers, musicians, actors, actresses, politicians—are deceiving and (by example) recruiting eight- and ten-year-olds as volunteers for service. The enemy has found a weakness in our values, has turned us inside out, and we are marching with a deadly cadence toward mass suicide.

The transmitters of our culture—our artists, athletes, television, radio, video, and music—are glorifying and adding glitter to the poison, which is making it socially acceptable as entertainment, a personal right and privilege, and inoffensive. Educators do not see it as the number-one competitor for the minds of our youth. We are losing by default, with little struggle. The Department of Education is spending $18 billion—but only $2.9 million (down from $14 million) on drug education.

My friends, we are losing our youth, our heritage, and our national integrity to the opium war. We must translate our feelings into fighting, our tears into sweat, our sorrow into sagacity, our burial grounds into platforms from which we say, "enough is enough"; platforms from which we say, "no more treasures of human triumph will be turned into tragedies and a trail of tears."

July 4, 1986, must become a declaration of independence from the external threat of the supply of death, and internal resistance to the concession to death. We will not let our ethics collapse, nor will we let our spirit surrender. We will fight back. We will resist. We will prevail.

When our top players are lost, we must not toss in the towel, lose by default, and let the enemy rejoice in our humiliation. New stars must arise, unknown to the enemy, driven by pride, love, and the law of compensation, and play better than we thought we could play, defy the odds, and win anyway.

In a strange and paradoxical way, the twin tragedies of two athletic treasures and heroes—Lenny Bias and Don—have given professional and college athletes the chance to become authentic heroes; a chance in death to lead the drive for renewal; a chance to redefine manhood and family responsibility; a man must not only make a baby, but provide for a baby and raise a baby; a man must develop his mind and his body; and a man must assess the odds and conquer. We must let the human spirit triumph over all foes—of evil or adversity.

When those who are perceived to be weeds are taken from the garden, we dismiss them as statistics. But those weeds are plants also. They are some mother's child. Sometimes God plucks a beautiful flower—a rose, yes, even a Rose Bowl champion—to get our attention.

Literally millions of our youth—lesser-known flowers than Don Rogers—are flirting with death or dying every day. It is a state of emergency. I average three to four high schools per week and I ask our children five basic questions. Do you know: (1) Someone who has died because of drugs? (2) Someone who is in jail because of drugs? (3) Someone who is on drugs? (4) Someone who has brought a gun or a knife to school? and (5) Someone who had to leave school prematurely because of pregnancy? They come forward in great numbers admitting their participation in drugs, alcohol, sex without love—making unwanted babies—and violence.

But with all the talk, countertalk and loose talk about drugs, that is not the central arrow piercing the hearts of family, friends, and loved ones on this occasion. We must go on what we know. We know he can't talk for himself. We know that he was born, lived, and died, and now deserves to rest. We know to capture the hearts of thousands of friends throughout the United States in twenty-three years is a fast pace and a special mission. The candle burned quickly, but oh, how bright was the glow. Today we celebrate his life and legacy.

Today the children mourn. I hope they learn. When old people die, there is the feeling that they have had their time, their chances, and their choices. Life may even have been tough. It may have been full of ups and downs and uncertainties. Still, they had their options.

But when a young person dies there is a feeling that God has robbed them. And yet, God sometimes uses our best people to get our attention. Jesus, God's only son, a good man, a young man, was crucified. Dr. Martin Luther King, Jr., a good man, a young man, shot down in cold blood in the prime of life. Mozart, Gandhi, Ernie Davis, Ben Wilson, and others—young, gifted, strong, admired—all taken from us in the prime of life.

Through the drastic intervention of death an unplanned family reunion has been called. Our schedules have been altered. In our state of trauma and pain, we are forced into a radical reevaluation of our lives. When the weeds, or so-called lesser plants, are plucked away, we ignore it. But when a rose or a tulip—a thing of special beauty and fragrance that we love—is taken from us, we take notice.

The fact is the so-called lesser flowers are drying up, withering and dying daily—red, yellow, black, brown, and poor white children—really are not lesser flowers. ALL children have their own purpose. God loves and cares for them all, and he put them here for a purpose. All children—male and female, rich and poor—are God's children, and they are all precious in his sight.

With all of his majesty, splendor, decency, and talent, if Don was vulnerable, all of us must beware. Don was one of the roses of his generation, one of God's superbly gifted people. He is now being used by God, in death, to save a generation. In death, his voice is louder and clearer. His sun was rising, generating heat and light. Then, at high noon, his sun was eclipsed. And then there was darkness. David said to Jonathan, while fleeing the wrath of his father, Saul, at our top stride we're just one step from death. It takes years to climb a mountain, but one slip or false step and we face oblivion. Life is finely tuned.

Don was born in the trauma of the best and worst of times. It was a time when Schwerner, Goodman, and Chaney captured the heart and pricked the conscience of the nation with their untimely deaths. It was a time when Dr. Martin Luther King, Jr., gave the vision for our country in his "I Have a Dream" speech. It was a time when President John F. Kennedy was killed. It was in a time and out of this mixture of joy and pain, hope and despair, that Don was born, bred, and developed.

To the family and friends, Don Rogers has been a blessing to our generation. His dying is a message unto eternity. We can feel good and smile through our tears because God forgives, redeems, and resurrects.

In the past, the various circumstances of the death of our young, whether in war or peace, have altered the course of our individual, national, and global lives. We must make Don's death the breaking point for the sacrifice of our youth by the hounds of hell.

You can be assured that we will not linger here. This tragedy will be transformed into triumph. The stone will be rolled away and resurrection, new life, and new hope will be the treasure that comes from this tragedy. This is not a PERIOD, that ends it for the Christian. This is the COMMA, as we pause in route to our new home.

The Scripture says: "And God shall wipe away all tears from their eyes; and there shall be no more death, neither sorrow, nor crying, neither shall there be any more pain: for the former things are passed away" (Rev. 21:4, KJV).

For those who remain, let us work. Let Don rest. He has a new home!

EVANGELIST FOR EDUCATIONAL EXCELLENCE

"Knowledge is the key to power, and power is the key to progress. With knowledge, you can live in harmony with the natural order and become God's partner. With knowledge, you can cultivate the social, political, and economic order. It was no accident that during slavery the highest penalty that a slave or slavemaster had to pay was if he or she were caught teaching a slave how to read or write. This implies that knowledge is the antidote to slavery and ignorance is the partner of slavery."

The Ten Commandments
for Excellence
in Education

In the fall of 1975, Jackson began to take his message
of ethics and excellence directly into high schools. By
the fall of 1976, he had developed his thinking into a
more structured and systematic form. This speech was
given at Operation PUSH's Saturday Morning
Community Forum on October 23, 1976.

Knowledge is the key to power, and power is the key to
progress. With knowledge, you can live in harmony with the natural
order and become God's partner. With knowledge, you can cultivate the
social, political, and economic order. It was no accident that during
slavery the highest penalty that a slave or slavemaster had to pay was if
he or she were caught teaching a slave how to read or write. This implies
that knowledge is the antidote to slavery and ignorance is the partner of
slavery. Without knowledge, someone can free you but you will run to
slavery. With knowledge, someone can attempt to enslave you but you
will escape to freedom. Knowledge is just that powerful.

We know that we need the pursuit of excellence as a way of bringing
legitimate pressure on the system in this country and the oppressive
systems of the world. We know there is some relationship between the
revolution and the laws of supply and demand. When there is a greater
supply of desire to be free than there is demand on the part of the
oppressor to grant freedom, there is a conflict; there's a confrontation.
When there is more water than dam, floods occur. When there's more
baby than belly, birth occurs. When there are more black athletes in
football, basketball, and baseball who have achieved excellence, not
only did we break into the game, but we became masters of the game,

captains of the game, coaches of the game—indeed, we became dominant in the game. They play us in football, basketball, and baseball not because of some great love for black people but because we are so excellent. If they want to win, they have to play us.

And so it must be in academics and in politics. Today if our political consciousness were more excellent, we would have sixteen million registered black voters rather than eight million. Needless to say, our mediocre attitude toward and poor understanding of politics has us struggling in a level of oppression that is totally unnecessary, but our demands for political options have outdistanced our supply of political consciousness. If we had excellence in economic consciousness, we would know more about finance and be as excellent as we are in romance. We would know how to study the laws of money, the laws of capital, so that no matter what system we were in we would survive.

We put emphasis on excellence because it can produce social change and has revolutionary value. And so it is that we raise these commandments.

1. *Education is a task requiring total community involvement. It cannot be left solely to the public schools.* A coalition of excellence of twenty-five to fifty members should be formed around each school. Such a coalition should include businesspeople, bankers, scientists, physicians, dentists, media persons, writers, disk jockeys, plumbers, carpenters, technologists, pilots—anyone interested in sharing. In other words, the "total involvement" concept. We can no longer leave our schools isolated and then make that isolated island quarantined, where only teachers and children show up every day. Rather, politicians, board members, superintendents, administrators, parents, preachers, and disk jockeys—the schools must be in the center of our socializing, politicizing, moralizing process and not stuck out on an island.

2. *Parents are the foundation of education.* They are the only ones whose first priority is children, and they are the only ones who can hold every part of the educational system accountable: students, parents, teachers, administrators, school boards, and politicians. Parents should come to school at the start of the year and work out a moral contractual agreement with the teacher stating what is expected of the teacher and the parent. The student, the teacher, and the parent must form a coalition. Parents should come to school to pick up report cards and review their children's progress weekly, monthly, or quarterly, as necessary. They should not show up in May while their children have been absent since September raising hell, and complain about not being involved. We just cannot do it that way.

3. *Public schools must define themselves clearly and say unequivocally what they stand for and believe.* At the beginning of each scholastic year, the

superintendent should give a major "state of the school" address in which he or she clearly defines educational goals, how the schools will operate, what the rules will be, what the goals will be, and what the nine-month timetable is. So if you come to school the first day and miss the next eight, when you come on day ten, you come in relationship to the plan.

4. *High performance takes place in a framework of high expectation.* Teachers' unions will need to review their policies and programs to make sure they are not protecting low-performance teachers from being singled out and being fired from the system. We cannot institutionalize mediocrity. New approaches might include the creation of union-run or -supported training for substandard teachers. But don't take the best teachers away from us and transfer them out and leave those who have to take that test four or five times, who come to work late and leave early—don't give them to us. If they can't cut it, they must cut out.

5. *The laws of convenience lead to collapse, but the laws of sacrifice lead to greatness.* Anything that is conveniently achieved has low market value. You win a gold medal because you sacrifice. You become successful in music, art, science, politics, athletics, marriage, and in life itself because you sacrifice. So sacrifice must not be seen as a negative. In addition, sacrifice must not be seen as punishment; it must be seen as therapy. The laws of sacrifice lead to greatness. Everybody cannot be famous because everybody cannot be well known. But everybody can be great because everybody can sacrifice and serve.

6. *The death of ethics is the sabotage of excellence.* Where there are no ethical standards, there is no excellence in achievement. If in your business people are trying to come late and leave early, which is un-ethical, you will never achieve excellence in productivity. If in your marriage you spend more time being dishonest and violating your ethical obligations than you do keeping your word, you will never achieve excellence in marriage. If in school you spend more time cheating than studying, the fact that your ethics collapsed means you will not achieve excellence. If in basketball you spend more time after practice drinking and smoking and not getting your sleep, the death in your personal ethics sabotages your capacity to be excellent.

7. *The full responsibility for learning cannot be transferred from students to educators.* You cannot teach anybody against their will. We must accept the premise that nobody can save us for us but us, and nobody can do the homework and schoolwork for the student but the student. The teacher can teach you, but you can only learn yourself.

8. *Requiring students to do things that are demonstrably beneficial to them is not inherently undemocratic.* Students are qualified to be students, but they are not qualified to teach themselves. Somebody must teach you,

even if it hurts. You must read even if you are sleepy. You must study even if you are tired. No football coach can develop a team while worrying about whether the members of the team might sweat or get dirty. Anything worth having is worth working for above and beyond the call of duty.

9. *Learning will not take place if a disproportionate amount of school time and resources must be given to maintaining order.* Principals therefore must prepare and distribute to students on the first day of school a written code of conduct. Students cannot be expected to observe rules that are unclear or unknown. Parents cannot be expected to support rules that are unclear or unknown or capriciously interpreted and administered. Teachers and administrators can operate effectively in this sensitive area only if policies and procedures are clearly stated.

10. *All human beings, and especially young people, need to be involved in activities that provide a sense of identity and worth.* Adolescents who cannot find identity and satisfaction in socially acceptable ways will find them elsewhere. Now what that means is this. It isn't enough to have Black History Month once a year. Every day must be another expression of the belief that we can make it. Our children must not only study black history and go to the Du Sable Museum of Afro-American Art, but they must also relate to community organizations. They must relate to black businesses. They must visit the black church. They must understand political processes. They must have voter registration machines in those schools. At graduation time we should put a diploma in one hand, symbolizing wisdom and knowledge, and a voter registration card in the other hand, symbolizing power and responsibility. We must not tack community identity on. It must be a part of the process.

The fact is, there's a law in the universe: whatsoever a man soweth, that shall he also reap. You may tell the doctor that you're well when you know you're sick. You may tell the lawyer you're innocent when you know you're guilty. You might tell your friend a lie, and your friend does not know any better. But there is a God, a twenty-four-hour God who neither slumbers nor sleeps. There is a God who is not mocked. You cannot fail to do your homework, flunk the test the next day, and come back and lie to your momma, making her eyes fill with tears because you didn't graduate and don't know very much. Whatsoever a man soweth, that shall he also reap.

So when you go to school, you need to know what the law is. You may be poor, but you have to know the law. That's why God said that it rains on the just and on the unjust. There are some laws that are so basic that, even if you have been oppressed, you still have to obey them. You can say, well, I've been treated unjustly and I never did see my daddy, and my mama's on welfare, and I have a lot of little brothers and sisters, and they're hungry, and I took this typing course, and I'm having problems. Well, we can give you pity, but, I declare, you cannot type with six fingers. You may have come from a bad situation, but typing has a way of objectifying those who have developed the orchestration of keys in their minds. That piano has no regard for your previous condition of servitude. If you don't know music, you can't make music on that piano.

The laws of finance. Those are some cold laws. They aren't white, they aren't black, they aren't Republican, they aren't Democratic. If you don't study finance, you will not know finance. I love our people too much to cripple them with excuses. I want you to get these down very good and to think about what this means over and over all week. Repeat this after me. "If you can conceive it and believe it, you can achieve it." The first one has to do with vision; that's why the Bible says without vision you perish (Prov. 29:18a). The first one says if you can conceive it—that means in your head—and in your heart if you can believe it, you can achieve it. The Lord told Abraham that he would give him as far as he could see. He didn't say as far as you can look—the Lord will give you as far as you can see. I'm not talking about eyesight; I'm talking about insight. The Lord will give you as far as you can see. Some mothers have seen five and six of their children graduating from college with no husband and no welfare, but they conceived it and believed it, and they achieved it.

Operation PUSH was six months old, new, and under suspicion by everybody. Some organizations that had been in town since year one were still getting kicked from pillar to post. The Lord showed us this building and said it's ours; just get it. We're not behind on the note, either. We conceived it and believed it and achieved it. Our students must know that if they conceive it, they can be what they want to be; they can do what they want to do; they can go where they want to go— if they conceive it. And teachers, if your students don't conceive it so clearly, wipe their windshields off. Reach up and knock down those clouds, those mental clouds of inferiority. Say, You're somebody, boy; you're somebody. You can make it. Tell that child, You might be in the slum, but the slum is not in you. You can be somebody; you're God's child. Tell that boy, tell that girl, that no child is illegitimate; all babies are legitimate. God legitimates life. You're somebody, and you can make it.

Before the Lord let the Israelites have Canaan, the Promised Land, he gave them the commandments. If you get in Canaan and don't have the laws, you can't make it. But we got to Canaan before we got the commandments. We have the right to vote but don't; have the right to go to school but don't; have the right to buy and sell to each other but don't; have the right to vote for each other but don't. I have figured out why. I know what the secret is: we got to Canaan before we got the commandments. Happy is he that keeps the law of the Lord (Prov. 29:18b). Except the Lord build the house, they labor in vain that build it. (Ps. 127:1).

You teach that boy and that girl how to read and write Monday through Friday and then you take that talent and teach some Sunday school on Sunday morning and teach character for a long time. I know black heroes are necessary. I believe in that. But when none of us had black heroes, we knew about Esther, and we knew about Joshua, and we knew about Moses. We knew about Abraham and Isaac and Jacob, and, even though we didn't identify with their Jewishness, they were men and women of character. Even though we didn't have any color on it, our character was strong. We didn't name our children strange names. My daddy's name was Noah not because my grandparents were trying to lock him into four or five thousand years of history but because Noah built an ark against difficult circumstances.

So if we want to bring about progress, we need to develop excellence by struggling against the odds. We have to learn the laws and develop our character.

Victim-Victimizer: Why Excel?

Jackson had been criticized by some who said that he was "blaming the victim" and letting the victimizer off the hook. This address at the March 5, 1977, Saturday Morning Community Forum of Operation PUSH was his response to these critics.

It is sad when people get so far down that they have to jump up just to touch the basement and when they do jump up they don't believe up is up because they've been down so long. I'm here to argue the case today, brothers and sisters, that we're not responsible for slavery, but we must accept responsibility for liberation. It is not to anyone else's self-interest for us to make adequate wages but us. It is not to anybody else's self-interest for us to take over their company but us. It is not to anybody else's self-interest for us to become mayor but us. It is not to anybody else's self-interest for us to become senators, for us to become president, but us.

Even as we argue this victim-victimizer argument, it is very clear in my mind that we are the victims and the oppressor is the victimizer. Now having said that, the oppressor is not going to run the race and give you his or her gold medal. You will have to conquer the odds and rise above your circumstance and win your own gold medal and then shout and sing, "How I Got Over." There are just some things that people can't do for you, that you have to do for yourself. Of all of your powers—your political power, your economic power, and your social power—no power is more fundamental than willpower. For if you get willpower, you'll get voting power and you'll get political power and you'll get economic power and you'll get social prestige. If you get willpower, you'll have a power that the boss can't fire. You'll have a power that jail cells can't lock up. If you get willpower, that will be a power that water cannot drown and fire cannot burn.

We have some politicians downtown now who have political power insofar as they can transfer a job from area A to area B, but because they don't have willpower, they can't stand for their convictions. They can have high political positions, but it can't be said to be power because when the heat comes their frost melts because they don't have the most essential of all powers—willpower.

Today I want to argue that our young people need their willpower developed. It's bad to be in the slums, but it's even worse when the slums get in you. If you get your willpower, you can be in the slums without the slums being in you. You can transform that slum; you can make flowers bloom in the desert.

Some of us have been down so long that we think that it is unfair punishment to demand excellence of our people. We think that it's punishment to tell our folks to excel, yet the only reason we can celebrate our heroes on the athletic field is because they excelled. They ran harder and longer and sweated more. They don't give any Olympic gold medals for pity or poverty. They give gold medals for winning in spite of your poverty and in spite of where you came from. They don't give most-valuable-player awards based upon where you came from but based upon what you did.

Why excel? Ignorance is an impediment to progress. That's why the victimizers tried to lock us out of school. If they can keep us ignorant, they'll keep us picking cotton rather than selling cotton. Ignorance is an impediment to progress. That's why it was illegal for us to read or write during slavery. Ignorance and slavery are copartners. If you keep somebody ignorant, you keep them in slavery. That's why Paul said you ought to study to show yourself worthy and approved. It's what will make you you and me me that nobody can take away. Take away my clothes power, take away my economic power, take away my social privilege, but deep down there's a me that really makes me me.

The system depends on ignorance. That's why we're fighting for excellence. They depend on consumer ignorance. That's why they make you buy what you want and beg for what you need. They need ignorance. That's why they keep us financially ignorant—so we can put our money in their banks rather than ours. Why do we bank there? Because we're ignorant.

Self-determination is our goal, and self-discipline, self-initiative, and self-awareness are necessary to get self-government. You can be walking around over oil, but, if you don't have information, you'll think it's greasy water. What does it matter if you have oil if you cannot mine it, cannot refine it, cannot sell it?

That's why we raise the question about teenage pregnancies. One high school in the city had five hundred freshmen four years ago and has fifty seniors today. Five hundred freshmen, fifty seniors—and they can't read and write. They are not trained to work their way on a job or to work their way off welfare. They'll always be hung-up because somebody early in their lives glorified ignorance and didn't tell them the value of a developed mind.

What we must do today is raise the expectation level of our people. Somebody says, Reverend, it's bad to raise their expectations, for if they excel and if their expectations are raised and opportunities are not there, they'll be frustrated. But you can be frustrated with information, and you can be frustrated without information. The difference is that if you're frustrated without information, you can't do anything about it. But if you're frustrated with information, you can do something about it. So the odds are on your side. There's no guarantee that you won't be frustrated, but you increase the odds of survival. If people with a college degree can't get a job, when they get mad they can do something about it. People who are carpenters and brick masons and mechanics, if they're unemployed, they can do something about it. Nobody can tell a skilled carpenter he shouldn't have a job because he isn't qualified. He knows better. You can't convince him he ought to be nobody when his skills make him somebody.

If you take people whose heads are down and whose hands are unskilled, you can suppress them easier. But if you raise the expectation level, you make the adrenalin flow. For example, there is this foolishness where we graduate students every year—100 percent graduate. All of them theoretically are going to college but only 20 percent actually go, and most of them don't graduate. They come out of college with a degree but are functionally illiterate. They walk around with this notion that if you develop your head you don't need your hands and if you develop your hands you don't have a head. The fact of the matter is, people have to be trained to work. Why? Not because of money alone. You need to work for self-confidence. Don't give me money; give me a job, and I'll make some money and have my dignity at the same time. If I don't use my mind, it will shrink and atrophy. If I use my mind, it will grow and multiply. Let me use my mind, use my hands.

Excel. Be so good until your enemies have to leave you alone. Be so good until they have to cut down high bushes to break down a path to your doorstep. Be so good until they might not like you but they have to respect you. Be so good until you're necessary. They're putting it in phrase language: talkin' about a "good thang man" and a "good thang woman." They're talking about sex and sex only. But beneath being a good thang man in the bed and a good thang woman in the bed, you have to be a good thang man and woman on your feet, at that desk, in that classroom. What does it matter if you have the right to engage in sex but are too hungry to have the energy to do it properly? Be a good thang man. Work early in the morning. Be a good thang man. Get a job; demand one.

I remember when I was in the first grade. There weren't any black writers then or any blacks on television or any black commentators. Blacks couldn't use the library, couldn't use the schools, couldn't be executives, didn't have banks. They had signs on lawns that said "dogs and niggers keep off." They put us down. All during the week, if you were walking the streets as a boy or if you were downtown working as a man, you would hear them saying that Nigger Joe is going to fight Billy Conn tonight. That nigger better not slip, he better not fall. They said all kinds of derogatory things about him. During the first stages of the fight, when Joe would start kind of slow, they'd start saying that that nigger ain't in shape and it seems like Billy's whuppin' him. There wasn't any television, and it seemed like Billy Conn was whuppin' him because they had one of Billy's fans announcing the fight. But by and by, because he had been running while Billy was walking and because he had been punching that bag when Billy Conn was giving press conferences, there was a connection between jaw and fist. And the good thang man emerged. Now what was significant about the good thang man was that no matter what they say about you, it doesn't matter unless it's true. Nothing they said about Joe Louis made him hit in the heart. Just because they say we ain't, we don't have to be ain't. Just because they say we cain't, we don't have to be cain't. Just be somebody anyhow.

People are so fickle. The same folk who say you aren't anything are vile when you establish without a doubt that you are something. That's why we have to excel. That's why we have to start producing merit scholars in our schools and make some people get off our backs. They don't mind our coming to the school as basketball players because they know that when we come the basketball team is going to get better. But they say that when we come into the math class the class gets held back.

Knowledge is the key that opens up the lock of slavery on your mind and makes your enemies leave you alone. If you have a better mousetrap and mice are worrying people, you'll be in command. The only protection against genocide is to remain necessary. As long as you remain necessary, there will be no door closed to you. But the moment you become unnecessary, all the angels and all the archangels won't be able to hold you.

That isn't just true in Western legend, it's true in your house. If you mess around and become unnecessary in your house, you're going to leave there. If you mess around and become unnecessary on that ball team, you're going to leave there. The only protection against genocide is to remain necessary. What is there about you that is necessary? Is it your service? Is it your mind? Is it your loyalty? Is it your attitude? What is it about you that makes you necessary?

Save Our Children: Administrators for Excellence

In this speech to the Council of Chief State School Officers, meeting in Phoenix on November 13, 1978, Jackson develops his views on the problems and solutions to the crisis facing public education in a fairly comprehensive way. Since 1975, he has given similar speeches across the nation to educational associations, parents' groups, and business and community leaders.

I am convinced that much can be accomplished—though certainly not everything—though creative, courageous, and competent administrative leadership in this country. Thus I have chosen to speak on the subject, "Save Our Children: Administrators for Excellence."

Education is confronted with a dual crisis. One crisis is external, and the other is internal. *Externally,* education is threatened by three things:

1. Racial trauma in and around our schools.
2. An assault on the public economy.
3. *Bakke* and Bakkeism.

Internally, education is threatened by:

1. The loss of moral authority.
2. Moral decadence.
3. Mass media diversion.
4. A crisis in effort.
5. Massive parental detachment.

I would like to discuss this dual crisis and then present several specific challenges to you as educational administrators and urge you to join us in an all-out assault on illiteracy and mediocrity in education.

External Impediments to Excellence

Race

Racial trauma in and around our schools is still the number-one impediment to an atmosphere conducive to educational development. If we are to save our schools, the first mountain to scale is the mountain of race.

Race has sapped our spirits and absorbs valuable energy. Race has brought tension; race makes many of us feel uncomfortable. Race makes some feel superior and others inferior. Race has brought negative publicity and images upon us. Race has divided families, communities, and our concept of justice. Race has split religious institutions and distorts the image of God. Race has wrought distrust and suspicion.

Race has caused us to build schools where we don't need them and pitted parents against parents. Race allows boards of education to waste taxpayers' money paying lawyers to fight immoral legal battles. Race has allowed politicians to exploit our emotions for their political gain, but at our educational expense. Race has polarized our children, forcing them to take sides. Race has stripped our teachers of moral authority and makes them less credible as teachers.

Racism, a philosophy of superiority, is untrue scientifically, immoral theologically, and unhealthy psychologically. Administrators, on this race question, we must *insulate* our children rather than *isolate* them. For if we don't, they will grow up and learn the truth, and they will turn against their parents, their leaders, and their society in bitterness and use pill power to *cop out* rather than willpower to *cope with*.

The PUSH for Excellence educational movement is not a departure from the historic struggle for equal educational opportunity. We stand firmly on the shoulders of the 1954 constitutional guarantees of the right of all of our children to have a desegregated education—even if it necessitates metropolitanwide desegregation. Administrators, you must become evangelists to convince the people in your state of the educational and social advantages inherent in cultural diversity. And you must make it administratively possible by including blacks and browns in key policy- and decision-making positions at every level of your administrations.

The country's agenda for desegregation today should be to: (1) aggressively enforce the present law, (2) desegregate the power, and (3) complete the task of changing people's hearts and feelings, which will alter their behavior and actions.

The Assault on the Public Economy

In the name of "high-sounding and noble causes," we are experiencing an all-out assault on the public economy. Using the cover of tax reform, of fighting inflation, of balancing the budget, and, yes, even in the name of quality education, the public sector is being undermined—and education will suffer drastically.

In California it took the form of Proposition 13 or the Jarvis Amendment. In Ohio and other states it took the form of rejection of bond issues for education. In Washington it took the form of Packwood-Moynihan tax credit legislation. In each case it may give the few short-term pleasure, but it will give us all long-term pain.

The analysis behind Proposition 13 was correct. We do need tax reform. But the solution was incorrect. It was an example of cutting off your nose to spite your face. The diagnosis was sound, but the prognosis reflected a national suicide complex. If you're having severe pains in your *left arm*, and the doctor's diagnosis indicates that you need an operation, and he or she puts you to sleep but amputates your *right arm*—when you wake up you will only have compounded your problem. You'll have a hurting left arm and a missing right arm. When the people of California spend their $5 billion surplus and the full impact of Proposition 13 hits them, they'll know that they still need tax reform, but Proposition 13 was not the answer.

Packwood-Moynihan-type legislation is also short-sighted and elitist because it is *regressive* rather than *progressive*. It would create a three-tiered educational system. A suburban school system essentially based on class, a private school system essentially based on race, and a public inner-city school system essentially based on rejection and alienation. The long-range consequences for the entire society of continuing and even increasing such a phenomenon will be disastrous for our society.

Rather than leading, President Carter is conceding to these negative forces. The president's psyche is split. On the one hand, he says all the right things and takes very small steps in the right direction, but his regressive economic policy is undermining his progressive rhetoric. He signed the Humphrey-Hawkins Full Employment Bill (which was simply a policy statement and a very limited plan, but not a full employment *program*), then three days later undermined full employment using monetary policy to prop up the dollar abroad. He launched an anti-inflation program but barely touched on the three basic causes of inflation: new world competition, economic concentration or oligopoly, and a bloated and wasteful military budget which produces dead-end or nonconsumable goods and is capital- rather than labor-intensive. Thus we have "stagflation"—high inflation and high unemployment at the same time. This year the federal government is spending $117 billion of our tax dollars on the military and $9 billion on education.

We strongly support the establishment of a separate Department of Education within the federal government if it means giving added national focus and a higher priority to education. But we must be careful not to allow a separate Education Department to become isolated and vulnerable to those forces that would destroy it. There is built-in structural inequity in the present financing of education, with 49 percent coming from local taxes, 44 percent from the state, and only 7 percent from the federal government. Both adequacy and equity are undermined by such an arrangement, and our present spending priorities would undermine its potential effectiveness. We cannot allow education to become the whipping boy for economic confusion and misplaced priorities.

We cannot educate in an economic and social vacuum. There is a tremendous amount of talk these days about how much we can cut, how much we must do without, but there is one thing that we must insist upon—that we cannot do without jobs. We must rebuild America's cities. We must provide adequate health protection and care for all of our citizens. We must provide quality education for all of our children. We must put America back to work because it costs less to employ our people—making them productive and giving them dignity—than it does to pay for unemployment compensation, welfare, and the personal and social destruction that comes from a hopeless, downtrodden, and unemployed people.

Bakke and Bakkeism

Why are we upset about the Bakke decision? Bakke and Bakkeism must be seen in context. A text without a context is a pretext. Legally, the Bakke decision represents the end of the period of the Second Reconstruction and lays the predicate for another century of struggle around the race issue. Black people are confronted with educational and economic gaps, and our goal is to catch up. This decision represents another external racial threat to our attempt to gain educational and economic equity and parity.

We are behind as a result of discrimination and denial of opportunity. There is 1 white attorney for every 680 whites, 1 black attorney for every 4,000 blacks; 1 white physician for every 649 whites, 1 black physician for every 5,000 blacks; 1 white dentist for every 1,900 whites, 1 black dentist for every 8,400 blacks. Less than 1 percent of all engineers are black. Blacks make up less than 1 percent of all practicing chemists. Cruel and dispassionate injustice set us back. We need creative justice and compassion to close the gap.

Bakke filed and won his case because the mass media erroneously convinced white America that blacks were making progress at white expense rather than seeing racial reparations as in the national interest. The Bakke decision was devastating, but not a fatal blow; the court did not leave us *un*protected, but it left us *less* protected. And this policy and tendency toward exclusion is both morally and economically more costly than inclusion. If a young man or woman goes to any state university in this country for four years, it will cost less than $20,000. If he or she goes to any state penitentiary for four years, it will cost anywhere from $50,000 to $100,000. Education and employment cost less than ignorance and incarceration.

Internal Impediments to Excellence

The Loss of Moral Authority

Educators must regain moral authority. Truth, like electricity, needs a conduit. It needs a conductor through which to travel. Educators and administrators are the conductors. If the educator has a healthy respect for the child, he or she can be a good conductor. But if the educator has exposed wires on race or ethics or character or caring, he or she will either blow a fuse or set off sparks that burn up a child's mind. The educator must love and care about those he or she is attempting to educate. Without sounding anti-intellectual, we must know that the issues of life flow from the heart, not the head. We must *be* the truth that we speak. We cannot teach our children against our spiritual will, using only our intellectual and administrative skills. We must share ourselves, not just our information. We cannot feed children with a long-handled spoon. We cannot teach what we don't know or lead where we won't go.

For without the reestablishment of moral, not merely legal, authority by educators, we cannot effectively challenge this generation to achieve its potential and become a greater generation. For if we challenge them to discipline *without* moral authority—that is, without our being believable, trustworthy, and caring—they will perceive it as punishment and react accordingly. However, if we challenge them *with* moral authority, they will perceive it as therapy and respond. Punishment and therapy both involve pain, but the reception and response are different.

We believe in competency tests and testing, while at the same time we're concerned about the motives of the tester. Tests should be used to diagnose and detect, not to delete and destroy. If the tester's motivation is to elevate, not eliminate, then the tester must have moral authority and be believed, or people will politicize the competency-testing issue and turn that which is essentially positive into something negative. Only when black-, brown-, red-, yellow-, and white-recognized leadership are full participants in the total process of testing—from conceptualizing the test to interpreting it—will we have the moral authority to test and be trusted. Functionally immoral people do not have the right to judge functionally illiterate ones. We agree, we should not discover in the twelfth grade that "Johnny" is reading at a seventh-grade level. We should know that in the eighth grade and then do whatever is necessary for the next four years to help him catch up.

There *must* be a revival of moral authority. This is the most critical element missing among educators today. Your analyses are correct and accurate. You have, in most instances, policies, plans, and programs that will work. It's not so much that you lack vision and concrete proposals as it is that you lack moral authority—nobody believes you!

Teachers cannot come to work as late as they can without a lesson plan, leave as early as they can, make as much as they can, and then sit on their cans. Moral authority demands much more.

Moral Decadence

Another internal impediment is moral decay and decadence. There is no such thing as value-free education. Nonvalues are values, but they are values leading to social decadence and decay. *The death of ethics is the sabotage of excellence.* If we are to lift ourselves out of this morass, we must go from the superficial to the sacrificial. We must lift our sights in order to see a new vision, and we must dig to new depths in order to. penetrate the superficial.

A steady diet of violence, vandalism, drugs, a teenage-pregnancy epidemic, alcohol and TV addiction have bred a passive, alienated, and superficial generation. The challenge is to close the economic and educational gap, and moral decadence diverts one from the goal of catching up.

A drunk army cannot fight a war for information and close the gap. Minds full of dope instead of hope will not fight for the right to vote and to fully register and vote as we must if we are to close the gap. A generation lacking the moral and physical stamina necessary to fight a protracted civilizational crisis is dangerous to themselves, their neighbors, and future generations. We need a sober, sane, and disciplined army to catch up.

In light of the internal decay, if we allow our children to eat junk, think junk, watch junk, listen to junk, talk junk, and play with junk—don't be surprised when they turn out to be "social junkies." We do reap what we sow. Everything that goes around, comes around.

Mass-Media Diversion

Whether we as educators know it or not, we are competing for the attention of our children's minds—and we are losing to the mass media. The mass media is the new primary educator in our society because it is the primary transmitter of knowledge, mores, folkways, values, and social trends. This is the first generation that by age fifteen has watched 18,000 hours of television and listened to many more hours of radio than that, while at the same time they have spent 11,000 hours in school and 3,000 hours in church. Thus, quantitatively, the mass media has greater access to our children's minds than the historic socializing agents (home, church, and school) combined—and qualitatively its impressions are deeper. If you don't believe me, check the posters on your son or daughter's wall and the T-shirts they are wearing—it's not a picture of the state superintendent of education. Entertainers, sports heroes, and other mass-media-created heroes are the models they are seeking to emulate.

What is being programmed into our children's minds through the media? Mick Jagger has an album out now entitled "Some Girls," and in a song by the same title he says: "French girls want Cartier; Italian girls want cars; American girls want everything in the world that you could possibly imagine; English girls, they're so prissy, I can't stand them on the telephone—sometimes I take the receiver off the hook—I don't want them to even call at all; white girls they're very pretty—sometimes they drive me mad; black girls just want to get f----d all night—I don't have that much jam." The Funkadelics have an album out now in which they sing about the "Doo-Doo Chasers," reducing human life to describing bodily functions and feces. The group Exile has a hit record out now entitled "I Want to Kiss You All Over," and Betty Wright has a song entitled "Tonight's the Night I Become a Woman," in which she describes in great detail her first sexual experience. We must call pornographic music what it is—child abuse. And television is no better. This season's programs may have slightly less violence on them, but the sexual exploitation has increased. They even have a name for it; they call it "T and A."

Our children are being programmed into premature heat, and the results are a teenage-pregnancy epidemic and rampant venereal disease. Eleven million teenagers are sexually active, and over 1 million teenagers became pregnant last year, including 30,000 between the ages of eleven and fifteen. Two-thirds of all teenage pregnancies were unplanned and unwanted, and one-third of all abortions were to teenagers. This "intercourse without discourse" is jeopardizing the welfare of this and future generations. These entertainers and celebrities have tremendous power and influence on our children's minds, and they must be challenged to accept responsibility that is in proportion to the power they have. We cannot stand idly by and allow them to divert an entire generation through a superficial understanding of life and the world.

Sex is too beautiful to be made ugly by ignorance, greed, and lack of discipline; and sex is too powerful to be left in the realm of mysticism and the superstitious. Sex education should not be avoided by calling it sex stimulation. It is media stimulation that is contributing most to the teenage-pregnancy epidemic, and only sex education, combined with moral education, will remedy this situation. We are sponsoring a "Reproductive Health and Health Careers Conference" in Chicago tomorrow and Wednesday, and we are prepared to take such a conference to other states as well. If you're interested, please feel free to contact our office.

A Crisis in Effort

It is clear that not everything wrong with our schools is rooted in economic, social, legal, and political elements. We are also confronted with a loss of the will to study and struggle. We need a revolution in values and priorities if we are going to turn the situation around.

The formula reads as follows: *Effort must exceed opportunity for change to occur.* For what does it matter if the doors of opportunity swing wide open and we're too drunk to stagger through them? What does it matter if our teacher is black or white if we're antisocial toward both? What does it matter if our teacher has a Ph.D. or "no-D" if we never show up for class? What does it really matter if we have a new book or an old book if we open neither? Motivation is at least as important as opportunity. For *with* motivation one can often learn in spite of the obstacles of opportunity, but *lacking* motivation the best opportunity in the world will pass you by.

Cognition and stimulation are compatible. That's why I don't apologize for getting excited and emotional when I share information, and that's why I use educational *and* motivational epigrams. It's both *interesting and true* that if you can conceive it, and believe it, you can achieve it. It's *inspirational and true* that it's not your aptitude, but your attitude, that determines your altitude, with a little intestinal fortitude or guts. It's *stimulating and true* that the laws of convenience lead to collapse, but the laws of sacrifice lead to greatness. Cognition and stimulation are compatible.

We must spend some time on the five Bs—blacks, browns, buses, budgets, and buildings—but we must spend an even greater amount of time and energy on the five As—attention, attendance, atmosphere, attitude, and achievement.

Massive Parental Detachment

The last internal impediment is massive parental detachment. Parents are the most critical element in a child's life. Parental involvement in the education of our children is absolutely essential and must be creatively planned rather than allowed to occur as an afterthought or accident.

Parents are the foundation of the school system (the starting point), not the bottom (the last stop). Life begins in the bedroom, is nurtured in the classroom, and culminates in the board room—in the various avenues of life. But parents are the beginning and foundation of it all.

Presently this most vital element is massively detached from our schools. Parental detachment is like a light without a plug or an oven without any heat. It is like a body without a soul and paper money without a gold reserve.

Too often politicians use our children as a political football to further their political careers. The first priority of board of education members is fiscal responsibility and management efficiency, at the highest level, and their reappointment or reelection, at another level. The principals' first priority, too often, is the progression of their career up the educational ladder, and teachers' first loyalty is to the union—the source of their economic security. Even the broader community (e.g., business and labor) are more interested in the end product (an efficient and productive worker) than they are in the child. Parents are the only adults whose first priority and vested interest is the child.

The recognition of this critical role that parents play shouldn't frighten them, but rather should serve to make them aware of the real power and responsibility they have. Parents are powerful because they birth the babies. They're powerful because they pay the taxes or the tuition to support the schools. Parents are powerful because they provide emotional security for children, and emotionally unstable children disrupt the educational process. Whether voted or appointed to office, the power of the board of education is derived from and granted by parents. Even striking teachers are powerful, not because of the union, but ultimately because parents respect the picket line.

Parents are the first teachers and the real enforcers of their child's conduct. They have the power to guide their child's study habits. Parents provide love, care, chastisement, and discipline and are the most important models in the child's formative years. In short, parents are the only element that can demand total accountability from the school and the child.

Parents must make room in their hearts, in their house, and in their schedule for their children. No parent is too poor, and no middle-class parent can be too busy, to take the time to raise a child while the child is a child. If parents don't take the time now, they'll have to take the time later to visit the counselor, the judge, or the jail.

A recent Gallup Poll found that discipline was perceived to be the number-one problem in both public and private education. However, the most interesting thing about the poll was that the same people perceived "parental detachment" as number ten on the list. What apparently was missed is that the resolution of number ten would virtually assure progress or the solving of the other nine concerns listed. No other one factor on the list could claim the same influence or have the same impact.

The Challenge to Administrators

The PUSH for Excellence education movement challenges the chief state school officers to coalesce with us in seeking massive parental involvement. Our programmatic goal for the first year was to restore order in the schools. Our second-year goal is to get hundreds, thousands, even millions of parents involved in the PUSH for Excellence. Our third-year goal will concentrate on academic achievement and character development.

We are asking parents—and you can aid us in asking them—to do four basic things which do not cost any more money, but they do require a change in our attitudes and priorities. We are asking them to:

1. Go to the school during the first week, meet their child's teacher, and exchange home phone numbers.

2. Monitor their child's study hours a minimum of two hours each day, with no radio, television, telephone calls, or social visits.

3. Go to the school and pick up report cards four times each year.

4. Pick up their child's test scores and discuss them with a trained counselor.

We challenge you chief state officers to join us in our efforts to implement the total involvement concept. That is, we must recognize that anything and everything that impacts upon our children's minds educates, and responsibility for education must be in proportion to the power possessed. Therefore we appeal to you to think of creative ways in which the religious community, the business community, parents, retired educators, the mass media, and many others can get involved.

The PUSH for Excellence movement challenges you to move beyond the general courses in civics and government and teach the basics and fundamentals of citizenship education. Last year, 3.1 million high-school seniors graduated, and virtually all of them were eligible by age and citizenship to vote last week. Yet most of them were not registered and did not vote. PUSH contends that upon graduation students must be given a diploma in one hand, symbolizing knowledge and wisdom, and a voter registration card in the other, symbolizing power and responsibility. And during their senior year they must be taught how to operate a voting machine. We must breed our children into citizenship education so that responsible citizenship becomes as natural as breathing, and graduation represents initiation rites into adulthood. Our children are not as apathetic or indifferent to voter registration as they are ignorant and fearful of a process and procedure that they don't understand. We are submitting a resolution to you for passage on this point, and we hope that you will give it serious consideration.

Last, we are challenging each of the state school superintendents to stay in touch with the grass-roots and day-to-day challenges by going back to the classroom to teach one class each semester. It will help to break up hardened educational arteries. Preachers must preach, doctors must practice, and educators must teach if they are to remain relevant. Educators who earned Ph.D.s in 1968 develop certain antique qualities unless they stay abreast. If professional educators fail to keep up or lose touch, they will become victims of educational atrophy.

Conclusion

We must fight for equity, ethics, and excellence because it is the only way that we can catch up and close the gap. Those of us who are behind must run faster because we are behind in a race for educational and economic equity and parity.

But we must close not only the quantitative gap but the qualitative gap as well.

We must close the gap with doctors, but doctors who are more concerned with public health than personal wealth.

Lawyers, but lawyers who are more concerned with justice than a judgeship.

Preachers, but preachers who will prophesy, not merely profiteer.

Journalists, but journalists who will ascribe, describe, and prescribe, not merely scribble.

Politicians, but politicians who seek to be of service, not merely seek an office.

Teachers, but teachers who will teach for life and not merely for a living.

Educators must believe in themselves, in their will, and in their skill to educate and administer effectively. We must believe in our children. Believe in our ability to teach them and their ability to learn.

We must believe that life is not accidental but providential, that it has meaning and purpose if we will but hold on and seek a new and brighter day.

Know that you are somebody, that you are God's child. For in the final analysis, we do not live by bread alone. We must know that unless God builds the house, they who labor, labor in vain.

We can teach our children—it is possible.

We ought to teach our children—it is our moral responsibility.

We must teach our children—it is today's imperative.

It's Up to You

Early on, Jackson spotted the teenage-pregnancy crisis and began to speak out on it. Unlike most of the speeches in this book, this speech was given to teenagers. Jackson delivered it at the "What's Happening" Teen Conference in Atlanta on June 19, 1978.

Good morning. I'm grateful for this privilege to participate in this youth congress, this fantastic national meeting with so many implications. This morning I want to speak on the subject, "It's Up to You," for it is important for you to get involved and to be a part of what's happening as you move toward making these decisions.

I want this area to my left to be Section A, and this area to my right, Section B. There are four steps in this ritual. Once we rehearse it one time, we will stand and do it all together.

The first part is called, "I Am Somebody." That is significant because if you don't feel that you're somebody, you won't act as if you're somebody, and you won't treat other people as if they are somebody. You must feel that you count in order to appreciate yourself and develop yourself in relation to other people.

People to my right, "I am"

ANSWER: "I am"

Now don't sound all scared and timid. I know better. "I am"

ANSWER: "I am"

REV. JACKSON: "Somebody."

ANSWER: "Somebody."

REV. JACKSON: "I am"

Answer: "I am"
Rev. Jackson: "Somebody."
Answer: "Somebody."
That's kind of mediocre. Try it, to my left.
Rev. Jackson: "I am"
Answer: "I am"
Rev. Jackson: "I am"
Answer: "I am"
Rev. Jackson: "Somebody."
Answer: "Somebody."

That's a little better. Give them a hand. That part deals with the question of self-appreciation and self-reliance: "I am somebody." The other is that it does not matter if we have the opportunity to live if we choose death. And so we say, "Down with dope; up with hope" because we cannot be what we ought to be if we push dope in our veins rather than hope in our brains.

Repeat this: "Down with Dope."
Answer: "Down with Dope."
"Up with Hope."
Answer: "Up with Hope."
"Down with Dope."
Answer: "Down with Dope."
"Up with Hope."
Answer: "Up with Hope."

You're kind of alive. I'm going to give you another hand. Now the third phase of it—and all of us are going to get involved with this—is that you must believe in your mind that you can do it. You must believe that you can do it. Don't let anybody convince you that you can't learn anything necessary for you to survive.

Repeat this: "My mind"
Answer: "My mind"
"Is a pearl."
Answer: "Is a pearl."
"I can learn anything"
Answer: "I can learn anything"
"In the world."
Answer: "In the world."
"My mind"
Answer: "My mind"
"Is a pearl."
Answer: "Is a pearl."
"I can learn anything"
Answer: "I can learn anything"

"In the world."

ANSWER: "In the world."

Now, take this last one. This is a very big one, maybe the biggest of all. Repeat this: "Nobody"

ANSWER: "Nobody"

"Will save us"

ANSWER: "Will save us"

"For us"

ANSWER: "For us"

"But us."

ANSWER: "But us."

This means that nobody is going to register you for you. Nobody is going to protect your body for you but you. Nobody is going to develop your mind for you but you. And if you don't develop your mind, you'll just be in bad shape, pitiful for the rest of your life.

"Nobody"

ANSWER: "Nobody"

"Will save us"

ANSWER: "Will save us"

"For us"

ANSWER: "For us"

"But us."

ANSWER: "But us."

Everybody stand. Give yourselves a big hand. Everybody stand. Now let's do the whole thing:

"I am somebody.

I may be poor,

But I am somebody.

I may be unskilled,

But I am somebody.

Respect me.

Protect me.

Never neglect me.

I am somebody.

Down with dope.

Up with hope.

My mind

Is a pearl.

I can learn anything

In the world.

Nobody

Will save us

For us

But us.
   Excel!
Excel!
Excel!
Right on!"

As you gather for this most important conference here in Atlanta, there are several points I want to wrestle with. The first point is that all of us cannot be famous because all of us cannot be well known. But all of us can be great because all of us can serve. Every now and then, I hear people brag about the new generation. It's not really anything to brag about being in the new generation because you didn't do anything to become the new generation. Your parents did something to make the new generation. You are the new generation without effort. So why brag about being new, when it's not the result of your work? Why brag about being black or being white? It's not the result of your work. You are a new generation without putting forth any effort. Your challenge is to become a greater generation, and you become a greater generation because you serve. If you feed more hungry people, you are a greater generation. If more people of this generation are educated, it's a greater generation. If the racial lines that separate us are overcome, we are a greater generation. And so our challenge is to be not just a new genera-tion, based upon birth, but to be a greater generation based upon work and effort.

Second, there's always the challenge of concentration. We used to have a saying some years ago in the freedom struggle, "Keep your eyes on the prize." If your prize is to develop your mind; if your prize is to develop your body; if your prize is to develop spiritual depth; if your prize is to grow up healthy, marry, and develop a family—if that is your prize, then don't let any activity divert you from your prize. When we are traveling, sometimes there are bumps in the road. Sometimes there are potholes in the road. Sometimes nails and broken glass may punc-ture our tire and delay us and divert us from the prize.

Mass-Media Diversion

One of the challenges of this generation is the threat of mass media as diversion. This is the first generation that, by age eighteen, has watched 18,000 hours of television and listened to more radio than that, com-pared with 11,000 hours of school and less than 3,000 hours of church. There's nothing that you need that you will ever achieve by being a mass-media addict. You will not learn to read, write, count, or think better simply by being a mass-media addict. And so you cannot become a victim of mass-media diversion. The same time you spend at night being entertained, you must commit to becoming educated. But that is a choice *you* must make. Part of my challenge is to lay before you what that decision is.

The other side of it, of course, is moral decadence, social decadence. In some real sense, premature pregnancy threatens this generation. Intercourse without discourse threatens this generation. Grabbing fire that's too hot for you to hold threatens this generation. There are two hallmarks of every champion: *discipline* and *character.* Sex is too beautiful to be made ugly by ignorance, greed, or lack of self-control, Sex as pleasure, sex as procreation, sex as fulfillment has its place. But sex is too beautiful to be made ugly by ignorance, greed, and lack of self-control.

On the other hand, not only is sex too beautiful to be made ugly by greed and ignorance and lack of self-control, sex is too powerful to stay in the realm of superstition. Our parents and teachers and preachers teach us about electrical wires because electrical wires are important, and they're dangerous. They teach us about cars because cars are important, and cars are dangerous. And we go to school and we learn who the presidents are, and that is important. We learn where the states are and what the capitals of the states are, and that is important. But in all of our studying, we must study ourselves, because we are more powerful than that car. We're more important than that state. We are more important than that car. We're more important than that electrical wire. So in all of our studying of the nation and of the states and of the presidents, we must study ourselves because sex is too beautiful to be made ugly by ignorance, greed, and lack of self-control, and sex is too powerful to be left to the realm of superstition.

One of the charges in this conference is to challenge you to make decisions. One decision I urge you to make today is that sex is not the only thrill in life. Sex is a thrill. But sex is not the only thrill in life. Twenty-five years ago when Senator Joseph McCarthy and the McCarthy movement were threatening free speech, a generation of youth rebelled and protested, fighting for free speech—and that was a thrill. When Rosa Parks sat down on the bus in Montgomery and Dr. King came to her rescue and then a whole generation fought to get a public accommodations bill, that was a thrill. When a group of students went to Selma, Alabama, and fought for the right to vote, that was a thrill.

Voter Registration

One of the resolutions I want you to pass here today has to do with voter registration. Virtually all of you will be eighteen when you become seniors in high school. Seniors are eligible to vote. A few years ago, we fought for the right to vote. When you go back across this nation, you should lobby at the various boards of education and make it mandatory that they teach you, during your senior year, how to use a voting machine; teach you who your alderman is; teach you where your precinct is; teach you who your elected officials are. Last year, 3.1 million high-school students graduated. All of them should have been registered to vote. The reason most of them did not register and vote was because they were not taught in school to register and vote. People are not born voting. People don't vote by instinct. People vote because they're taught to vote. You three or four thousand students here today, when you come across that stage and graduate, if you have a diploma in one hand (symbolizing knowledge and wisdom) and a voter registration card in the other hand (symbolizing power and responsibility), you will not only be a new generation, you will be a powerful generation, a generation to be respected, a generation that will get a response!

Now some of us get confused because sometimes we measure our manhood and our womanhood by violence and sex. In other words, if I can knock somebody down because I've got muscles, I am a man. I am tough. Or if I can engage in sex as often as I want to, I am a man; I am a woman. But I want you to know today that if someone is sick with fever and about to die, if someone stands there, 6'6" and cannot even give the person an aspirin, that person is not manly enough or adult enough or tough enough to make a difference. Somebody 5'3" might show up with a medicine bag under his or her arm. That person has the ability to save the person who is sick. You are not a man because you can kill somebody; you are a man because you can heal somebody. A man must be able to function. You're not a man because you can make a baby. Test tubes can make babies. You are a man because you can raise a baby and provide for a baby and develop a baby's life. A man is a man by a functioning definition. "I am a man if I can produce, protect, and provide."

In the same way, you are a woman by a functioning definition. Girls can make babies, but it takes women to raise them. The emotional maturity required to raise a baby means that babies really shouldn't have babies. If you cannot handle that load, then don't pick it up in the first place. *You* must make that decision!

Brothers, I want you to repeat this after me. "I am a man. I will produce; I will protect; I will provide."

Sisters, repeat this: "I am a woman. I will produce; I will protect; I will provide."

Now let me raise this next point with you. There's a scripture I used to read when I was much younger, but I didn't quite understand it then. "God causes it to rain on the just and the unjust alike." I didn't understand that too well because I knew that God was merciful and he helped people who couldn't help themselves. But the older I got, I finally learned what that verse meant. It meant that even though God loves you, you must live with the consequences of your decisions. In other words, if a little baby falls in a bathtub full of water, that baby will drown and must live with the consequences of that decision. If a six-year-old innocent, wonderful little child steps in front of a moving car, that child will most likely be killed because that child must live with the consequences of that decision. You who make the decision to put dope in your veins rather than hope in your brains or fill up your nose with cocaine or float around in angel dust—you may be black or white or rich or poor, but you must live with the consequences of your decisions. And that is why it is important that the church, the home, and the school teach us our options so we can know what decisions to make, whether to choose the high road or whether to choose the low road.

I repeat: sex is too beautiful to be made ugly by ignorance, greed, and lack of control, and sex is too important for us to be ignorant of it. We need to learn sex education in the first grade, second grade, third grade, fourth grade, and fifth grade! We need to learn about our sex organs just as soon as we learn about our other organs. We learn that if something is hot, it'll burn you. So don't touch it. We learn that if something is cold not to stay up against it too long—you'll freeze. We learn that if something tastes bitter, to spit it out of our mouths. We learn about our senses at ages 2, 3, 4, 5, and 6. There's no reason why we should cut ourselves off to the reality of our sex. We need to remove the superstition and the taboo and the foolishness. Sex is too powerful for us to leave in the realm of superstition.

Finally, I want to challenge you on this question of philosophy. I was listening not too long ago to a song that is an interesting kind of song to me. "You Light Up My Life" is beautiful. And for a long time, I was merely impressed with the melody. And there were some other songs that I had argued were damaging. Songs like "Shake Your Booty," "It's All Right to Make Love on the First Night," and "Let's Do It the French Way" because I knew what that implied. And this song eventually closes on this line: it talks about "How can it be wrong when it feels so right?" Now that's an interesting proposition, because a whole lot can be wrong with something even though it feels right. That's just like saying how can not doing homework be so wrong when it feels so right? How can not developing my mind be so wrong when it feels so right?

If you go further in school, you will learn the philosophy called "hedonism." It deals with short-term pleasure and long-term pain. You remember this: *the laws of convenience lead to collapse, but the laws of sacrifice lead to greatness.* Those who sacrifice for the Olympics get the gold medal. Those who sacrifice and go to medical school get the medical degree. Those who sacrifice and go to law school get the law degree. Those who are able to live with the laws of sacrifice are able to settle for short-term pain but enjoy long-term pleasure. Too many of us, unfortunately, end up with short-term pleasure and long-term pain.

We must make a decision. You can either use willpower on the inside and cope with or use pill power and cop out. If you've got willpower, just because it rains, you don't have to drown. If you have willpower, just because a mountain is high, it doesn't mean you can't climb it. If you've got willpower, just because it's cold, it doesn't mean you will freeze. We must develop willpower and cope with, rather than pill power and cop out. We must know the difference between sweat and tears. Sweat is wet; tears are wet. Sweat is salty; tears are salty. But progress comes through sweat. Progress never came through tears. When life gets difficult, there's nothing like reaching down on the inside, sweating for that which you believe.

Finally, I want you to know that there's nothing more dangerous than to be trapped with a shrinking mind and an expanding behind. You must develop your mind to protect your behind, your body, and your soul. *You* must make that decision. Nobody can make it for you. *You* must make that decision. I want all of you to repeat this now:

If my mind can conceive it, and my heart can believe it, I know I can achieve it.

Down with pill power. Up with willpower. Down with dope. Up with hope.

It's not my aptitude but my attitude that determines my altitude, with a little intestinal fortitude.

My mind is a pearl. I can learn anything in the world.

I am somebody.

Nobody will save us for us but us.

Right on!

PEACEMAKER

"History teaches us that ultimately might is not right; right is might. Peace is possible. Peace is imperative. The nuclear race must end. It is too costly, too dangerous, and too likely to take place. We must choose the human race over the nuclear race."

In Pursuit of Peace—
A More Excellent Way

President Carter and Soviet President Brezhnev had just signed SALT II (Strategic Arms Limitation Treaty) and it was being sent to the Senate for ratification when this speech was made. (SALT I was completed and ratified in 1972.) The Senate never ratified SALT II, but Presidents Carter and Reagan voluntarily agreed to operate within its limits, at least until mid-1986. This speech was the commencement address at the University of Rhode Island, Kingston, Rhode Island, on May 27, 1979.

Students and graduates of the University of Rhode Island and students from other colleges and universities around our nation, you are a new generation. But that, in and of itself, is no accomplishment. You're new by birth, not because of any effort or choice on your part. However, each generation has the opportunity, even the obligation, to receive the torch from the last generation and carry it forward. Generations of students before you accepted the critical challenges that confronted them.

In the early 1950s, McCarthyism threatened free speech, and students were in the forefront of resistance. In the 1960s some citizens were denied basic citizenship rights, and students, black and white, led the struggles for public accommodations, voting rights, and open housing. In the late 1960s and early 1970s the nation was confronted with a war for which we never found a moral justification, and students rose up to say, "No, we won't go." These generations were great because they saw and accepted the challenges of their generation. Not everyone can be

215

famous, because to be famous is to be well known. But everyone can be great, because greatness lies in service, and everyone can serve.

This generation of students has the same opportunity and obligation. You must discover the great issues of your day and meet them, if you are to be a great generation—and that is your challenge. But if you are to meet them you must move from massive detachment to massive involvement, from the paralysis of media diversion to education and edification.

One of the great issues confronting us is the massive arms race. No person who cherishes human life, including his or her own life, can afford to be unconcerned or aloof with regard to this important development. The huge military budget, eating away at the social fabric of this society and the world economy like terminal cancer, is reason enough for every student in America to be concerned.

The world's people pay a huge bill for the arms race—approximately $400 billion a year. At the same time, on any single school day, some 200 million children around the world are not in school, mostly because their families are too poor to send them or their country is too poor to provide classrooms for them to attend. The contemporary arms race is both wasteful and dangerous, and humankind can afford neither. The human race and the nuclear arms race cannot coexist.

The grim urgency of the matter is underscored when one reflects on official U.S. nuclear policy, including collaboration with the apartheid-fascist regime in South Africa. Along with several Western European countries and Israel, Congress continues to support a policy of extending financial assistance to South Africa in the fields of uranium extraction and processing, the supply of nuclear equipment, the transfer of technology, the training of nuclear scientists from South Africa, and general financial support for South Africa's nuclear program. The possibility of Nazi Germany having the capability of producing nuclear weapons was a nightmare for the world to contemplate in the 1940s. Now that same nightmare is threatening to become a devastating reality again in the 1980s as their successors in South Africa come ever closer to being able to produce nuclear weapons—if they are not there already—because of Western financial assistance.

The specific contribution that the people of our country can make to this international effort at this moment in history is to insist that the U.S. Senate ratify the SALT II agreement without delay or crippling amendments. We have a moral obligation to insist on this as the only country whose government ever used an atomic weapon against another people.

For the next several months the Senate and the American people will debate the merits of ratifying the second phase of the Strategic Arms Limitation Talks (SALT II) with the Soviet Union. There are few issues more critical to our two countries and the world than that SALT II be ratified. The choice is not between a perfect treaty and guaranteed peace and security but between an imperfect treaty in an imperfect world and *no* treaty.

Ratification, not rejection, is in the national interest of both countries. Ratification, not rejection, will contribute to a wiser use of our and the world's limited resources. Ratification, not rejection, will contribute— even if only in degree—to greater world economic stability (i.e., lesser inflation and greater employment). It will do so because the process of needlessly squandering our human, technical, and economic resources on capital-intensive, nonproductive, noneconomically cyclical, and nonsocially useful hardware will be slower *with* SALT II than *without* it.

Today I want to discuss four basic concerns regarding the coming SALT II treaty and debate.

How Did We Arrive at SALT II?

With the discovery, development, and military use of the atom in World War II against the Japanese at Hiroshima and Nagasaki, it became apparent that humanity could now develop the capacity literally to destroy itself. Thus the nuclear arms race began. Building on the work of Presidents Truman and Eisenhower, President Kennedy signed the Test Ban Treaty in 1963, the first agreement with the Soviet Union to stop the poisonous testing of nuclear explosives in the atmosphere. Five years later, in 1968, under President Johnson, the United States, Russia, and other nations signed the Nuclear Non-Proliferation Treaty, which was designed to prevent the spread of nuclear explosives to other nations.

In 1972 President Nixon signed the SALT I agreement, the Anti-Ballistic Missile System, or ABM Treaty, which, for the first time, limited the development of defensive missile systems; and a five-year Interim Agreement which placed agreed-upon limits on the number of offensive weapons. In November 1972 negotiations began on SALT II, which are now completed and will be unveiled and voted on shortly by the U.S. Senate.

What Is SALT II?

The SALT II treaty consists of three basic parts: (1) a *treaty* to last until the end of 1985 which sets limits or equalizes strategic nuclear vehicles, Multiple Independently Targeted Reentry Vehicles (MIRVs), heavy bombers, and Intercontinental Ballistic Missiles (ICBMs); (2) a shorter-term *protocol* that will expire on December 31, 1981, which, until then, bars deployment of certain types of missiles; and (3) a *joint statement* of principles and guidelines for subsequent negotiations on SALT III.

In addition, the treaty contains a commitment about the development and use of the Soviet Backfire bomber, an agreed-upon memorandum listing the number of strategic weapons deployed by each side according to different categories, a set of provisions dealing with quantitative and qualitative limits on the development and deployment of missiles, and verification measures.

Why Is SALT II Necessary and Desirable in Spite of Its Limitations?

National Interest

The first obligation of any government is to provide for the common defense. PUSH is convinced, after the reading and research that we have done, that SALT II fulfills this obligation. Secretary of Defense Harold Brown and others have assured us that we have the capacity to survive any first-strike attack from the Soviet Union and respond with a devastating attack of our own that would destroy them as a functioning society. That, I understand, in military terms, is called "deterrence." For security purposes, in addition to *actually having* that capacity, the Soviet Union must *perceive* us to have that capability so that there will be no miscalculation of judgment. By the same token, America must not only be secure, but Americans must be convinced and feel that we are secure.

Black America must not remain aloof from the SALT II debate. The two major targets of any Russian attack would be against our military bases and installations and our major metropolitan centers—both of which are occupied in disproportionate numbers by black people. As with most things, blacks are a weather vane in this society. That is, we receive the first and the most of whatever is bad and the least and last of whatever is good.

Morally Sound

It is morally sound for the U.S. Senate to ratify this treaty. If we reject this treaty, other nations of the world would lose faith in our commitment to negotiate, compromise, and cooperate in the Strategic Arms Limitations process. The considered judgment of world opinion would be against us. Rejection of ratification would give the Soviet Union a propaganda tool that could be used against us around the world. We are morally obligated to ratify this treaty.

An appeal to the world from the Stockholm Peace Conference has urged all governments to cooperate in outlawing nuclear weapons and ending the arms race. That was also the underlying seed of the World Disarmament Conference convened at the United Nations last spring. The power of world public opinion, mobilized, can aid in putting an end to the arms race.

Verification

Most critics have focused on the issue of verification, that is, can the U.S. effectively monitor whether the Soviet Union is abiding by the terms of the treaty? The Carter administration claims that, even with the loss of our monitoring bases in Iran, verification can still take place because of the "size and nature of activities we must monitor and the many effective and sophisticated intelligence collection systems which we in America possess." Actually, without oversimplifying, the real question regarding verification is whether there are greater verification possibilities with or without a treaty which sets a framework and lays ground rules for verifying compliance. Attempts to verify without a treaty could lead to even greater mistrust, uncertainty, and miscalculation.

Equivalence

Some argue that we should not ratify the SALT II agreement because we are negotiating from a position of weakness. However, most experts agree that during the last two decades, and at tremendous economic and social cost to their society, the Russians have reached a point of "essential military equivalency." One of the fundamental problems facing America's leaders and the American people is psychological. We have gone from a position of a 10-to-1 advantage in 1960 to a state of essential equivalency, and psychologically we're having trouble adjusting to dealing with others as equals. We have gone from a "monopoly of power," where we lived over people, to a "balance of power," where we are being forced to live with other people.

The Soviets weakened their total society because they used so much of their national resources to catch up with us militarily. Domestically, they have suffered agriculturally and industrially, and there is consumer unrest. Because of the increased militarization and the resultant repression, increased resistance periodically (and increasingly) is manifesting itself in Soviet society. Ratification of the SALT II agreement will aid and strengthen the moderate and peace elements in the Soviet society, thus reducing the need for us to compete with them militarily, and will aid the possibility of greater peaceful cooperation. The pursuit of peace and disarmament represents strength, but the continuation and escalation of the arms race really represents weakness.

Linkage

Some argue that we should refuse to ratify SALT II because of Russian adventures around the world and because of their own internal violations of human rights. Such a linkage would slow, prohibit, and further delay the process involved in trying to de-escalate the nuclear arms race. Disarmament is much too important to be sidetracked by such linkage.

Process vs. Solution

Even with ratification of SALT II, the arms race will continue, but at a slower pace and in a more predictable fashion. We tend to want final solutions, but SALT II represents a small step in the right direction in a continuing process. This strategic arms limitation agreement is not a panacea for all of the ills accompanying the proliferation of nuclear weapons. Only an international treaty providing for total and complete disarmament would accomplish that. SALT II contributes significantly to that process because it recognizes that any new escalation of nuclear weapons production is a threat to all and must be avoided. That is the beginning of wisdom in this matter and the beginning of the end to the madness that otherwise could engulf us all.

Nuclear Holocaust

Failure to ratify the SALT II treaty increases the instability in the world and will cause a tremendous escalation of the arms race and associated costs (perhaps an extra $30 billion on the part of the U.S.). Many of us have failed to come to grips with the awesome destructive potential of nuclear weapons. For example, one relatively simple Titan II missile carries *three times* the destructive power of all the explosives detonated during World War II and the Korean War combined. When one realizes that there are thousands of these nuclear devices on both sides, it requires little imagination to consider what would be left of the world should they ever go off. The brush with disaster at Three Mile Island provides a small insight into the aftermath of a thermonuclear war.

Amendments

Some senators are contemplating adding amendments to the treaty, while the Carter administration insists that it be accepted as is. This treaty is too important to be jeopardized by unacceptable, one-sided, and unilateral amendments. If there are amendments to the treaty, they should be part of the continuing negotiating process, and thus acceptable to both sides. Any amendments that are not subject to compromise, and thus which would jeopardize the treaty itself, should be avoided.

Change

Developments in communication and technology, population shifts to metropolitan centers, and the rising independence and expectation of underdeveloped nations have caused increasingly rapid changes in the

relationships between nations. We should expect this process to continue and even escalate in the 1980s. Matthew Nimetz, counselor of the
Department of State, said in Atlanta on April 6, "We are witnessing a
massive decentralization of international management which has become more democratic in process, but more strident in tone, more
uncertain in direction, and more chaotic in appearance." In such an
atmosphere of change and uncertainty, we must increase the stability
and predictability of the nuclear arms race.

Priorities

We must ratify the SALT II treaty in order to enhance the possibility
that we can rechannel our national resources toward our domestic needs
rather than continuing to waste them on an arms race that literally no
one can win.

The Pursuit of Peace—
A More Excellent Way

The U.S. must make the economic, political, military, and psychological
adjustment of being a world power but of not dominating the world.
Military power is not the only form of power in the world. Some believe
that might is right, but actually right is might. If we're going to compete,
and we must, let us not think that the most lasting form of security is
military. Arms may be able to enforce quiet, but they can never establish
peace. Justice is the prerequisite for peace—at home and abroad.

Excellence is doing your best—as an individual or a nation—against
the odds. We ought to seek to be first in the world, but first in moral
excellence, first in service to others, first in justice and compassion, first
to discover the cure for cancer, first to feed the hungry in our country
and around the world, first in ideas and ideals, first in diplomacy and
statesmanship, first in helping to build political institutions and structures in the world that can sustain rapid economic and technological
modernization and change.

We need not be afraid to compete, nor should we fear competition,
but let us compete to heal, to prolong and improve the quality of life, not
to kill and jeopardize life through a ridiculous and wasteful arms race.
Let us compete to reconcile rather than to separate. Let us compete to
accommodate rather than to alienate and annihilate.

But we in the human rights movement—whether in the peace and
disarmament division or the civil rights division—must not ourselves be
naive. We must not shy away from that which is necessary to move us
along the path toward our ideals and goals. That is, we must not shy
away from power and the ambiguities that accompany it. We cannot
have peace in the world until we get a piece of the world. There is no

conflict between power and human rights. In fact, power is the prerequisite to secure human rights, because power is simply the ability to
achieve purpose.

So what must our agenda be? The human rights movement—the
peace forces, the civil rights forces, indeed all forces seeking to improve
the quality of life—must join hands and coalesce. In that coalition, we
must distinguish between our private organizational agendas and the
coalition's major public policy agenda and be willing and able to distinguish between major and minor agenda items.

We can't shift from killing abroad to healing at home unless we
coalesce. We can't provide quality and equality of education for all our
own people unless we coalesce. We can't provide quality health care,
safe and sanitary housing, economic security, adequate and healthy food
for all of our citizens unless we coalesce. We must coalesce to slow and
eventually end the arms race so these human rights issues can be
attended to.

But the external issues and struggle are only part of the dialectic.
There is a system without and a system within. To fight for these
humane causes requires a sane, sensitive, and sober generation. A
generation high on drugs, pickling its brains in alcohol, engaging in
intercourse without discourse, using the means of violence and vandalism to express their protests and alienation is too morally wicked and
physically weak to win the battle.

There must be a balance between the external and the internal. The
external must be the focus for economic and political struggle, but the
internal must guide and sustain you over the long haul. The "me"
generation must become the "we" generation and stop reflecting in the
mirror and begin looking out the window. When you look out the
window, let me suggest some things at which you should look.

First, we must look to end the cancer of increased racial polarization
in our society. We must make a conscious effort and go beyond the call
of duty to overcome the estrangement and alienation that presently
separate blacks, browns, and whites. It will not be easy, and it will cost
us time, money, and effort. But if we don't, it will cost us more socially,
politically, and economically.

Second, we must look at the crisis of unemployment. A combination
of political power and dramatic direct action around the theme "Put
America Back to Work" must greet every candidate in every primary
come 1980, and we ought to look seriously at the possibility of a massive march on Washington around the same theme on August twenty-
eighth of this year—the sixteenth anniversary of the 1963 March on
Washington.

Third, we need to look at the potential strength of the youth vote.

There are 3.1 million high-school seniors graduating this year. Kennedy defeated Nixon in 1960 by 118,000 votes. Nixon defeated Humphrey in 1968 by 550,000 votes, and Carter defeated Ford in 1976 by 1.7 million votes. The power of 3.1 million high-school graduates alone is greater than the combined pluralities of three presidential elections in the last sixteen years. We must insist that—as an educational function—at all high-school graduations, our students should come across the stage with a diploma in one hand and a voter registration card in the other.

If you add to this number, college students and working and unemployed youth, young people potentially have the power to determine the next president and congress and to determine the course of this nation. College presidents should insist that, along with an academic transcript, students should submit a copy of their voter registration card. Any person coming across this stage today who is unregistered to vote has a driver's license but isn't going anywhere.

Fourth, when students look out the window, they should see the need to struggle for and develop alternative renewable energy resources and technology that will allow for continued economic stability in a safe and healthful environment.

Last, we must look for an adequately planned and funded urban policy. We must rebuild our cities; they are the centers of modern society. There has never been a suburb without a city. It's not exclusively a race question because more whites live in cities than do blacks and browns. Cities are the cornerstone of our civilization, and they must be saved and rebuilt.

This is a workable agenda. It's one that we can do—it's possible. It's one that we ought to do—it's the moral thing. It's an agenda that we must do—the imperative of now.

But we must have faith. Faith in ourselves, faith in our fellow human beings, faith in the future, and faith in a power beyond ourselves. If we have faith, the future is ours and cannot be denied or taken from us. If we have faith, disciplined minds, and developed characters, there is no limit to what we can accomplish together.

Thank you very much, and God bless you.

Foreign Policy—
But Not Foreign Values

While he was a candidate for the Democratic party's 1984 presidential nomination, Jackson was invited to speak at the United Nations by the ambassadors to the UN from the African states on January 27, 1984. Jackson indicated from the beginning of his campaign that one purpose of his candidacy was to raise issues that otherwise would not be raised. African policy was one of those issues.

I come before you today as a public servant, not as a perfect servant. I come to engage in dialogue, to learn, and to share. I do not presume to know all of your problems, thus I do not presume to have all of the solutions. I know there are many crises on the great continent, and, while I do not have the answers, I do have a concern, I do have a will to listen, I am willing to learn and to share.

I do bring a set of values, an attitude, and a philosophy to foreign policy. It is an approach of mutual respect, of reciprocity, of talking, of negotiating conflicts, and of measuring human rights by one yardstick. I argue that the first step in foreign policy is to count the foreigners. There are four billion people in the world—two billion Asian (one-half of them Chinese); one of every eight people on earth is African. Early U.S. history was perverted by counting those of us who are of African descent as three-fifths human and those of European descent as seven-fifths human. As a result, it imperiled our nation at its foundation and stunted its growth and global outlook. Peace requires justice and that we play the game by one set of rules.

My approach to foreign policy is to engage in negotiations, not confrontations. World leaders must initiate positive action, not just engage in negative reaction. Thus I urge an approach of presidential initiative. An American president ought to meet African leaders, visit the African continent, and learn and share. Our foreign policy ought to reflect diplomatic sharing, and agricultural, economic, technical, and cultural exchange. If we are to remain the hope of the free world, our challenge is not military escalation but a worldwide war on poverty, disease, and illiteracy. Domestic policy is foreign policy—they are interrelated. That's why my campaign has as its theme: justice at home and peace abroad. We must give peace a chance.

I need not tell you that we live in perilous times. I need not tell you that the vast majority of humankind wants peace, economic and social justice, and the right of self-determination. This very institution was designed and built by the nations of the world, including the United States, to implement these goals. We in the United States have had a very special interest and mission in creating the United Nations. Our people have come from all corners of the globe, from Africa, Europe, Asia, and the Americas. Our nation indeed is a mini–United Nations.

As I travel around this country and talk to the people in the towns, cities, and factories, they all tell me how important it is that we learn to live with the rest of the world, especially because we are fast becoming a genuinely interdependent world. The electronic media bring to our living rooms the wars in El Salvador, Lebanon, and Angola. The people of this country know and want a continuing dialogue with the rest of the world, and they see the United Nations as a forum where this dialogue can take place. I would like to assure you that the political gimmick to punish this or that international organization is nothing more than political gimmickery. After all, it is somewhat humorous when a major power like ours begins to punish an international organization devoted to uplifting the small farmers of the world. The real American tradition is to stand by the seashore and wave people to come in and share our bounty, not to wave them goodbye.

I want, however, for you to understand that there is a great moral debate going on in this country as to what kind of nation we want to become. After all, we have been a major world power for just a few decades. We have not had the time to digest and understand this grave moral responsibility. It is for this reason that during this campaign I want to talk about the moral responsibility for being a major world power. There is the dilemma of making every crisis in the world our own crisis. Once we make it our own crisis, we are called upon to provide quick and immediate solutions. Unfortunately there are no quick and easy solutions for difficult and sometimes insoluble problems.

When we become frustrated and incapable of finding solutions, we take the easy way out by engaging in political gimmickery. When gimmickery fails, it sometimes leads to paranoia, and indeed, as the American political theorist Richard Hofstadter has told us, we develop a paranoid style of politics. It is my intention and the intention of the vast majority of the American people to make sure that this paranoid style of domestic politics is not exported to the world. What I stand for today is a new approach to politics not only domestically but also internationally. This paranoid style that we have pursued has confused the vast majority of the nations, especially the newly independent countries. We should not only cease being the police of the world but, more important, we should not and cannot become the bully of the world.

The struggle for internal democracy by the people of this country did not prepare us to become either policemen or bullies. The democracy that we have struggled for internally must be reflected internationally. You will forgive me if I draw from my early training as a preacher when I say that we need a new vision of the global community. That vision must involve an understanding and acceptance of each nation or culture as having an integrity and authenticity that cannot be trampled upon. That is why my former teacher Martin Luther King, Jr., spent so much of his time teaching us about peace and nonviolence—not because he was afraid but because he saw the need to unite love and will to preserve humanity. Such a new vision is essential today if we are to preserve the human race, especially since we know that the paranoid style can only lead to war and annihilation.

Such visions, I am sure you are going to tell me, are unlikely to resolve the many practical problems that confront us. But before I turn to the practical problems, I want to remind you where excessive realism has taken us during the past forty years since the inception of this institution. Realism without a vision is an empty process.

I think we need to have a new framework to deal with the world's problems. There is a dangerous tendency today to move away from seeking multilateral and regional solutions and toward relying entirely on bilateral solutions. If there is going to be any meaningful solution in the Middle East, Central America, and South Africa it must involve the countries in those regions, especially the regional organizations like the front-line states, the Organization for African Unity, the Contadora group, and Middle Eastern regional groupings. We certainly must see these groupings as partners rather than adversaries.

Indeed, the time has come for us to give up the anachronistic view of John Foster Dulles that the nonaligned movement, for example, is immoral. All these regional organizations must be harnessed if there is going to be genuine peace. The time has come for us to stop seeing the nations of the world as mere pawns in a giant chess game being played by two powers. If there is going to be any progress, this very fragile institution, the United Nations, must be strengthened and used creatively to bring about peace. The time has come for the nations of the world to stop using this global body cynically, to laud it when it is useful to them but to condemn it when it is against their interests. History has taught us that multinational institutions are difficult to build and easy to destroy, and the major powers have an additional responsibility to see that these international organizations are preserved and protected.

I want to turn now to look at some crisis points in world politics and, second, to make some comments on the role of the United States in the efforts to bring about social and economic justice and, finally, to see how this can be accomplished within the framework of a global arms race and the threat of nuclear war.

Several crisis points in the world today threaten our global peace and security. Our interdependence makes us recognize the necessity of resolving these crisis points so our children and our grandchildren can live in a more just, equal, and peaceful world. There are at least three critical regions in the world today where the United States can make a difference. We need to devise a new strategy of leadership for ourselves, one that takes into account our historic heritage—our anticolonial origins, our multinational population, rich in the cultures of all the peoples of the world, our internal struggles for social, economic reform, and justice.

The crisis in southern Africa needs our attention. This is 1984. For the people of Namibia, 1984 means one hundred years of colonialism. For decades the U.N. has attempted to negotiate the independence of Namibia with the Republic of South Africa. Never before has the world come so close to achieving a solution as in Security Council Resolution 435. But the government of South Africa continues to place stumbling blocks on the road to Namibia's independence. The government of South Africa introduces conditions that must be solved prior to addressing Namibia's independence. The government of South Africa is delaying the independence of Namibia. The United States must not find itself a party to South Africa's obstructionist plan. We must not find ourselves supporting a government that violates the basic principles of the U.N. charter.

The world has long recognized the inhumanity, immorality, and injustice of apartheid. The global community has sought to isolate the apartheid government. In every other part of the globe, nations have made steps toward achieving greater social, economic, and political justice for their people. South Africa chooses to stand still, even to step backward. In every other part of the globe, nations have given up or are giving up their colonies. South Africa chooses to stand still or step backward. The preconditions and extraneous issues raised by South Africa only delay Namibia's independence. The United States must not find itself a party to the delaying process. We can play a major role in developing a new strategy which should be undertaken under the auspices of the United Nations and include the South West Africa People's Organization (SWAPO) as the sole and authentic representative of the people of Namibia. My country is South Africa's number-one trading partner and is in fact a strategic economic military ally. This is a source of shame and despair. This is the despair of the earth, not the hope of the free world.

Let us not find ourselves here in 2084 discussing Namibia's independence. One hundred years is too long a time for the Namibian people to wait. With our own history founded in an anticolonial struggle, the United States should recognize the aspirations of the Namibian people and all peoples of the world still under colonialism. For if Namibia's independence is not won by multilateral diplomatic efforts, it will be won by armed struggle, which poses a greater threat to global peace and security.

Fundamental Questions to Be Raised

• Why has the mighty United States of America not made a greater impact on Africa? Why is there no single state in Africa that this country can show to the nations of the world, and to herself, as a shining example, a very beautiful demonstration, and an excellent model of American rugged capitalism, of the free-enterprise system in a democratic society?

• Why is it that the United States—with all her glorified direct aid and technical assistance to developing countries, her handsome contributions to the World Bank, International Monetary Fund, United Nations specialized agencies such as the Food and Agriculture Organization (FAO), the United Nations Educational, Scientific, and Cultural Organization (UNESCO), UNDP, the World Health Organization (WHO), and her self-assumed role in the defense of the free world—does not have a large following in Africa today? Why is her influence not greater than it is? Why is she not more highly respected?

• The U.S. policy for Africa must be structured on the basis of a clear determination:

What America wants and needs from African states.
What Africa has to offer the U.S.
What Africa wants and needs from the U.S.
What the U.S. has to offer Africa.
What are the challenges to a U.S.-Africa partnership?

What have been and still are the road blocks to better U.S.-African cooperation, trade, partnership, and friendship?

Some Cardinal Principles to Be Observed in Developing a U.S. Policy for Africa

• All U.S. citizens are not European descendants.

• Over twenty million American citizens trace their ancestry to Africa.

• Africa has to be considered as important to the U.S.A. and as much a part of the U.S.A. and as much a part of U.S. foreign policy as are European nations, Israel, Japan, Canada, Russia, Latin American states, the European Economic Community (EEC), the Organization for Economic Cooperation and Development (OECD), North Atlantic Treaty Organization (NATO), and the General Agreement on Tariffs and Trade (GATT).

• The U.S. government should identify the similarities between the struggle of blacks in America and the struggle of blacks in Africa, particularly in South Africa. These are the common struggles for: (1) political and civil franchise, (2) economic emancipation, (3) human rights, (4) self-respect, and (5) the basic opportunities and responsibilities of all first-class citizens of any democratic nation.

• U.S. treatment of its black citizens will impact favorably on or impede the respect, trust, confidence, or audience and reception accorded the U.S. government by African leaders.

• Significant strides with respect to race relations and civil rights have been made in the U.S. since the 1960s. The U.S. government needs to capitalize on this in its contacts and dealings with African nations. In the meantime, it should continue to make even greater strides and progress toward achieving the ideal "rainbow" nation, making the U.S.A. a true melting pot and weaving a beautiful national quilt of races, varied cultural origins, religious persuasions, colors, political parties, geographical distribution, income levels, professions, and occupations.

• A true "rainbow" coalition can improve African confidence and trust in America.

Vital Economic Considerations

• The U.S. should accord the same preferential treatment to friendly African governments as it does to friendly European governments, Canada, Japan, and to certain Latin American nations.

• The U.S. government should support and participate in the African Development Bank as fully as it does in the Inter-American Development Bank.

• The U.S. government should offer support to Economic Community of West African States Fund for Cooperation, Compensation, and Development (ECOWAS) comparable to what it gives to the EEC.

• One or more African nations should be included in the GATT and the OECD.

• The United States should seriously encourage and expand free and fair trade with African nations instead of sparingly feeding African nations teaspoons of pitiful aid with strings attached as compared to what the U.S. gives to nations on other continents.

• The United States should provide aid to Africa for productive economic development programs and projects of the same magnitude provided to Israel and for the reconstruction of Europe after the Second World War. More money is provided to Israel alone in aid, grants, and loans than provided all black African nations combined. More loans are made to Mexico and Brazil than to all black African nations combined. This imbalance is unfair and creates an atmosphere unconducive to peace because it perpetuates poverty, disease, ignorance, fear, hate, bitterness, international terrorism, and unrest in the world.

Basic Political and Social Considerations

• Africa seriously needs UNESCO, WHO, FAO, International Bank for Reconstruction and Development (IBRD), United Nations Conference on Trade and Development (UNCTAD), International Labor Organization (ILO), but it especially needs UNESCO at this time.

• African nations do not need more military buildup.

• African nations are capable of becoming trusted U.S. allies. Liberia has been a faithful and valuable ally of the U.S. since 1847, as faithful as any other U.S. ally.

• African nations can become strong, profitable, and dependable trading partners with the U.S.A.

• There can be rich and valuable cultural, social, and commercial exchanges between Africa and the U.S.A.

• African nations (through the Organization of African Unity [OAU]) and the U.S. should work out a protocol of division of labor in industry, agriculture, trade, and commerce.

• Likewise, Africa (through the OAU) and the U.S. must work out a protocol or treaty of cultural and social exchanges.

The Importance of Firsthand High-Level Direct Personal Contacts in Africa with African Leaders

• The United States should send small, senior-level missions to selected African states to consult with and obtain the views, counsel, and advice of heads of state; appropriate ministers of government; president, African Development Bank; secretary general, OAU; executive secretary, United Nations Economic Commission for Africa (ECA); managing director, ECOWAS Fund; African business executives; and private Africans.

• U.S. leaders should undertake fact-finding missions to Africa to consult with the same levels of Africans to learn how they view African-American relations, U.S. government policies toward Africa over the years, and what they believe would strengthen U.S.-African relations in the areas of economic cooperation, trade, international politics, and the struggle for world peace.

Thank you for the opportunity to speak before you today. American-African relations are important, but they are seldom discussed in this country. Thank you for providing this platform. I hope these ideas can become the framework for further dialogue.

American Options on Apartheid

Following a seventeen-day visit to South Africa in the summer of 1979, Jackson was invited to testify on September 6, 1979, before the U.S. House of Representatives Subcommittee on Africa, Committee on International Relations.

Chairman Solarz and members of the House Subcommittee on Africa. First, I want to express to you my sincere thanks on behalf of the Board of Directors of Operation PUSH and our South African delegation for the invitation extended by you to present testimony on our recent trip to South Africa.

In its oversight and legislative functions, this subcommittee of the International Relations Committee of the United States House of Representatives can do an enormous amount of good in helping to shape our nation's foreign policy and, in particular, our relationship to South Africa, and in making that foreign policy consistent with the human rights sensitivities of the American public. This is particularly important, in my judgment, because the clock of history is ticking away in South Africa. We have reached the countdown stage in the long struggle between the forces of freedom and institutionalized racist oppression. The United States, in its own national interest, is required by historical circumstances to choose sides in that struggle, and it would be very unwise, to say the least, for our country to be on the side of supporting moral bankruptcy and institutionalized racism.

Mr. Chairman, as you and the distinguished members of this committee well know, much has been written and said about conditions in South Africa. The range of national and international organizations that have addressed the problem of apartheid is quite extensive, and the information they have published is considerable. This range includes such international bodies as the United Nations Special Committee on Apartheid and the World Peace Council, and national organizations like PUSH, the American Committee on Africa, Clergy and Laity Concerned, the NAACP Task Force on Africa, and the International Freedom Mobilization, which last April convened a summit conference of black religious leaders on apartheid at the UN Church Center in New York.

Of course, this legislative body has access to voluminous amounts of published information by these and other organizations. In addition, many persons with particular expertise on African and international affairs are available to this committee. One calls to mind Mr. Johnny Makitini, the North American Representative of the African National Congress of South Africa (ANC); Bishop H. H. Brookins, Chairman of the Board of PUSH, who presided over an Episcopal District of the AME Church in Lusaka earlier in this decade; Dr. Samih Farsoun, the current president of the Association of Arab-American University Graduates, who is professor of sociology at the American University here in Washington, D.C.; and Mr. Randall Robinson, Executive Director of Trans-Africa, to mention only a few such persons.

The focus of my remarks today will be on observations made in connection with our seventeen-day visit to South Africa in July of this year, and in this context I will also address specific questions of interest to this committee that were raised in Chairman Solarz's letter inviting our testimony.

Our three-member delegation made this trip in response to an invitation from the United Congregational Church of South Africa and from the general secretary of the South African Council of Churches, Bishop Desmond Tutu. During this trip our delegation talked with people living in squatters' camps, as well as executives of U.S. corporations. We met with factory workers in Port Elizabeth, scholars from various universities in South Africa, leaders of the Natal Indian Congress in Durban, "banned" leaders like Mrs. Albertina Sisulu, high-school students from Soweto, clergy attending the annual conference of the South African Council of Churches in Johannesburg, and many others, including many who have experienced arbitrary detention by the police for long periods of time. We spoke at a mass meeting, which the press estimated drew 15,000 people, at the Regina Mundi Catholic Church in Soweto and had similar meetings in each city we visited.

We came away from this trip with strong impressions both of the hope and sense of determination that are so alive in the hearts of the people as well as with a sense of the tragedy of apartheid. Above all, as citizens of these United States, we feel the urgency of the need for our country to have a coherent Africa policy which is understood by the people of that continent as well as by the American people.

Mr. Chairman, I first want to attempt to describe, in some measure, the South African arrangement. The apartheid system in South Africa is brutally enforced by the police and upheld by racist laws which represent a daily violation of the humanity of the black population in South Africa. We talked with a number of business leaders among white South Africans who fully agree with that estimate. Apartheid, as we know it, is a political system. The South African government does not recognize black humanity. There are 25 million people in South Africa, 18 million officially classified as blacks; 2 million "coloreds"; and another half-million classified under apartheid definitions as Indians. In addition, there are 4.5 million whites, and though all are classified as white, in terms of the existing power relationships in South Africa, the 2.5 million Afrikaners rule the country and do not share power with either the 20 million nonwhites or the other 2 million in the English-speaking white population.

One could say, "Well, this is bad, and we oppose it, but what does this have to do with U.S. foreign policy?" The U.S. involvement with that racist regime—the economic, political, diplomatic, military, and cultural ties between our government and the apartheid regime of South Africa—constitutes a partnership of serious import.

The United States has official diplomatic relations with the South African government. This legal cover allows 350 U.S. business corporations to operate there. The highest returns in the world on foreign investments are in South Africa, and 15 to 17 percent of total U.S. foreign investment is there. The greatest share of this investment by U.S. companies is concentrated in five U.S. corporations—General Motors, Ford, Caltex, IBM, and Mobil. These 350 U.S. corporations employ about 60,000 blacks—mostly in menial, low-paying jobs with no union—and another 40,000 whites, mostly in upper-salary, white-collar occupations and managerial positions.

These circumstances put the U.S. government and our corporations in an uneasy partnership with South African apartheid. Sixty thousand black jobs and no union or citizenship rights cannot serve as a trade-off or a buffer for the quest for full and equal citizenship rights for 20 million black people in South Africa. The partnership between the United States and South Africa is an uneasy one because it represents the most blatant violation of President Carter's human rights policy. Diplomatic recognition of the apartheid regime by the United States paves the way and sets the climate for business investment and market outlets. It also encourages other nations to relate to South Africa, since they have our example to follow.

Mr. Chairman, in your letter of August 10, among the questions you asked is, "To what extent are alternatives to apartheid and separate development being seriously considered by the South African government?" My observation is that they are not being considered at all. Apartheid and separate development are two sides of the same coin. The regime in South Africa is making some cosmetic changes in some of the grossest expressions of apartheid and is gambling on these changes to help them escape world condemnation and censure. Through this tactic, they hope to preserve all of the basic functions and operations of the system of apartheid. "Separate development" is an updated version of this policy, which, in content, is designed to strip the majority of South Africa's black population of any suggestion that they are citizens of South Africa by imposing a paper citizenship on them in the Bantustans. On the other hand, there does exist some degree of flexibility in attitudes in the white community, which is worthy of note.

Our observations of the South African scene convince us that the economic system and the political system there are on a collision course. The economic system needs trained workers; apartheid will not train them. The economic system needs people who work and pay taxes and consume. With millions of blacks unemployed, they cannot pay taxes, and they cannot consume. So the few whites who are working have to pay extremely high taxes for the military and the police apparatus needed to control the unemployed. Apartheid is failing the economic system.

The economic system needs money, bank loans, and investments from the outside, but the uncertainty of the system of apartheid makes investment more difficult to come by. South Africa's expanded trade and diplomatic relations with Israel, which are designed to circumvent the effects of world economic sanctions, will not succeed either.

In my discussions with business leaders, I learned that the apartheid regime needs a growth rate of 7 percent a year. From their own capital they can generate 3 to 3.5 percent a year—or about half of what they need. The system needs $600 million to $2 billion a year in new capital to grow. If we insist upon disinvestment because of disenfranchisement and only support investment when there is full enfranchisement, then we could make a valid contribution to the liberation of black people in South Africa. For we would force the business order into conflict with the political order, and adjustments would have to be made. This is not unlike what happened in our own nation a hundred years ago when the rural capitalism of the South confronted the industrial capitalism of the North. That was the basis of the Civil War—deciding which economic system would prevail. In South Africa, change will not come because their consciences burn because of the enslavement of blacks. Change will come because we stimulate a confrontation between the economic and the political orders.

There is hope because there is academic unrest. White leaders are hemmed in by apartheid as well. Tyranny is similar to cancer. Racism, hatred, and fear are like cancer. If they ever come near the heart, they soon go all over the body. Tyranny cannot be localized. So the white academic leaders are saying, "Reverend, the fact is, we don't have academic freedom. Books are banned. We can't do research on energy supply. We cannot do research on our own government. Our freedom has been taken," these white people are saying, "by apartheid." The same cancer that was designed to eat up black folks is now climbing up higher into the broader body politic. These white academic leaders at universities told us they were prohibited from doing research into police behavior or the judicial process; their access to books is limited, not by money, but by government policy. So they are seriously restricted in their academic pursuits. They are not free to look into the functions of foreign corporations and informed us that Section 2 of the "Terrorism Act" prohibited any South African citizen or "noncitizen" (i.e., blacks) from arguing the case for disinvestment, under penalty of a minimum of five years in prison.

We met with church leaders. Some blacks had paid for a church. The church property was confiscated. They then had to rent the church that they already had bought. But Bishop Desmond Tutu is now preaching civil disobedience, arguing that the church must make a higher witness and be willing to face a crucifixion in order to get a resurrection. The very involvement of a visible church, with black and white clergy, which by definition breaks the law, is hope.

It is in these developments that there may be some hope or prospect for peaceful change in South Africa. Nevertheless, it must be underscored that apartheid is violence, daily violence, implemented by brutal terroristic methods. It is a state of war against the human rights and citizenship of the black majority population and a repression of the rights of most white citizens.

What do South African blacks think U.S. companies should be doing? They think they should be disinvesting. We talked with dozens of workers in American-owned plants, and none of them was willing to compromise a few token concessions, of an affirmative action type, as a substitute for their full human rights in South Africa. If an American company were to give a plant to black South Africans today, the white minority government could take it back tomorrow.

Apartheid is an authoritarian form of government for blacks and a limited democracy for whites. Apartheid, the official policy of the government, will not grant citizenship to the majority of the population.

STRAIGHT FROM THE HEART

Black Africans do not have the right to vote. Black Africans have no official power. They are in the pre–*Dred Scott* days, because a black has no right that a white is bound to respect. They run parallel societies. They are separate, but there is no pretense of their being equal. In South Africa, blacks cannot live in the city. Blacks cannot own any property. Coloreds can get property on a ninety-nine-year lease. In the downtown areas, there are areas of "colored preferential," which means that blacks cannot work downtown, except when there are not enough coloreds to go around.

The $5.7 billion of direct or indirect investment that U.S. corporations hold in South Africa is an economic pillar for the apartheid regime. The attitudes of these U.S. corporations are such that we can understand South African blacks saying that they should disinvest.

For example, we met with the leaders of the Mobil Corporation of South Africa at Mobil House in Cape Town. Mr. Nichols is their chief representative. It should be noted that as recently as 1971, after eighty-five years of operating in South Africa, the Mobil Company had a situation in which all nonwhite employees were making the absolute minimum wage, and none was in any advanced training program. Mr. Nichols opened his remarks in our conversation by putting forward a distinction between apartheid and separate development. It seems that Mobil is opposed to apartheid, at least in giving lip service to same, but does not take the same position on separate development, which, I have noted earlier, is apartheid's alter ego.

Mobil employs 3,000 workers, of whom about 1,600 are white. After ninety-three years in South Africa, Mobil has one African district manager and eight sales managers out of a managerial force of about two hundred. When we asked the company leadership if the oil they sell to the South African government is resold to Rhodesia (and was thereby in violation of the embargo that is supposed to be in effect), they replied that the South African "Official Secrecies Act" prevents them, by law, from answering any questions regarding where they get their oil or to whom they sell it. Furthermore, he said that the General Law Amendment Act of 1974 requires them to apply to the Minister of Economic Affairs to get permission to answer questions like the one we were asking, and they informed us that they could not continue the conversation unless we changed the subject. This is an example of the extent to which U.S. corporations accommodate to the rules of the apartheid regime and, at the same time, are, in effect, willingly held hostage to the regime's legislation.

We visited Ford in South Africa, in Port Elizabeth, and found that 80 percent of its labor force is nonwhite, but 88 percent of its supervisors and managers are white. This is another example of the employment pattern of U.S. corporations, which fully fits into the design of apartheid, in that they provide a majority of white workers with the best paying jobs and thereby make them beneficiaries of apartheid rather than allies of the black workers in a common effort to improve conditions for all. We asked the representatives of the Ford plant management if their company was in compliance with U.S. Commerce Department Regulations issued in February of 1978 regarding sales to the South African government.* Their reply was the following: "Our company has told us that these regulations apply to U.S.-origin products only but that products licensed elsewhere can be sold to the South African government." They went on to say that about 10 percent of their sales are to the South African government and that they hesitate to refuse sales because the government has the power to effect a general boycott of Ford products in the South African market.

We visited the Port Elizabeth assembly and manufacturing plant of General Motors of South Africa. I believe General Motors has been in South Africa since 1924. Today, 52 percent of their labor force is non-white. They have one African foreman and no black employees in such white-collar jobs as the timekeeping department. We asked the leaders of the GM plant how they would describe their relations with the South African government. Their response was, "Good. The South African government is a big customer."

So these giant U.S. corporations have good relations with the apartheid regime. But the indigenous African National Congress of South Africa, founded in 1912, is banned by that same regime, and their leaders are either in exile or in jail on Robben's Island. The National Convention Movement is banned. The black people's Convention Movement is banned, and Steve Biko, its founder, assassinated. African trade unions are banned. The Natal Indian Congress, founded by Gandhi, enjoys only semilegal standing, and some of its leaders are among those individuals banned. Banned, Mr. Chairman, by the same government that General Motors, Ford, and Mobil say they have good relations with and, in the case of the latter two, who say that the government is a good customer.

So South African blacks think U.S. companies should be disinvesting. "Is there a role for U.S. private investment in South Africa?" your letter asked me. Not if they are in partnership with the official policy and regime of apartheid and separate development and are willing hostages to apartheid law and customs. And that is their present posture, as it is the posture of the U.S. government.

---

*Among other things, these regulations prohibited U.S. firms from supplying military equipment to the South African government.

Mr. Chairman, as a matter of emphasis I wish to underscore again the point that South Africa, as an apartheid regime, does not recognize black humanity. It does not recognize us legally. No black in South Africa has citizenship status or any protection under the law. No right to vote. No right to protest or assemble. Only citizens have that right, and blacks are not citizens by the operational definition of apartheid. Economically, we are not recognized. We experience either low wages or no wages. No African union is recognized. Businesses there are shielded by business protection acts externally and official secrecy acts internally. Socially, blacks are in the category of the "untouchables." Apartheid assumes that black people cannot dream, hurt, or aspire. Apartheid destroys family life. Religiously, apartheid assumes God made a creative error when he made a black man. The human community cannot coexist with apartheid. It is a moral illegitimacy that we must fight.

Now in terms of assessing current U.S. policy toward South Africa, it is clear that the United States is a partner with South Africa with its capital in the form of investments and loans. And capital attracts capital. The United States contributes to the social acceptance of South Africa. U.S. companies exploit cheap labor. U.S. companies abide by South African law. Ford and General Motors sell cars and trucks to the government of South Africa, thereby circumventing the intent of the Commerce Department's regulations by getting parts from Britain and England but producing paramilitary equipment for South Africa. South Africa makes $1.2 billion a year from the sale of the gold krugerrand, and more than half of this amount, roughly $600 million, is money or foreign exchange earned by South Africa from sales in the American market. The United States and South Africa exchange scientific personnel. The United States collaborates with South Africa in the expansion of South Africa's nuclear capabilities, including the development of uranium capability. So America must make a decision about South Africa. The United States must determine which side of history it chooses to be on.

Mr. Chairman, in your letter of invitation you asked me to comment on how black political leadership in South Africa and the black community there responded to the proposed changes embodied in the Riekhert and Wiehahn reports.* The information we received suggests that, with respect to the Wiehahn Commission Report, it is obvious that many of the recommendations sound very good. I would say that there is a wait-and-see attitude on the part of black leadership because, as you probably know, it is an old ploy of ruling circles in white minority regimes to

---

*Two recent South African reports on apartheid recommending changes within the apartheid system but not its abolition.

respond to the uprising of a people by creating a commission. Then the commission comes forward with a white paper, and this white paper proposes that things be looked into further. The issuance of the white paper is usually accompanied by a great many demogogic speeches, and then the paper is promptly shelved and no more is heard about it. Because by that time, they hope, the so-called natives will have calmed their restlessness. This is one of the classic styles of Western parliamentary rule, so we know that the Wiehahn Commission Report does have some very positive recommendations.

Of course, again if one looks at the details, we need to take into account that South Africa is an industrially developed society. Thus there is really no necessity for any government in South Africa that wishes to conform to democratically accepted norms of behavior to reinvent the wheel. Since all industrial countries have a generally accepted set of labor relations that govern the democratic rights of their laboring population (to have unions, organize, and these sorts of elementary rights), it is not necessary for South Africa to invent anything new. So the Wiehahn Commission Report suggests that they know what needs to be done with respect to establishing universally recognized norms of relationships between labor and business. The question is, what will it take to make them do it?

However, one must also look at the Wiehahn Commission Report from the standpoint of a couple of their recommendations. They say that all persons, irrespective of race, color, or sex, who enjoy permanent residence in South Africa and who are in fixed employment, qualify for membership in a registered trade union. Now that is very interesting, because those qualifications, of course, mean that the large pool of migrant laborers—people classified as migrants, not as permanent residents—would not be covered under the Wiehahn definitions. People from Mozambique, Angola, and so forth who work in the coal mines would not be covered. The question then becomes, who enjoys permanent residence in South Africa? If the Bantustan proposal is pushed further, this would mean that a majority of black people would not be given permanent residence in South Africa. So, whatever changes the Wiehahn Commission represents, it would not apply to them.

It is also interesting that one of the clear provisions of the Wiehahn Commission Report is that the closed-shop practice is suspended. That is, the union protection pattern which has, in all industrial countries, protected the right of industrial unions to organize, is suspended, and no further agreements in South Africa for closed shops may be permitted. The National Manpower Commission will be instructed to investigate the need for this practice to be retained, but, as of now, the closed shop as a union protection instrumentality is abandoned in South Africa, even under the Wiehahn Commission Reports.

So again, the fact remains that this report is perceived as an evolutionary process by which South Africa eventually will arrive at some universally recognized standards of democratic rights for working people. The possibility that such a thing will eventually happen under apartheid is as good as the possibility that it will never happen. So again I emphasize that the black leadership that we talked with seem to have a wait-and-see attitude with respect to it because there is no basis for looking to it as some type of Emancipation Proclamation.

The same is true of the Riekhert Commission Report. We can dispense with it for the time being by saying, categorically, that since no legislation implementing the Reikhert Commission recommendations is expected before 1980, we will simply have to wait and see what legislation is formulated that represents implementation of this report before we could place any real judgment on it. But, at any rate, it is hardly a point on the agenda at the moment simply because there is not going to be any legislation covering their recommendations before 1980, if at that time. So it is clear that neither of these reports represents much with regard to the ills that plague South Africa. It is the will for freedom among the South African people themselves, combined with international pressures, that will ultimately decide the course of events in that country.

Now I will respond to the other question you raised about the issues involved in the controversy surrounding the world championship boxing match set for October 20 in Pretoria. This is a major sporting event in South Africa. South Africa has gold power and military power, but South Africa does not have world acceptance. Seventy nations of the world have said that apartheid is an international crime against humanity. In South Africa, blacks must operate with passes and permission slips. There is no policy of multiracial sports in South Africa. Even when there are mouthings from the top of the government, at the very bottom every city still has the right to determine whether or not to obey the statement. Thus it amounts to states' rights.

In Pretoria, where the fight is being held, if a black person were to go there on any occasion other than the night of the fight, that person would have to use a pass to get in, would have to sit in a section for blacks only, would have to use lavatory or toilet facilities for blacks only—as distinguished from colored, Indian, and white. They could not use any of the social areas. And, without a special permit, they would be locked up going home because no black can be on the street after 9:00 P.M. To be found on the street thereafter is to break the curfew laws.

But, because South Africa wants to change her face and attract money—as opposed to changing her heart and bringing human rights to all human beings—on the night of the fight, for this massive international facelift, South Africa will give blacks a one-night rendezvous with dignity. One night, they can come to the fight without a pass. One night, they can use the toilet of their choice. One night, they can sit any place, while the cameras of the world—operating between the developed cities—in that one-night rendezvous with dignity, can say, "Things are not what they ought to be in South Africa, but they are getting better. Therefore we should invest money in South Africa."

We in PUSH have joined with other human rights organizations in a commitment to fight to stop that fight. The reasons behind our commitment and determination are the following:

First, a heavyweight boxing match held in South Africa fills the most desperate need that the apartheid regime has for world acceptance. The sports route is the main highway through which the regime hopes to gain acceptance and reduce world criticism.

Second, multiracial sports is a myth in South Africa. It is nonexistent. So NBC-TV will be televising a sports match in South Africa which makes it a party to selling a fraud to a worldwide audience. The Pretoria Stadium arrangement to which I just referred underscores this fact.

Regardless of the outcome of the fight, the apartheid regime will gain from this event if it is held in Pretoria—international prestige, tax receipts, and a propaganda victory that will make it more difficult to isolate South Africa from participation in the 1980 Olympics, which is only ten months away. So the timing of this fight is very important to take into account. The leaders of the few organizations which still enjoy legality in South Africa feel very strongly about having this fight cancelled. The one thing they asked of us in Durban and elsewhere was that we would put forth every effort to see to it that this fight was cancelled.

Finally, Mr. Chairman, regarding recommendations that we have arrived at in relation to our partnership with South Africa. Our delegation met with President Carter on August 9, 1979, and we submitted the following recommendations to him:

• We urged him to instruct the Commerce Department to monitor closely the activities of General Motors, Ford, Caltex, Mobil Oil, and IBM in South Africa. The purpose of such monitoring is to establish that these companies are in full compliance with the intent of the U.S. Commerce Department's regulation 135, regarding the selling of supplies to the South African government, and also with regard to maintaining the embargo against Rhodesia. This requires, at a minimum, strict monitoring of activity by the executive branch of the government.

• We asked that the Justice Department look into the scandal now

shaking the South African government—the Rhoodie investigation,*
with which we are all familiar. We asked that the attorney general
investigate the use of South African government funds to influence
election campaigns in this country, such as the defeat of Senator Dick
Clark of Iowa, former head of the Senate Foreign Affairs Subcommittee
on Africa. We feel that the American public needs more information on
this, as well as an investigation into the South African government's
attempts to use their funds to buy up U.S. news media and influence
public opinion here.

● We recommended that any further negotiations between the United
States and South Africa on the SASOL project to convert coal into liquid
fuel be based upon the condition that universal adult suffrage and full
citizenship for the black majority population of South Africa be recognized and established as a matter of law. We would not continue any
negotiations on the SASOL project with South Africa until there was an
understanding and a commitment to extend these democratic rights to
the black majority population.

● We recommended that he convene a White House conference on
Southern Africa within the next six months. This level of focus on the
situation in that region of the world would help to mobilize public
opinion and help shape a coherent U.S.-Southern African policy. The
present policy of imposing economic sanctions on Zimbabwe-Rhodesia,
which is changing to majority rule, while being in partnership with
South Africa is a blatant contradiction in U.S. foreign policy.

This point is extremely important, as are the others, with respect to
the executive branch of the government in the light of the resignation of
Andrew J. Young. I think we all recognize the enormous contribution to
public awareness that he made during his tenure as ambassador to the
U.N., and it has made the work of all of us easier. The great debt that we
owe to this distinguished public servant can only be fulfilled if we renew
our efforts to place our country on the side of justice and human rights.
The acid test of this posture is our relationship with the racist, apartheid
regime of South Africa.

Also, it seems to me that the Congress has some very concrete things it
can do, and I want to include in our recommendations that the United
States Congress legislate that the sale of the krugerrand in this country
be banned. The vast amount of foreign exchange that the South African
government earns from the sale of the gold kruggerrand covers its oil bill
and its defense budget, and those are two very significant items in
apartheid's survival. So the banning of the sale of the krugerrand—

---

*Rhoodie, a South African government official, set up a fund to buy influence in the
United States. Among the activities investigated were an attempt to purchase the *Washington* (D.C.) *Star* and the channeling of funds into several U.S. political elections.

which, for us, also adds to our problems of a trade deficit, adds to our problem of a balanced budget, and contributes to the high price of gold on the world market because of the speculation in gold—would be a role that the Congress could play in helping concretely and in setting a climate that says, "This partnership with South African apartheid is being dissolved."

It is very important for the Congress to contribute to such a climate because the Congress, according to the Constitution, is supposed to be the most representative of the three branches of government. A variety of activities tell us where public opinion in America is on this question: church organizations making their appeals through stockholders' resolutions on disinvestments; the student movements on major college campuses for disinvestment of university funds from corporations doing business in South Africa; mass-based movements against bank loans; and the summit conference of black religious leaders. The American people oppose apartheid, and they will support concrete actions by the government in breaking the relationship with apartheid. But the president and the Congress must act. So I am appealing to the Congress today to take steps that will give some leadership to this mass sentiment. One concrete step that could be taken is that the Congress could legislate against the sale of the krugerrand in the American market. We urge that you do so.

Finally, Mr. Chairman, if I may be permitted a very personal word. Some persons in South Africa were critical of us because they said, "You haven't been here long enough, and you don't understand apartheid. There are just some things you don't understand." And there may be some things that I do not understand about South African apartheid, but I doubt if there are many. For you see, when we arrived in the airport and I saw the signs "Black" and "White," that was nothing new for me; it was simply a reminder. I told the press, when they challenged me, "You apparently don't understand. I was born and bred in apartheid—not in South Africa but in South Carolina. I have an advantage on you. I've known apartheid from both sides. I grew up under apartheid but, with the help of God, rose above it. I know your side, but I also know the underside. So I understand rejection. Separate schools by law is nothing new to me. It's a reminder. Teachers making dual salaries, while black teachers make less by law, is a reminder. The African National Congress (ANC) is banned in South Africa, but the NAACP was banned in America. They call ANC communist, but they called the NAACP communist. I know rejection.

"This division by color is nothing new to me. I waited tables. I catted and shined shoes while the white boy was the cashier. I grew up where it was against the law for a black boy to know what a white boy knew. I know about signs in buses reading, 'colored from the rear.' I know about 'three-fifths human,' *Plessy v. Ferguson*—'separate but equal'—*Dred Scott*—'a black person has no rights that a white person must respect.' " I told them, "Maybe y'all don't know me, but I know y'all."

Change is going to come in South Africa. Whether it will be essentially economic, political, and peaceful or whether violent and relatively sudden is yet to be determined. That lies largely in the hands of those with power in Pretoria. I am also convinced that the United States, for moral, economic, political, national interest, and national security reasons, ought to help facilitate the change there. We should use our diplomatic, economic, political, and military leverage to foster change for black and white South Africans.

Chairman Solarz and members of the committee, I wish to thank you for the opportunity to share with you our experience and views relative to our recent visit to South Africa. Your patience and interest in a rather lengthy testimony is very much appreciated.

Peace Through Justice:
The Crisis in
Central America

As part of his campaign for the Democratic party's presidential nomination in 1984, Jackson went to Mexico. The most important purpose of that trip was to focus on the international debt crisis. At that time, Mexico, along with Argentina and Brazil, were the Western hemisphere nations most threatened with bankruptcy. Jackson delivered this speech May 28, 1984, at the Universidad Nacional Autonoma de Mexico in Mexico City.

I came to meet with you today with greetings from my own country, with greetings from the thousands of people in the United States who do not want to see an expanding war in Central America, with greetings from all those who want to see an end to the arms race. I come here to Mexico this day because I have been encouraged by the way in which Mexico, along with the other Contadora nations—Colombia, Panama, and Venezuela—has taken the initiative in attempting to resolve the current Central American conflict in a peaceful and just manner. It is such a just resolution that not only I but millions of Americans have desired for so long. I also come here because I believe that for too long too many of my countrymen have viewed the relationship between our two countries in a unilateral manner. Hence many have felt that you had much to learn from them, but they little from you. And there is probably no more timely situation than the current conflict in Central America for the United States to look to what you have to offer in terms of the search for peace.

I should add that all too often we have both oversimplified and overgeneralized about each other. To do so helps neither and hurts us both. We must realize that the complexity of the United States is like the complexity of Mexico or any other country. It is full of contradictions and inconsistencies. Thus the United States is the mining of the harbors of Nicaragua, but it is also the Rainbow Coalition. The United States is the support of racist and repressive regimes in South Africa and El Salvador, but it is also the civil rights struggle of Martin Luther King, Jr. The United States is support for the hated Somoza contras in Honduras and Costa Rica, but it is also ten thousand Mexican Americans, blacks, and progressive whites marching in Los Angeles last week to stop the repressive Simpson-Mazzoli immigration control bill. The United States is budget deficits and their corollary of higher interest rates, but it is also the young Americans here tonight on their way to Nicaragua. Just as there are dangers in the U.S. oversimplifying and overgeneralizing about the Third World, so too there are dangers in the Third World over-simplifying the peoples and context of the United States. Neither of our realities is unidimensional.

President Reagan would have the people of the United States believe that the struggle in Central America and Latin America is a struggle between the United States and the Soviet Union. He would convince our people that this is a life-and-death struggle between the forces of light and the forces of darkness—that all those who love freedom must be willing to commit endless military and financial resources to the govern-ment of El Salvador, to turning Honduras into an American military base, to financing the contras seeking to overthrow the government of Nicaragua. He seeks to make the isolation of Cuba one of the chief goals of United States Latin American policy.

Even my Democratic opponents, Walter Mondale and Gary Hart, accept far too much of Ronald Reagan's analysis of the problems in Central America. They both think that our nation should keep military advisors in Central America. They both have declared that our country should not seek to establish diplomatic ties or trade with Cuba. They both would continue to increase our nation's military budget, a budget which has grown 60 percent in real terms in just the last four years. Fully 62 percent of our federal budget will go to the military in 1984. In the last five years we have poured $1.8 trillion of the world's resources into military spending. A world in which 2 billion people live on incomes below $500 a year, 600 million people have no jobs, and 11 million babies die before their first birthdays because of inadequate health care. The huge increase in our military budget has created huge budget deficits for the United States. It has caused interest rates to soar, greatly worsening the international debt crisis. The results have been disastrous for the world community. Our interest rates and the world debt crisis endanger our relationships with our closest allies. It has caused untold hardships around the world, as austerity programs widen the gap between rich and poor. We have seen food riots in Santo Domingo and Haiti. The recent report of the Inter-American dialogue, which includes leaders from throughout Latin America and the United States, reports that 1983 was the worst year for Latin American economies in fifty years.

I believe that the United States can and must seek a new direction, a new foreign policy, a new military policy, a new policy in Central America. Most of the people of the United States want to see peace. They do not want to see American troops sent to Central America. They do not want to see more and more of their tax money spent on the arms race—on deadly missiles that could destroy the world thousands of times over. But before we can direct our nation on a path toward peace, we must succeed in fully exposing the myths, the false vision, of the conflict in Central America put forward by Ronald Reagan. Your nation, the understanding and experience of your people, has much to contribute in defeating Ronald Reagan's myths.

You are closer to your own history of revolution than my people are. You can help to tell them that the struggle in Central America is not a struggle between the Soviets and the United States but a struggle between people who have been oppressed for generations and those who still seek to exploit them, backed by United States weapons and death squads. There were 5,142 civilians murdered by government forces and paramilitary forces last year in El Salvador. More than 38,000 murdered since 1979. It took the Nicaraguans years to overthrow the hated dictatorship of Somoza, who was supported until the very end by the United States government. Now we ally ourselves with those who seek to overthrow the Nicaraguan revolution. We supply them with millions in military aid. We have actually directed the mining of the harbors of Nicaragua, the invasion of Nicaragua from the north and from the south. We have separated ourselves from the decent opinions of humankind. We are making a name for ourselves as international terrorists by allowing Ronald Reagan to continue to pursue policies which reflect his vision of the conflict in Central America.

I believe we must completely reverse Ronald Reagan's policies in Central America. My goals, which have been further strengthened by my visit here, are:

• We must end the war waged on Nicaragua. We must engage in negotiations with the government of Nicaragua so we may assist them in their attempt to build a more just society and encourage their development of democratic institutions. We should encourage the development and spread of their health and literacy programs. They provide a model for the whole hemisphere.

• We must dismantle the military complex under construction in Honduras and terminate our semipermanent exercises there. We already have undermined very weak democratic institutions in this, the poorest country in Central America.

• We must begin a process of negotiations in El Salvador designed to bring a halt to the violence, to develop an interim government involving all parties which can sponsor truly free elections. We must end all military aid to El Salvador immediately and condition any further economic aid on serious negotiations with the FDR-FMLN. We can no longer afford to support death squads against peasants, students, priests, nuns, and trade unionists. We must ally ourselves with the many seeking justice in their own land. We must look to the leadership of the Contadora group in helping to bring about these negotiations toward a peace based on justice.

• We must maintain the cut-off of military assistance to the Guatemalan government, guilty of repressive policies toward its own people. We must help provide aid for Guatemalan refugees in Mexico who have fled the violence in their homeland. This is not a burden that Mexico should have to bear alone.

• We must support the thousands of Costa Ricans who marched in the streets against the militarization of their country by the contra forces supported by the United States. We must stop pressuring the Costa Rican government to abandon its principled position of neutrality, its attempts to resist militarization. Costa Rica does not need or want military aid from the United States. We must base our relationship with Costa Rica on trade, on plans for economic development that meet the needs of the Costa Rican people, and ensure a mutually profitable relationship between our countries.

• We must normalize our relationship with Cuba. We trade with the Soviet Union, give credits to Eastern Europe, military assistance and nuclear power plants to China, and then say we cannot even recognize this small island, our next-door neighbor. Nothing could be more self-defeating. We have pushed Cuba into the arms of the Soviet Union, just as we are now doing with Nicaragua. Nothing could be further from our real interests. We have much to learn from the Cubans. They have much to learn from us. It is time for a spiteful policy to become a sensible one. We need to encourage trade and economic, cultural, and social exchanges between our peoples.

The policy I seek for Central America would promote economic, cultural, and social development that would meet the needs of the vast majority of the people, not of a handful of bankers and multinational corporations. I would seek to strengthen those regional programs, governments, and institutions that are acting to narrow the gulf between rich and poor, between peoples of different color, between men and women. I would seek programs to deal with the international debt crisis that did not expect the poor to pay the price for the mistakes of banks and governments. I would support limited commodity agreements to help Central American countries stabilize export earnings. I would seek to stop the arms race, the budget deficits, and rising interest rates in the United States which have worsened the financial crisis everywhere.

We seek to build a Rainbow Coalition in the United States of people who have a new understanding, a need to work together to solve their problems, to stop the arms race, to meet human needs. Your perspective, your vision strengthens us. I thank you for your inspiration and support.

Forty Years Later—Liberation, But Not Yet Joy

On the fortieth anniversary of the end of World War II in Europe, a variety of activities was scheduled in Europe. Among these was a visit by Ronald Reagan to the graves of S.S. troops at a cemetery in Bitburg, Germany, and an address to the European Parliament. Jackson also spoke to the European Parliament, visited a Nazi concentration camp, and was the principal speaker at an open-air rally in the heart of West Berlin on May 8, 1985, attended by about fifty thousand people. This speech was given at that rally.

Forty years after the celebration of the surrender of the Nazi terrorists, we gather, hands across the sea, lovers of peace, coming together across race, region, sex, religion, and ideology to find common ground in our commitment to life and our resistance to the slaughter of human beings. Today we remember that we must never forget. With all of our passion and with all of our pain, we cannot resurrect the dead, but if we learn from their death—and behave differently—we can rob death of its sting and add immeasurably to the worth of their lives.

Today, forty years later, May 8, 1985, the scene of desecration and death is before us. Today the source and scope of death in this war make us tremble. Today the solution to this madness remains a challenge to us. The scenes of historical shame stand as landmarks that should remind us of humankind's low moments. For Jesus it was Calvary. For the Jews it was Nazi Germany. For President John F. Kennedy it was Dallas. For Dr. Martin Luther King, Jr., it was Memphis. The blood of the innocent bids us to come, look, and listen. It cries out for us to finish the unfinished business—to stop racism and anti-Semitism. We must stop this perversion of the human character forever—that their dying be not in vain. We must measure human rights by one yardstick and make room for everybody in the human family.

We must never forget nor remove these ancient landmarks—the places where the victims lost their lives, the victimizers lost their souls, and a nation lost its innocence in the government conspiracy to exterminate a people. Our collective burden will last as long as pain lasts—the loss of families, the brands on bodies, the conspiracy of silence, and the nation whose doors were closed. We must remember lest we forget. And if we forget, our tongues should cleave to the roofs of our mouths, and our hands should lose their cunning.

The scope of death is estimated to be fifty million people. The source? Unbridled racism! Racism cuts through the ideologies of East and West, Jew and Gentile, Asian and African. We must forever be reminded that where there are master- or superior-race theories, they have genocide as their logical conclusion. They colonize, occupy, oppress, and kill. Down with facism yesterday, today, and forever!

The Third Reich was finally rejected on ethical grounds and was fought on military terms. We forever must put ethics over economics, dignity over dollars, and persons over property. Wherever racism manifests itself, the seeds of insecurity, ignorance, fear, hatred, and genocide are always present. Thus the same ethical grounds for rejecting the Third Reich in Germany must be employed to reject the Fourth Reich in South Africa. Many of the S.S. troops went from Germany to South Africa—and all of their philosophy went there.

Forty years ago today the Nazi troops officially surrendered. But Nazism has not surrendered; it has simply shifted. Thus, in some measure, the germ of genocide was not buried at Bitburg, it was transferred to Johannesburg. Shifting the site of the cancer is inadequate. We must root the death germ out of our body politic. If it simply shifts or remains dormant, in the right economic or leadership climate it will rise again. This generation cannot resurrect the dead of 1945, but it can save the living of 1985. We must roll the stone away and go forward. Although we must remember, we cannot go forward looking backward. We must revive our spirits, redeem our neighbors, and move on to the higher ground of love, mercy, peace, and justice.

The issue for this generation is not guilt or innocence for today's or yesterday's atrocities but the responsibility for both and the will to act differently based upon our knowledge. This day we must choose another course that the human race might be spared this nightmare again. Yesterday it was Nazism and slave camps. Today it is apartheid in South

Africa and missile deployment in Europe that reduce the planet to a death camp.

I come here today representing the National Rainbow Coalition, a progressive political organization pulling together people across lines of race and sex and region and religion who are seeking to find common ground. We seek a new direction. We seek to shift our nation and our world from a history of racial battleground to economic common ground and on to moral higher ground. One of the critical lessons to be learned is that we will either learn to live together as brothers and sisters or we will perish apart as fools.

On a given day, Mr. Reagan and Mr. Gorbachev are the two most politically powerful men in the world. The weight is upon their shoulders to make peace and justice the imperative and transcendent issues of this hour. The most fundamental lesson to be learned from the Second World War—apart from the fact that unbridled racism started the war—is that both superpowers had to come together to stop the war and put the world on another course. It is just as true today. And the fact of nuclear deployment makes the imperative even more urgent. Until there is a meeting at the wall of leaders with a sense of mutual respect which can afford each other mutual security, we will not know peace. I look forward to having a discussion with Mr. Reagan and Mr. Gorbachev to make such a moral appeal.

I come to Berlin today in part because this is the scene of the pain of war and the celebration of victory. The war is over, but forty years later the joy has not been restored. Until families are restored and the wall of separation is removed, we will not have joy. The wall is not a solution. It represents tension and fear and shadows. It does not represent relief and courage and sunlight. In so many ways its function today is archaic because the overriding issue of our day is the real possibility that the nuclear race will wipe out the human race. That wall cannot spare us that growing nightmare. The nuclear buildup is too dangerous, it's too costly, and nuclear war is too likely to take place. For those who are running the war race, the danger is that one of them might win but not be able to take the victory stand to pick up the trophy. There will be no winners in a nuclear war. Thus we must bury the weapons and not burn the people and freeze the planet. The superpowers must see where our interests converge and come together.

Europe forty years after the end of World War II must resist becoming a colony in the superpower nuclear chess game. Europe must resist being a permanent laboratory for missile terror. Europe must resist becoming a space colony for star wars and moon monuments. Just this last week Mr. Mitterrand recommended an African foundation to help wipe out hunger and end the hunger holocaust in the Sahel, in Ethiopia, in Somalia, in the Sudan, and in thirty-one of fifty-one African nations. It was a step in the right direction.

We must congratulate President Mitterrand for his African foundation initiative to relieve the hunger holocaust taking place in Africa today. Tens of thousands are dying in Somalia, the Sudan, and Ethiopia—even as we speak. Mr. Mitterrand's putting focus on Third World trade, as opposed to just Third World aid, also was a step in the right direction. When he made it a precondition for trade talks, it was a step in the right direction. The $700 billion debt the Third World nations are now laboring under creates such real tensions North and South that any of them could trigger a war between East and West. We must use trade and aid in a deliberate plan to assist the developing nations to become self-sufficient and self-reliant.

We who gather today must face the fact that there is rising racism and anti-Semitism in the United States and Germany—and it is a threat. Nazism is dormant; it is not dead. Without progressive leadership and better economic conditions, blind obsession with communism and toleration of racism can set us back forty years. Let us not forget that Hitler was not a communist. He was a racist. Everything has changed, yet in many ways nothing has changed. We were blind to Hitler's racism. The logical conclusion of all racism is genocide. Inherent in every cell and seed of racism is a combination of insecurity, ignorance, fear, and hatred that can explode and wipe out a people.

Our delegation just had a very significant meeting with the head of the Jewish community in West Berlin, Rabbi Heinz Galensky. We agreed that blacks and Jews have in common the necessity to fight racism and anti-Semitism. We agreed that Israel has a right to exist with security within internationally recognized boundaries. We agreed that there will be no peace without Palestinian justice, lest we institutionalize war permanently. We agreed to help form an international commission to help honor the black GIs for their service without honor and recognition. And we agreed to condemn the revival of racism and anti-Semitism in the U.S. and Europe in the aftermath of Bitburg. It was a delightful and frank meeting.

As we look upon options forty years later, clearly blacks and Jews— victims of racism and anti-Semitism—have every reason to allow our interests to converge and reach out to the rest of the human family. Racism is such a blind cancer that it does not stop in one neighborhood. We must not forget that 50-plus million people were killed in the Second World War. And thus, just as there was a world war forty years ago, there must be a world commitment to peace forty years later. We are not unmindful of the death of 20 to 22 million Russian people;

9-plus million German people; 8-plus million Polish people; 6-plus million Jewish people; 4-plus million British people; 3 million Gypsies; 400,000 Americans; perhaps 100,000 Senegalese; and millions of others, including Japanese, Italians, French, and Slavs. We are mindful of the scope and devastation of that war. We do not want it to occur again.

I must appeal to you as a son of a black American veteran of the Second World War. My father and his brother served in one of three all-black segregated infantries. Black soldiers had an especially difficult task—fighting for democracy in Europe in 1942, 1943, 1944, and 1945, without having the right to vote in America until 1965. They were inspired to fight, not for the freedom that they had, but for the freedom that they hoped for. Many of us hoped that their investment for freedom in Europe would gain freedom for us at home. These gallant men left their families in America, and all too many left their lives in Europe. Oftentimes they were used as shock troops, they had no rights at home, and they never got their Marshall Plan or reparations.

It is also significant that in some instances the German troops would land and dress up as American soldiers, decoys, but then attack and panic the village. The only thing that distinguished the American soldiers clearly—thus relieving the people's fears, giving the people a sense of security and direction—was the black American soldiers. It was clear that they were not Germans.

Also, we now find that, at least at Dachau and Buchenwald, black American soldiers arrived first and were recognized by the concentration-camp victims as playing that role. This morning Mr. Galensky reminded us that at Buchenwald black American soldiers were among the very first soldiers that he saw. That is a very significant role, but their gallantry and service remain unrecognized by both Europeans and Americans. And yet the story of their contribution must be known and appreciated before the final chapter can be completed. The burden of war was shared by all. So must the glory of liberation and triumph. So we appeal to our friends in Europe to express in some special way your thanks to those heroes of the Second World War who never got recognized for fighting in that war while it took so long for them to get a measure of civil rights at home. For these and other reasons, I'm delighted, in a very special way, to be here today.

Yesterday I went to the Struthof concentration camp along with Dr. Bruno Kreisky and a distinguished delegation of European citizens, and today I went to Polotzonseo. As a result of these two visits, an uncharacteristic, indescribable level of pain and trauma came over me. I have seen electric chairs. I have seen gas chambers. I have witnessed assassinations. But I have never experienced the chill and the tremor of the human heart as I did today upon looking at a death camp up in the mountains set aside for the exclusive purpose of exterminating people based on their race and/or their religious beliefs. One can never go to a death camp and return the same. We must say to policies of genocide, "Never again." But also, "Why in the first place?" We must look at the scene to be reminded lest we forget. We must study the source and the scope so we can be determined to end the death germ of fascism. In every germ of fascism is a combination of insecurity, ignorance, fear, hatred, and genocide.

A few possessed of this spirit are buried at Bitburg, but many more are doing business in South Africa and South America. The challenge of this generation is not to resurrect the spirit of the S.S. at Bitburg but to declare human rights in Johannesburg. We cannot just shift a cancer from one part of the body politic to another. We must root it out.

Forty years ago we declared the end to a reign of terror that tore at the soul and seam of the human family with such devastation that we still tremble. Forty years ago this continent lay in waste, in blood and ashes. Forty years later the phoenix has emerged from the rubble with a new lease on life. The stench of death has given way to the fragrance of life. Our coming together today across various religious, national, and racial lines is a sign of hope. Red, yellow, brown, black, and white—North and South, East and West—we are all precious in God's sight. It is even clearer today that we must either learn to live together as brothers and sisters or we shall surely die apart as fools.

Let the course that we choose this day be our emblem of honor to the lives that perished here.

The approach of no-talk policies, preemptive strikes, starvation, and asphyxiation through trade embargoes, superpower intimidation through threats and money-market manipulation must give way to the most basic link in civilization—communication. Policies of mutual respect and the Golden Rule must prevail. "Do unto others as you would have them do unto you" is infinitely more powerful than gunboat diplomacy, Manifest Destiny, and the arrogance of power. History teaches us that ultimately might is not right; right is might. Peace is possible. Peace is imperative. The nuclear race must end. It is too costly, too dangerous, and too likely to take place.

The solution challenges us this day. The moral imperative of this hour demands that we act before it is too late. We must choose the human race over the nuclear race. We must restructure the Third World debt, which is the fuse of this day's bomb. We must free South Africa so that God and the world might know that we are serious about justice and mercy. We must fight apartheid and fascism in South Africa.

We must choose negotiations over confrontation and choose developed minds over guided missiles. We must spare Europe the role of being the world's permanent site of the missile-countermissile chess game. And we don't need to shift the missiles from Europe to outer space. We need to destroy them before they destroy us. We must burn the weapons and not burn the people and then freeze the planet. As opposed to star wars and moon monuments, there must be earth wars where we use our best economic thoughts and techniques and the energy of our youth to wipe out poverty, ignorance, and disease.

We must be aggressive for peace. Wipe out malnutrition in the world. Put grain in our silos, not missiles. We must listen to John Lennon and "Give Peace a Chance." We must study war no more, beat our swords into plowshares and our spears into pruning hooks. Every crisis gives us the opportunity to shed light upon darkness and offer a better way en route to higher ground. Suffering breeds character, character breeds faith, and in the end faith will not disappoint.

Let the course that we choose be our emblem of honor to the lives of the innocent that perished here.

CORPORATE AND CULTURAL CRITIC

"Never in the history of humankind has a majority with power engaged in programs and written laws to discriminate against itself. The only thing whites are giving up because of affirmative action is privilege—something to which they were not entitled in the first place. This nation went out of its way to enslave us as a group but now wants to free us through individual effort and merit. We need a solution that is consistent with and comprehensive of the problem."

What Does the Government Owe the Poor?

This interview first appeared in *Harper's* magazine in April 1986. It appears here in a slightly edited form.

The following conversation between Charles Murray and Jesse Jackson took place at the Harvard Club in New York City.

Charles Murray is a senior research fellow at the Manhattan Institute for Policy Research. He is the author of *Losing Ground: American Social Policy, 1950–1980,* which criticizes the effects of social programs on the poor. He was formerly chief scientist at the American Institutes for Research, where he evaluated government programs involving urban education, welfare services, child nutrition, day care, adolescent pregnancy, juvenile delinquency, and criminal justice.

CHARLES MURRAY: How can government help the poor? The problem is that, so far, we haven't been very good at it. During the late 1960s and early 1970s, we began a major effort to bring people out of poverty, to educate the uneducated, to employ the unemployable. We have to confront the fact that the effort to help the poor did not have the desired effect. In terms of education, crime, family stability, the lives of poor people have gotten worse since the 1960s, and we have to explain why.

During those years we, in effect, changed the rules of the game for poor people. Essentially we said, in a variety of ways: "It's not your fault. If you are not learning in school, it is because the educational system is biased; if you are committing crimes, it is because the environment is poor; if you have a baby that you can't care for, it's because your own upbringing was bad." Having absolved everybody of responsibility, we then said: "You can get along without holding a job. You can get along if you have a baby but have no husband and no income. You can survive without participating in society the way your parents had to." And lots of young people took the bait. So the question remains: What, if anything, does the government owe the poor?

JESSE JACKSON: I'm as unimpressed with boundless liberalism as I am with heartless conservatism. Creative thinking has to take place. But to begin to think creatively, we have to be realistic: about the role of government, for example.

We cannot be blindly antigovernment. The government has made significant interventions in many, many areas for the common good. Without public schools, most Americans would not be educated. Without land-grant colleges, the United States would not have the number-one agricultural system in the world. Without federal transit programs, we would not have an interstate highway system. Without subsidized hospitals, most Americans could not afford decent medical care. And the government has played a significant role in providing a base for many American industries. The defense industries, for example, may be considered private, part of the market, but many of them are almost wholly supported by government contracts.

Now, we consider spending the public's money toward these ends to be in our national interest. When we saw the devastation in Europe after World War II, we devised the Marshall Plan—a comprehensive, long-term program. Had the Marshall Plan been a five-year investment program—as the War on Poverty essentially was—Europe would have collapsed. But we determined that the redevelopment of Europe was in our national interest. That's an instance where a vigorous government investment made something positive happen.

But when we shift from the notion of subsidy as something that serves our national interest, to that of welfare, the attitudes suddenly shift from positive to negative. In this country there is a negative predisposition toward the poor. We must learn to see the development of people who are poor as in our national interest, as cost-efficient, as an investment that can bring an enormous return to every American. The government definitely has a big role to play.

MURRAY: I agree it has a role. There are some things government can do, and one of them is to ensure that a whole range of opportunities is available to everyone. For example, in my ideal world, whether a child lived in the inner city or in the suburbs, everything from preschool to graduate school would be available to him—free. In this ideal world, if someone really looked for a job and just couldn't find one, perhaps because of a downturn in the economy, some minimal unemployment insurance would be in place to help him.

Opportunity should be assured, but attempts at achieving equal outcome abandoned. What would happen if you took away all other government-supported welfare, if the system were dismantled? Well, believe it or not, a lot of good things would begin to happen.

JACKSON: The notion of "opportunity" is more complicated than it sounds. For example, some people are poor because of government. When a nation is 51 percent female yet can't get an equal rights amendment passed; when many women still cannot borrow money with the same freedom men can, cannot pursue their ideas and aspirations in the marketplace because they are not equally protected—that amounts to government interference, too, but on the side of the status quo. Many blacks and Hispanics cannot borrow money from banks, on subjective grounds—because some bank official doesn't like their color, or because whole neighborhoods are red-lined so that money will not be loaned to anyone living there. Government must be committed to the vigorous enforcement of equal protection under the law and other basic principles; without that enforcement, it is not a government handout that's the issue as much as it is the government's shoving people into a hole and not letting them out. When Legal Aid is cut, and the poor no longer have access to the courts, that's an example of government playing a role in perpetuating poverty.

MURRAY: If you try to rent an inexpensive apartment in my hometown of Newton, Iowa, even if you're white, you may very well not be able to rent that apartment, on "subjective grounds." I mean, you come to the door, and because of the way you act or the way you look or whatever, the landlord says to himself: "My apartment's going to get trashed." These subjective grounds often have a basis in fact. And it's real tough for people renting out apartments—and maybe even for banks—to operate in ways that enable them to make money if they aren't permitted to make these kinds of subjective judgments.

JACKSON: Dr. Murray, the farmer wearing his bib overalls who walks up to that apartment door and is rejected for the way he looks is not a victim of racial prejudgment. That man could put on a suit and get the apartment. Blacks can't change color. The idea is that bankers choose not to make loans to blacks institutionally.

Now, I'm not just throwing around a charge here. John H. Johnson, the president of Johnson Publishing Company, which publishes *Ebony*, is perhaps the most established black businessman in the country. Yet several banks turned down his loan application to build in downtown Chicago. Maybe the most established black businessman in the country was turned down for a loan simply because of the institutional racism of banks. And so we need laws enforced, we need the government to protect people who are black or Hispanic or Asian or Indian or female, from the bankers' ability to do that.

A lot of people, to this day, are simply locked out. Until 1967, there had never been more than a couple of black car dealerships, because the automobile industry's policy was not to allow a black to invest in a car dealership or to learn to run one in any neighborhood, black or white. So blacks now have fewer than 240 dealerships out of the 22,050 in this country. Blacks always had the ability, but they were locked out by race, even if they had the money. Operation PUSH confronted Ford as late as July 1982, when there were fewer than 40 black automobile dealerships out of 5,600. Ford finally agreed to grant 30 new black dealerships in one year, which they had previously claimed was impossible. Well, those 30 dealerships are still operating, employing an average of more than 50 people each, and those jobs represent the alternative to welfare and despair.

MURRAY: If you say that in 1960 blacks as a people were locked out, well, I have no problem with that. But that is no longer accurate. Let's talk about black youth unemployment. Are you saying that America's black youth are marching resolutely from door to door, interviewing for jobs, and that they are getting turned down because they're black? If so, then a jobs program ought to do wonders. The Comprehensive Employment Training Act (CETA) ought to have done wonders. But it didn't.

JACKSON: The private economy, by being so closed for so long, has pushed many people into the public economy. There's just no reason why, in a population of thirty million blacks, there are only two black beverage-bottling franchises. You can't explain it by lack of ambition or an unwillingness to take risks, because for the past twenty years blacks have been the top salesmen in that industry. A lot of people got locked into poverty because of the government's failure to enforce equal protection under the law. Until the Civil Rights Act of 1964 and Lyndon Johnson's executive order of 1965, beverage companies could get lucrative government contracts to operate on U.S. military bases around the world, even though they locked out a significant body of Americans.

MURRAY: I'm not in a position to argue with you about wholesalers and franchises. But I don't think we can assume that if blacks gain more access to entrepreneurial business positions—which I'm all in favor of—it will have a fundamental effect on poverty and the underclass.

JACKSON: If there is an artificial ceiling limiting the growth of the so-called talented 10 percent—I use the term advisedly—then it compounds the problem of the disinherited 90 percent. If where we live, our money won't "spend" because of red-lining, which becomes a de facto law; if where we live, our money cannot buy a car franchise or a beer franchise or a soft-drink franchise—which are some of the great American ways out of poverty—then blacks are effectively locked out of the private economy. And so, just as the political grandfather clause locked blacks out of the political system, economic grandfather clauses have effectively locked blacks out of the economic system. Blacks today can take over a town politically, because its population is mostly black. But the economic territory—the entrepreneurial opportunities, beyond mom-and-pop businesses, which allow a people to develop a leadership class in the private economy, which in turn begins to lift others as it hires them and trains them—is still closed. Blacks who worked as salesmen and saleswomen for the first generation of black entrepreneurs now have franchises of their own, because they have access to the franchise head. But that has not happened historically.

MURRAY: Why is it that the Koreans and Vietnamese and all sorts of other people who come here with very few resources do well, including West Indian blacks? They come here, start businesses, and manage to earn a median income which rivals or surpasses that of whites. I'm not trying to say racism doesn't exist. I'm saying it doesn't explain nearly as much as it ought to.

JACKSON: Do not underestimate the impact of 250 years of legal slavery followed by 100 years of legal segregation. The damage it did to the minds of the oppressor and the oppressed must not be played down. When I grew up in South Carolina, I could caddy but I couldn't play golf. That's why I can't play golf now; I could have been arrested for hitting a golf ball at the Greenville Country Club. I could shag balls, but I couldn't play tennis. I could shine shoes, but I couldn't sit on the stand and couldn't own a stand at the train station. I could wait tables, but I couldn't sit at them; and I could not borrow money to build a competing establishment.

The other groups you mentioned have not known that level of degradation. The Cubans came to Miami as beneficiaries of a cold war between this country and Cuba; we used money and subsidies to induce them to come here, and those who came were in large measure from a class that had some history of business acumen. Many of the Vietnamese were beneficiaries of the same kind of cold-war policy.

Now, shagging balls and not playing tennis, caddying and not playing golf, not voting and seeing others vote—all of this had the cumulative effect of lowering people's ambitions and limiting their horizons. Let me give an example. I saw a story in USA Today last summer headlined "More Blacks Graduating from High School, Fewer Going to College." A young lady from Chicago was quoted in the story, and I decided to meet with her and her mother. It turned out she had a B+ average, was a member of the National Honor Society—the whole business. I said to the girl, "Do you want to go to college?" She said she did. I said, "Well, have you taken the SAT tests?" She said she hadn't. "Why not?" "Well, the counselor told me that since I couldn't afford to go to college, that stuff was a waste of time." In other words, she was being programmed for failure, taught to be mediocre, programmed downward.

Once I discovered what was happening, I went on the radio and asked any high-school student—black, white, brown—who had every college qualification except money to come to Operation PUSH. Seven hundred fifty young people came with their parents; we have placed 250 of them in colleges, including that young lady. But if that young lady hadn't gone to college, she would have been written off three or four years later; people would have said the family was subsidized, dependent; she didn't go to college; now she's pregnant; and the whole cycle begins again. She was programmed into lower ambition, programmed away from college. Yet many schools, especially the better ones like Harvard and Columbia, provide scholarship money. But so many students don't know this; it's a well-kept secret. Those who have, know; the circle remains essentially closed.

MURRAY: Getting that information out would serve as an incentive. I know how I'd spend money on educational programs. I'd put up a bunch of posters saying that anybody who gets such-and-such a score on the SAT will get a free ride through college. I'm willing to bet that I'd get more results from my program than the government would get by trying directly to improve the schools.

JACKSON: There's a role for that kind of motivation. There's also a role for increasing opportunity. Often it's not lack of ability or ambition that locks people out, but lack of information.

MURRAY: I'm worried, because I'm starting to agree with you too much!

JACKSON: Just give me time, you'll be all right.

MURRAY: Oh, I think we'll find some things to disagree on. I come from an all-white town. I went back to visit this Christmas, and I said to myself, "I wonder what poverty is like here in Newton, Iowa." So I got in touch with the human services people and spent some time riding around with a caseworker. And as I listened to this caseworker describe what her problems were, I realized that if I closed my eyes, I could have been listening to a caseworker in the South Bronx. The problems were indistinguishable from what are usually considered "black problems."

JACKSON: Yes, we must whiten the face of poverty. It's an American problem, not a black problem. But the face of poverty in this country is portrayed as a black face, and that reinforces certain attitudes. I mean, John Kennedy holds up a sick black baby in his arms and people say,

"Gee, he's a nice guy." He holds up a sick white baby in West Virginia and people say, "We've got to do something about this."

Of the thirty-four million people living in poverty in America, twenty-three million are white. The poor are mostly white and female and young. Most poor people work every day. They're not on welfare; they're changing beds in hospitals and hotels and mopping floors and driving cabs and raising other people's children. And there is no basis for taking a few people who cheat the system as examples, and using them to smear millions of people who by and large work very hard.

MURRAY: The welfare queen is not the problem. And the dynamics of dependency operate pretty much the same for both blacks and whites. For example, I did some checking on what the out-of-wedlock birthrate is among poor whites. Guess what? Middle-class blacks don't have much of a problem with out-of-wedlock births, just as middle-class whites don't; but poor blacks and poor whites alike have a big problem with it.

Now, when I visit a school in inner-city Washington, I see a couple of different kinds of kids. A lot of kids are sent out of their houses every morning by their moms and dads, who tell them, "Get that education. Study hard. Do what the teacher says." And these youngsters go off to school and study hard, do exactly what the teacher says, and still graduate a couple of years behind grade level—not because they're stupid, but because of what has happened to the school systems during the past twenty years. A great deal of energy and attention has been spent catering to the kind of kid who, for whatever reason, makes it real hard for the first set of kids to learn.

So I think we need to reintroduce a notion which has a disreputable recent history in America: the notion of class. A good part of our problem can be characterized as one of "lower-class behavior," which is distinct from the behavior of poor people.

JACKSON: In other words, the Watergate burglars, though white, male, and rich, were engaging in "lower-class behavior."

MURRAY: No, but if you talk about the danger posed by the increase in crime, it so happens that it is not the rich white folks who are suffering.

JACKSON: Back up now, back up. You introduced a phenomenon there, Dr. Murray, about "lower-class behavior." I suppose that means low morals.

MURRAY: You added that.

JACKSON: Well, I guessed that's what it means. What does "lower-class behavior" mean?

MURRAY: The syndrome was identified long ago, although the term is more recent. People in the nineteenth and early twentieth centuries would simply talk about "trash," for example, and later there was the concept of the "undeserving poor." The sociologist who did the Elmstown study certainly recognized the syndrome, as did Edward Banfield. It is characterized by chronic unemployment due to people working for a while and then dropping out, unstable family life, and so on.

JACKSON: But you know, Dr. Murray, you made a distinction here on this "lower-class behavior" and I was trying to get a definition of it, but I did not get it. I'm sorry, I haven't read all those books you mentioned. But I suppose it means immoral behavior.

MURRAY: I'm not using words like "moral" and "immoral."

JACKSON: Well, I guess it means violence against people, unprovoked violence—lower-class behavior. Sex without love, making unwanted babies—lower-class behavior. Taking what belongs to other people—lower-class behavior. Filling your nose full of a lot of cocaine, driving drunk—lower-class behavior. That's not lower-class behavior, Dr. Murray, that's immoral.

It seems to me that whether it is stealing in the suites or stealing in the streets, whether it is happening in ghetto, barrio, reservation, or suburb, we should condemn lower-class behavior. Cain killing Abel, brother killing brother, is lower-class behavior because it's low morals, it's unethical, it's not right. Whether they're welfarized or subsidized, people should not engage in lower-class behavior. Is it more moral for a business executive to sniff cocaine than a welfare recipient?

MURRAY: If you are saying that rich white people can be lousy, I agree. But my point is that if we continue to pretend that all poor people are victims, if we do not once again recognize in social policy the distinctions that have been recognized all along on the street, we will continue to victimize those poor people who most deserve our respect and our help.

Parents, black or white, who are working at lousy jobs but who are working, paying the rent, teaching their kids how to behave—yes, those people are behaving differently, and certainly in a more praiseworthy way, than parents who fail to do those things. Poor people fall into very different classes, distinguished by differences in work behavior, such as chronic unemployment whether there are jobs or not. And there are differences in child rearing. Working-class people pay a lot of attention to how their children are doing; they talk to them, ask how they're doing in school. But there are children who come to school at the age of five and do not know, for example, the words for the colors; nobody's talked to them, they've been utterly neglected. Finally, when there is divorce among the working class the man takes continued responsibility for supporting the children. Lower-class behavior, on the other hand, is characterized by serial monogamy or promiscuity and a failure of the man to take responsibility for his children.

JACKSON: Dr. Murray, the lady who lived across the street from us while I was growing up ran what they call a "bootleg house." She was a woman of high character; she was a seamstress, and all her children graduated from college. But on the weekend people came over to her house to drink and gamble, and so Mrs. X was considered an outcast. Now, another lady named Mrs. Y, who lived about three blocks from us, owned a liquor store; because she was white she could get a liquor license. Mrs. Y was an entrepreneur, Mrs. X was a moral outcast. But something told me early in the game that the only difference between Mrs. X and Mrs. Y was a license.

Men and women would come over to Mrs. X's house sometimes and have sex down in the basement; promiscuity, also a sign of lower-class behavior, and another reason why people looked down on her. Well, I began working at the hotel in town; I was paid to carry in the booze for the men who would meet women there, often other people's wives, sometimes even their friends' wives. They'd each leave at a different time and by a different door to maintain their respectability, but I knew where they lived because I used to cut their grass and rake their leaves. This is distinctly lower-class behavior—sleeping with other people's wives.

MURRAY: No, engaging in sexual behavior, even promiscuity, does not make you lower class. What makes you lower class is having kids you can't or don't take care of.

JACKSON: Now, Dr. Murray, are you saying that a lawyer who has sex with his partner's wife and uses a prophylactic is engaging in behavior that's higher class than that of someone who does the same thing but does not have the sense or ability to use a prophylactic?

MURRAY: Look, I'm not against sex. I'm not even necessarily against sex outside of marriage.

JACKSON: Now, don't get too swift on me here. The act of going to bed with another man's wife is adultery.

MURRAY: Fine.

JACKSON: It ain't fine. It's immoral. It's lower-class behavior, and whether it takes place in the White House, statehouse, courthouse, outhouse, your house, my house, that behavior is unethical.

MURRAY: But that has nothing to do with what I'm saying.

JACKSON: It shows a certain attitude: If you do something and it's subsidized, it's all right. If others do it and it's welfarized, it's not so good.

I was in inner-city Washington several months ago, talking to a gym full of high-school kids. I challenged those who had taken drugs to come down front. About three hundred came down. Next day the

Washington Post published three pictures and the headline "Jackson does phenomenal thing—kids admit drug usage." Editorial: "It's a great thing that Jackson did, but you know he has a special way with black kids." Next day I went to a school in Maryland—in one of the richest counties in America, about 97 percent white, single-family dwellings, upper middle class, and all that. The principal said to me, "Well, you can make your pitch, but of course it won't work here." So I made my pitch. I said, "Taking drugs is morally wrong, except in controlled medical situations; it's morally wrong and ungodly." Six hundred students were present. I said, "Those who have tried drugs, come forward." About two hundred came forward. This was a junior high school; these kids were thirteen, fourteen years old. The principal was in a daze. Now that's lower-class behavior and upper-class economic status. Rich folks embezzle and poor folks steal; rich folks prevaricate and poor folks lie. But I think a lie is a lie is a lie.

MURRAY: If we agree that lying is lying and stealing is stealing, that doesn't help the little old lady who is trying to get from her apartment to the grocery store without getting her Social Security check ripped off. If we take the attitude that white-collar crime is just as bad as street crime, so let's not go after the street criminals when we let the embezzlers get away, the problem is that we ignore that little old lady, who is not in much immediate danger from embezzlers. Poor people, first of all, need safety. We'll take care of the white-collar criminals as best as we can, but first I want to make it safe in the neighborhoods. And if that requires putting a whole bunch of people behind bars, let's do it.

JACKSON: We should remember that four years at a state university in New York costs less than $25,000; four years at Attica costs $104,000. I am more inclined to take these young kids and lock them up in dormitories, give them years of mind expansion and trade development. It costs too much to leave them around for years without education, hope, or training.

The present welfare system should be replaced with a human development system. As presently constructed, the welfare system has built-in snares; there's no earn-incentive, no learn-incentive to get out. Assume you are locked into this box: a girl with a tenth-grade education and a baby. If she's making, say, $200 a month on welfare, why not provide some positive incentives? If she went back to school and got her junior-college degree, she should get $240, $250. Why? Because that's making her employable, moving her closer to the market, where she can earn her own money. She can go back to junior college and study computer science, or learn cosmetology or business. The way it is now in most states, if she went out and found a job and made $200, they would take away $200 from welfare. So why earn the $200? Maybe if she earns $200 she should keep at least $100.

The point is that incentives to earn and learn must be built into the system. As it is now, if the young man who fathered the child doesn't have a job but comes back to live with the mother, she loses her check. So there's an incentive to keep the father away. And one of the few ways she can get any extra money is by engaging in an activity that may get her an extra child.

Now this young girl—white, black, Hispanic, Asian, Native American—is the victim of a system that is not oriented toward human development. We must take away the punishment and threats and disincentives and move toward a sense of optimism and increasing options.

MURRAY: One part of me endorses what you're saying in principle. But when I think of all the practical difficulties I get depressed. Most of all, it is extremely difficult to make much progress with youngsters who already have certain behavior patterns. If we go to a poor part of New York City, white or black, and pick a hundred kids who really have problems—drugs, illegitimate kids, the rest of it—and I say: "Here's a blank check; hire the best people, use the latest technologies, do whatever you can." At the end of three or four or even five years, if you start with seventeen- or eighteen-year-olds, maybe you will be able to point to ten or fifteen out of that hundred who show any major signs of getting somewhere.

Human beings aren't plastic. We don't know how to deal with certain kinds of problems after a certain age. The only route we have is prevention. So if you're hearing me say we're going to have to write off a generation, you can certainly back me into that corner.

JACKSON: Dr. Murray, I have seen these same kids, who you say can't do anything, volunteer for the army, and in six to eight months they are building bridges, assuming responsibility. Why? Because it's an effective program that teaches, inspires, and sets clear goals.

So many young people step into sex and have babies because of ignorance, lack of discipline, and the like. If there was sex education before the fact, as well as the teaching of moral values, then there'd be less debate about abortion after the fact. Today, there is this whole group of people who love the fetus; they march across America to save a fetus and march right back to cut off aid for a baby.

Aid to women for prenatal care has a lot of value. The Head Start program saved a whole generation. The drive to wipe out malnutrition by Senators McGovern and Hollings in the food stamp program actually worked; it brought about balanced diets where there had been none. We should drop programs that aren't working, not those that are.

MURRAY: It is beginning to percolate into the consciousness of policy makers that we just don't know how to affect large numbers of people who are leading blighted lives. The only way we can deal with this is by prevention.

JACKSON: I agree that there are ways to change this situation without just paying another top-heavy layer of overseers and administrators who'd be sending paperwork back to Albany. I would take five hundred young people and say, "How many of you would like this neighborhood to be cleaner?" Most hands would go up. "How many of you would like to have windows in your buildings in the wintertime?" Hands would go up. "How many of you would like to make $12 to $20 an hour?" Many hands. "We'll teach you how to be a mason. You can lay bricks and not throw them. You can learn how to be a glazier, how to be a plasterer. And at the end of this time, we'll get you certified in a trade union. You will then have the skill to build where you live; if the floor's buckling in your gymnasium, you can fix it."

And so these young men and women would be empowered and enfranchised: they would much rather make $20 an hour than be on welfare. Just to do things for them while keeping them economically disenfranchised is no systematic change at all. And, Dr. Murray, people who can lay bricks and carpet and cut glass have no intention of going back on welfare.

MURRAY: I should point out that in my ideal world, by God, any black youngster who wants to can become a glazier, any poor youngster can learn a trade. And, Reverend Jackson, in my ideal world I would also clone you, because I've heard you speak to these kids.

JACKSON: But why do you think black kids everywhere are playing basketball so well? I submit to you that they're playing basketball and football and baseball so well and in such great numbers because there is a clear and obvious reward; there's a carrot. Do this and you'll be in the paper, on the radio, on television. And you'll get a college scholarship. And if you're real good, you'll get a professional contract. So these same kids that you say are unreachable and unteachable will gravitate to a carrot if they can see it. There must be a way out. And right now we must come up with ways out.

MURRAY: Yes, education and training opportunity—the carrots—are absolutely central. But once you have those, you have to have a support system, and this is where we've got a real problem. For example, let's say a youngster graduates from high school without many skills. He gets into a good job-training program, one that will really teach him a skill if he buckles down. But the youngster has never learned good work habits, so he flunks out of the training program. For that youngster to come out of high school ready to take advantage of a training program, there must be changes in the school he came from.

Now, what about the youngster who is offered an opportunity but who is below average in intelligence? I mean, half the country is below average in intelligence, and in industriousness.

JACKSON: Does that apply all the way through the government?

MURRAY: Let's just say this youngster is no great shakes, not much of anything. How is this youngster going to have a life that lets him look back when he's sixty and say, "Well, I did O.K., given what I had. At least I always supported myself and raised my kids and so on." The only way that eighteen-year-old kid is ever going to get to that position is by taking jobs that aren't much fun and don't pay much money. In order to reach the point where he feels good about supporting himself and his family, he's got to survive those years of eighteen, nineteen, twenty, when kids want to do things which make a whole lot of sense when you're that age but turn out to have been real stupid by the time you're thirty. Here is where, after you've provided the opportunities, which I am for in abundance, you've still got to worry.

JACKSON: But Dr. Murray, democracy must first guarantee opportunity. It doesn't guarantee success. Now, why do you think these ghetto and barrio youngsters are doing so well in athletics?

MURRAY: Because they see people just like them, who came out of those same streets, making a whole lot of money doing it.

JACKSON: So successful role models are a great motivator.

MURRAY: They make a huge difference. Now, how do we get the Jesse Jacksons of the world to be more visible role models?

JACKSON: Well, I've been working on that for a few years. But the point is that where the rules are clear, even though the work is hard, the locked-out tend to achieve. Ain't no low-class and high-class touch-downs. But there are no black baseball managers and no black profes-sional football coaches. Why? Because in those areas where the deci-sions are made behind closed doors and where the rules are not so clear, those who are locked out don't do well.

That is basically true in the private economy: the more subjective the rules, the less the penetration. When people go behind closed doors to, say, determine who the dean of the medical school will be, eight people who are doctors, all of them graduated from the same school, tend to come up with someone from the same lineage. Why are there so many blacks in government employment? Because if you do well on the test, you can get in, and the rules of seniority are established.

MURRAY: In 1983, the New York City Police Department gave a sergeant's exam, and 10.6 percent of the white candidates passed but only 1.6 percent of the blacks. So it was decided that even though the rules were clear, some blacks who had failed the test would be promoted in order to fill a quota. Now, either you assume that the test measured nothing relevant to being a sergeant and that skill is randomly distributed, so it didn't make any difference that a whole bunch of blacks were arbitrarily promoted despite the fact that they didn't pass the test, or you assume that the test did in fact measure abilities that are important to advancement. If that's true, a few years down the road very few of the black sergeants will become lieutenants. This ensures, in an almost diabolically clever way, that no matter how able blacks become, they will continue to be segmented, and whites will always be looking at black co-workers who aren't quite as good at their jobs as the whites are. You build in an appearance of inferiority where none needs exist.

Now, your son went to St. Albans and my daughters go to National Cathedral. These are among the finest schools in Washington. Your son, when he applies for a job, doesn't need or want any special consideration. The fact that he's black is irrelevant.

JACKSON: You're making dangerous comparisons here, Doctor, which tend to inflame weak minds. My son is not a good example because, like his father, his achievements are above average. The fact is that all of America, in some sense, must be educated about its past and must face the corrective surgery that is needed.

When there's moral leadership from the White House and from the academy, people tend to adjust. When Lyndon Johnson said—with the moral authority of a converted Texan—that to make a great society we must make adjustments, people took the Voting Rights Act and affirmative action and said, "Let's go."

There are a lot of positive examples around the country where integrated schools have worked, where busing has worked, where affirmative action has worked, when that spirit of moral leadership was present. The same school where the national guard had to take two blacks to school in 1961—the University of Georgia—is where Herschel Walker won the Heisman Trophy. Later he was able to marry a white woman without protest in rural Georgia. Why? Because people had been taught that it was all right.

MURRAY: You've got the cart before the horse. By the mid-1960s, white folks finally, after far too long, had had their consciousnesses raised. They said to themselves, "We've done wrong. We have violated a principle that's one of the taproots of America; we haven't given people a fair shot just because their skin's a different color." A chord was struck that triggered a strong desire not only to stop doing the bad things but also to help people make up for lost ground.

The additional response was, from the very beginning, sort of pushing it. The principle that had actually been violated was that of the fair shot; but the black civil rights movement isn't feeding off that important nutrient anymore. It's gone beyond that. Today, when white folks aren't making public pronouncements, I hear far too many of them saying things which are pretty damned racist. I see a convergence of the old racism, which is still out there, with a new racism, from people who are saying, "Well, gee, it's been twenty years now. You'd think they'd be catching up by now."

JACKSON: They're getting strong signals from the highest pulpit in the nation. When the White House and the Justice Department close their doors to the Afro-American leadership; when the Congressional Black Caucus cannot meet with the President of the United States, when the government closes its doors to the NAACP, the SCLC, the Urban League, Operation PUSH; when the White House will not meet with the Conference of Black Mayors; when those who work in the vineyards daily will not even engage in the dialogue you and I have engaged in today—that's reprehensible behavior. It sends out signals that hurt people. When leadership is present, people behave differently.

MURRAY: In addition to spending a lot of time talking to white people in general, I also spend a lot of time talking to conservatives. And I happen to know that their passion for a colorblind society is not just rhetoric.

JACKSON: Are you a consultant for an optometrist? Because the only people who would benefit from people going colorblind would be optometrists.

Nobody wants to be that way, man. We don't need to be colorblind; we need to affirm the beauty of colors and the diversity of people. I do not have to see you as some color other than what you are to affirm your person.

MURRAY: I mean that the ideal of giving everybody a fair shot—of not saying to anyone, "Because you're black I'm going to refuse to give you a chance"—is something which a lot of conservatives feel more passionately about than a lot of your putative friends do.

JACKSON: But if two people are in a one-mile race and one starts off with a half-mile head start and one starts off at point zero—O.K., now let's take the chains off, every man for himself—well, such a race is not just. We are starting out behind. I mean, of the top six hundred television executives, fewer than fifteen are black.

MURRAY: I had a talk with somebody from one of the networks a few weeks ago, as a matter of fact. He said to me: "Well, we figured we ought to have a black producer, so we went out and hired the best one we could find. But he really isn't very good, so we do most of his work for him." Now, insofar as people aren't allowed to be TV producers because they're black, that's bad. But insofar as white people go around saying, "We had to get our black TV producer, so we brought in someone who can't make it on his own," they are not doing blacks a service.

JACKSON: Man, for most of my life, I have seen black people train white people to be their boss. Incompetent whites have stood on the shoulders of blacks for a long time. Do you know how impressed I am when a white rock singer who is selling millions of records explains how he got his inspiration from a black artist, who can't even afford to come to the white man's concert? A few months ago *Time* said in an article that Gary Hart was the only Democrat who has run a coast-to-coast campaign. I was on the cover of *Time* twice during the 1984 campaign. But Hart's the only one. Isn't that a strange phenomenon? It's like Ralph Ellison's invisible man: they look at you but they don't see you.

By and large, the black people the White House sees are those one or two exceptions who did something great. They take a Hispanic kid or a black person and try to impose that model on the nation. I could take the position, "Well, if I can make it from a poor community in South Carolina, explain to me how a white person can be in poverty," and it would be absurd. But I could argue it and get lots of applause.

MURRAY: I'm willing to grant that we shouldn't make so much of the exception if you grant me that just because folks may be against certain kinds of programs, it doesn't mean that they're mean-spirited, or don't care about problems.

JACKSON: If we can avoid the demagogy and turn debate into dialogue and stereotypes into creative thinking, we can begin to develop ideas. I mean, I agree that this welfare system hurts people fundamentally. Many of the things that come from this administration, like the enterprise zone idea, have a lot of validity. If an enterprise zone creates a green line, instead of a red line, where if you live in that area you get certain incentives—that idea has merit. It may mean that a young man or a young woman teaching school will want to move to a district because of a tax incentive, or perhaps a doctor or a lawyer will want to move his or her office there. You establish an incentive for people to locate there, through the tax system or otherwise, you begin to shift capital, and the people who live there have first option on the new jobs. But the administration has never really discussed this idea with those who would have to communicate with the masses about it.

So that idea has merit. Together we could make sense of such an idea. I'm anxious to open up the door of social policy, and I'm impressed with this opportunity today.

Black Americans Seek
Economic Equity
and Parity

One of the main purposes of SCLC's Operation Breadbasket and of Operation PUSH was to develop black consumer power to negotiate for jobs and economic development opportunities in the private sector. Jackson has signed over a dozen moral covenants—sometimes referred to as non–legally binding trade agreements—with major corporations such as Coca-Cola, Seven-Up, Burger King, General Foods, and Avon. At the signing of the covenant with Heublein on March 16, 1982, Jackson made the following statement, which succinctly states what his approach to the private sector has been. Among other things, Heublein owns Kentucky Fried Chicken.

Economic growth, development, trade, and aid are economic issues of great concern to many people. The economic consciousness of the poor, despised, and rejected of the world, including black Americans, has increased to the point that these are now emerging as our concerns also.

Black America is an underdeveloped nation within a developed nation. To develop, black America must put forth a plan, a formula for development. The plan is for black America to renegotiate its relationship with corporate America. The formula is reciprocity—our share of community dollars reinvested for the institutional economic development of our community.

Corporate America already recognizes black America as a nation within a nation but defines us in such a way as to divert attention and

dilute our power. Corporate America defines us as a "special market"—
an addendum to its business—and thus it has always been able to take
us for granted. By defining us as a special market, it continues to relate
to black Americans as essentially consumers and workers but never as
copartners in development, production, ownership, and shared wealth.
Today's agreement points toward a new way of viewing and relating to
black America by corporate America.

Corporate America has procurement contracts and services it renders;
black America has productive capability, labor, and consumer dollars it
spends. That combination provides a basis for renegotiating a new
understanding and economic relationship around mutually beneficial
economic needs and interests. Because we pay taxes, we have a right to
demand our share of a $750 billion public economy. But we have
determined not to put all of our eggs in one basket. There is a $3 trillion
private economy that is immediately vulnerable to our disciplined appe-
tites and consumer dollars. We must use our dollars to fight for dollars.
The one-way trade relationships must end. We have a right to both
private and public trade and aid.

The black American economy is an unexplored treasure chest in a
wrecked ship that now must be opened, inspected, and liberated. What
does that market represent?

- Twenty-six to 30 million people;
- Seventeen million eligible voters;
- Thirty million dollars per month paid in union dues;
- Millions of dollars contributed to pension funds;
- Billions of dollars paid in local, state, and federal taxes;
- A $145 billion English-speaking consumer market immediately
accessible;
- The most educated minds and the best trained labor force of any
developing nation in the world;
- A link and a bridge to the markets of other nonwhite developing
economies (e.g., a half-billion Africans).

Yet, this well-trained labor market is not utilized, and this huge
consumer investment in the private sector is not reinvested to develop
the economic institutions in our community. Neither Russia nor
China—nor both of them combined—does $145 billion of business
with corporate America. Therefore we must not only use our seventeen
million eligible votes to cast a ballot every two or four years, but we
must vote for dignity every day with our dollars.

Black America suffers from a budget deficit that is the result of a trade
imbalance. We must balance our trade and reduce our budget deficit by
expanding private trade in addition to public aid. Historically black
America has had a "free-trade" policy—we have not put up trade

barriers or import restrictions in our community. But corporate America has taken advantage of our free-trade policy by exploiting us and adopting a restraint-of-trade policy against us. We have traded with them and helped to develop their businesses, but they have not traded with us and helped to develop our businesses. While in the relatively recent past we have received some aid and no trade, under the current political climate black America is receiving reduced aid MINUS trade, when what we need is free trade PLUS aid.

Blacks are looking for actions that will stop the restraint of trade now being practiced by the private sector against the black community. It wants an end to the economic grandfather clauses—perpetual contracts. There are approximately 4,200 independently owned beverage franchises in the soft-drink, beer, wine, and spirits industry—but less than 10 are black-owned. There are 22,500 auto dealerships; only 86 are black-owned. The tobacco, furniture, and most other industries have the same pattern. Corporate America has conducted an industrial lock-out against us. If you think the baseball lock-out of Jackie Robinson was immoral and foolish, the industrial lock-out and rejection of the black American economic market and its potential for development is absolute economic nonsense. We have ideas, energy, and money to invest and risk.

This covenant represents economic growth for Heublein and economic development for black America. It will not hurt corporate America, and it will help black America. Heublein is simply recognizing the existence and potential of the black American economy and pointing the way for others to do the same. This covenant represents three critical principles which must be taken into account as corporate America renegotiates its economic relationship with black America:

• *Reciprocity.* Our fair share must be the new criterion and standard. Reciprocity means mutual benefit. The black community needs economic reciprocity, not just social generosity. It needs investment for business and community development, not a paternalistic relationship. The new focus will be on an economic relationship versus solely a social relationship. The reinvestment of a fair and equitable return on the black consumer dollar is the demand. Jobs are not enough. Full employment with no pay is slavery, and employment without ownership is colonialism. Reinvestment of consumer dollars in the community of their origin is required.

• *Development Plan and Formula.* Underdeveloped nations require development plans and development formulas. Heublein and other corporate giants do not just bring jobs and money to underdeveloped nations. The Nigerians must own, run, and sell Heubleins, Seagrams, Somerset, Coca-Cola, Pepsi, Royal Crown, and 7-Up in their country. Development requires new rules—not just new rulers—that are designed for national development. Whoever does business in Nigeria or Mexico must comply with those nations' development plans and formulas. Black America can settle for nothing less.

• *Institutional Economic Development.* There must be a concentrated focus on institutional economic development by black America. Basic black economic institutions—banks, savings and loans, insurance companies, newspapers, radio and television stations, advertising agencies, and more—must be built. We must focus on the "supply side" as well as the "demand side" of the economic ledger. It is not enough to have affirmative action on the demand side—jobs and consumer protection. We must have affirmative action on the supply side—our share of ownership, wealth, and control.

Corporate America can adopt three basic attitudes in renegotiating its relationship with the black consumer and black businessperson. First, it can see it as essentially negative, fight it, and concede only out of economic necessity. Second, it can see it as a necessary evil and enter into the negotiations in a state of psychological and economic schizophrenia—torn, divided, uncommitted, and passive. Third, it can see it as a positive opportunity and approach black America as it approaches other economic markets—as a $145 billion economic common market to be developed and traded with.

Heublein has chosen the third alternative. They saw the business sense and economic potential of the black American common market, creatively responded to our challenge to come forth with a plan, and aggressively pursued this agreement. They want to forcefully and aggressively join with PUSH to promote and publicize the new economic relationship that has been established between black America and Heublein, with the hope and belief that others will join them.

The covenant includes ten specific areas where Heublein plans to increase its business relationships with black individuals and firms:

1. A $10 million Capital Formation Program to enable blacks to open twenty-four Kentucky Fried Chicken stores over the next three years. Heublein will guarantee leases on these restaurants.

2. The company will also make available eighty-eight additional KFC franchises to qualified investors who want to become owner-operators. Operation PUSH has volunteered to help KFC identify qualified applicants.

3. A pioneer in the use of black advertising agencies, Heublein is increasing its expenditures with these agencies by 50 percent, to $4 million this year, and will increase another 25 percent to $5 million the following year.

4. Heublein is increasing its loan agreements with black-owned banks

by 50 percent this year, to $4 million, and will increase its commitment to at least $20 million over the next five years.

5. The company has placed 15 percent, or $42 million, of its group life insurance with a black-owned insurance company. The annual premium is $165,000.

6. In addition to the services of various minority professional companies and individuals it already retains, the company committed to hire a black law firm and a black CPA firm in the next year. The company has already engaged a black-owned consulting firm to identify other professional firms and individuals with the expertise the company needs.

7. Blacks already account for 16.4 percent of Heublein's management workforce, but programs for providing upward mobility opportunities for blacks will receive even greater attention. Heublein's fourteen-member board of directors includes a black and a woman.

8. About 20 percent of Heublein's contributions of more than $1 million a year are directed to minority organizations. The company, however, will explore other opportunities such as research grants to black educational institutions and support of the Martin Luther King, Jr., Center for Nonviolent Social Change.

9. Heublein will purchase $9.8 million in goods and services in 1982 under its Minority Purchasing Program and plans to increase this to $11.5 million in 1983, with similar increases over the succeeding years. Over the five-year period, the company targets to spend $75 million under the Minority Purchasing Program.

10. The company stands ready and willing to work with qualified black enterprises in the distribution of its beverage products within the framework of laws and regulations.

In conclusion, I especially want to thank Heublein's president, Mr. Hicks B. Waldron, for his commitment and creative leadership and to express appreciation to Dr. Lisle Carter, who helped guide the negotiations, and also to thank Mr. Ed Byrd and Mr. John Cox and the members of the negotiating team for Heublein for the positive, constructive, and professional manner in which the negotiations proceeded. Also, a special word is due the Rev. B. W. Smith, chairman of PUSH's National Selective Patronage Council, for his guidance and inspiration along the way, and to Attorney James Felder, Mr. Joseph Gardner, the Rev. Willie Barrow, and the Rev. George E. Riddick, chief negotiators for PUSH.

Thank you very much.

Save the Family Farm and the Farm Family

Jackson's general approach to social issues includes trying to establish common economic or political ground between people who have been divided or who have not seen their common interests. In this speech, given to the Saturday Morning Community Forum of Operation PUSH on January 26, 1985, Jackson seeks to link what he often refers to as "the rural feeders" and "the urban eaters."

This week about two thousand family farmers will lose their farms. Also this week, forty-seven farmers got arrested here in Chicago protesting corporate greed. Small towns in Minnesota shut down on Monday, January 21, so twelve thousand farmers, businesspeople, townfolk, and school children could rally at the state capitol. In short, our nation's rural communities are being destroyed, and they are resisting.

We city folk know about urban decay. We know about hunger, about malnutrition, and about joblessness. A number of studies conducted by hospitals and health departments are showing that significant numbers of poor and hungry children are failing to grow properly. They are too short for their ages and too thin for their height. Here in Chicago, one study found over 20 percent of our children failing to grow properly.

We know there is a crisis in our cities. Farmers are here today to tell us that there is also a crisis in the country—rural America is in crisis too. Our mutual circumstances have us bound together. Our religion draws us together. We live at a time in world history when the very existence of the human family is threatened—by famine and hunger, by misuse of our natural and human resources, by greed and avarice, and by nuclear holocaust. Rural farmer, urban dweller, and former sharecropper, white producer and black consumer—all of us share a common legacy of economic exploitation and a common commitment to dignity and life. Our values bind us together: to get our economic house in order, to feed the hungry, and to clothe the naked. We need to house the homeless and provide jobs for the jobless. We need fewer guns and more butter. We need to keep our family farmers on the land. We need fewer missiles and more housing, fewer submarines and more subways.

The Bible teaches us that we must judge character by how we treat the least of these; that we judge a tree by the fruit it bears, not just by the bark it wears. Our society has elevated greed and profit to sanctified levels. Last year ninety thousand corporations made a profit and paid no taxes, and one hundred thousand individuals made $100,000 or more yet paid no taxes, while poor folks making $2,000 below the poverty line paid taxes.

The same misguided values that motivate many to personal greed have also led our nation to squander its precious resources. Perhaps no area of national policy better illustrates this point than our rising military budget. Our trillion-dollar deficit is in no small measure directly related to the unbridled escalation in defense spending. What's more, we are spending more and more on military hardware every day, yet we are less secure than ever in our history. Defense spending also generates fewer jobs than any other area of public spending, and it produces little of utility to our society—no food, no clothes, no housing, no medical equipment or supplies; in short, nothing of social or redemptive value. Yet each year we spend more on the military budget and cut spending in health, housing, and education to make up the difference.

We must choose to meet people's needs instead of corporate greed. Our very lives are at stake. Our national priorities must be reordered. True national security rests in our people and their well-being. And when the despised and rejected come together, we can choose a new path of life and health and turn from the current path of death and destruction.

Today, while he poses as a great defender of traditional American values, Ronald Reagan is presiding over the end of one of our most basic and cherished traditions—family farming. During my campaign for the presidency of the United States, I met with family farmers from across the country: farmers in Missouri who wore brown paper sacks over their heads while protesting our government's policies for fear of government retribution and farmers in the deep South who told me that there would be no more black-owned farms at all by the end of the decade.

All over our fertile land, our nation's farmers are telling a grim tale. In the most productive farmland in the world, we see farm foreclosures and forced liquidations at record levels. Twenty thousand farmers went out of business in both 1982 and 1983, and as many as eighty thousand farms may have gone under in 1984. Nearly a third of farm borrowers from the Farmers Home Administration are delinquent in repaying their loans. Suicides, mental illness, family disruptions and break-ups, and death in many forms are destroying the family farm and the farm family. Rural towns are becoming ghost towns. These social costs are too high.

How did we get to the point where young farmers can no longer begin farming? It is important to note the irony of an absurd economic system where *our food producers are going broke because they are producing too much food in a world full of hungry people.*

Some facts:

● Between 1972 and 1975 the consumer price index for food went up 48 percent.

● However, the amount Americans were paying for food that actually went to farmers increased by only 8 percent.

● Between 1973 and 1975, after-tax profits for food corporations rose by 54 percent—which, more than any other component, accounted for the rise in the nation's food bill.

● By the end of the 1970s, commodity prices went down, but the price that consumers paid in the store stayed high.

That means that both farmers and consumers were getting the raw end of the deal. Farmers got less for their products—in fact, not even enough to meet production costs—while consumer prices stayed high. In the meantime, food companies made profits to the tune of 54 percent.

During this same period we were told over and over again that the solution to farmers' problems was to export. Again, let's look at some facts. With encouragement from government and private lenders, farm-ers planted more and more, increased their credit, and exchanged earned income for borrowed dollars. Farm debt quadrupled to about $215 billion today. The price of farm supplies went up, the price of land tripled during the 1970s, and interest rates soared. Our "cheap farm price" policy, coupled with our "produce for greater exports" policy, created an inflationary spiral of selling more and more and getting less and less.

By 1982 net income per farm had sunk to one-half of what it was in 1979. In 1980 farmers' profit per acre was less than one-third of what it was in 1973.

The debt crisis faced by the American farmer is no different from the debt crisis faced by Third World countries, which totals more than $700 billion. The structure of the international debt crisis is the same as the structure of the farmers' domestic debt crisis here in America. Third

World countries are forced to grow cash crops to sell on the world market to pay off their loans to the International Monetary Fund (IMF) and the international bankers. Thus food is no longer produced for consumption at home. In that sense, the American farmer and the Third World farmer face the same problem. Both produce for export to pay off their loans while folks at home are forced to endure budget-cutting austerity programs and go hungry.

Our rural farmers who are overproducing are going broke, while the urban unemployed and the poor starve. That's the nature of the contradiction and the crisis.

Who isn't going broke? Working families in the cities, the unemployed, and small farmers are suffering tremendously. But what about the large grain companies? I'm sure that Cargill, Continental, Dreyfus, and Bunge are doing quite well. It's hard to know exactly, because these companies are not subject to public accountability under Securities and Exchange Commission laws. They can undercut prices whenever they choose, and we'll never know what the real deal was.

What farmers need is parity and not charity. No one is looking for a handout. Unemployed workers need to go back to work, and farmers need to farm. When people lose their land, are hungry and malnourished, starvation is sure to follow. The demand for 90 percent of parity for storable commodities means simply that farmers must get a fair price for what they produce. They must be able to meet their production costs so they can continue to provide us with an abundant and healthful food supply. All those who work are entitled to a livable wage in return for their labor—and farmers are no exception. It is to everyone's benefit to keep the family farmer farming. And guaranteeing a fair price is a key ingredient in that process.

What would 90 percent of parity do to the price consumers pay for food? The grocer in the food store gets more for the coupon on the box of Rice Krispies than farmers get for the rice in that same box! Farmers get 5¢ for the wheat in a $1 loaf of bread. With 90 percent parity, prices might go up a few pennies to consumers but nowhere near as much as they will if we have no more family farmers and are subject to the prices of the large corporations.

Ronald Reagan says let the free market solve all of our problems. But the free market has never been free or friendly to farmers. What he really means to do is to let the large conglomerates dominate agriculture. What Mr. Reagan means by "free enterprise" is ruthless, cutthroat competition among small farmers, resulting in fewer and fewer corporations controlling our entire food production system. Then we will truly see monopoly price fixing. Prices will soar. We will see even more destruction of our land and depletion of our water supply. Family farmers are the most efficient farmers, partly because they care about the land. They care about preserving our resources for our children and for our children's children.

While I was campaigning in Nebraska in 1984, the North American Farm Alliance donated beef to help feed the hungry in Omaha. That beef was a good example of what is happening to our farmers, ranchers, and our food system. The retail price of that beef had risen from 14¢ a pound in 1965 to over $1 per pound today. Farm prices go down, while food prices go up, and the spread between the two is getting bigger and bigger. We have starvation and financial collapse amidst abundant production. We have a distribution problem. We have a problem of justice. We have a moral problem. Under the present arrangement, no matter how much farmers produce, hunger, malnutrition, and starvation are on the increase.

We are at the point where, unless policies are changed, family farming will be gone forever. And with the family farm will also go our small towns, small businesses, jobs, schools, and our rural churches. We live in an interdependent society and an interdependent world. As the farm goes, so goes the city. We do not exist in separate oceans—one called "rural" and another called "urban"—and we are both in the same boat. When our small farms disappear, these proud, independent, but disillusioned and angry farmers will swarm to our cities to compete with black, brown, and poor unemployed workers for jobs that no longer exist—jobs that have been eliminated by automation or shifted to cheap labor markets abroad by the same corporate interests that took their farms.

In the 1960s America responded to the hungry. We expanded the school lunch program for children and the Food Stamp program for the poor. We started a supplemental feeding program called Women, Infants, and Children (WIC) for pregnant mothers and their babies. And we created meals for our elderly citizens. Serious hunger as a national problem was virtually eliminated.

But ten years later, doctors went into these same poor areas and found that hunger and malnutrition are again becoming rampant. But it is no longer 1967 or even 1977. It is 1985, and hunger and malnutrition have returned as serious problems in America—and the current direction is toward more misery.

Hunger, of course, is related to poverty. And poverty is significantly higher today than in any year since 1965. Today 35.3 million Americans are in poverty—an increase of 6 million since the beginning of this decade. Since 1979, 3,000 children a day have fallen into poverty! And with poverty comes hunger. I must remind you that of those 35.3 million, 24 million are white, 11 million are black, Hispanic, Asian, and

Native American. The poor are mainly white, mainly young, and mainly female. We must remove the Al Jolson mask of poverty and show it for what it is—a mainly white, female, and young phenomenon. But whatever color, race, or religion hunger strikes, hunger hurts. When a baby cries at night because it went to bed hungry, that baby does not cry in color, sex, or religion. It cries in pain. We must have a personal commitment and build the political will to ease that pain.

Problems of this magnitude do not just happen; they have causes. Hunger and malnutrition in a wealthy nation don't just happen. They are caused.

A study recently completed at the Harvard School of Public Health concluded that hunger has returned to America as a direct result of conscious government policies. As the economy weakened, as unemployment increased, as poverty rose dramatically—in other words, as the needs of the American people increased—our government turned its back on our most needy, helpless, and vulnerable citizens.

• With poverty and unemployment at record levels, the 1982 tax act shifted $20 billion from families already in poverty and gave an extra $64 billion to those who already made over $80,000 per year.

• With unemployment at the highest level since the Great Depression, over 8 million on the official rolls—95,800 more than when Reagan took office—1 million Americans were cut off from Food Stamps, and 20 million had their benefits reduced.

• With poverty increasing, 3 million children were dropped from the school lunch program.

• With malnutrition already a serious problem, health care for poor Americans was cut substantially.

This is America in 1985. Hunger has returned because the very programs which once virtually eliminated it were weakened and cut at the time they were needed the most.

Today we have a crisis in America. We are a nation adrift. Our spiritual power and the power of our people are in jeopardy. Nothing points this out more sharply than the presence of hunger in a land of plenty. It is a question of priorities. We can share our food with Africa and save the family farmer as well. We must see agriculture, not bombs and missiles, as our most strategic defense, for it supplies the most fundamental human needs and creates allies who never forget who came to their aid in a time of crisis.

Now is the time for leadership. Now is the time to choose. We can choose two CVN Nuclear Attack Carriers that cost $3.4 billion each, or we can take that $7 billion and restore every federal nutrition program cut by the Reagan administration. If we did, we would have enough money left over to increase Food Stamp benefits by 25 percent and still be able to expand the school lunch program.

Food and steel are the backbones of our national industries. Last week I joined the Steelworkers Union and unemployed steelworkers in the Mahoning Valley just outside of Pittsburgh where over 200,000 jobs have been lost. In 1984 alone, 2,000 high-paying steel jobs were exported to slave-labor markets in apartheid South Africa. At the same time, here in Chicago, you rallied at the U.S. Steel South Chicago Works plant to protest the loss of jobs there—jobs down from 20,000 at its peak to just 600 now. We were in Pennsylvania protesting plant shutdowns at the Duquesne Works.

Together we have a common interest in a new economic agenda. Together—farmers and steelworkers, rural and urban, black and white, male and female, young and old—we have a responsibility to save our farms and to ensure our steel industry's ability to grow. Both affect our national security. Both are sources of life. Both represent our children's future.

We must demand tripartite ownership. What's good for Chrysler, what's good for Continental Bank, that same formula can save the steel industry: (1) government capital and tax credits, (2) equitable worker concessions (if necessary), and (3) competent industrial management. We must demand a moratorium on farm, home, and small-business foreclosures until there is economic recovery. We must insist on debt restructuring for our family farmers so they can continue to plant. The 1985 Farm Bill must move toward the goal of 90 percent of parity prices for storable commodities, coupled with supply management to ensure that we produce what we need.

The problems of Rainbow poverty, Rainbow unemployment, and the Rainbow loss of our family farms present us with the Rainbow challenge of 1985. Each of these elements of the Rainbow Coalition of the rejected crosses lines of race, sex, religion, and national origin. As people who love our children, who care about the future, who respect the earth and all of God's precious gifts, we must commit ourselves to ending hunger and malnutrition, to ending unemployment, and to saving the family farm and the farm family. Together we can save the farm and save the cities. Apart we can save neither.

Equity in a New World Order: Reparations and Reciprocity

This speech was Jackson's presidential address to the ninth annual convention of Operation PUSH in New Orleans on July 16, 1980. In this speech, evidence can be seen of Jackson's international travels and activities during the previous year. Representatives of both Israel and the Palestine Liberation Organization, as well as of many Arab and African nations, were in attendance.

Operation PUSH was born in controversy, and it remains in the forefront of controversy because it attempts to remain relevant and on the cutting edge of the critical issues of our day. PUSH is a controversial organization because it consciously identifies with the poor, the rejected, and the oppressed, and any organization that so identifies itself will have mixed views about it. PUSH consciously seeks social, economic, political, and legal justice and is striving for a more humane and peaceful nation and world in which to live—and God knows that this is controversial.

PUSH, as a national human rights organization with national and international concerns, is concerned with the quantity *and quality* of our lives and refuses to be limited solely to so-called black or ethnic concerns. Don't do us any favors by turning the ghetto over to us. We are grown and responsible. We want to share and participate at every level in the burdens and the responsibilities of helping to create a new national and world order.

The purpose of this convention is to take stock and evaluate what the organization has done over the last year, to analyze the state of affairs for black and poor people in 1980 and beyond, and to give direction and project an agenda and program for the coming year.

PUSH's ninth annual convention is meeting at a critical and strategic time. This is a national election year, with the Republicans meeting this week and the Democrats meeting early next month. At the present time, black and poor people are confronted with the serious dilemma of reduced and very limited political options. We are meeting in the middle of a planned economic recession that apparently has not yet hit bottom.

We are meeting at the conclusion of a decade of moral decadence as well. Recall the national nightmares of Vietnam, Watergate, Koreagate, and other official corruption and misconduct. We are meeting after a decade of economic decline and stagnation when the economic gap between blacks and whites has increased. We are meeting on the threshold of the 1980s, when the economic prospects appear bleak, when the aggressive actions against blacks by the KKK, the police, the Nazis, and other right-wing groups have dramatically increased, and when the social tolerance by blacks is growing thin, as witnessed by the racial unrest in such cities as Wichita and Miami.

We meet in New Orleans while one of our premier leaders, Vernon Jordan, lies in bed in New York, recovering from an assassination attempt. That assassination attack may very well have been an attempt by extreme right-wing provocateurs to trigger riots across the country so that a "law and order" candidate—a messiah of repression—could then sweep in and "save the people."

It happened with Nixon in 1968, and it may very well have been attempted again in 1980. Or it may have been an attempt by extreme left-wing provocateurs to achieve the same end so that, in their words, "the contradictions in this society would be heightened," which they see as necessary "prior to the revolution taking place."

As the PUSH convention meets in New Orleans, we are at a crossroads. The two Chinese characters that combine to form the word "crisis"—danger and opportunity—are again appropriate. We are confronted with a decade of decision. If we make certain decisions, we will face a decade of greater danger. If we choose other options, the 1980s can be a decade of greater opportunities. Before we get to that, however, let's look briefly at what PUSH has been doing and has accomplished over the last year.

What PUSH Has Accomplished

In order to keep new blood, fresh ideas, and a broad base of leadership responsibility alive in Operation PUSH, Bishop H. H. Brookins, who so ably served as our national board chairman for nearly four years, stepped aside, and Mayor Richard G. Hatcher, who so inspired and challenged us yesterday, willingly accepted the board's nomination and election as its new chairman. The organization officially and legally changed its name to People United to *Serve* Humanity, from *Save,* as it has continued to expand and grow under the able leadership of Rev. Bill Thurston. PUSH now has a presence in nearly sixty cities across the country.

Immediately following last year's PUSH convention in Cleveland, Jack O'Dell, PUSH's International Affairs Director, and I led a delegation on a seventeen-day tour of South Africa. We discovered several things. South Africa, a nation of 25.5 million people—19 million black, 2 million mixed-race people called "colored," 500,000 Indian, and 4 million white—has great human and national treasures. But the ruling white minority apartheid fascist government has turned South Africa into a tragedy.

We also discovered that America is in partnership with the South African government. U.S. diplomatic recognition gives South Africa international social acceptance and paves the way for American business investment. Five American companies—General Motors, Ford, Caltex, IBM, and Mobil—are the major investors in South Africa's fascist-controlled cheap labor market, where U.S. investment constitutes 17 percent of all foreign investment, and where companies reap the highest profits in the world. The United States, through Ford and General Motors, is involved in selling military equipment to the South African government through technical legal trickery, circumventing the intent of a Commerce Department regulation prohibiting such supplies. The United States engages in nuclear collaboration and has joint military contingency plans with South Africa. In short, America is a partner with South Africa in supporting the oppression of our brothers and sisters in South Africa.

America is on a collision course and seems willing to choose the 4 million Afrikaners of South Africa over the half a billion blacks that constitute the rest of Africa. Such action is immoral, it is economically unfeasible, it is politically dangerous, and it threatens our national interest. Black and other concerned Americans must join the international community in supporting economic sanctions against South Africa and pressure our government to stop vetoing such proposals in the U.N. We must never choose short-term dollars for the few over long-term dignity for the many. Every presidential candidate must be asked to state his position on this question. We must ask mayors and city councils, governors and state legislatures to boycott South African goods. The struggle must continue in South Africa until all 25 million people have full citizenship rights. Until that time, blacks from South Africa should be granted the same refugee status by the U.S. Immigration Service that it grants to Soviet Jews, Cubans, and Asians. You should be aware that this year the federal government requested $510 million to process and resettle the following immigrants to this country: 168,000 Asians; 63,000 Eastern Europeans, mainly Soviet Jews; 20,500 from Latin America, nearly all from Cuba (although well over 100,000 actually came); 2,500 from the Middle East; and only 1,500 from Africa. Racism and an outdated cold-war policy have never been right and no longer are tolerable.

My wife, Jackie, Rev. B. W. Smith, Rev. E. V. Hill, Jack O'Dell, and I also led delegations to the Middle East on two different occasions. On the first trip, a peace mission, we went to Israel, Jordan, Egypt, Lebanon, and Syria. On the second trip we went to Saudi Arabia and Kuwait. After these two extended trips to the Middle East, this tinderbox of both hot and cold war, I am still convinced that peace is possible, but it will require a new formula. Blacks have a vital interest in peace in the Middle East because in a hot war we will die first and in a cold war over oil we will be unemployed and will freeze first. The human rights community is too silent on the Mideast crisis. This country has a national interest in peace because the Arab states produce 43 percent of the West's oil and have $155 billion in fiscal reserves. Without firing a single shot, the Arab countries can throw the entire world into an economic tailspin. Thus peace is necessary if economic and political chaos is to be averted.

There are obstacles to peace on both sides. An element on the Arab side must have the courage to recognize that any long-term solution to current problems is going to be primarily political rather than military. Continued aggressive acts by the Israelis also constitute a major obstacle to peace: (1) the continued policy of encouraging settlement in the West Bank, (2) the continued occupation of East Jerusalem, and (3) the refusal of Israel through negotiations to grant full autonomy and self-rule to Palestinians living in the Gaza Strip and on the West Bank, in keeping with the Camp David accords.

Peace in the Middle East is going to require a new formula that reconciles five basic interests:

• Israeli security within internationally recognized boundaries, as set forth in U.N. Resolution 242.

• Palestinian justice that recognizes their rights to self-determination and a homeland. There will be neither peace nor justice without the involvement of the PLO in the Middle East negotiations. One hundred sixteen nations of the world recognize the PLO as the legitimate bargaining agent of the Palestinian people.

• Respect for the territorial integrity of Lebanon. The preemptive strikes must stop.

• Normalized ties with the Arab world. America can no longer ignore the 100 million Arabs of the Middle East.

• The return of East Jerusalem. Jerusalem is a city holy to three major religious faiths, and it must not be closed to one of them.

The Peace Now movement in Israel is an encouraging sign. A comparable group of Palestinians must assert itself. Both groups should converge at the Jordan River and determine to study war no more.

Peace is possible, and the formula we have been enunciating is one that more and more people have come to see as providing a pathway out of the current stalemate. World opinion and recent events are now shifting toward our position. In June the leaders of the European Economic Community (the Common Market) adopted a stance similar to ours. Now the U.S. government must join those challenging the present stalemate.

It is in our country's national interest to help break the cycle of fear, terror, and nonnegotiation. The continued no-talk policy is an international absurdity. We lost 50,000 American lives in the Vietnam War, and, even though we discussed the size and shape of the negotiating table in Paris at great length, we never stopped talking. The Palestinians, including the PLO, have not taken American lives. Yet we refuse to talk with them because of a secret agreement Henry Kissinger entered into in the dead of night in September 1975. America's role must be to reconcile the warring factions. We must provide for both what neither can provide for the other: sufficient military security and economic aid to develop peacetime economies and rebuild the countries.

We are concerned about the American hostages in Iran. It is morally right that our hostages be returned. To violate the sanctity and diplomatic immunity of embassies could lead to international anarchy. We have communicated this message directly to Ayatollah Khoumeni and his emissaries. On the other hand, we reject the attempt to impose a gag policy to cover up the American role in Iran over the past quarter of a century. We resent the attempt by the U.S. government to impose bans on the right of American citizens to travel in foreign countries, including Iran. Ramsey Clark was right about America's responsibilities to seek the truth and to speak the truth to the American people about what the American government did there. He had the right to go there, and he was right to go there. Further, without lessening our concern for the American hostages in Iran, we should not allow our attention to be diverted and forget about the 25 million black political hostages and the over 50 million economic hostages being held captive in this country because of a plan by this country's economic militants.

Again, we are concerned about the Russian invasion of Afghanistan. Just as preemptive strikes into Lebanon by Israel and South African strikes into Namibia set dangerous precedents, the preemptive strike of Russia into Afghanistan must be condemned. It is interesting that when

PUSH protested South Africa's heavyweight Kallie Knoetze fighting Bill Sharkey in Miami we were attacked and criticized for mixing politics with sports. The two, they said, were and should remain separate. Now, however, they justify politicizing the Olympics. It's inconsistent. Black young men and women could give America as much of a thrill this summer running fast and jumping high on the athletic field in Moscow as the white boys did this winter playing hockey in Lake Placid.

Some people might say, "Now, Reverend, all this travel and talk about foreign affairs is good, but aren't you missing the point? What about us down here in the ghetto?" Well, this separation between foreign and domestic policy is a false distinction. White people think their jobs went to Harlem and Watts and the South Side of Chicago through some sort of reverse discrimination. Black people are wondering which way the yellow went. Multinational corporations are expending capital and moving plants and jobs to foreign cheap labor markets in the automobile, textile, rubber, shoe, and electronics industries. Baseballs that used to be made in upstate New York are now manufactured in Haiti, where workers are paid 25¢ a day. American corporations exported $157 billion in capital last year. The flight of capital is an economic hemorrhage that must be controlled. There is a direct relationship between foreign and domestic policy. Every foreign item purchased is an international act. Every product we make and export is an international act. We are citizens of the world. No man is an island. Open your eyes and your minds; this is a new day. Blacks need to convene an international conference on foreign affairs in October to broaden our people's vision, to educate the American people, and to influence American foreign policy.

Also, just to set the record straight, PUSH did not abandon its direct domestic concerns. At the critical and strategic times in the presidential primaries, we went into various states, raising the issues of jobs and justice. You didn't read about it or hear about or see it on the television because we were locked out by the major news media. But you need to know that we spent three days in Iowa and drew bigger crowds than any of the candidates. We went to New Hampshire and spoke to an overflow crowd of students at the University of New Hampshire. We went to Alabama, Louisiana, Illinois, Pennsylvania, South Carolina, Missouri, Virginia, and other states, raising the critical issues of jobs and justice before each of their primaries. This effort culminated with a National Youth Pilgrimage for Jobs, Peace, and Justice in Washington on May 17, with 17,000 people present. We went to Miami in support of the Haitians and to interpret the riots in Miami. We were at the side of Vernon Jordan within hours after he was shot to demand to know not only *what* shot him but *who all* was involved in the shooting. So we have not abandoned domestic concerns; we have remained on the case and on the cutting edge of domestic concerns.

Although they were Chicago struggles, each of the crises I'm going to describe had a national impact or implications. With the attacks on the public economy symbolized by Proposition 13 and the balance-the-budget hysteria, employees working in the public sector have been especially vulnerable to our economic crisis. Our middle class, unlike the white middle class, is essentially built on the public economy. Thus attacks on the public economy disproportionately affect us. Thus when the Chicago Transit Authority workers, headed by two black union officials, went on strike and Mayor Jane Byrne attempted to break that union and those black men, we stood by the workers and helped to mediate a settlement. When the Cook County corrections officers went on strike, they asked us to represent them in the negotiations, and we were able to negotiate a number of benefits for them. They continue to meet at Operation PUSH on a weekly basis under the direction of Rev. Mrs. Willie Barrow. When the Chicago school system came up $700 million short and the teachers went out on strike because they were being asked to sacrifice disproportionately, PUSH established a variety of alternative programs that served more than 14,000 students in more than 75 sites across the city. As the *Chicago Tribune* concluded, "Of the large private community groups, Operation PUSH probably moved the earliest to identify and coordinate alternative schools."

Last, when the 4,000 firefighters went on strike and 22 people from our community lost their lives in fires, PUSH organized the 400 black firefighters as leverage on the city and on the union. Those 400 black firefighters had the power to sustain or break the strike. The union had to decide how important the black firefighters were to their cause. Through the leverage of the black firefighters, we were able to mediate and resolve the strike—something which the mayor, the union, and state and federal mediators failed to accomplish. The media was so racist that they refused to give us credit, and in fact they attempted to give the credit to Senator Kennedy on the eve of the Illinois primary. If you had read the Chicago papers or had watched television immediately after the settlement, you would hardly have known that we were involved in the dispute. But we're alive and well and on the case. We are present.

The Nature of Our Crisis

In times like these, it's important to be present. We can no longer use the single-bullet approach. We must use a shotgun approach. We must be present in a variety of ways on a wide range of issues because we are faced with a civilizational crisis. There are many factors that make up this civilizational crisis that currently confronts us. In many ways, it is easier to analyze the crisis than it is to design ways of resolving it. When we spend all our time analyzing our problems, too often we get trapped in the paralysis of analysis. So I don't want to discuss the crisis in all of its dimensions. I simply want to highlight four aspects that cannot be avoided.

We do not need to be told that racism and racial trauma is the fundamental flaw in the American character. We experience it daily. What we do need is an understanding of its many manifestations and how it permeates every aspect of American life. Racism is a philosophy; it elevates skin color to the level of religion and becomes the focus of people's ultimate allegiance. Racism becomes institutionalized in the social, economic, legal, and political structures of the society. We understood how to fight the Southern redneck because his racism usually was personal and involved a direct act. We are not as prepared to fight the impersonal violations and indirect acts of institutionalized racism. It was easier to be outraged at four black children being murdered in the bombing of a Birmingham church than to come to grips with an infant-mortality rate in one community on the South Side of Chicago that is higher than that of Calcutta, India.

One of the ways this institutionalized racism is manifest is that the news media do not consider the condition of the black community to be newsworthy. The income gap between whites and blacks has widened. Segregation is greater in the North now than it was twenty-five years ago. Police brutality is still one of the major sources of irritation in the black community. Black teenage unemployment never fell below 35 percent during the entire decade of the 1970s. And more. Yet little media attention was focused on these forms of racism because they were impersonal and indirect. Yet we were affected directly and very personally.

Now I want to discuss an issue that isn't very popular in Louisiana, generally, and that's confusing to a lot of blacks, in particular—the Equal Rights Amendment. The ERA has several dimensions to it: legal, economic, social, and racial. PUSH takes the position that the humanity of women must be affirmed and given equal protection under the law. Economically, women should be paid for the work they do. The issue is not your personal social relationship with your husband or wife or boyfriend or girlfriend—your individual roles can be negotiated. But the issue of roles is academic for the 60 percent of our children who are born in poverty in single-parent families where one parent is mother, father, breadwinner, and homemaker. The women's movement thus far has been led by upper-middle-class white women who have been contemptuous of black women. PUSH supports ERA, and that is one issue, but PUSH also supports black women within ERA, and that is another issue. Oppression by skirts is no less oppression than oppression by pants. Black women at this convention must organize and demand to meet with the leaders of the National Organization for Women and the National Women's Political Caucus to deal with their racial insensitivity and arrive at an understanding. The state legislature of Louisiana needs to affirm the humanity of all its citizens by ratifying the ERA.

Second, this nation is confronted with an economic crisis. The potential gross national product (GNP) not produced due to inadequate economic performance in the eight years between 1957 and 1964 totalled $256.6 billion. But between 1970 and 1976, a mere six years, the American economy wasted $381.6 billion in production (in constant dollars). Stagflation—high inflation and high unemployment at the same time—is not the result of government spending, so we can't solve stagflation by balancing the budget. In reality, it is the other way around. During the 1974–78 period, federal revenues went down as a result of high unemployment, but federal responsibilities went up. In the four years from 1970 to 1973, federal deficits totalled $58.1 billion. In the five succeeding years from 1974 to 1978, they were $212.6 billion. Thus the huge and unprecedented deficits of the 1970s came after stagflation and as a result of it, not before.

Institutionalized racism is manifesting itself through the current planned recession. This government is not opposed to planning because Paul Volker and the Federal Reserve Board conspired with the president and Congress to bring about the current recession. What this government opposed, with the support of private industry, is planning for a full-employment economy. We must be wise as serpents and harmless as doves and examine carefully the various economic proposals being presented to solve our dilemma. For example, many are touting John Anderson's 50-cents-a-gallon gasoline tax proposal as new and innovative. In reality, it's one of the most regressive proposals put forward. The cost of reaching the goal of conservation is paid by the consumer, and especially the poor.

Energy. Energy will remain a dominant economic and political issue in the 1980s. Blacks cannot remain on the sidelines of this debate. PUSH opposed the deregulation of domestic oil and opposes the deregulation of natural gas. PUSH opposes the building of nuclear power plants because they are capital- rather than labor-intensive, environmentally dangerous, and threaten the health and safety of too many Americans. PUSH opposes the synthetic fuels program—again, because it is capital- rather than labor-intensive and will only increase energy supplies by the equivalent of 500,000 barrels of oil per day by 1987. PUSH opposes the continued reliance on nonrenewable fossil fuels. Instead, PUSH supports a massive and serious conservation program because, dollar for dollar, investments in increasing the energy efficiency of buildings, industries, and the transportation system will save more energy than expenditures on new energy facilities will produce. This applies to both rich countries and poor countries.

Second, PUSH supports the rapid transition to renewable energy sources, including solar, wind, water, biomass, and geothermal. PUSH supports such programs because they mean jobs for our community. We could put America back to work insulating our houses. PUSH supports these programs because they are environmentally safer, they don't threaten human health as much, and they do not require a reduction in our standard of living—although they may require some changes in our style—and they generally improve the quality of life. The programs we oppose, we oppose in large part because they place the heaviest burden for solving our energy problems on those least able to bear it—the black, the poor, the young, and the unorganized. We support the programs we do because they make possible and more likely economic justice and racial harmony.

Last, the crisis of war and peace. The arms race threatens the goals of economic justice and racial tranquility. The world cannot afford to spend $400 billion annually arming itself to kill when what is needed is a program to heal. That money is needed to clothe the naked, heal the sick, and feed the hungry. We need a war, but a war on poverty, ignorance, and disease. SALT II must be put back on the nation's agenda. We presently are threatened with a return to a cold war with the Soviet Union. Our mutual paranoia is fraught with danger. A return to the cold war will mean a return of McCarthyism as well. We need to end our no-talk policy with the Russians over Afghanistan and call a summit to discuss Afghanistan and the growing tensions it is spawning in the Middle East. Talk and negotiations are the only alternatives to fear and mistrust and the miscalculations that could result in a nuclear holocaust.

PUSH opposes the reinstitution of registration for the draft and will actively support those who choose to resist. If our national security is genuinely threatened, we ought to come to our nation's defense, and we ought to do it voluntarily. But we have not been convinced that our national security is at stake, and thus we think registration for the draft is linked more to campaign security than to national security. They deliberately planned a recession that leaves us unemployed and then whip the country into a frenzy over foreign policy. The game plan is clear. We all know that they have two alternatives for us when we're unemployed: send us off to war or lock us up in jail. They are creating the climate for the former, and they are acting on the latter. There are 550,000 Americans in jail—about 400,000 black and brown (at a cost of $17,305 a year per person). As if that's not enough, the federal government is now embarking on a five-year plan to expand the prison population another 300,000. Racism, I tell you, manifests itself throughout these various crises that we must confront.

Equity in a New World Order: Reparations and Reciprocity

It's not enough to lay out the problem and to accentuate the negative. Analysis is necessary, but it's no solution. The real question is what are we going to do about it? We didn't come to this convention simply to say that we met, that we fellowshiped. We came here for a purpose. Why do we need such a convention, and why are we here?

First, we are here to crossbreed information. Second, we are here to solidify our leadership, to educate our membership, and from this platform, through the media, to engage in mass education. Third, we are here to synthesize our vision and our agenda. We must leave here with operational unity and around one essential message to be carried out through the different vehicles and instruments that each of us represents. In an orchestra, there are many instruments: the violin, the kettle drum, the tuba, the French horn, and the trumpet, and they are all necessary and important instruments. A symphony, however, requires that each instrument perform its part in harmony with all other parts. In other words, the transcendent agenda of the symphony must supersede any particular instrument's agenda if the whole orchestra is to get over.

There are many instruments in the PUSH orchestra. Some instruments are called PUSH Buffalo, some PUSH Cleveland, some PUSH-EXCEL, while still others are called "confused"—just waiting for the word. But all of these instruments are in the PUSH orchestra, and all are necessary if the PUSH symphony is to get over. Our job at this convention is to determine the content—the agenda—for the PUSH symphony and then to send each instrument forth to play its part in harmony with all other parts. The goal is one song. We'll always have many sounds and voices.

In 1980 the Democrats have an agenda—to stay in power. The Republicans have an agenda—to get in power. Blacks must have an agenda, and that agenda must transcend either of these instruments. Some Jews are Democrats and some are Republicans, but all support the state of Israel. They have a transcendent agenda. We have two political parties but only one economic order. This one economic system feeds both political parties so that whichever delivery system is out of power, their transcendent agenda is still in power. Blacks must have a transcendent agenda so that whoever is elected to the White House in November, we are not in the outhouse come January.

There's a lot of negativism, pessimism, and cynicism in the black community and the country today. It's understandable, but negativism, pessimism, and cynicism never built or changed anything. Even within the chains of limited economic and political options, we are not impotent, although we are far too dependent. If we were impotent, we wouldn't have any power. We do depend on others to do a lot of things for us, but we are not powerless. We have power, but much of it is potential power, unrealized power, unused and underutilized power. We needn't shy away from power because power is simply the ability to achieve purpose. We need power.

Two tangible factors keep us dependent and in bondage. If we ever overcome these two obstacles, independence and freedom will be ours. The first and most basic factor is spiritual—a desire and a will deep in our souls to be free. The second is mental. We need developed minds to guide our struggle for freedom. With pure hearts and changed minds, then neither the lure of money nor the threat of death and jails can turn us around. If our attitudes are inclined toward freedom and if our minds are committed to it, then social, economic, and political freedom will be the byproduct. Too often we try to work this process in reverse. Yet—the body heals from the inside out, and Jesus' primary focus was on changed hearts and minds. Historically, and in most instances for necessary and justifiable reasons, most of our civil rights organizations have been supported financially largely from outside the black community— by the labor movement, by white liberals, and most recently by major white corporations. When the struggle for freedom was essentially a horizontal one—a quest for citizenship rights—both conscience and an enlightened economic self-interest led these groups to support us morally and financially. Now, however, as the struggle for freedom has shifted from the horizontal to the vertical plane where we seek upward mobility and equity—our fair share—many of our closest allies of the past have abandoned ship and in some instances now actively oppose us.

Thus it is only right and necessary that during the 1980s we shift from dependence to independence. We cannot and should not expect our oppressors to finance our struggle for freedom. Our unrealized and underutilized power must be released. We now must support our own organizations and institutions. We no longer can fight for freedom looking pitiful. And freedom is worth the investment.

What untapped sources of power do we have? We have six levels that we must concentrate on in the 1980s, and two words must be the watchwords that guide our struggle through the '80s—*reparations and reciprocity.*

A decade ago James Forman raised the question of *reparations* for us in light of the black experience in America. Many people reacted negatively and tried to dismiss the thought; but he was correct. We need repair for the damage done to us because of slavery, segregation, and discrimination. We need not apologize for seeking reparations. Creative justice demands reparations. If reparations are still being given to Israel by Germany for damage imposed on Jews under Hitler, and if because of an uneasy conscience America is giving $5 million a day to Israel in reparations, then reparations are justified for us. Court cases clearly show the government can be sued for reparations when it is found to be abusive. In this month's decision in *Fullilove v. Klutznick,* the Supreme Court concluded that a special 10-percent set-aside program for minority businesses and contractors in a public works program passed by Congress was constitutional. However limited the context of the decision may be, the Supreme Court thus has affirmed reparations as an appropriate and constitutional legal principle.

The other word, *reciprocity,* has to do with a fair return on investment. We want our fair share in return for our 10 million votes. We want our fair share for our $125 billion in disposable income. We want our fair share of economic security in return for our serving disproportionately in the armed services, protecting this country's national security. We want our fair share of television shows and news coverage and our fair share in the print media for the papers we support directly and, through patronizing their advertisers, support indirectly. Reparations and reciprocity are our watchwords for the 1980s.

Self-reliance is consistent with both reparations and reciprocity. We must see self-reliance as a revolutionary concept. We must fight economically, politically, legally, spiritually, and journalistically for self-reliance and self-determination. It is what Jesus talked about when he said, stop looking for salvation to come from without, because "the kingdom of God is within." It is what Gandhi meant when he told the Indians to stop looking to the British Parliament for independence and call upon *satyagraha,* "soul force." It is what Dr. King meant when he said, "better to walk in dignity than to ride in shame." It's a spirit that says "I will" when they say "you won't." It's that something on the inside that says "I can" when they say "you can't." It's not rational, but neither is it irrational; it's supra-rational. Self-reliance and self-determination are positive qualities in a people, and when these qualities are mobilized then nothing is beyond achievement for them. Self-reliance does not mean less government responsibility; it means developing the power from your own resources for greater government accountability.

We have six levers of untapped power on our way to self-determination. First, we have *mind power.* Second, we have *votes.* We have 10 million registered voters and 17 million potential voters. Third, we have *money*—$125 billion collectively. Fourth, we have *marching feet*—we can

302

JESSE L. JACKSON

engage in direct action. Fifth, we have *pens and voices*. We must write and articulate our own story. Last, we have *moral power.* Our cause is morally right.

First, mind power. There is nothing more powerful than a fully developed and made-up mind. That is why we started and are expanding our PUSH-EXCEL program. That's why we support the black colleges—they have developed a specialty in developing black minds. They are superior to all other institutions in reaching the unreachable, in teaching the unteachable, and in healing brokenness. This year our emphasis will be on massive parental involvement in education. PUSH-EXCEL's goal is to involve the maximum number of parents in the education of their children. PUSH-EXCEL advocates such mass involvement of parents by seeking to enlist parents to do four specific things critical to their children's education: (1) at the beginning of school, to visit their children's teachers and exchange home telephone numbers; (2) to monitor their children's study for two hours each night without interruption from radio, television, telephone, record player, or social visits; (3) to pick up their children's report cards at the end of each grading period; and (4) to pick up their children's standardized test scores and discuss their progress with school counselors.

Achieving these goals does not require expenditure of massive additional funds; instead, it essentially requires a new priority and effort on the part of parents and all others engaged in the educational task. The fundamental role that PUSH-EXCEL should play is the conscious and systematic organization of parents to affect the totality of a child's educational experience. This is critical because parents are the first teachers and the real enforcers of their children's conduct. They have the power to guide their children's study habits. Parents provide love, care, chastisement, and discipline, and they are the most important models in their children's formative years. If there is a crisis in values in our schools, then parents are the only element that can solve this crisis. If children sit in the classroom unmotivated, then parents are the keys to restoring motivation. Parents are the only ones whose first priority and vested interest is in the welfare of their children.

From a broader perspective, if parents do not birth children, there is no school at all. If parents do not lend their moral support to public education, the system cannot survive. If they don't pay their taxes in support of public education, schools are inadequate or nonexistent. Parents directly or indirectly elect school-board members who set educational policy and should hold administrators accountable. Parents, as members of the broader society, reap the spiritual and material benefits that accrue to society as a result of a successful educational system. In short, parents are the only ones who can demand total accountability from both children and the school system. Parents, as the motivators of students, and preachers, as the motivators of both—you are the keys to developing strong black minds.

Second, we have 10 million registered voters and 17 million potential voters. Twenty-three percent of the total black vote is in the 18- to 24-year-old age bracket, yet they have the lowest registration and voter turnout. We cannot allow our young people to cop out. Too many people have suffered and died so that we could have the right to vote for us to allow them to be that irresponsible. Nonparticipation may be understandable, but it's not acceptable. We must go after the youth vote. Through our idea of linking the presentation of a high-school diploma and a voter registration card, PUSH has registered over 10,000 18-year-olds in Chicago, over 12,000 in Los Angeles, and thousands more in other cities across the nation. With the ballot, we determined who the Democratic nominee and the president would be in 1976, and hands that picked cotton in 1960 will determine who the president will be in 1980.

President Carter was involved in two elections in 1976: one with white voters and another with black voters. He lost the first election by 2,480,000—a considerable margin in a modern presidential election. Fortunately for President Carter, he won the second election dramatically. He got about 90 percent of the black vote so that, rather than losing the election by 2.5 million votes, he won by 1.7 million. Some argue that Carter is the only option black people have in 1980. That's not true. Blacks can vote Republican; blacks can vote Democratic; and blacks can stay home. We must be motivated by positive economic change, not by fear of the negative. A trip from the frying pan into the fire will not make things cooler. Since the black vote will determine who the next president will be, what the Democrats need in 1980 is not just the black vote but the enthusiastic black vote. So we have more options than most people think we have. We must negotiate this power wisely. We will be the difference in 1980. We can go Democratic, we can go Republican, we can go for a compromise candidate, or we can go home.

In any event, since blacks constitute 25 percent of the Democratic party, we should never again give the Democrats our blind loyalty. We must demand reciprocity, and we must demand it in the only way politicians will understand it. In 1984 black people must run for the Democratic nomination for president. The appeal will be broad-based and not limited to blacks, but black people must seek the presidency in 1984. We must organize enough political power to make the Democratic party and the nation respect us and then leverage that power to achieve our legitimate goals of equity and parity. Never again should we allow ourselves to be taken for granted by one political faction and written off by another. We will meet with Governor Reagan and President Carter. Both have sought meetings with us. We shall put forth an agenda that deals with the need for private job creation, business development, expansion of black colleges, and zones to build government installations with tax and labor incentives for private sector businesses.

Third, we have economic power. We have $125 billion in disposable personal income. At present, only 10 percent of this is spent in the black community. We have the margin of profit in many consumer industries. We must demand reciprocity and then leverage that $125 billion to achieve it. While the *Fullilove* decision is important, the major source of capital which will enable the black business community to survive and thrive is the major private economic institutions in our nation. Their combined assets total $500 billion. It is this $500 billion of capital investment that fuels American businesses. This capital—accumulated and controlled by major insurance companies, labor union pension and welfare funds, and other vast economic institutions—must be invested in the development of black America. Presently none is invested in black businesses, and without that capital, there is no way for black businesses to expand. Unless black businesses can grow, inflation will make it impossible for black businesses to become self-reliant and for the black community to achieve self-determination. It is part of American law, as contained in the Community Reinvestment Act, that a substantial amount of these funds must be invested in the community from which they came. We are 30 percent of the Teamsters. They have $2 billion in their pension and welfare funds. We want reciprocity. The United Auto Workers have a little less than $1.6 billion in their pension fund. We are 38 percent of the UAW. We want reciprocity. There is $500 billion to be invested in American businesses. We want 10 percent. We demand reciprocity. I didn't say "welfare"; I said "reciprocity." I didn't say "Lord, have mercy"; I said "reciprocity." We will seek through our board to meet with the heads of these unions.

PUSH is organizing a national boycott and consumer protection conference to be held in Gary, Indiana, August 21–22. We are putting together a list of 100 companies and financial institutions in the private sector and labor unions that we're going to target. We're going to demand reciprocity—our fair share.

We cannot limit our concern solely to American corporations. The world is too interconnected for that. At least at General Motors and Ford and Chrysler we have some black representation at various levels of the company. But we do not have such a position in these foreign industries in Japan and Germany that are knocking American workers out of jobs. We must demand reciprocity. Of American foreign investments, only 3 percent are in Japan. Of Japanese foreign investments, 23 percent are in the United States. Japan's rising oil prices and lower currency values will likely result in Japan's having a $12 billion trade deficit this year. They may try to export their way back to a balance of payments, largely through the American market. We must demand reciprocity from Japanese and West German industries just as we demand reciprocity from American corporations. We have a meeting next Tuesday at 10:30 A.M. with the Japanese Ambassador to the United States to discuss economic reciprocity.

Fourth, we have marching feet. Our march in Washington on May 17 marked the beginning of our return to the streets in organized, disciplined mass protests. We must dramatize our plight and sensitize and educate the American people in support of our cause.

Fifth, we have pens and voices to tell and interpret our story. There are 133 TV network executives in this country; only 2 are black. There are 1,769 daily newspapers; only 6 have blacks in executive editorial positions. The mass media rank among the worst of the racist institutions in our country. They will not tell our story fairly. We must support the black press in a new and aggressive way, and we must demand reciprocity in the white press. We must demand our fair share of television news coverage and programming. We must sharpen our pens and refine our ability to argue our case through the mass media.

Last, we have the knowledge that our cause is morally right. Ultimately, might does not make right; right makes might. We must never concede the fact that at its center our struggle is a moral struggle. The black church—whatever it is and ain't—historically has been and today remains the greatest contributor to sustaining us and allowing us to progress.

We must reject racism. Racism has as its root the notion that some are preordained for heaven. Likewise, racism teaches that others are preordained for hell.

Sexism is intellectually unreasonable. It is psychologically painful to the oppressed. It will be the basis of political obituaries for those who don't understand it.

We must have a new vision—a character with ethical content. We cannot equate shack-ups with marriages. We cannot equate foul speech with free speech. We cannot fight to lower the liquor-drinking age. We cannot use gambling and chance as a substitute for a sound economy with choice. We must move beyond the political realm to the prophetic realm. We who care must represent the new people. We must be possessed of a strength that jail cells cannot lock up, that bullets cannot kill, that water cannot drown, and that the status quo cannot discourage.

When the storms of life rage and our enemies mount against us, we must use willpower and cope with, and not pill power and cop out. We must put hope in our brains and not dope in our veins. And we must know that we will win the proposition of human rights for human beings everywhere because it is right and it is God's will.

Hold your heads high! Just because it rains, we don't have to drown!

Hold your heads high! When it's dark out, the stars can be seen most clearly.

Hold your heads high! We are victims of second-class treatment, but we are first-class people.

We may be in the slums, but the slum is not in us!

God has space for us, a time and a place for us! God has purpose for us!

Through it all, we've learned to trust in him! Our burden is heavy, our suffering is great. But God is the source of energy. Don't give up—feel tired! God didn't bring us this far to leave us!

Let us march on until victory is won!

Environmental Justice:
A Call to Action

Jackson gave this speech to the Citizens Conference to
Stop Acid Rain, held in Manchester, New Hampshire,
on January 6, 1984.

Our campaign is a moral and political crusade to
transform the quality of American life. We want to restore a moral
quality to the political decisions that affect our lives at home and the
decisions that affect the lives of our brothers and sisters around the
globe. We want to set our nation on a course where the full spiritual,
moral, and physical resources of our people can be realized. We want to
end the exploitation and oppression of the many by the few.

We emphasize the themes of participation and equality, historic values
of American life too often sacrificed to a political and social system that
has denied true access to the rejected majority of blacks, Hispanics,
women, environmentalists, and the proponents of peace.

The laying waste of the resources of our planet may be seen as part
and parcel of a social and economic system that sacrifices the welfare of
the many for the short-term economic interests of the elite few; that
mortgages the future to the present; and that destroys or threatens to
destroy the most precious gifts of the Creator. Those gifts include the air
we breathe, the water we drink, the food we eat, the mountains and
forests that inspire awe in our hearts, and the companionship of our
hundreds of thousands of fellow travelers on this spaceship earth.

We care about these things for two reasons:

First, we care about them for their own sake. We realize that we
cannot live in harmony with one another if we cannot live in harmony
with the world around us. We cannot learn to tolerate and appreciate

the differences among the peoples of the earth if we do not cherish the diversity of nature.

Second, we recognize the injustice that the destruction of our environment brings about. Ecological harm is not distributed evenly throughout society. It is the poor, the elderly, and minorities whose drinking water is the most polluted, whose air is the most dangerous to breathe, whose food is the least nutritious, whose jobs are the most hazardous. It is the coke-plant worker, not the steel-mill owner, who suffers levels of lung cancer seven times above the average. It is the housing project tenant who breathes air containing carcinogenic compounds at fifteen to thirty times the background rates.

It is the poor, locked up in the terrifying slums of our inner cities, who face today the ecological holocaust that the affluent may, for a short time yet, be able to escape. This campaign unequivocally calls for a complete reversal of existing environmental policy.

We call for a reauthorization of the Clean Air Act, including new and stronger provisions for the control of toxic air pollutants, and, as I will discuss shortly, for the elimination of acid rain. We call for the reauthorization and strengthening of the Clean Water Act and the passage of the Safe Drinking Water Act.

We demand the prompt elimination of toxic-waste sites and the aggressive enforcement of the Toxic Waste Superfund program. We call for the phasing out of all existing nuclear power plants and an end to construction or licensing of new plants. We are in complete opposition to any attempt to attack the National Park System in Alaska, and we oppose auctioning off our precious national lands to the highest bidder. We stand for preserving such resources for generations to come. Indeed, our campaign is one to give speech to those without voices, and there are none in greater need of a voice than the unborn generations who will inherit the planet.

We believe that by solving our environmental problems, by following "soft" energy paths, and by encouraging conservation we can resolve many of the international conflicts and problems in the world. The Middle East is a flashpoint for hot and cold war in the world because of the unnecessary dependence of our country and the world on nonrenewable petroleum resources. The solution is not the amassing of ever-greater armies to fight over these dwindling resources. The solution is to commit now to the development of nonpolluting, renewable technologies.

A caring and egalitarian foreign policy and a willingness to share our resources with the rest of the world can bring about an end to the destruction of the environment taking place in the rain forests of Brazil and the ever-growing deserts of Africa. It is only the inexorable pressures of poverty, disease, and hunger which fuel such tragic events. The solution lies not with the poor masses of the world but in a change of heart by our own nation, a nation which can never live in security and peace so long as our 5 percent of the world's population continue to consume one-third of the resources of the entire globe—no matter how many nuclear weapons we stockpile.

We are here tonight because acid rain epitomizes the environmental crisis we face. Like no other issue, acid rain reminds us that there is no such thing as "away." The seemingly insubstantial yellow plumes of sulfur dioxide emitted from the supertall smokestacks of America's utilities and smelters do not simply dissipate harmlessly into the air. Instead, these plumes return to the earth in the form of an incredible twenty-five million tons a year of poisonous sulfuric acid.

The ecological effects of acid rain provide eerie confirmation of Rachel Carson's prophecies in *Silent Spring*. Brook trout no longer crack the unnaturally glassy surface of dying lakes in the Adirondacks. They are vanishing, along with the crayfish and frogs, the loons and the king-fishers. The chorus of spring peepers has been silenced, and blight is killing the trees of the forest.

Here in New Hampshire, the name "Granite State" has taken on a new and frightening significance. Since granite does not neutralize acid rain, the state of New Hampshire has been particularly ravished by this poison from the skies. One study has suggested a 50-percent decline in red spruce growth in New Hampshire and Vermont in recent years. Red spruce are especially vulnerable to acidic mists, clouds, and rain.

It has been estimated that acid rain is already producing damage on the order of $5 billion a year to the New England economy as a result of declines in sportfishing, agriculture, forestry, and building damage. This annual cost exceeds the total cost of cleaning up acid rain.

Most important, acid rain may be creating an insidious health problem of enormous proportions. The Office of Technology Assessment estimates that the inhalation of sulfates may cause 50,000 excess deaths per year. Acid rain may be leaching deadly lead, cadmium, and copper from our drinking-water pipes and aluminum and mercury from our watersheds.

Delay will only increase the magnitude of the damage and the cost of the cure. We cannot wait until thousands of children have suffered irreversible lead poisoning. We cannot wait until the fishing and tourist industries in New England have been completely devastated.

We cannot wait until relations with our good and close neighbor, Canada, have deteriorated to the point of open hostilities. It has been a hallmark of our campaign to energetically attack those problems which create divisions among nations and disharmony among people. There is

310 JESSE L. JACKSON

no better place to start than in our own backyard; it is appalling that American intransigence on the issue of acid rain is causing serious deterioration in our relationship with Canada.

We therefore commit our campaign to the strongest, swiftest, and fairest possible action against acid rain. Most important, this campaign calls for a much bolder, more imaginative, and visionary approach to use of the Acid Rain Superfund dollars.

It would be tragic to spend billions of dollars only on scrubbers, merely to support a brutally polluting, capital-intensive technology owned by the utilities but subsidized by the rate payers through their utility bills and by coal miners through the destruction of their lungs and their lives. We believe that a significant portion of the Acid Rain Superfund should be used to encourage conservation and the development of safe and renewable energy sources. This approach would reduce sulfur dioxide emissions by vastly decreasing the need for electrical generation from nonrenewable fuels.

For instance, we would launch a major program to rebuild and insulate homes, thus reducing energy use, reducing sulfur dioxide emissions, getting people jobs, and improving the housing stock of our nation. In our view, this is a far better way, all things being equal, to spend a billion dollars than to just build scrubbers and give them to the electric utilities.

We would launch a major program to build solar heating devices and install them across America. These too would greatly reduce the need for coal-fired utilities, would provide thousands upon thousands of jobs, would reduce utility bills, and, most important, would give the poor more control over the technologies that affect their lives. It would be a giant step toward beginning to decentralize our economy and the source of power in our society. Our campaign, after all, stands for empowering the poor.

We would begin a massive replanning and remolding of our nation's cities to achieve pleasant, livable environments for all our citizens, without the massive waste of energy which now occurs. We would encourage policies to rebuild our inner cities, create diversity, and end the ever-increasing suburban sprawl that is responsible for the use of so much of our petroleum supply and is productive of so much of the nitrogen oxides, which are another important cause of acid rain.

In all such uses of Acid Rain Superfund dollars, first priority should be given to providing jobs to coal miners and others whose livelihood now depends on the coal industry.

With acid rain, as with all things, there is a negative and there is a positive approach to the problem. There is a way of looking at acid rain only as a problem, only as another source of loss, of sadness and of pain.

The capture of Lieutenant Robert Goodman was a personal tragedy for him and his family and a source of pain for our nation. The administration in Washington reacted by sweeping this problem under the rug. We saw the capture of Lieutenant Goodman in a different way. We saw it as a human situation, as a symbol of how people could set aside political differences and political tensions and get to the human root of the problem. We thought that by making a personal and moral appeal to the Syrian leadership we could get the stalemate off dead center, break the cycle of pain, and begin the cycle of healing.

In the same way, the problem of acid rain can be the source of an environmental breakthrough. Some would sweep this problem, too, under the rug. Others would look solely to expensive and complex technology owned by the utility companies as the total solution, leaving the power relations in our society intact.

I support all needed stop-gap measures, but, at the same time, I would go much further. I would take the problem of acid rain and use it as the fulcrum by means of which the entire environmental policy and direction of this nation may be leveraged and changed. Then we will do much more than restore life to dying ponds; we will do much more than restore fertility to our forests; we will do more than staunch the economic bloodletting of our tourist, forest, and fishing industries.

We will begin to transform our society into one in which people live in true harmony—harmony among nations, harmony between men and women, harmony among the races of humankind, and harmony with nature. In the final analysis, that is the goal of our Rainbow Coalition. I urge you to join with us in our moral crusade to bring about the reconciliation our society so desperately yearns for and so urgently needs.

An End to
Corporate Blackmail

Jackson gave this campaign speech in Akron, Ohio, on
May 7, 1984.

Our theme as we cross this great state of Ohio has been
the need for a new direction: a new commitment of the American government to the American people. We have said that the government must
act immediately to stop the kind of corporate warfare we have seen being
waged on the people of Ohio who have built America's great industries:
steel in Youngstown, rubber here in Akron, automobiles, the machine
shops.

You built these industries with your sweat and blood and tears. Great
corporations made their profits off your labors. Now they have abandoned you and your cities, leaving behind a shrinking tax base and city
services that can no longer meet your needs. A proud work force is now
forced to stand in unemployment lines to seek minimum-wage jobs that
will not support your families. These corporations have not shown you
the respect or the concern that you and your communities deserve. The
government has given them tax breaks, and they have used those tax
breaks not to reinvest in American industry but to buy other industries,
to merge with one another, to move to slave-labor markets abroad. The
state of Ohio looks like a battlefield, with closed plants as memorials to
those who fought for decent wages.

You know all too well the losses you have suffered. The official
unemployment rate in Akron stands at 11.9 percent, not counting your
youth, not counting your discouraged workers. One-third of Ohio's
unemployed have been out of work for more than two years. The
number of people on general relief doubled in the last year. That figure

312

represents people who have been out of work so long that they have fallen off the unemployment rolls. Unemployment has become a way of life for one of the proudest work forces in the country. Since 1950, 25,000 jobs have disappeared in Akron. Goodyear production alone is down to 4,000 from a wartime high of 19,000. And the losses continue. Northeast Ohio has lost 115,000 payroll jobs since 1979. In 1983, 6,500 Fortune 500 jobs were lost in northeast Ohio. There are 137 hunger centers in the five-county area around Akron. They are distributing enough food for 20,000 people to receive a three-day supply each month. Home and farm foreclosures are up 50 percent.

You are the victims of multinational corporations that have sought higher profits elsewhere at the expense of your communities. Since 1945 these corporations have invested more than $200 billion dollars abroad. That gives them the third largest gross national product (GNP) in the world. These corporations represent the increasing concentration of economic power in this country. At the end of World War II, 45 percent of manufacturing assets were controlled by the 200 largest firms. Today they control 60 percent. Today 1 percent of all manufacturers control 88 percent of manufacturing assets and make 90 percent of all manufacturing profits. The rich have gotten richer, and the poor have gotten poorer.

The rich richer, the poor poorer is the story of the last ten years and the story of the economic recovery that we now hear so much about. We hear from Walter Mondale that the story of the Chrysler bail-out was a great success. The workers gave up a billion dollars in concessions. The taxpayers paid a billion. And now Chrysler is making record profits— $705 million in the first three months of this year, more than it has ever earned in a full year. The directors are setting aside $51.6 million in bonuses for more than 1,400 executives, and Lee Iacocca is talking about buying a bank. The stockholders are happy. The executives are happy. But what has happened to the workers? Chrysler used the bail-out to pay off one-third of its work force. Chrysler cut 52,000 workers from its work force this year while it made such record profits. What has happened to our communities? According to the terms of the bail-out and present tax law, *Chrysler does not even have to begin paying any taxes until the beginning of 1985.* And yet you, the workers, pay taxes on your unemployment benefits while you try to make your house payments!

I stand before you today as a candidate for the presidency of the United States because I believe that we must put an end to government policies that favor corporate power over the needs of working people and their communities. We must put an end to an unfair and unjust tax structure. Last year 90,000 corporations that made profits paid no taxes. Before World War II, corporate income taxes accounted for 34 percent of all federal receipts. Today they account for no more than 13 percent.

Corporate America must once more start to pay its fair share. A just, equitable restructuring of our tax system would provide our nation with $50 to $70 billion dollars a year.

A just, equitable tax law is just one step for a government that would arbitrate fairly between multinational corporations and the American people.

We must look at every aspect of United States foreign and domestic policy that has favored the rich over the poor, the few over the many. As a nation, we must change direction.

We must look at our foreign policy. In 1978 Goodyear announced that it was ending production at the last plant making passenger tires in Akron. One month later, the company announced that it was investing $34 million in a new tire plant employing 2,000 people in Chile. Goodyear left Akron to take advantage of cheap slave labor in Chile. The people of Chile do not want to be slaves. Just as much as the people of Akron, the people of Chile are a proud people with a long history of democracy, a history of strong unions. They did not want to be exploited by multinational corporations any more than the people of Akron wanted to lose their jobs. They elected a president, Salvador Allende, to protect their interests. The government of our own country chose to spend millions and millions of dollars to overthrow the government of Salvador Allende, to establish the dictatorship of Augusto Pinochet Ugarte, a dictatorship that shoots down students in the street for chanting "Bread, Peace, and Justice," a dictatorship that has done everything in its power to break Chile's trade unions. Now we see our government, our CIA, repeating the same process in Nicaragua, attempting to overthrow the legitimate government of another people, a people trying to work out their own destiny after years of exploitation and injustice at the hands of Somoza, another U.S.-supported dictator. We see our government lending thousands and thousands of dollars in military aid to a government in El Salvador, where death squads have killed thousands of trade union organizers, where many workers make 50 cents a day.

Our present foreign policy serves no one but multinational corporations seeking cheap labor markets abroad. It does not serve the people of this country. It does not serve the people of other lands. It runs the risk of war in countries around the world where people are rising up against exploitation and oppression. It puts our nation on the wrong side of history. It drains our nation's resources into military adventures abroad, when we so desperately need to be increasing our own security at home by rebuilding our cities, our roads, and our bridges, putting our people to work, educating our children, cleaning up our environment.

A new foreign policy; a new domestic policy. These are the themes of my campaign, a campaign that we have called a crusade to restore a moral quality to the decisions that affect our lives, our environment, our working conditions, our relationships with people around the world.

I hope you will join me in this crusade. Together we can set new goals, a new agenda. We have great resources. We can put people to work meeting human needs. We can clean up our environment. We can aid the development of the people and the economies of other lands. We have a long way to go. We have only just begun. Together we can re-direct this nation.

Excellence in the Press: Freedom, Fairness, and the Future

Jackson gave this speech to the annual convention of the Associated Press, meeting in Cincinnati, Ohio, on June 3, 1978.

Today I want to speak as briefly and to the point as I can about three issues affecting all of us, but especially the press: (1) freedom of the press; (2) fairness in the press; and (3) the role of the press as it relates to the future of our society. Thus I have chosen for a title: "Excellence in the Press: Freedom, Fairness, and the Future."

Freedom of the Press

The First Amendment to the Constitution says: "Congress shall make no law . . . abridging the freedom of speech or of the press." We must never allow the right to a "free press" to become a cliche, to be taken for granted. The price all of us must pay to protect this right is eternal vigilance.

We must not only have the right of a free press, but we must use that right. I generally agree with Tom Wicker's "law" in his new book, *On Press*, that one should "learn everything you can and print everything you know." I say "generally" because even Wicker adds in closing that "there really isn't a rule that applies to every case and that's why journalism isn't a profession for people with weak nerves."

My point is really one that grows out of my own religious understanding that if God gives you a talent and you fail to use it or if you abuse it, you will lose it. The principle is no less true with the issue of "freedom of the press." Therefore I urge that we continue together to fight for the freedom of the press—even if it means going to jail on occasion—and that we not allow the government or anyone else (even civil rights leaders) to intimidate us into compromising this precious right.

Several recent developments disturb me a great deal. In January 1975, Senator Roman Hruska (R-Neb.)—the absolutely worst senator at the time—and Senator John McClellan (not exactly a freedom fighter himself) introduced legislation to rewrite the Criminal Code. This legislation, called S–1, written in the climate of the Ellsberg controversy, was clearly designed to restrict the freedom of the press. Journalists, civil rights activists, and others rightly exposed the threats inherent in S–1. We now have the "son" of S–1, S–1437, and although it is a vastly improved bill, I urge that we keep an eye on this legislation since the law is our basic protection.

Just this week we have seen the highest court in our land—despite protection in the Constitution given explicitly to the press—rule that police may go unannounced to a newspaper office with a search warrant and look for evidence of a crime, even if no member of the paper is suspected of the offense. The political use of this ruling is coming, so you might as well prepare for it. Journalists may need to be prepared to go to jail en masse rather than to submit to this tyranny.

Be clear, it is not hard to find a judge who will issue such a warrant. Sources will not be as available if they know that, even though the journalist will not reveal his or her source, they may be "accidentally" discovered in one of these fishing expeditions, as Justice Stewart points out in his dissent. Do not underestimate the impact that this decision by the Nixon Court is going to have on the freedom of the press. I doubt if Watergate and other crucial issues would have been exposed if this law had been in effect at that time.

Last, I support the idea that, along with the executive branch of government, the legislative and judicial branches, as well as the regulating agencies, need more exposure, which can only come through greater access by all forms of the news media to their domains. Radio and television, along with print journalists, should be permitted in Congress, in court rooms, and in the regulatory agencies to share with the American public their deliberations, decisions, and the process involved.

Since the founding of our nation the executive, legislative, and judicial branches of government and its citizens have struggled to suppress, preserve, modify, or interpret the First Amendment to the Constitution—"freedom of the press." The press has become so powerful—especially since television—that it is often referred to as the Fourth Estate.

What is the essence of the power of the press? Why is it so powerful? I suggest it is because of the power to assess, the power of appraisal. If a person buys a diamond ring for $10,000 and decides to insure it, the insurance company will insist upon an independent appraisal. So an appraiser closes one eye and through a glass expands the other. If the appraiser says it has an imperfection, it may only be worth $2,000. On the other hand, the appraiser may say it is perfect, making it worth $20,000. Ultimately, then, power is in the eye of the appraiser.

The press, as appraiser, has the power to determine, in large measure, who gets seen and how they get seen. What it projects shapes our concepts and attitudes and affects how we think and feel about each other. Who gets projected is itself a form of power—nonappearance represents nonimportance—and in large measure casts who we are.

Fairness in the Press

The press, in defending its institution, concentrates almost exclusively on the legal questions concerning freedom of the press. As important and necessary as this is, it is nonetheless a limited understanding of the total question. Freedom is both the *right* and the *ability* to exercise options. To have the legal right to go to any university or live in any neighborhood without the ability to pay the tuition or the house note is not truly freedom. It is an empty promise or an illusion. Often it is argued that freedom and responsibility go together. The missing element in both, however, is the necessity of power to exercise freedom or assume responsibility.

There is no such thing as "objective" or "unbiased" reporting, only "fair" reporting. Those coming closest to being objective and fair are those who are most aware of their biases. Thus freedom *in* the press— the power to decide relative to appraisal—is a prerequisite for freedom *of* the press. Not a prerequisite in the legal sense, but in the sense of fairness. For without fairness in the press, freedom of the press is limited in its vision. One has the freedom to see but cannot see.

Black people find themselves in a country with the legal and constitutional guarantee of freedom of the press but lacking the actual power to exercise that right because there is not freedom in the press. As a result, all Americans, but especially black people, suffer through distortion and deletion. Journalism has used its power of appraisal to mentally disenfranchise us.

What do I mean? In light of the argument just made, the first question is, "Who is appraising us?" and the second, "How are they appraising us?"

Who is appraising us? In a word, the decision makers in both the program and news departments of television are white and male with a suburban and an economic middle- to upper-middle-class mentality or perspective—"bias," if you choose. In addition, the industry is privately owned and monopolistic—excluding blacks on both counts.

The *Hollywood Reporter* (October 1977) listed the top executives at the three major networks: ABC listed 40, CBS 49, and NBC 44, for a total of 133 executives. Of the 133 network executives, only 1 was black—Mr. Peter Andrews of NBC—a scandalous eight-tenths of 1 percent.

The absurdity and injustice of who appraises us can be illustrated by recent major television productions. Although ABC's "Roots" set television viewing records, few know that there were no black producers, assistant producers, writers, or directors involved. The only thing black in "Roots" were the actors seen on the screen. And even there, two white actors received more money than all of the black actors combined. NBC's "King" also had a white producer, Abbey Mann. Can anyone imagine NBC's "Holocaust" with all black producers, assistant producers, writers, and directors and none who was Jewish or white?

In one sense television is the most powerful journalistic medium since most people get their news from television. Therefore, access to people's minds makes it powerful. But that is not totally true because television itself gets its essential news from print journalists, and print journalism is the most racist branch of journalism today. Of the 1,769 daily newspapers, there are only 5 or 6 blacks in executive editorial positions. Out of 40,000 print journalists, only 1,700 (4 percent) are black. So television news originates from the most racist form of journalism in the nation. Presently, print journalism is saying, "Do as I say, not as I do," and the end product is hard to swallow.

The question of blacks moving into the industry horizontally as well as moving vertically, up to decision-making positions, is not only a philosophical problem of fairness, nor is it simply a moral and statistical question to be answered with more black bodies. It really strikes at the heart of journalism.

The fundamental thing that journalists have going for themselves is their believability—their ability to deal in truth with integrity and fairness. When journalists lose their moral authority, their believability, they have lost their most precious jewel. In materialistic terms, their commodity is no longer salable.

To a certain extent, the news media have already lost much of their moral authority with the black community. For example, we have watched how the news media have twisted and perverted the issues relative to affirmative action, especially the *Bakke* case, using code words ("reverse discrimination," "preferential treatment," "quotas") to perpetuate myths rather than to inform the public with facts. I shall return to this point shortly.

One of the consequences of the press's loss of credibility with the black community is that many blacks have transferred their nonbelief in what the press says on affirmative action and many other issues that affect us to such issues as Idi Amin and his slaughter in Uganda. Since the news media so callously (if not consciously) misstate and misrepresent the facts and us in so many ways, many blacks feel that the situation in Uganda is just another instance of the white press distorting and attacking a proud and defiant black African leader whom white people can't control. That is the price the news media pay when they lose their moral authority and believability. If a journalist or if journalism itself loses moral authority, even the Constitution and some laws cannot save you.

The second question of *how* television appraises us is equally disturbing. Television's major violation of us is a consistent combination of distortion and deletion which projects us as less intelligent, more violent, less hard-working, and less universal than we are.

First, it appraises us as less intelligent than we are. We may be underrepresented in the professions because of a denial of opportunity, but we are represented in every profession in American society—doctors, lawyers, bankers—yet we are seldom projected as such.

Second, it appraises us as more violent than we are. It seems that only when we rob, rape, or kill somebody are we newsworthy, and it is not counterbalanced with a more holistic appraisal of us. In the last thirty years, two of the four Americans who have won the Nobel Peace Prize were black—Dr. Ralph Bunche and Dr. Martin Luther King, Jr.

Third, we are primarily workers. We work longer, harder, and often, but not always, at the most menial jobs, making less money than anyone. We are concentrated in the heavy-duty and certain service industries. We are 30 percent of the auto workers, steel workers, and teamsters; 35 percent of public transportation and postal workers; and 40 percent of the hospital, sanitation, and laundry workers. Yet television's projection of us almost makes welfare, poverty, unemployment, and blacks synonymous.

Last, television generally does not project us as being universal persons but as limited to ethnic concerns. It constantly refers to our leadership as "black leaders" (rather than "leaders" whose blackness is self-evident), which has the effect of keeping us in a "black box" rather than allowing us to speak and be heard on all issues as others do. Too often when we try to address ourselves to international or economic issues, we are met with the question (in effect, if not actually), "By what authority?" The classic example may be Dr. Martin Luther King, Jr.'s speaking out against the war in Vietnam.

To the degree that journalism accurately and fairly informs and educates the public, to that same degree will it retain its moral authority and believability. Right now, as far as black people are concerned, it has been weighed and found wanting.

The Future of the Country

In my experience, journalists too often try to argue that they don't make value judgments or interpret the news, they merely report the news—leaving the false impression of "objectivity" or "value-free" reporting. There is no such thing as value-free journalism. Nonvalues are values, but they are the values of decadence and decay. Every journalist, by definition, is involved in a subjective-objective process. The degree may vary, but all journalism is advocacy journalism. What must be done, it seems to me, is that we must become as self-conscious as we can about about our values and point of view.

Freedom and fairness must be seen within the context of our broad national objectives. The news media made a judgment about McCarthyism in the 1950s. Journalism made a judgment about legal segregation in the South and decided that we should not, indeed could not, exist as a nation—half slave and half free. The news profession made a decision about Vietnam and about Watergate because it had a sense of the nation's objectives and what it ought to represent in the world.

We have argued in our recent education program that the truly educated person goes through several stages of development. First, they must be exposed to the subject matter. Second, they must remember that to which they have been exposed. Third, they must internalize it. Fourth, they must develop convictions about it, and, last, they must apply it. Journalism is no different. You can't jump over the fourth point about convictions in the name of objectivity and nonvalues and pursue our broad national objectives.

That may be the reason the nation's press has so miseducated the public on affirmative action and *Bakke*. The question is essentially a moral one. Is our society going to implement its creed of one society, with liberty and justice for all? Affirmative action and even minimum quotas do not represent "reverse discrimination" and "preferential treat-ment," as Bakke claims. To argue such is to see affirmative action out of context, and a text without a context is a pretext.

Actually, "reverse discrimination" in the American context is illogical and a contradiction in terms. Never in the history of humankind has a majority with power engaged in programs and written laws to discrimi-nate against itself. The only thing whites are giving up because of affirmative action is privilege—something to which they were not entitled in the first place. The issue is not reverse discrimination but the reversal of the effects of historic and present discrimination.

Blacks are not making progress at the expense of whites, as news accounts tend to project, because there are 49 percent more whites in medical school today and 64 percent more whites in law school than at the beginning of the affirmative action programs some eight years ago.

If we lose the *Bakke* case now before the Supreme Court, my advice is that we rebel. We sat in at lunch counters when they locked us away from food for our bodies, and if they lock us away from the food of information for our minds, I suggest that we begin sitting in on university campuses all across this nation, demanding that they serve us some information. I recommend that we engage in boycotts and sit-ins of selected businesses who refuse to hire us and promote us in equitable numbers. I suggest that we engage in the drama of street demonstrations to dramatize and educate the American people. If Bakke wins, we should not concede this injustice with a conspiracy of silence.

You say, "Well, why do you resist being judged on merit?" We do not resist being judged on merit, but America resists judging us on merit. Being born black in the United States is to be born with demerits. We were not enslaved and are not discriminated against because individually we lacked merit. We were discriminated against as a group because of our race. It is more subtle, but no different, with the discrimination today. This nation went out of its way to enslave us as a group but now wants to free us through individual effort and merit. We need a solution that is consistent with and comprehensive of the problem.

We argue for special protection because we have, in this society, a special problem—racism. Free citizens ought to be able to live without fear of loss of rights or life—yet we needed federal troops in the South after the Emancipation Proclamation to protect us. After these troops were removed in 1877, America entered its most violent period, and we were the victims. We needed a special amendment to the Constitution, the Thirteenth, to guarantee our citizenship.

After education was made mandatory in this country, we needed a special law (the *Brown* decision in 1954) to guarantee our equal educational opportunity. Citizens have the right to use public facilities, but we needed a special law in 1964 to gain access. Citizens have the right to vote, yet we needed, and still need, a special law (the 1965 Voting Rights Act) to ensure our right to vote. Even now it must be renewed in 1982 rather than having been guaranteed into perpetuity. We need the special law of the 1968 Open Housing Act, not because we lack merit, but because we need protection from racism. We would like to be judged on merit, but the special problem of racism has given us demerits; thus we need the protection of special laws.

Another suggestion I might make to the news media for the future, in our attempt to accomplish our broad national objectives, is to develop peripheral vision. We tend to have myopic vision relative to the various administrations that come into power. We speak of the Kennedy years, the Johnson era, the Nixon saga, and the Carter administration. That is the single view, and even a necessary one, but we must broaden our perspective on the powers that affect our lives.

We must be concerned about a business community that last year invested $164 billion—$32 billion of it abroad—thus contributing to the flight of capital and jobs. We must be concerned about a union establishment that resists our employment and upward mobility and refuses to even train us. We must focus on a Congress that is more indebted to us than Carter is yet refuses many of the programs he does send up. Our concern must encompass a Supreme Court that has shifted the burden of proof from the effects of discrimination to the intent to discriminate, thus winning cases becomes more expensive and more difficult. The mass media themselves, as documented earlier, must increasingly become the focus of attention.

We fight for freedom of the press, fairness in the press, and for the future because of the broad national objectives of life, liberty, and the pursuit of happiness for all persons. PUSH is not morally neutral or objective on these matters. The only reason I can come here and challenge you today is because of the freedom inherent in our national objectives.

Just as freedom of the press is worth defending and struggling for, so is educational and economic equity and parity. That's what our PUSH for Excellence program is all about. We cannot remain detached from the rising crime rate, the lack of voter registration and voter participation experienced over the last decade, the growing estrangement between blacks and whites in this country, and the continuing gap between the rich and the poor. We must research, report, and expose the structural and institutional impediments that are perpetuating these injustices.

For the press, then, freedom is not simply a right and a privilege, it is a duty. You, more than any other institution, are the trustees of the nation, because no one else gives their opinion so openly and so regularly. The press fights for itself and its domain (freedom of the press) rather vigorously, but the founder of my religion taught a universal principle that we should love our neighbors as ourselves. He didn't naively suggest that we ignore our own self-interest. Neither did he say we should be satisfied once our interests were secure and protected, but rather that we should struggle to secure the same for our neighbors.

In conclusion, I know that there is a dialectic involved. Part of the reason the press was able to do its job in the 1960s is because we were actively engaged in dramatizing the injustice being done to us. That's the reason I argue that victims may not be responsible for being down, but they must be responsible for getting up. They must be responsible for initiating change, determining strategy, tactics, and timing, and be disciplined enough to make it happen.

In a racial society, we know that we must pursue excellence just in order to be considered average. Effort must exceed opportunity for change to occur. We must return to militant, nonviolent, mass direct action to dramatize and educate the American people to our plight.

In the final analysis, we ask from the press, not any special favors, but simply the reporting of our plight with accuracy and fairness. For we believe that in the end might is not right, but right is might. We believe that the pen is mightier than the sword, that a nation's conscience can be stirred and moved if the truth is told with conviction and with power.